Japan '79

JAPAN '79

A New York Times Survey

Introduction by
Edwin O. Reischauer

Edited by
Mitchell Rapoport and Joshua Fogel

Arno Press
A New York Times Company

New York, 1979

© 1977, 1978 by The New York Times Company.

© 1979 by Arno Press Inc.

Book Design: Sam Woo

Assistant Editor: Marie Stareck

Library of Congress Cataloging in Publication Data

Main entry under title:

Japan '79 : a New York times survey.

    Includes index.
    1. Japan —Politics and government —1945-
—Addresses, essays, lectures. 2. Japan—Economic
conditions—1945- —Addresses, essays, lectures.
3. Japan—Foreign relations —1945- —Addresses,
essays, lectures. I. Fogel, Joshua. II. Rapoport,
Mitchell. III. New York times.
DS889.J345.1979   309.1'52'04   78-66158
ISBN 0-405-11753-1

Manufactured in the United States of America.

Contents

Preface

Japan 79 is the first in a series of yearbooks designed to fill a need for current, reliable information on a subject of continuing importance. The book provides coverage of issues and events in Japanese business, political and diplomatic life between August 1977 and July 1978. It also reports on the differences between Japanese daily life and our own. The medium is *The New York Times*, from which more than 200 authoritative articles are reprinted exactly as they appeared in the newspaper. The articles—a mixture of on-the-scene reporting and informed analysis—record day-to-day Japan and outline emerging trends.

Professor Edwin O. Reischauer, in his general introduction (page ix) comments on the major issues of the Japanese news year and on those Japanese institutions which have shaped them. Each of the volume's 10 chapters opens with an introduction reviewing the principal themes which are explored in greater depth by the articles that follow. The stories within each chapter are arranged chronologically, except for the occasional clustering of initial and follow-up reports. (In chapter one, for example, an August 11, 1977, article on a volcanic eruption is succeeded by a report on the same theme from November 22.) The index (page 235) is the reader's guide to the wealth of information contained in the volume.

Japan 79 is designed as a practical reference for scholars, travellers, business people and others who need current information about Japan. Yet the book reveals as much about Japan as it does about America's *perceptions* of a land and people linked to us politically, commercially and historically.

Special thanks are due to Sam Woo, the book's designer, and to the *Asahi Shimbun*, the German Information Center, Japan Air Lines, the Japanese Consulate General (New York), the Japan National Tourist Organization, the Japan Trade Center, the United Nations photo office and the White House photo office for use of photographs.

Introduction

In 1974 Arno Press published as part of its series "The Great Contemporary Issues," a large volume entitled simply *Japan*. This book consisted of facsimile reproductions of the major newpaper stories that had appeared in *The Times* between the years 1852 and 1974. It provided a fascinating glimpse of the amazing evolution, triumphs, and vicissitudes of Japan over a span of almost a century and a quarter.

During this long period and at an increasing pace in recent years, Japan has become a country of great significance in the world. This is dramatically illustrated by the fact that the original volume covering 122 years is now followed by this sizable collection of *New York Times* articles about Japan drawn from one single calendar year, August 1977 through July 1978. The articles are grouped topically, with the individual items in each section then placed in rough chronological sequence. Clearly, there is a need for an annual volume of this sort for the many persons who wish to keep up with what is happening in Japan and in our relations with that country.

Today Americans are most engrossed by problems of the economy, and these quite naturally predominate in our relations with Japan. Domestically we are plagued with rapid inflation, widespread unemployment, a slow growth of productivity, high taxes and interest rates, and myriad other problems that are aggravated by these conditions. In our foreign economic relations, a widening deficit in our trade balance and a steep fall in the value of the dollar loom as major problems.

Japan is in some ways central to many of these issues. The dollar's weakness in relation to the yen has been perhaps the most startling aspect of its decline, and the soaring excess in Japan's trade balance with us has been one of the most disturbing elements in our trade deficits. Major American industries have felt threatened by Japanese imports. In 1978 steel, once the pride of the American economy, feared that it was being overwhelmed by Japanese imports and the automotive industry felt threatened, remembering how most motorcycle production had earlier passed into Japanese hands. Japan is the most serious competitor of the American computer industry, which is well aware that much of the production of televi-

Introduction

sion sets and other earlier phases of the electronics industry has come to be dominated by Japan.

Economic frictions between the United States and Japan are now so severe and the complexity of economic problems in both countries and throughout the world so great that tremors are beginning to be felt in the whole international economic system. It seems quite clear that adjustments of some sort must be made, but exactly what needs to be done is by no means obvious. There can be no dispute, however, that the huge economic relationship between Japan and the United States lies very close to the epicenter of these economic instabilities. The United States and Japan are the two largest global traders and have developed between them by far the largest trans-regional trade. This in turn has given rise to some of the greatest and most perplexing economic frictions.

The central position of the United States in the economic problems of the world is not surprising. As one of the world's largest countries, generously endowed by nature, it has quite understandably become the richest country in the world. But Japan is a mere twenty-fifth the size of the United States, with only half its population and very meager natural resources. One would scarcely expect it to have become the third largest economy in the world, exceeded only by the two super-states, the United States and the Soviet Union.

Japan's amazing economic position can only be explained by the skills of its people and the excellence of its economic system. Wholly aside from the problems encountered in the Japanese-American economic relationship, the organization of Japanese industry, the drive of Japanese businessmen abroad, the relationship between labor and management, and the high quality of the Japanese workers are all matters of very great interest to Americans. Who can tell what hints for the solutions of our own economic problems we might find in the remarkable record of the Japanese.

For all these various reasons, the economy is the aspect of Japan that has attracted our attention most in 1978, as is clearly illustrated by the make up of this volume. Five of its ten sections specifically treat economic and trade matters. One section entitled "Japan's Economy" deals with the Japanese economy as a whole, and another on "The Business World" concerns the organization of the great business enterprises which have been so successful in

developing both Japan's domestic economy and its export trade. "The Japanese Abroad" deals primarily with the successes as well as the problems of the Japanese businessman when he ventures into the outside world. "Trade Relations with the United States" focuses in on this largest of fundamental problem areas, which is the one that naturally concerns us most. "The Steel Controversy" singles out this most abrasive issue of the year 1978 in Japanese-American trade relations.

Other sections deal at least in part with economic issues. "The Energy Crisis" is an even greater economic problem for the Japanese than for us, because Japan must import close to 90 percent of its energy resources. One particularly difficult aspect of this problem is the controversy that peaked in 1978 between Japanese desires for American uranium in order to develop more efficient nuclear breeder reactors and American fears that this step might lead to an increased threat to nuclear proliferation because of the production of plutonium. Another aspect of the problem is Japan's search for increased imports of oil from China and gas and coal from Siberia to help offset its overwhelming dependence on Persian Gulf oil, which is a problem for the Japanese far greater than America's troubling but much less crucial reliance on Middle Eastern oil. The section on "Trade and Diplomacy with Asia and the U.S.S.R." also bears in part on these key economic problems.

The American concern with Japan, of course, is not limited to economics. In our relations with Asia, Japan looms larger than any other country. It constitutes a major part of the world trading system we have done so much to develop since World War II. It is one of the very few and by far the largest of the democratic, open societies of the trans-Pacific part of the world. Our Mutual Security Treaty with Japan is much the most important commitment we have in that whole half of the world. American bases in Japan underlie our entire military presence in the area. In short, Japan is decidedly our greatest strategic interest outside of Europe and the Middle East. Problems of its defense, its relations with its neighbors, the attitudes of its people toward us, and the mutual ability of Americans and Japanese to understand each other are matters of prime concern. These are dealt with in the section on "Japan's World Role" and also in part in the section on "Trade and Diplomacy with Asia and the U.S.S.R."

Back of the problems of trade, security, and international alignments lie the development and health of Japanese society and politics. These are treated in sections "Japanese Society" and "The Political World." In these domestic areas of activity, the coverage of foreign journalism is likely to be more sporadic. Significant developments usually take place slowly and in a somewhat amorphous manner, making them more difficult to write about and seemingly less "newsworthy." The foreign reader is likely to perceive such matters as being less immediately relevant to him and also more difficult to comprehend than are foreign relations and trade.

Since there was no major election during the period covered, "The Political World," not surprisingly, is devoted to articles on hijackings by Japanese terrorists and the great protests and rioting that accompanied the opening of Tokyo's new international airport at Narita. Both of these topics were important news items, but they probably represented more the fading fringes of Japanese politics than its developing core.

Once the role of huge numbers of student activists was an important element in the on-going confrontation between conservatives, who were in solid control of the Diet, the Japanese Parliament, and the various opposition parties collectively known as the "Progressives." More recently this confrontation has faded considerably, and student activists have shrunk greatly in number and influence. As they have declined, however, they have become more desperate and violent, but as a result they have also become more peripheral to the political process, shunned by "Progressives" as well as by conservatives. Many of the student terrorists have been driven abroad by the efficient Japanese police, and their hijackings are more likely to represent the last flickerings of past conditions than any wave of the future. Only at Narita has the combination of genuine local farmer opposition to the use of land for the airport and wide dissatisfaction with environmental pollution by heavy air traffic permitted the continuation of a large-scale student-led protest movement. It seems unlikely, however, that many such demonstrations will continue in the future or become again an important part of the political process in Japan.

As for mainstream political life, the most noteworthy trend in 1978 was a continuing and perhaps growing convergence of the Japanese voters near the

Introduction

center of the political spectrum. This has forced a similar convergence of the various parties, seen more in their actions than in their words, which remain less changed because of past history and the sometimes greater commitment of politicians than average voters to traditional ideological stands.

This trend toward the center has been accompanied by the decline of the two major parties, the ruling conservative Liberal Democrats and the Socialists, and the tendency for minor parties to grow and new splinter groups to break off, not toward the extremes of politics, but toward the center. The Liberal Democrats have declined to the point where they have only a tiny majority in either house of the Diet and do not control all of the Diet committees. Their impending loss of a majority has long been predicted and was once expected to herald a radical shift to the left, but such a change no longer seems at all likely. As the Liberal Democratic Party has declined, it has developed the typical Japanese skill of cooperation with others and a smooth transition toward more or less formal coalition governments of the center, embracing many if not all of the Liberal Democrats, seems likely. Old problems of political confrontations between left and right—particularly the question of alignment with the United States —have also faded to a large extent, and newer problems of pollution and slower economic growth, which once seemed to threaten a new polarization of politics, have brought unexpected cooperation among the various parties on a largely nonpartisan basis. All this means that Japanese politics in 1978, as during the past four years, has become progressively calmer and more stable.

Behind these developments lies the convergence of the Japanese people toward a political consensus of the center and, more fundamentally, a steady movement toward a society of remarkable stability. The great majority of the people see themselves as middle class. They overwhelmingly support their constitution, even though it was a product of the postwar period when America occupied Japan. They are pleased with their highly egalitarian

social system, and its leadership by an educational meritocracy. They complain of the rigors and ruthless competition of their educational system but are proud of its openness to all and its results. The Japanese are now perhaps the world's best educated people, with 90 percent of Japanese youth completing the twelve intense years of formal schooling that lead to graduation from senior high school. The Japanese seem to be a well satisfied, reasonably affluent, consumer-oriented mass society, with the usual emphasis on mass spectator sports and other mass activities, with which Americans are so familiar.

At the same time, Japanese society bubbles with vigor and liveliness. It shows tremendous cultural vitality and also variety. It displays, at least to the foreign observer, a bewildering juxtaposition and mixture of internationally familiar elements with others which are strange to him, deriving as they do from Japan's distinctive cultural heritage. Japanese society is evolving and changing at a rapid pace—perhaps as fast as anywhere in the world—but at the same time it retains an extraordinary degree of order and stability. The Japanese have reason to be proud of themselves and are indeed almost complacently self-satisfied. Yet this does not prevent them from agonizing over what it means to be a Japanese and wondering anxiously if they may not be losing their identity. The obvious answer of the outsider would be a resounding "No," but the Japanese themselves have serious doubts on this score.

All in all, Japan is an extraordinarily complex, diverse, and fast changing country. It does not lend itself to easy newspaper coverage, which is inevitably piecemeal in nature. But the section in this book on "Japanese Society" does afford many glimpses into the richness of the mix that makes up modern Japan. It, of course, cannot be comprehensive, but it does present excellent illustrations of at least some of the facets of the complex whole.

A volume like the present one meets a very real need. Scholarly books and analyses tend to trail years behind the

onward march of events. Television, newspaper, and magazine coverage usually leaves only quickly fading impressions. A permanent collection of solid news reports from the recent past offers a useful midway stage in the recording of knowledge.

For Americans, such a record is particularly important concerning Japan. The earlier volume of articles from *The Times* entitled *Japan* shows how extremely remote and unimportant that country seemed to Americans, at least in the early years of their relations. But that is hardly the case today. Japan seems to impinge on our lives at almost every turn. The contacts between the two countries are huge. The problems they raise are vitally important. On the other hand, our knowledge of Japan remains very thin. It is unquestionably far greater than it was only a few decades ago, but it is still entirely inadequate for the needs of the present.

Despite Japanese fears that they may be culturally overwhelmed by a largely Western international culture, they remain extremely distinctive and separate—perhaps too much so for their own good or the good of the world in general, including ourselves. Their language helps isolate them from the speakers of the Indo-European languages of the West or the other major language families of the world. Their ideographic writing system isolates them even more from all countries except the two—China and Korea—which share in part that unique writing system. Their long isolation from the outside world in premodern times has built up psychological barriers that linger on between them and others.

In no other relationship in the world is there a greater contrast between the importance of the contacts and the difficulty of communication and understanding than there is in the relationship between the United States and Japan. There is a pressing need for special efforts to overcome these barriers and develop greater mutual understanding. This volume is to be welcomed as a significant contribution to this important effort.

Edwin O. Reischauer

In marked contrast between ancient and modern Japanese tradition, a pedestrian clad in a kimono walks toward a Tokyo office building.

Chapter 1

Japanese Society

When most foreigners visit an overcrowded industrial city like Tokyo, it is quite possible that they will fail to perceive the distinctive alter-ego of Japanese society, a characteristic which sets Japan apart from the rest of the world. Although young Japanese no longer observe all the religious customs to which their grandparents were devoted and despite a preference for Western rock 'n' roll over Noh incantation, many of Japan's traditional social institutions continue to survive little changed by new cultural phenomena.

These social institutions have been based upon order and cohesiveness, the tightly knit Japanese family organization extended to a national way of life. Until recently, many of the conflicts within other industrialized societies were seemingly absent in Japan. Steadily, however, friction arising from social discrimination, the role of women in a traditional society vis-à-vis that in a modern industrial state, and the increasing threat of environmental pollution and its subsequent social ramifications—common sources of dissension in the United States and Western Europe—are becoming a common part of Japanese life.

Japan is also unique in its unusual ethnic cohesiveness. Only the Koreans, numbering about 600,000, less than 1% of the population, can be considered a recognizable minority group. The majority of Koreans now living in Japan are the remainder of a much greater number brought in during World War II to work in Japanese factories. Although closely related ethnically to the Japanese, the Koreans continue to experience severe discrimination. In recent years, they have become increasingly militant in their demands for social equality. Another element of Japanese population, the *burakumin*, descendants of an ancient pariah class, have also begun an organized campaign against discrimination, with the aid of student radicals.

Japanese women still tend to live for their families and through their husbands. Slowly, however, this situation is changing. Only under the postwar American occupation were women given the right to vote. In mid-1977, during the national elections, a Women's Party entered the races in many Diet (Parliamentary) districts. The Women's Party platform asserted that women be allowed to rule Japan because Japanese men, the traditional rulers, had failed. Although this party captured no seats, its very emergence reveals a rip in the tight social fabric of male-dominated Japan. Paradoxically, however, arranged marriages are still common throughout Japan.

The Japanese government has done little to resolve the problems of industrial pollution. For cities beset by smog, automobile fumes, traffic congestion and an energy shortage, the Cabinet suggested bicycles as an answer to the evils engendered by motorized traffic. A seemingly endless sea of bicycles parked in Japanese cities, many illegally, has created its own, peculiar problems. One small step, however, in the dismal fight against the destruction of the natural environment has been a recent campaign to protect non-smokers in a society that claims the world's highest *per capita* tobacco consumption.

Japanese live in the shadow of natural disasters. Earthquakes, volcanoes, floods, fires and typhoons have all caused extensive physical damage and have left their mark upon the Japanese psyche. Many Japanese live with the real or transmitted memory of a 1923 quake in the Tokyo area which left 150,000 dead and countless others homeless. In August 1977, Mt. Usu, a volcano on Japan's northernmost island of Hokkaido, erupted and caused massive evacuations in the area of Toyako Onsen as well as large-scale damage to agricultural communities. In November, the same area was rocked by a series of earthquakes. In January 1978, an earthquake struck the Izu peninsula south of Tokyo, leaving 25 persons dead. Five months later, a quake hit Sendai, a city of 600,000, killing 21 and rattling windows in far-off Tokyo where subway service had to be halted. Such earthquakes raise concern in Japan, as in California, that the next will be the big one.

Troubled by the major problems resulting from rapid (and highly successful) industrialization, juxtaposed against a background of traditions often incongruous to modernization, Japan has unusually strong tendencies to measure itself—nervously—against other industrial nations. This characteristic is best revealed by turning to an example in the realm of sports. Baseball is by far the most popular sport in Japan, introduced with overwhelming success by the Americans. On September 3, 1977, Japan's baseball hero, Sadaharu Oh, hit his 756th homerun, breaking Hank Aaron's lifetime mark and electrifying the entire Japanese nation. Immediately, a controversy emerged as to whether Oh's homerun total was, in fact, comparable to Aaron's. Do Japanese pitchers throw as hard as American pitchers? Are not Japanese ball parks smaller than those in the United States? Is Oh really Japanese after all? "Oh", it seems, is the Japanese pronunciation of his Chinese father's surname, Wang. The legitimacy conflict coloring Oh's stunning accomplishment highlights Japan's identity crisis, as well as its fluctuating self-assurance.

Japanese Society

Erupting Volcano
Damages Big Area in North Japan

A hiker observes a volcano in Japan.

BY ANDREW H. MALCOLM

TOYAKO ONSEN, Japan, Aug. 10—On Sunday this was a bustling summer resort community of more than 5,000 people.

Yesterday, it was a ghost town.

Mount Usu, a 2,385-foot extinct volcano overlooking this northern Japanese town, has come to life again. In the last three days two new craters, each about the size of a football field, have spewed out millions of tons of rocks, sand, sludge and ash, turning large areas of the rich agricultural island of Hikkaido into a lifeless gray. So far, a downwind swath twice the size of Massachusetts is affected, including 119 towns and cities. Every breeze carries the dust and damage farther.

Because of the prompt evacuation of more than 10,000 area residents and the departure of additional thousands of tourists, there have been no deaths reported. But damage to private and public property, farmland, crops ready for harvest, buildings, businesses, wildlife and lumber resources is expected to top $10 million, officials say. "It's all so far beyond any human calculations," said Yasushi Niki, a town official who donned a helmet against a rain of rocks to help preside over this deserted community. Few Japanese, including the residents, who left yesterday in a military caravan, realize the full extent of the disaster.

Yoshiro Tazawa, director general of the National Land Agency, toured the area today and said he was "surprised" at the extent of the destruction. A full governmental ministerial meeting is planned later this week on specific relief efforts.

But with sharp earthquakes continuing every few minutes here and further eruptions possible, the military and police have cordoned off the hardest hit area, which can be reached only by back roads where volcanic dirt and ash fell knee-deep in some places.

Today, to visit the area of Lake Toya, which was famed for its lush wilderness in a heavily urbanized nation, is suddenly to enter a stunning monochrome world where all color has been bleached out and everything is white or gray.

Green forests are gray. Blue water is gray. Brown houses are gray. Blacktop roads are gray and covered with the fist-sized and head-sized stones that the volcano has hurled thousands of feet into the air since it first erupted Sunday morning. An All Nippon Airways jetliner with 317 persons aboard was forced to return to Chitose Airport, which serves Sapporo, Hokkaido's capital, situated 50 miles to the northeast, after one early rock shower shattered cockpit windows.

Several times the volcano's black,

roiling smoke has climbed to 40,000 feet, where winds carry the ashes for distances of 120 or more miles.

Lights are necessary here even at midday to see through the clouds of dust raised by the slightest movement. In the nearby town of Sobetsu, to which wary residents have been permitted to return, firemen this afternoon seemed to be painting the landscape with their hoses as they washed down buildings, vehicles and streets, with each watery sweep restoring more of the original color.

The streets here stand empty and deserted except for earth-movers and dump trucks, commandeered by Japan's Self-Defense Forces to help haul away huge piles of the refuse.

A few persons, mumbling into once-white gauze masks, shoveled and hoed the volcanic gravel off roofs and half-buried cars, some of which had been covered with blankets and boards as flimsy protection before the residents' hasty departure.

Wildlife Left Without Food

But the ash and dust were everywhere—on food, furniture and floors. "For decades," said Yuiko Shimizu as she shoveled out her grocery store, "you live a normal life here and then this happens and you don't expect it and you don't know what to think."

Overlooked for the moment was the countryside, where deer, bear and pheasant, among other animals, are now denied food. The only sound here today, apart from that made by human activity, was the cawing of crows.

Officials said it would take millions of dollars and a half-dozen years to restore the soil's fertility. Much of the surface of Lake Toya was covered with dust and light-weight pumice rocks,

which tinkled together like ice cubes in a glass. Fishermen downstream expressed growing fear over what would happen to their livelihood when rains carried the ash into fish-breeding places and shellfish beds.

Still unknown is the future impact on tourism, which brought three million visitors to the area annually. In July and August in Toyako Onsen alone tourism amounted to a daily business of $750,000.

Ironically, the disaster began on the weekend of a local festival dedicated to the volcano, which had been dormant since 1910. The Japanese, with an animist religious history, traditionally revere such powerful mountains. Mount Fuji is one such natural monument, and many other mountains retain a special semireligious aura.

Mount Usu also serves as a local tourist attraction. Last Saturday there were earthquakes every seven or eight minutes. But thousands of tourists had gathered, so a big fireworks display, representing an erupting volcano, went on as planned by Hideo Ano, festival chairman.

By Sunday morning, when preparations for the second day's events began, the quakes were coming every two or three minutes. And then at 9:12 A.M., a moment everyone here remembers, the eruption began.

"I looked up," said Shigenobu Kondo, "and suddenly this giant pillar of black smoke shot out of the mountain. But there was no sound at first. It was the strangest thing."

"I was absolutely terrified," said Masae Togawa, "and those earthquakes came so often. Oh, there's another one now." And she paused while the remaining windows in her home rattled loudly.

In one 24-hour period officials here measured 1,480 earthquakes. Shortly before noon Sunday the ashes began to fall. "It was as dark as night," one resident recalled. Everyone remembers giant rumblings like thunder on Sunday night. The evacuations began Sunday and ran through the sporadic eruptions until late yesterday.

"That was the worst," Mrs. Shimizu remembered. "Everything was shaking and then suddenly some little stones fell. People ran out to see them. They were still warm. And then big rocks came down and everyone had to run. See, it shredded my awning."

Eruption Dies Down

Only wisps of steam seeped from the mountain top today. But the frequency of earth movements far below increased, and Yoshi Katsui, a Hokkaido University seismologist, said the mountain's latest eruption might take months to develop fully. Showa Shinzan, another nearby volcano, had intermittent eruptions for 18 months during the World War II years.

"It's still far too early to think of the end," said Mr. Niki. "We haven't fully grasped the beginning yet. But it's strange. We think of that thing as just a mountain. It's been quiet so long you take it for granted. But not now."

Then he chuckled. "You know, I was playing golf when it happened," he added. "We had a city tournament and I had a bad first nine holes when I looked up and saw it. Now, we'll get to start all over again."

But it will not be very soon. The entire golf course now lies under three inches of ashes.

August 11, 1977

A Busy Volcano
Has Unsettled Japanese City

By ANDREW H. MALCOLM

TOYAKO ONSEN, Japan — In this city, the pictures on the walls hang crooked. Every few minutes all conversations halt while residents look up at their ceilings and the buildings shake.

More than three months after Mount Usu, the nearby volcano, roared back to life to bury this northern resort city under tons of ash and rock, Toyako Onsen is now threatened with a plague of earthquakes. One occurs every three minutes as a mass of molten rock a mile underground slowly seeps its way toward the main crater.

Above ground, the material damage from the initial eruption came to more than $127 million. Emergency crews have hauled away much of the debris that the volcano sent up to eight-mile heights to drift and settle over an area twice the size of Massachusetts.

Officially, this city's complete evacuation has ended and its citizens have returned. The cautious residents have united in a well-organized if somewhat bizarre self-help program to draw back the three million tourists who visit here each year and whose money is its economic lifeblood.

Toyako Onsen's troubles began at the

peak of last summer's tourist season. At 9:12 A.M. on Aug. 7, the weekend of the annual volcano festival, Mount Usu, a 2,385-foot-high volcano that had been dormant since 1910, began belching thick gray, black and yellow clouds of smoke thousands of feet into the air. Soon after, sludge, ash, pebbles and hot rocks began plummeting from the sky. The streets of Toyako Onsen were no longer a place to stroll.

The tourists fled. Military caravans evacuated more than 10,000 residents of the area. The city was deserted and the surrounding countryside was smothered by up to two feet of volcanic refuse.

There were no deaths, but crops and timber on thousands of acres were destroyed. Windows and cars were smashed and thousands of fish perished in the once-crystal-clear lake, parts of which still turn ashen after each rain.

Disaster and Opportunity

"This has been a terrible disaster," said Mikio Takezawa, the mayor, "but it's been a good opportunity, too, to forget about our petty little rivalries and rebuild a sense of belonging between neighbors."

"Our big concern" said Kyuichi Maetani, secretary general of the Tourist Association, "is that our disaster has been so well covered by the Japanese media, but our complete recovery has not. We want to tell people. . ." then he paused to look at the ceiling while another quake rattled his office.

"We want to tell people," he continued, "that it is safe here now."

There are those who disagree. The police, for instance, would not lift their roadblocks until late September. A 10 P.M. business curfew lasted even longer and hotels are still required to keep 35 percent of their rooms unoccupied to be available for evacuated citizens.

They also worry that Toyako Onsen may become known mainly as a great place to spend an earthquake. Many tremors are small and noticed only by a group of seismographs now stationed here. Several dozen others each day, however, start with a sharp jolt and seem to last a brief eternity.

The New York Times/Nov. 22. 1977

Hospital Torn in Half

The earthquakes have literally torn in half the nearby Sankei Psychiatric Hospital. The 265-patient facility at the volcano's base is deserted now, its vertical beams tilted and its cement buckled. Crows fly through the shattered windows of the superintendent's office as each day one building wing drifts a little farther away from the other.

Local businessmen stress that the movements underneath their town have declined from 1,500 a day to around 400 a day—but this is still about 400

more than many people would choose to experience in a lifetime. As a result, visitors have stayed away in droves.

Above the city, on the mountain where steam still roars from dozens of fissures, a new peak is growing about 16 inches every day. The surrounding towns each want to name it for themselves, but a special monitoring team pays more attention to an underground mass of molten material, known to scientists as magma, measuring roughly 2,000 feet by 3,000 feet.

"We're not so worried about lava shooting out," says Michiya Yoshidome, one of the monitors, "but this magma is on the move up. That's what is causing the quakes as it breaks through the rock layers. Our major concern is if it hits an underground river. Then you've got vast quantities of water striking magma at maybe 1,000 degrees centigrade and instantly boiling. That pressure could build suddenly and you'd have a very dangerous vapor explosion."

"Nobody knows about the future," Mr. Takezawa said, "but for the layman, things seem much less dangerous now."

Then he looked up through the crisp, early winter air here and pointed at the volcano.

"When I saw it erupting," he said, "the first thing I thought was how simply spectacular it was. You know, you don't see such a beautiful scene often in your life—fortunately."

November 22, 1977

Korean Factions Clash in Tokyo

TOKYO, Aug. 13 (AP)—Korean supporters and opponents of President Park Chung Hee clashed today in Tokyo in a brawl that left 19 persons injured, eight of them seriously, the police said. Authorities said about 300 Korean supporters of the Park Government had disrupted an anti-Government conference, hurling bottles at the dissidents and overwhelming guards and the police.

August 14, 1977

Japan Mourns War Dead and Fetes Spirits of Ancestors

By ANDREW H. MALCOLM

TOKYO, Aug. 15—These are the days for the dead in Japan.

Through religious and historic coincidence, the times for remembering deceased ancestors and those who died in Japan's most recent battles fall together in the middle of August. The accompanying mixture of prayers and tears and festivals and dances makes for some bittersweet midsummer moments in this homogeneous nation, which, although it is the size of California, often seems more like a giant small town.

Observances for victims of the atomic bombs began 10 days ago. The hometown prayers, food offerings and dances to greet returning spirits of the dead began over the weekend throughout Japan. And today at dozens of official memorial services, millions of Japanese, including Emperor Hirohito, bowed their graying heads to feel once again the painful emptiness caused by World War II, which ended at noon 32 years ago today.

But this year, the first in which the

Thousands of people in Nikko participate in a large-scale Bon dance called "Waraku Odori."

Japan National Tourist Organization

postwar generation constituted a majority of Japan's 113 million people, as in other recent years, there were signs that many others, most of them younger, did not share the traditional intensity of feelings for the war dead. "It seems the children have grown more distant and pay little attention," said Yae Ando, a widow.

A Happy Buddhist Rite

Almost everyone in Japan, however, pays attention to O-Bon, a Buddhist holiday introduced to this country in the seventh century. Once a somber religious rite observed only by noblemen, it has become a common happy summertime rite of reunion when families gather to pray and greet the spirits of the dead, who are said to return on the 15th day of the seventh month of the lunar calendar.

The families offer prayers for the souls' peace, token foods for their nourishment and lanterns and bonfires to light the way to and from the spirit world. Joyful folk dances by people of all ages clad in summer kimonos go on well into the night to the sounds of flutes and drums.

Together, families visit the sites where their ancestors' ashes are buried. They clean the grave and pray there and pour rice wine over the stones. Incense is burned too, and if a parent

was especially fond of a particular brand of cigarette, a lighted one may be left behind.

In old rural Japan this observance was a simple gathering. But in modern urban Japan, with families spread all over the archipelago's 3,927 islands, mid-August is turned into a transportation nightmare with trains, buses and roads jammed well beyond capacity. Single domestic airline flights have waiting lists of more than 1,200 people, many of whom take their vacation days in conjunction with the holiday.

Some 5,800 of those travelers, however, were coming to Tokyo as representative members of the families of Japan's 3.1 million war dead.

"No matter how many years pass," said Hatsuko Fukumoto, a war widow whose husband died in Manchuria, "on Aug. 15 we always feel sad."

The site was the Nippon Budokan, frequently the scene of martial arts combat, including the bout last year between Muhammad Ali, the boxer, and Antonio Inoki, a Japanese wrestler. Today the cavernous hall was hung with black, offset only by the Rising Sun flag and carpets of yellow and white chrysanthemums. An orchestra played somber themes as the mourners, most of them dressed in black and aged in their 60's and 70's, were ushered

to their seats.

Alone on the stage sat the Emperor the 75-year-old symbolic leader, who took responsibility for the war when he surrendered to the victorious allies in 1945. Empress Nagako was absent because of back trouble.

Still 'a Pain in My Heart'

"Thirty-two years have passed since the end of the war," said the Emperor, "but I still feel a pain in my heart when I think of the many people who perished in the last war."

Today the voice of the Emperor, which the ordinary Japanese people heard for the first time in his radio speech announcing the surrender, was soft and frail, like the many elderly politicians and officials who also spoke. They included Eiichi Nishimura, who appeared on behalf of Prime Minister Takeo Fukuda, the first prime minister to miss this service since it was instituted in 1963.

Mr. Fukuda, whose wartime duties in the Finance Ministry had included advising the puppet government in China and working out the budget for imperial troops in Indochina, was in Singapore today during a two-week good-will tour of six Southeast Asian countries, each of which suffered at Japan's hands in the war.

The strongest voice at today's hour-

Japanese Society

long ceremonies was that of Hide Teruya. "The day we shall never forget has come again," said the 67-year-old widow, whose husband, Seizen, died in fighting on Tinian.

Mrs. Teruya spoke directly to the cenotaph and to the spirits. "Please look at us and your sons and daughters who have grown to be the support and driving force of modern Japan," she said. "When we see these young people enjoying an affluent life free from care and worry, we realize again how important and valuable human life and peace are. You, the war dead, please rest in peace."

By then hundreds of the older persons wept openly or buried their faces in their hands. "Sometimes I pray for peace," said Mrs. Ando, whose husband's troopship was torpedoed while on the way to New Guinea, "but mostly I think that if we hadn't had a war, then my husband and I would still be leading such a happy life together." Her son, now 36, remembers his father only vaguely as a man who gave him a toy once.

The couple had been married just four years when Setsuji Ando was lost at sea. "But," said his widow, who like most of those there never remarried,

"I think of him every day and I pray." Then she walked out to a bus for the scheduled sightseeing tour of Tokyo.

Among those impatiently waiting to get into the hall were Kimihito Okumura and a band of friends eager to practice kendo, a form of stick fencing. Kimihito, 14 years old, was the only one in the group with a relative killed in the war, an uncle who died long before his birth.

The youth was aware of the memorial service. "But I have no particular feelings about it," he said. "We have a tournament tomorrow."

August 16, 1977

Sunken Ship Becomes Trove for Japanese City It Attacked

By ANDREW H. MALCOLM

ESASHI, Japan—One day more than a century ago, the Kaiyo Maru, the three-masted flagship frigate of the Japanese Navy, appeared offshore here with cannons blazing to attack this prosperous northern city as feudal lords fought against their overthrow and the modernization of Japan.

On that night, Nov. 15, 1868, in one of the many storms that seem so crucial in Japanese history, the Kaiyo Maru ran aground and sank into memory.

Now from below—rotten and rusted —the fabled Kaiyo Maru is successfully returning, piece by piece, to conquer through affection and nostalgia the city it could not subdue by force.

At the same time the sodden vessel has ignited thoughts of those two universally exciting words: sunken treasure.

Katsuji Sumiya, a diver, started the latest flush of excitement one day not long ago when he was working in about 20 feet of water in Esashi Bay. A glint from a partly buried object the size of a fist caught his eye. Mr. Sumiya held the thing up to his mask. It was dirty. It was heavy. It was gold.

A Piece of National History

"I said: No, this can't be!" he recalled. But it was. The chunky object— over two and a half pounds of solid gold—is worth more than $5,600, apart from its antique value.

The ancient ship's reincarnation as a piece of national history, a symbol of local pride, and maybe some day a profitable tourist attraction, continues daily now with the raising so far of more than 8,000 items—old binoculars, knee-high leather boots, watches,

The New York Times/Aug. 19, 1977

navigational instruments, coins, cannonballs, cartridges made in Belgium and huge cannons still loaded for firing.

The science club at Esashi High School is restoring the treasure-trove for a municipal exhibition that is attracting growing crowds from all over Japan. And every night Hideo Yamamoto takes the gold bar to a bank in a plain brown envelope just in case some "outsiders" get any dishonorable ideas.

Forgotten for the moment are the town's troubles—the deteriorating herring catches, the continuing economic centralization of life in Japan's bigger cities and the irresistible draw they have for Esashi High School's graduates. The population has fallen to 14,000, half the total when the ship sank, but these days the town is exulting in the surprise, the promise and the mystery of the sunken treasure.

"Everybody knew a ship was out

there somewhere," said Mayor Giichi Honda. "Kids and professionals would go diving to look for it all the time. But of course no one ever found it. And no one ever dreamed there was such a wealth of things down there. Who knows what else there is?"

Ship Ordered From Netherlands

The 240-foot-long ship was ordered in 1863 from Dordrecht, the Netherlands, because the Civil War in the United States tied up shipyards there. It cost $400,000 and arrived in Japan just as the 260-year rule of the Tokugawa shoguns, the military chiefs, was crumbling.

The Kaiyo Maru fought against some of the Emperor's forces in the Pacific Ocean near Osaka and rescued the last shogun from imperial troops near there. From Tokyo, then called Edo, the ship and seven others fled to Hokkaido, the northernmost of Japan's main islands, to regroup, unsuccessfully as it developed.

Under Emperor Meiji Japan then moved to enter the modern world and build the third largest economy in only 100 years.

"If they hadn't lost their main warship here," the Mayor said, "and they went on to victory, then Japanese history would have been drastically different."

After the ship sank, a few items including a giant anchor and a cannon were dragged onto the beach. But over the years local inhabitants lost track of the wreck. It was covered with mud and sand. Unknowingly the town even built a long cement pier on top of part of the vessel. But in 1975 the local board of education, with financial support from the central and provincial governments, began a major search and recovery effort that will cost far

5

more than the ship did.

It is thought to be the first such salvage project in Japan. "I believe," said Yuko Kobayashi, the science teacher who supervises the renovation of the discoveries, "that Japanese marine archeology is beginning right here in our town."

'Like Unraveling a Mystery'

"It's like unraveling a mystery," said Hideki Urasaki, a student. "As I chip off the mud and shells I imagine what each part was and where it went and how it worked."

City officials hope to build an exhibition center for the artifacts, possibly a concrete, ship-shaped underwater museum of the sunken vessel situated coveniently near the local restaurants, inns and bars of this 700-year-old regional commercial center. However, the projected cost is $5.6 million, "and that might be a bit much for a small town like this," speculates Fujio Ishibashi, head of the board of education.

For others here the wreck of the Kaiyo Maru recalls more from the past than it portends for the future. "When I was a little boy," said Toshiyoshi Konya, who is 66 years old. "I used to crawl into the same bedding with my grandmother and she'd tell me all the stories about how she saw the ship arrive and the cannons and shells and fires and how she fled into the mountains with her money and food in a pot on her back.

"Esashi didn't have any samurai for protection because it was only a business center," he said.

Mr. Konya remembers helping to pull the one anchor up the hill, where it stood upright until the Japanese Army confiscated it during World War II for scrap iron. "When we were little," he said, "we used to lie in the curved part and look out at the sea and up at the trees. Those were different days then. But I firmly believe there are two more anchors down there somewhere.

"We're going to find them some day," he said. "And then the children of Esashi can lie on the old iron anchor on the hillside once again."

August 19, 1977

Japanese Women Find Forum in Film Maker's TV Show

By ANDREW H. MALCOLM

TOKYO, Aug. 26 — The television show opens with a view of the woman guest. Her identity is hidden from viewers by camera angle or rippled glass, but she is obviously sobbing and wiping her eyes.

A female announcer tells the story of this 36-year-old woman, how she was married 15 years ago, how her husband was stricken and bedridden soon afterward, how they have not had sexual intercourse for a decade, how strongly the woman wants her own child yet how torn she is between her own desires and needs and loyalty to her husband.

"I need your guidance, please," she implores.

Switch to the moderator: "Among the various problems we are consulted about here," he says, "the most painful are those involving illness when normal marital relations are impossible. Today's is such a case."

The woman's identity remains hidden, but who is the man? A psychologist? A doctor? Maybe a minister?

A 'Dear Abby' Approach

No. The moderator of this "Dear Abby"-type program is none other than Nagisa Oshima, the 45-year-old avant-garde Japanese movie director whose latest film, "In the Realm of the Senses," has aroused the critical attention of moviegoers, critics and censors and added fire to a continuing global dispute over the difference between a statement and an obscenity. The cinematic controversy centers on whether the film, which graphically depicts the literally all-consumng, insatiable love of a Japanese couple, the man's murder and his vivid castration by a devoted mistress, is art or pornography.

Artistic statements aside, certainly Mr. Oshima's largest audience consists of Japanese housewives, whose washing machines, automatic rice cookers and other labor-saving devices have given them the time in recent years to reflect on their social position in Japan and, through television, to see how women live and work elsewhere.

One result of this time to reflect has been the widespread growth and popularity of daytime counseling programs for women. Mr. Oshima's 30-minute live "School for Women" is about the most popular of them, drawing more than nine million viewers nationwide every Wednesday morning at 9, the precise time millions of husbands are reporting to work.

Except for confidential chatter with female friends, a shelter for battered wives and the marriage counseling of a small band of foreign Christian missionaries, there are virtually no organized outlets for women's guidance —except for these television shows, which are swamped with mail from women who want to appear and get help.

'An Invaluable Insight'

Mr. Oshima is frank about the show's corporate purpose. "It's to raise the station's ratings and earnings," he said. "But for me, it is an invaluable insight into lives as they are lived on the ground and not high in the sky. I'm sure it has affected my film work." It also provides him with a regular income (which he won't disclose) in Japan's precariously financed film world.

Mr. Oshima sees himself as "principal" of his women's school. With the help of a lawyer and three laymen, he listens to the problems of each week's anonymous guest, asks questions and suggests solutions. "Often just talking about the problem helps considerably," he said. "There is no one else to listen to them."

Under the panel's questioning, the unhappy, childless wife said she had been doing her best, listening to her husband's daily tales of aches and pains and suppressing her desires for sex and a baby—and also for a divorce— because it seemed like abandoning her spouse. "I just feel so awfully lonely," she said.

By the program's close, the consensus, including Mrs. X., was that a divorce was desirable to let her start a new life. "I'm sure your husband has been watching this," Mr. Oshima said, "and now he knows how you feel and perhaps now you can have a real talk about the problem."

In his five years on the Asahi Network show, Mr. Oshima, who is married and the father of three, has detected a sharp change in the problems presented.

"The women used to be always the victims," he said. "They were beaten or abused or seriously unhappy. They just wanted to know how to cope. However, now they want to change things. I call it 'dissatisfaction disease.'"

He describes the typical symptoms as follows: An intelligent young woman works for several years then marries and quits work to raise babies. A few years later the child enters school and the woman suddenly finds herself alone, surrounded by the walls of an apartment. The ambitious husband is gone mostly, and their interests drift apart.

"That's when the women," Ms. Oshima said, "ask themselves the question: 'What kind of life is this for me?'"

Displays of emotion and heart-to-heart talks between husband and wife are not openly prized in Japan. Even Mr. Oshima doesn't consult or confide in his wife before a family decision; he informs her afterward.

Indirection Is Much Favored

Traditionally, in Japan the basic bond between husband and wife is believed strongest when unstated. Shared silences are far more meaningful than a flood of words. Even when speaking, implication and indirection are much favored, not explicitness. In a static society this was adequate, and still is for many.

But Mr. Oshima and other observers

see increasing modern-day marital problems in Japan as the changing assumptions, ambitions and understandings of women undermine traditional foundations. The men feel threatened and the women misunderstood.

"Sometimes I get very depressed about all this," said Mr. Oshima, who occasionally is sought out on the street by troubled women. "Of course," he noted, "Japanese men have their own problems. But for them the bar girls and mama-sans play the same counseling role. They listen. They sympathize. They console. And maybe they suggest solutions. They're just not on television."

August 29, 1977

Oshima's Troubles

TOKYO, Aug. 26— The controversy surrounding his film, "In the Realm of the Senses," is only part of the trouble that faces Nagisa Oshima.

The Tokyo District Public Prosecutor's Office earlier this month indicted the director and Hajime Takemura, president of Sanichi Shobo Publishing, for selling and possessing obscene literature and photographs. The indictment is based on a book about the movie, which contains pictures from the film and script excerpts. Officials said the book needlessly arouses sexual desires and violates good sexual morality.

"That's absurd," Mr. Oshima said. "The book is even more obscure than the censored movie. Things only look obscene if you try to hide them, and that's what they're trying to do."

To satisfy Japan's censors, who found Mr. Oshima's film to be pornography rather than art, the same effort to "hide" was taken. The film version here has been given a moving, blurry fuzz covering any part of the screen showing any private parts of the anatomy. In this film, that makes for a lot of blurry fuzzes for $3.30 a ticket.

August 29, 1977

Oh Surpasses Aaron With 756th Home Run

By ANDREW MALCOLM

TOKYO, Sept. 3—Sadaharu Oh hit the 756th homer of his Japanese baseball career here tonight, making him the most prolific home-run hitter in professional history.

The 37-year-old first baseman for the Yomiuri Giants hit his 755th home run last Wednesday night, tying the number that the retired Henry Aaron achieved in setting a major league mark in the United States. Oh's homer tonight, an arching 328-foot shot into the right-field stands of Tokyo's Korakuen Stadium, ignited nationwide celebrations by millions of cheering fans, who have adopted Oh as a Japanese national hero—even though he is actually Chinese and cannot vote in Japan.

Oh has said, "I don't think I would do as well in American baseball," but comparisons are difficult to draw. Japanese parks are slightly smaller than those in the United States, and coast-to-coast travel takes a more severe toll on American ballplayers. On the other hand, Oh has had to achieve his feat in considerably shorter seasons played in Japan.

Joe DiMaggio, a frequent visitor to Japan, had rated Japanese baseball quality as somewhere between the American triple-A minors and the major leagues. Other American observers also believe that Oh faced pitchers less effective than those who threw to Aaron.

Tomorrow Oh, the shy, modest son of an immigrant Chinese noodle vender, will meet Prime Minister Takeo Fukuda

to receive a special Japan medal of honor. Then he will proceed to the ballpark to resume his left-handed assault on the 800 home-run goal.

But tonight, even as chanting fans bearing banners converged on his modest Tokyo home, Oh, bathed in spotlights, stood hatless in the middle of the field and told a hushed, hoarse crowd: "As long as my body can stand it, I will swing a bat and hit more home runs, with everybody's help."

To make matters even better, the historic home run helped Oh's Giants, the perennial pennant-winners in Japan's two-league, 12-team professional baseball system, to top the second-place Yakult Swallows, 8-1, and keep a 14-game hold on first place.

The 'Oh Shift'
The homer came in the bottom of

the third inning, with none on and one out. Oh, who has been hitting .321, had walked his previous time at bat, a tactic opposing pitchers have taken 2,180 times during his 19-year career. The Swallows also had gone into the "Oh shift," in which players move to the batter's right.

The count was 3 and 2. Oh, who admits he still gets tense before every game, nervously tapped his shoes with his bat, spit into his ungloved hands and faced the Swallows pitcher, a 28-year-old, five-year veteran named Yasu-miro Suzuki.

As the ball left Suzuki's hand, Oh lifted his right leg in his distinctive one-legged "flamingo" batting style. The pitch was supposed to be a sinker. But Oh slammed his right foot down hard and swung the bat around waist-high. The ball rose into the muggy air, along with 55,000 screaming fans.

Four seconds later Saneyoshi Furuya, a 25-year-old office worker who was at his fifth game in five days hoping to see the big homer, caught the ball. In return for it, the Giants gave him a new autographed ball, bat and a trip to a hot springs spa.

"I knew instantly that it was gone," said a smiling Oh, who held his arms up high and circled the bases slowly, as his coach had instructed, so he could savor the achievement. Oh jumped on home plate with both feet and was mobbed by teammates. "Now I can sleep well tonight," he told them.

Pitcher Declines 'Honor'

Confetti, streamers and fireworks flew while Suzuki, the pitcher, watched quietly. Continental Air Micronesia, a United States airline, had offered the pitcher of home run No. 756 a trip to Saipan. But a disappointed Suzuki declined tonight.

Absent from the crowd were Oh's wife, Kyoko, and their three daughters.

Sadaharu Oh demonstrates skills to fans on his day off.

Oh, who is protective of their privacy from his fame, had them watch on TV at home. But his aging father, Shufuku, 76, and his mother, Tomi, were in their reserved seats as usual. And Oh presented them with his prize bouquet. "At last," said the elder Oh, "the pressure is off."

Oh will get a substantial bonus on top of his $240,000 salary for a 130-game season. He will also receive an oil painting, a new car, an electric organ, a spa trip and 756 bath towels.

"I've been wearing the uniform of the Yomiuri Giants for 19 years," Oh told the crowd. "I've had my difficulties and disappointments. But thanks to your strong support, my dream has been realized. I am a fortunate man."

Oh, who like Babe Ruth began his career as a pitcher, has been the premier Japanese player almost from the day he graduated from high school and signed with the Giants. He has hit four home runs in one game, seven in seven consecutive games and 13 with the bases loaded, including one in the opening game this year.

September 4, 1977

Wow! Oh!!

By Shigeru Makino

TOKYO—Sadaharu Oh, the famous slugger for Japan's Yomiuri Giants, has hit his historic 756th home run, putting him ahead of Hank Aaron. Yet American baseball circles maintain that Oh's record is not a world record—a view shared by many average citizens as well.

At the same time, I hear that there is a suggestion that a Japanese team, namely the Yomiuri Giants, be admitted to the United States major leagues, to generally benefit the game and make it truly international.

As for whose record is recognized, Oh's or Aaron's, I don't think it matters one bit. And on the matter of changing the league lineups, I don't think it's a good idea.

First, Oh's record: Japanese players use smaller baseballs, it is said. They play in slightly smaller fields. And Oh hit pitches thrown by Japan-ese pitchers while Aaron faced stronger American hurlers.

What puzzles me is the way some Americans carp at such trifles about Oh's home-run achievements. Whether or not to see Oh's 756th home run (he now has 761) as the world's record is just a matter of comparing figures, and will never establish which man is the world's No. 1 hitter. Such meticulousness on Americans' part seems to me to derive from confusing plain figures with real power.

Japanese Society

We Japanese have had a similar experience. When a Frenchman beat Japan's judo champion at the world tournament not long ago and snatched the championship from Japan, we didn't want to admit that he was stronger than our man.

However, we learned that such a development would not necessarily drag judo down from the seat of a Japanese national sport. Likewise, Oh's 756th home run does not degrade at all the athletic achievements of Aaron. They both have excelled. Aaron's record is Aaron's; Oh's is Oh's. What we should do, then, is just admire their individual greatness respectively

I spend every March in Florida taking a look at the spring camps of the major league teams. What I have learned from these experiences in the Grapefruit League is that the average power of Japan's professional baseball teams is Triple A class. Of course, we have Oh and a few other players who could easily compete on the major league teams of another nation. But,

on the average, I'd say a Japanese player might be ranked, unfortunately, as Triple A in both power and speed.

Hal Breeden, an American outfielder playing with Japan's Hanshin Tigers, is a good example. He has so far hit more than 30 homers this season alone here, although he only hit 21 during his four years in the American majors.

"Internationalizing" baseball by including one Japanese team in the American major leagues is a proposal that looks interesting and amusing. But there are too many problems for it to be realized.

There are mechanical problems—the size of the ball is smaller, and the travel costs and jet lag would be great. But, more importantly, the departure of any single team—and especially if it is the widely followed Yomiuri Giants—would so disrupt Japanese professional baseball and its schedule as to require dissolution of the two leagues, which is of course impossible.

You can see the importance of base-

ball here by the jubilation that greeted Oh's world record home run. Not only baseball fans but the entire nation got so excited that even Prime Minister Takeo Fukuda awarded him a national decoration.

Maybe we got a little too excited over Oh's recent homer. But I'd hope that this would be understood by the American people who sometimes have the same crazes. This kind of enthusiasm should promote further baseball coordination between our two baseball nations instead of turning us to arguments over Oh's record.

Shigeru Makino is a sportswriter and baseball commentator on television. A former infielder for the Nagoya Dragons, he spent 14 years as head coach of the Yomiuri Giants. While he was coach, the Giants won 11 championships, nine of them in a row. This article was translated from the Japanese by the Tokyo bureau of The New York Times.

September 24, 1977

Tokyo Greets 'Pele Brigade' As Superstars

By ANDREW H. MALCOLM

TOKYO, Sept. 9—Typhoon No. 9, packing winds of more than 125 miles an hour, was bearing down on the Japanese islands today. But it is hard to believe that any winds could sweep this city the way Pelé and the New York Cosmos have, even before their two exhibition games against Japanese teams.

The 25-member Cosmos party — minus Steve Hunt, who returned to England because of "homesickness," according to Coach Eddie Firmani—arrived here last night after two games in the Caribbean area, a one-day layover in New York City, and a 16-hour flight to Tokyo.

Just for walking off the airplane, the team grabbed prominent Page One displays in Japan's national sports daily newspapers.

"HERE COMES THE PELE BRIGADE!" screamed the red ink at the top of the Tokyo Chunichi Sports newspaper, which devoted its entire page just to the arrival. "King Pelé and Emperor Beckenbauer Compete in Dream Game," another yelled.

Flashbulbs Galore

At a news conference today, every movement of a team member, especial-

ly Pelé, ignited the flashbulbs of dozens of Japanese photographers.

"We are deeply honored," Coach Firmani tried to say over the staccato stutter of snapping shutters. Pelé had only moved his hand.

Tomorrow at the invitation of the Japan Soccer Association, the Cosmos will play the Furukawa Electric Company team, Japan's national corporate champions. On Monday there is a soccer festival in Osaka followed by a night game Wednesday against the Japan All-Star team.

Then it is on to a game in Peking, one in Shanghai, one in Calcutta and a return to New York City Sept. 26 to prepare for Pelé's last match against his old Brazilian team, Santos, Oct. 1.

Both games in Japan will be televised nationally, as were filmed portions of today's circus news conference, which was conducted in Japanese, English, German, Spanish and Portuguese.

The Cosmos are only the latest in a series of American athletic teams that have made the long trans-Pacific flight to compete before Japanese fans. Foreign sports here are heavily merchandised by newspapers, equipment manufacturers and television stations, which broadcast some British football and National Football League action months and even years after the games were played.

Big Profits Expected

The Cosmos' tour here is expected to be very profitable. Tickets, which range from $8 to $15, are selling well, and then there are Cosmos binoculars, Cosmos keychains, Cosmos paperweights, Cosmos sun visors, Cosmos pens and Cosmos pencilboxes.

The National Stadium, scene of both games, holds 65,000 people, although heavy rains from the rim of the approaching storm may cut into attendance. What will you do, one reporter shouted, if it rains tomorrow?

"We'll play with umbrellas," said Pele.

There is little doubt where the focus of the Cosmos tour here is. In fact, it isn't called the Cosmos tour. It's the "Pele Sayonara Game in Japan."

Pele was asked if this was definitely his last retirement. "I have an invitation to play on the moon," he said, "but nothing else on earth."

Franz Beckenbauer, Giorgio Chinaglia, Carlos Alberto and other members admitted they had fallen victim to jet lag, that disorienting discomfort when your body tells you it is midnight in New York when it is only 1 P.M. in Tokyo. "We all got up at 4 A.M.," Chinaglia said.

"This is one of my biggest worries," Firmani said later, "we've been traveling so much. I don't know if there is

9

enough time to recuperate."

"We'll be ready tomorrow," said Chinaglia.

The coach ordered an hour's calisthenics and running this afternoon at a borrowed Tokyo athletic field. "It's to take the airplane out of our bodies," said Julio Mazzei, assistant coach.

First, however, the Cosmos had to extricate themselves from a besieging. beseeching crowd of newsmen. But this time the Japanese journalists did not want quotes or photographs. They wanted autographs.

September 10, 1977

Cosmos Draw Record 65,000 In Tokyo Game

TOKYO, Sept. 14 (AP) — Giorgio Chinaglia, Jadranko Topic and Nelsi Morais each scored one goal as the Cosmos of the North American Soccer League defeated an all-Japan squad by 3-1 tonight before 65,000 spectators, Japan's biggest soccer crowd ever.

Pele, star of this and one previous "Pele Sayonara" game in Japan, a 4-2 victory over the Furukawa Electric Company team, missed an excellent scoring chance when his second-half free kick missed the goal by three feet.

The 36-year-old Brazilian retires Oct.

1 after a game between the Cosmos and Santos of Brazil, his former team.

Tonight's attendance at National Stadium beat the previous record of 53,516 set May 26, 1972, when Santos played an all-Japan team at the same park. It also marked the retirement of Kunishige Kamamoto, Japan's No. 1 player, after 13 years.

Chinaglia Opens Scoring

Chinaglia scored the first goal 16 minutes into the game and Topic smashed in a rebound shot that struck the left goal post seven minutes later. Morais scored the visitors' final goal with nine minuets left. Japan's only score came with six minutes remaining on a kick by Keizo Imai.

After the game, Pele and Kamamoto exchanged uniform jerseys. Then the Brazilian star gave his spiked shoes to Kamamoto.

In a brief farewell message to the Japanese fans—in Japanese—Pele said: "Mina sama domo arigato gozai mashita," which means "Everyone, thank you very much."

September 15, 1977

Bread? Let Them Eat Rice

By HIROTAKA YOSHIZAKI

TOKYO

It probably had to happen sometime. And now it has. Japan is making bread—with rice.

"We wanted more people to eat rice," said Akio Takaoka of the government's food agency.

"And we wanted to cooperate with the government's policy to encourage people to eat more rice," said Kenichi Miyazaki of the Yamazaki Baking Company, Japan's largest.

A result is an oblong-shaped loaf of bread that looks like a loaf of bread, cuts like a loaf of bread and tastes faintly like a bowl of rice.

Another result is to help use up Japan's growing surplus of rice, the only major food this island country produces enough of. Consumption of rice has been steadily decreasing in recent years, reflecting a drift in taste away from rice and toward meat and wheat.

In the last two decades, for instance, the per capita consumption of rice in Japan dropped 26 percent while that of meat rose a dramatic 580 percent, milk

A farmer tends his rice paddy.

Japan National Tourist Organization

730 percent and butter and cheese 880 percent. Last year's rice harvest produced a 2.6 million ton surplus, and this year a three-million-ton surplus is expected.

In fact, rice has been so abundant that farmers once received incentives not to grow it. More recently, the Education Ministry reintroduced rice into school lunches, and the food agency initiated an "eat more rice" campaign.

Now comes rice bread. It not only helps consumers to eat more rice but could also decrease costly imports of wheat. Japan buys 96 percent of its wheat overseas, mostly from the United States.

"Besides, in terms of nutrition, rice bread is superior to the bread made from wheat alone," said Akira Matsuda, a spokesman for the Japan Baking Industry Association. "It contains more vitamin B-1, B-2, and minerals."

The bread is from 14 to 20 percent rice flour. Other ingredients include wheat flour, yeast, sugar, water, shortening and powdered milk. The color is somewhere between white bread and whole wheat. The taste and odor vary somewhat according to baker, but generally it tastes like white bread with a light rice flavor and added chewiness.

What added to Japan's drive to develop rice bread was the fear of a possible food crisis, especially after the United States' temporary restriction on soybean exports and the oil crisis in 1973.

Despite the government's zeal and the bread industry's cooperation, however, the new brand of bread is not yet selling like hot cakes. Although 40,000 loaves are sold each day, that is only two percent of total bread sales in this nation of 113 million people.

The price of rice bread is almost 20 percent higher than conventional bread. A 14 ounce loaf of rice bread costs 53 cents here while the same size of regular bread is 45 cents.

September 14. 1977

In Japan, You Can Buy Almost Anything From a Vending Machine

By ANDREW H. MALCOLM

TOKYO, Oct. 24—Japan, the powerful economic giant whose energetic postwar recovery built the second largest economy in the non-Communist world, has now become No. 2 in a new category of industrial achievement—vending machines. But not without problems.

No one kept track of the exact moment that this island nation's vending-machine census surpassed West Germany's battalions of mechanical dispensers.' But Japanese vending-machine vendors have now populated this narrow nation's narrow streets, lanes, alleys and hallways with more than 3.2 million machines. That is seven times the number clicking away in 1967.

In the same decade, Japan's human population grew by only 13 percent.

But since Japan's area is about the same as California's, that makes for more vending machines per cubic coin here than any other country. The United States, for instance, has one machine for every 53 people; Japan has one for every 36. There is even an annual vending machine manufacturers' trade fair that ended here last week after displaying 600 different machines from 45 manufacturers.

Vending Machine Says 'Thanks'

Row upon row from Hiroshima to Hokkaido, these bright-eyed electric salesmen peddle everything from tickets to teas, from stockings to noodles, from batteries to fish. The machines are the only residents of some highway rest stops. And one automatic vendor in Sapporo reportedly even thanks patrons politely.

The social significance of this Japanese trend has yet to be fully plumbed here. Many see the growth as another part of the depersonalization and standardization of urban Japanese life, while investors have marked vending machines as one of the nation's hottest growth industries.

The growth has in recent years created a whole new class of absentee entre-

In Japan, vending machines sell everything from stockings to noodles.

Japan Air Lines

preneurs whose total business is conducted for them by machine. Japanese vending-machine sales last year totaled $6.4 billion, or about $60 per person.

This compares with $9.8 billion and $40 per person for the roughly four million vending machines in the United States.

This rapid success has also brought problems to Japan in the form of machines that spit boiling water over the hands of unwary patrons, machines reluctant to part with wares and unstable machines that topple on passers-by, fatally in two cases.

'Pornography' Issue Raised

But the fastest growing sector of the Japanese vending-machine phenomenon has now become the center of a nationwide social and legal controversy. It concerns the 11,000 machines that sell what in Japan are called "pornographic magazines," publications that display photographs or drawings of partly nude women. So far, no one is questioning the need for such magazines, which are bought or perused by millions of readers of all ages at newsstands.

What has aroused the outcry among some parents, politicians and police officials is that any child with the proper coins can buy the publications.

The heated controversy, which has now entered several local assemblies, has lead to recent newspaper headlines such as: "Irresponsible Vending Machines Criticized" and "Pornography and Vending Machines: What Should Be Done? What Can Be Done?"

Nara Prefecture has banned such so-called "porn machines." The police in Osaka have seized a number of the machines, while other bodies have begun deliberations to brand some of the publications "harmful to the healthy growth of juveniles." One new Nara ordinance prohibits the sale of contraceptives in vending machines within 220 yards of a school building.

But the need for legal regulation of such machines is so new in Japan that legal responsibilities are divided among several Government ministries, and there are few specific rules to enforce.

Definition of Obscenity Imprecise

The Tokyo police have been able to seize some "porn machines" because they occupy part of a public throughfare. But there is no enforceable definition of what constitutes exhibition of "obscene pictures and other materials," a criminal-code violation that could bring a two-year jail term and an $8,000 fine.

A Tokyo metropolitan police spokesman said the department preferred the vague definition because it kept prospective pornography publishers uncertain of what they could publish.

tain of what they could publish.

One compromise solution is to cover the machine's lighted display glass with an opaque film that can be seen through only at night, when presumably youngsters are at home in bed. Nighttime in Japan is when many of the machines do their best business.

Except in the bar-filled nightlife quarters like Tokyo's Ginza or Shinjuku, most stores, and especially the thousands of family-run neighborhood shops in Japan, are shuttered by 7 or 8 P.M. Even most public pay phones are unplugged by then and taken indoors until morning.

Thus, anyone running out of milk, beer, cigarettes or ice would have to wait until dawn without the help of the vending machine. In Japan the machines also sell golf balls, fortunes, pantyhose, hamburgers, bags of rice, cans of corn soup, popcorn, whisky, fishburgers, rice balls, dried fish, noodles, lemon tea, brandy tea, whisky tea, sake, cold chocolate milkshakes, fruit juice and cans of coffee black, coffee with sugar, coffee with milk, coffee with both or coffee with liquor.

October 25, 1977

Data-Loving Japanese Rejoice on Statistics Day

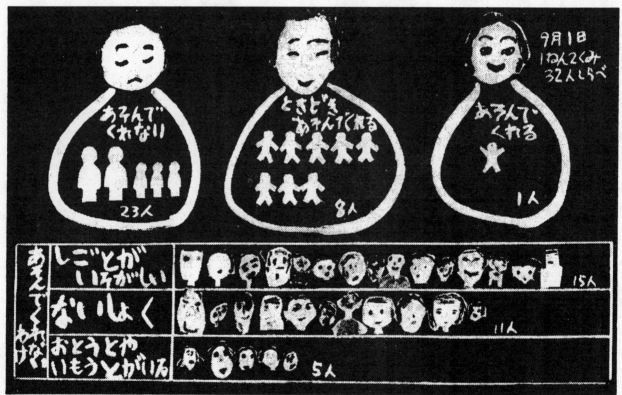

The New York Times/Hirotaka Yoshizaki

Prize-winning graph in Japanese contest was done by five 7-year-olds. Chart told how often classmates' mothers played with them (never, sometimes, always) and gave reasons (too busy, she works, looks after siblings).

By ANDREW H. MALCOLM

TOKYO, Oct. 27—This month, the 10th one of the year, the 72-year-old Takeo Fukuda, this nation's 13th postwar Prime Minister, leads the 113 million citizens of Japan in marking the fourth anniversary of a very special event in the official life of Japan—Statistics Day.

Japan, a 2,600-year-old nation that consists of 3,937 islands covering 145,267 square miles, was a relative latecomer in the official compilation of numbers used throughout the world today to portray national characteristics.

In fact, it wasn't until after World War II, during the American military occupation, that Japan began applying the same methodical diligence to the collection of statistics that it would apply to its remarkable postwar reconstruction. As one result of that rebuilding, Japan now boasts the third most powerful economy in the world.

But there is likely no nation that ranks higher in its collective passion for statistics.

In Japan, statistics are the subject of a holiday, local and national conventions, awards ceremonies and nation-wide statistical collection and graph-drawing contests.

"This year," said Yoshiharu Taka-hashi, a Government statistician, "we had almost 30,000 entries. Actually, we had 29,836."

Four years ago, in an effort to broaden public understanding of sta-tistics and to provide a public relations focus for the work, the Cabinet set Oct. 18 as National Statistics Day. Since then the number of Statistics Day observances has increased so much that one day cannot handle the load. So October has become a kind of statistical observance season.

Numbers sometimes seem to domi-nate life here. The national census is taken every five years, twice as often as in the United States. On school re-port cards children, who are referred to as second son or third daughter and so forth, are graded on a scale of 1 through 5 or 10. In Japanese the months have no names, just numbers.

Last month, when Sadaharu Oh, the baseball player, broke Hank Aaron's career home-run record of 755, a Japa-nese newspaper ran a lengthy series of articles on him. But the series con-tained not one single word, only num-bers. It was a statistical record of every time Mr. Oh had come to bat in his 19-year baseball career.

When a malfunction or strike delays or cancels some of the thousands of trains that daily stitch these islands together, the railroad companies pro-duce precise totals of the number of passengers inconvenienced with a certi

tude that can come only from the knowledge that no one else is counting.

In Japan, every day's news on televi-sion and radio and in the newspapers is dominated by statistics—the yen's value is increasing, the stock market is declining, exports are up, imports are down, foreign exchange reserves are growing, so are foreign criticisms, the cost of living, the number of bank-ruptcies, unemployed, the size of sav-ings accounts and the importance of statistics.

On Oct. 18, 1870, two years after the end of feudal Japan was pro-claimed, the Meiji Government, in what is believed to be this nation's first mod-ern compilation of statistics, ordered all prefectural governments to submit statistics on their local products regu-larly.

But it was not until after World War II that the science of statistics really got started here. Under the influence and encouragement of American occu-pation forces, the Japanese Govern-ment standardized and consolidated its statistical operations—for the first time—in the Statistics Commission.

The central Government's statistical role has been reorganized several times since. Moreover, the National Statistics Law, which aims at "securing the truthfulness of statistics, eliminating the duplication of statistical investiga-tion, consolidating the system of statis-tics and planning to improve and devel-op the statistical system," has been amended 11 times.

"In a modern society," noted Mr. Takahashi, "statistics have become a necessity." In addition to the obvious statistical categories, the central Gov-

ernment now compiles figures on such things as the success rate of the artifi-cial incubation of chicken eggs, the number of railroad cars produced, the volume of mail from overseas, the size of children's monthly allowances, the number of baseball gloves imported, and the frequency of toothbrush usage.

Four years ago, however, the Gov-ernment began to notice a statistical decline in the cooperation rate of its citizens, many of whom were apparent-ly unconvinced of the numbers' neces-sity. Thus National Statistics Day was established.

This year's national theme is "Statis-tics are the beacon for our happy life." Entries in the statistical graph contest were screened three times by judges, who gave first prize this year to the work of five 7-year-olds. Their graph creation, titled "Mom, play with us more often," was the result of a survey of 32 classmates on the frequency that mothers play with their offspring and the reasons given for not doing so (the most often heard excuse: "I"m just too busy").

Tomorrow, 2,500 Government em-ployees involved with statistics will gather in the city of Fukui for Japan's main statistical rally. The highlight will be an address by Prof. Takashi Iga on "The kinds of statistics needed for the economy of the future." He says he will speak for about 60 minutes.

But there is one figure that won't be included: Officials do not yet keep statistics on the number of statistics they keep. "We don"t know," says Mr. Takahashi, "they are countless."

October 28, 1977

PERFORMERS IN JAPAN LINKED TO DRUG ABUSE

Many Prominent Figures Involved, Stunning Fans—
Fears of a New Epidemic Voiced by Officials

TOKYO, Nov. 5—The entertainment world has been shaken in recent days by the interrogation, arrest or conviction of a dozen prominent Japanese on charges of having violated strict laws against narcotics and marijuana.

The highly publicized incidents, which stunned fans in this predominantly con-servative country, heightened official and private concern that the nation might be entering another cycle of increased use of drugs. Modern-day Japan has not been hit by one of the epidemic surges of ad-diction that have swept Western nations and that now appear to be gripping West-ern Europe.

The problems increased in the early 1960's and again in the early 70's, but their scale, relatively small by interna-tional standards, was also small in rela-tion to the population of 113 million. This was attributed in part to national homo-geneity, a pervasive law-enforcement ap-paratus, traditional respect for authority and stringent enforcement of tough laws, including life sentences for pushers and required "cold turkey" withdrawal treat-ment for apprehended addicts.

Rise in Arrests Is Noted

In recent months, however, the authori-ties have begun to express growing con-cern over a reported increase in the abuse of drugs. According to the Ministry of

Health and Welfare, which has estab-lished a panel to design improved diag-nostic and treatment systems for addicts, the number of arrests under the Stimu-lant Drug Control Law jumped from 1,619 in 1970 to 10,919 last year, reportedly the most in two decades, and the increase is said to be continuing. The Tokyo police force has established a special force of 1,100 people to expose trafficking routes.

The most famous performer involved in the recent arrests is Yosui Inoue, a popular 29-year-old folk singer, who earned more money than any other Japa-nese singer (over $300,000 a year) in 1975 and 1976, according to the Tax Adminis-tration Agency. Charged with possession of marijuana, he pleaded guilty and was sentenced to eight months in prison, the term being suspended for two years.

Yasuko Naito, 27, another popular singer, was arrested on suspicion of violating the Hemp Control Law for having given marijuana to still another well-known vocalist, Naoko Ken, 24. So far Miss Ken has only been questioned by the authorities.

Miss Ken's face and those of other popular entertainers touched by the investigations have virtually disappeared from the taped musical programs that dominate television. Although only a few of the performers have been convicted, they are already being excised from lucrative commercials.

Agent Accused as Smuggler

Another famous entertainer arrested for marijuana possession is Akira Nishikino, 28, also a singer. Others were arrested or questioned regarding hashish or stimulant drugs, which according to some estimates may have about 100,000 addicts in Japan.

In addition, Akira Ota, a 30-year-old booking agent , was arrested on charges of having tried to smuggle in a large quantity of marijuana. The police, it is reported, also found a notebook belonging to Mr. Ota that contained the names, some of them in code, of more than 120 entertainers.

One resulting trial has seen an unusual defense argument. In Kyoto the lawyer for Ko Akutagawa, a 44-year-old artist charged with having grown marijuana in his backyard, argued that an individual's right to smoke marijuana comes under the pursuit-of-happiness provision of the Constitution. His counsel maintained that marijuana was not harmful and that it was unreasonable to punish those found with small amounts.

These incidents have prompted a rash of editorials and self-examination in the news media. One newspaper, the English-language Japan Times, noted the effective police control of narcotics smuggling and the traditionally scant market. "Today," the paper continued, "the law enforcers are still effective, but we may well wonder if the basic social controls have not weakened."

November 6, 1977

Graffiti, 141 Giant Eyes Along River Bank, Hint at Changing Japan

By ANDREW H. MALCOLM

KYOTO, Japan — Katsuo Nakagawa was strolling along the famous wooded banks of the Kiyotaki River here one day admiring the bright autumn colors when, suddenly, he could not believe what he saw. There, staring back at him from the river were 141 giant eyes —pink ones, white ones and black ones —painted on rocks.

Such incidents, whether merely malicious mischief or artful expression, have been unheard of in Japan, so the mysterious eyes were reported to the police and a full investigation was launched. The result has been a bureaucratic, legalistic and artistic debate that reveals something of the social workings and values of a changing society.

It has also become a severe headache for Yoshihiro Imaeda, a seasoned detective who for a quarter of a century has dealt with simpler wrongdoings like murder and arson. "This," said Superintendent Imaeda, "is a very unusual case."

The complexity arises because almost everyone with a stated opinion denounces the painted eyes as offensive to the rural river's natural beauty but there does not seem to be any law prohibiting them. While newspapers and officials call for stern action against the culprits, policemen and prosecutors are hesitating since any acquittal could endorse the legality of similar freelance graffiti anywhere.

Avoiding a Bad Loss of Face

"We must be very cautious in this

The New York Times/Hirotaka Yoshizaki
Eyes painted last September on rocks on the Kiyotaki River in Kyoto, Japan

case," a prefectural official explained. "If we lost it would be a bad loss of face, and it might encourage others to pull the same stunt."

The mysterious tale of the painted eyes began in September when Mr. Nakagawa, as he has once or twice a week for three decades, went to the river to sing his favorite folksongs far from complaining neighbors. Like millions of others he regards that particular river area, called Takao, as one of the most picturesque in Japan—especially in fall, when the maples turn the steep hillsides into bright hues of red and gold.

Restaurants, tearooms and sake shops, some built on stilts, line much of the mossy, gracious gorge where the river trickles among the rocks on the northwestern outskirts of this ancient Japanese capital. Though there is a mass of trash—plastic bags, bottles, cans and papers—sloshing there, it is the bizarre eyes, some neat, some sloppy, that offend many.

"One or two might be O.K.," said Akira Asano, a longtime Kyoto resident, "but that many and that bright and in Takao. I mean, really—it's such bad taste."

"They must be crazy people, that's all," said Takeshi Izawa, who is the official in charge of maintenance of the river. "The eyes are awful and primitive. I think they just wanted some media attention. If so, they must

14

be happy because they sure got it."

No Billboards, No Advertisements

He immediately checked the River Law, but found no provision against painting rocks. Similarly the Scenic Preservation Law and the Ancient Capital Preservation Ordinance. Officials even checked the outdoor billboard regulations, but it was decided that rocks are not billboards and eyes are not advertisements.

Superintendent Imaeda, calling the case unprecedented, commented: "The legislators who wrote all these laws never expected this sort of incident. Such crimes were unimaginable here."

The police, the prefectural government and the prosecutor are meeting to consider the next move. Only after they have reached a consensus will the prefecture file a complaint, the police launch an official inquiry and the prosecutor place charges.

Overlooked for the moment is that the authorities have no idea who painted the rocks. They know only that the act took about five gallons of oil paint and several hours to complete and will likely require blowtorches to undo at substantial taxpayer expense. They speculate that four or five young people were involved, which happens to

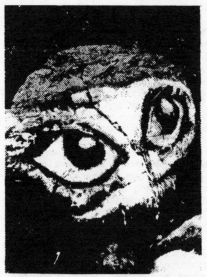

A city official called the eyes "awful" and suggested they had been painted by "crazy people."

coincide with the number spotted in the area just before Mr. Nakagawa went out singing.

For many the painting reflects the decline in group standards and the urbanization that have been overcoming Japanese cities.

Cold Cement, Not Beautiful Wood

"For one thing," said Mr. Asano, who has lived all of his 38 years here, "the buildings are getting taller and they're made of cold cement instead of beautiful woods. We're not so kind to each other any more either. Sometimes even local people speak harshly to one another. And people move more often too. We used to know everyone, but now there are some neighbors I don't know. It doesn't seem right."

Superintendent Imaeda sees the changes reflected in crime statistics for this city, whose 1.4 million residents make it Japan's fifth largest. "The total number of felonies is still going down," he said. "The number of murders is staying the same—33 so far this year—but the so-called fun crimes, those committed with no motive other than thrills, they are increasing. I think it's the frustrations of modern life."

Meanwhile, the painted eyes remain on the rocks in case they are needed as evidence. The perpetrators' remain at large. The sightseeing throngs come to see the leaves but go away remembering the eyes. Mr. Izawa, sitting in his Government office, shook his head: "I don't understand it. Nothing like this has happened before."

November 10, 1977

At 79, Suzuki Tempo Is Still Agitato

By ANDREW H. MALCOLM

Shinichi Suzuki demonstrates the Suzuki Method to a young student.

MATSUMOTO, JAPAN

HE moves with more effort now and is a little hard of hearing in one ear. But the experienced hands and quick fingers still draw the same mellow sounds and energy from the violin, and his eyes still light up at the sight of a child.

"I just like children," says the old man. "That's all."

Of course, that isn't all. For the man is 79-year-old Shinichi Suzuki, whose Suzuki Method has revolutionized musical instruction around the world. The method claims more than 300,000 students, two-thirds of them in the United States, where President Carter's wife, Rosalynn, and their daughter, Amy, began their joint Suzuki Method violin lessons recently. About 20,000 students and their parents are enrolled at 83 Suzuki schools throughout Japan.

The Suzuki Method, which Mr. Suzuki prefers to call the Mother-Tongue Method, was given birth about four decades ago when Mr. Suzuki observed that Japanese youngsters branded by schools as "dumb" had mastered their complex mother tongue through their own ability and their family's instinctive encouragement. He decided the same approach could be taken to music.

Every March, 4,000 of the children are selected for a mass string concert in Tokyo. The young musicians have no joint rehearsal nor do they use sheet music. "A child learns to speak before he can read," Mr. Suzuki says. "Why shouldn't he learn to play an instrument before he reads the music?"

As a youth, Mr. Suzuki was not musically inclined, but he used to play with violins all the time. He said he would bash his brothers with them in chases through their home in Nagoya, where his father ran the Suzuki violin factory.

Mr. Suzuki worked there a while, too,

but it was not until he was 17 years old, when he was so moved by Mischa Elman's recording of Schubert's "Ave Maria" that he began to teach himself the violin with his typically fierce determination.

These days he rises at 3 A.M. for six hours of listening to student tapes mailed from all over Japan. He records comments on each and sends them back. "Teaching is my hobby," he says, "I just do it all the time."

Mr. Suzuki, who favors a white shirt and a tie under an old gray cardigan sweater, takes one day off each year—New Year's.

"My husband never relaxes," said Waltraud Suzuki, his wife. "That's the trouble with him. When he has some spare time, he plays the violin more. He's always trying to find a new way to teach a point to a particular student."

At 9 A.M., Mr. Suzuki begins a 10-hour day at his Talent Education Institute (3-10-3 Fukushi, Matsumoto City, Nagano 390, Japan), where his students range from toddlers to Suzuki Method teachers like Linda and Roger Stieg of Lansing, Mich., who sold many of their belongings to study here for two years. Tuition is $47 a month plus $90 for registration.

Mrs. Suzuki has also learned to put up with her husband's carelessless about money and an absent-minded behavior that may lead him, for example, to put his hearing aid into a suit pocket just before the suit is sent out for dry cleaning.

Ideally, the child's musical education begins at birth, Mr. Suzuki says, with the mother regularly playing records or tapes of fine music near the crib. Around the age of 2, they begin their lessons along with their mothers, who play a central role in the musical education.

The child sees and hears the mother learn and practice and eventually, with his imitative motivation built up, is permitted to start, using a special 1/16th-scale violin. The children, accompanied by a parent, receive individual instruction, but in front of other children and parents, to help instill a sense of confidence and accomplishment. Criticism and suggestions are always linked to some positive achievement.

"I really like it," said 6-year-old Satoshi Hikari. "It never gets boring." Each day he practices one hour before school and another hour afterward. With his sister, Chinatsu, he also listens to records daily. She has just turned 3 and practices five minutes at a time several times a day.

"Talent is not inherited," Mr. Suzuki said as he knelt on the floor to get closer to his pupils. "The potential of every child is absolutely unlimited. And these children know when you believe that. You can see it in their eyes when we're communicating one living soul to one living soul. I learn so much from them."

The Suzukis are now involved in plans for an American tour next spring with 200 of their young Japanese pupils. They hope for a meeting with Mr. Carter. Mr. Suzuki has a message he wants to deliver to the President and others.

"I want to tell everyone," he said, "that this method is not education of the violin. It is education by the violin.

"We are not only nourishing a child's sensitivity to music but also to humanity. Through Mozart, for instance, he can also learn a high morality."

"If we could use this same method of teaching positively all kinds of things right from birth," he added, his excitement rising. "If everyone followed this method, then we wouldn't need any police or soldiers or war."

But Mr. Suzuki, eager to complete his thought, could no longer wait for his remarks to be translated from Japanese. He tried it in English.

"If mother good heart then baby good heart," he said. "If mother not good heart, then baby catch that, too."

He described his plans for a research institute to apply the Suzuki Method to all levels of teaching children, starting with mothers during pregnancy.

"I think," Mr. Suzuki said, "that I must postpone my retirement until I am 110."

November 13, 1977

October, Not June, Is the Time of Year To Marry in Japan

By ANDREW H. MALCOLM

TOKYO, Oct. 17—The first time Yoji Morita met Tamiko Minemura they were not permitted to speak. Ten days later they were engaged by telephone. The other afternoon they were married over a cup of rice wine. It was, according to Japanese custom, the most important day of their lives.

It ended an arrangement process that began with two fathers exchanging snapshots over a cup of coffee. And it reflected some of the slow, but deep and profound social changes creeping across this land of 67.7 million adults, 63.3 million of whom have been married.

This year a million more Japanese couples will marry. During October alone, the most popular month for weddings, one couple exchanges vows every 12 seconds, around the clock.

Such an entrenched and popular social institution—with little divorce—perpetuates the important stabilizing role of the family in Japanese life. With all its accompanying ritual, gifts, celebrations, trips and other expenses and purchases, this role supports a marriage industry whose annual income has been estimated at more than $6 billion.

Weddings Still Intensely Personal

The Morita-Minemura marriage accounted for about $13,600 of that sum, according to details provided during several hours of unusual interviews with the couple, their families, relatives and guests.

For all their expense and pageantry, individual marriages in Japan are still intensely personal affairs, involving only the family and the closest of friends. The planning arrangements, Shinto ceremony, reception and emotions involved are experiences rarely shared with outsiders.

The idea for this wedding blossomed last winter in the mind of the bride's father, Ryosa, who decided that at 25, his daughter had reached marriage age. "If you have someone in particular," he told her, "please introduce me to him. Otherwise I have some potential husbands in mind."

Miss Minemura did not like the idea. "But I said to my father," she recalls, "'please do whatever you think best.'"

Soon afterward her father set up a coffee appointment with Kazuo Morita, a long-time office friend. During the conversation Mr. Minemura mentioned his search for a suitable son-in-law and produced a color photograph of his daughter, in a kimono, the kind of photo taken traditionally each New Year's Day.

"Please do with this what you think proper," Mr. Minemura told his friend. Mr. Morita showed the photo to his wife, who found the young woman most pretty. Both felt it was time that their only son, who is 34, was married. They awaited the right moment.

On March 20 their son returned in a fine mood

from a skiing trip. His father showed him the photo and suggested a meeting. "My mother liked her picture," the young man recalled, "so I agreed."

The next day father and son called on the young woman's family. Everyone sipped green tea; no one spoke but the fathers, who discussed the weather, sports, business—everything but marriage.

The young persons took glances at each other. "I thought she was not very shy," Yoji Morita said.

"I thought he was very quiet," Tamiko Minemura said.

After two hours Miss Minemura walked to the train with the two visitors and she and Yoji Minemura spoke to each other for the first time—about skiing. She was invited to dinner that night, and accepted. Yoji Morita later escorted Tamiko to her home alone.

In a week, he called for a dinner date. Three evenings later, he telephoned Miss Minemura. He recalls that conversation: "I said I was wondering if she would like to get together or join me in our lives. I would never use the word marriage, but I meant it."

Thinking It Over

Miss Minemura knew exactly what the caller meant. "Naturally," she said, "his proposal was not a surprise, because our dates were based on the assumption that we might get married. However, I told him I would think it over."

"I had pretty well decided already," she continued, "but, of course, I discussed it with my parents. They asked if I thought I could get along with him. Three days later I telephoned Yoji-san and said, 'Yes.' Of course, I told my father first."

Thereafter, every Wednesday night after work, Mr. Morita, who produces television commercials for the Tokyo Broadcasting System, met Miss Minemura, who is a bank teller for Dai-Ichi Kangyo, for dinner and a walk, so they could get to know each other better.

Sometimes, and always in private, they held hands. On a bicycling trip, Miss Minemura began calling Mr. Morita by his first name, a gesture of intimacy that he noticed immediately but, until his wedding day, could not bring himself to reciprocate.

In May the families exchanged gifts and money, sealing the engagement. The wedding was set for October, which is to Japanese brides what June is to American brides. The date was picked for its luck, according to the lunar calendar.

It was agreed that the bride's family would pay half the wedding and reception expenses while Mr. Morita would split the other half with his father.

On the appointed day the bride arose early to pack and pay her farewell visits to the neighbors. At 2:30 P.M. she arrived at the Meiji Kinenkan wedding hall to apply her white facial and neck makeup and don the large black wig and colorful formal kimono that she had chosen for the Shinto service.

A bride and groom at a modern Japanese wedding. The bride is wearing a traditional wedding kimono while the groom is dressed in western attire, as is customary.

Consulate General of Japan, N.Y.

The hall, once the historic site of a constitutional conference, is now the most famous of 150 Tokyo wedding centers.

The 20-minute ceremony began at 4:30 with ritual purification and chants, prayers and dances by the four priests and two priestesses. Three times the bridegroom and then the bride took three sips of sake. He slipped a gold band on the third finger of her left hand; she slipped one on the third finger of his right.

Vows for a Life of Sharing

Mr. Morita read his vows, which bind the couple to love and respect each other, to have a family and to share pain as well as pleasure for their entire lives. "We wish the gods may bless us forever," Mr. Morita intoned. His new wife simply spoke her first name — "Tamiko"—as a verbal signature.

Downstairs Kuniyuki Nagata, the photographer, lined the wedding party up on a platform and then took individual photos of the couple. "Move the fan up a little," he said; "Tilt your head more. More! That's it. Hold your breath. Thank you! Next?"

At the reception, 67 guests drank beer and saké and consumed eel, shrimp, mushrooms, jellyfish, eggs and melons. Thirteen waitresses, working their third reception of the day, hustled the food from the elevators to the tables.

"The timing of the courses is very important," said one, Takako Kanasugi.

"It is a very moving day for me," said the bridegroom's father. "You know, he is my only son." As usual here, the newlyweds will live with the bridegroom's parents. It is no longer a thing of shame in Japan for a man's wife to work, so both will continue their jobs, at least until the first of "at least three babies" arrives.

Each month young Mr. Morita will give his father $200 of their combined monthly salaries of $1,069 to help pay for rent and food. The mother-in-law will cook during the week, the new wife on weekends.

After cutting one piece of real cake that had been placed on the side of an eight-tiered plastic cake, the couple retired to change clothes. Then the hall's announcer read aloud a poem to the parents, and their children offered bouquets of gratitude for the years of rearing. The mothers wept. The fathers cleared their throats frequently.

"I think," said the bride, "that our love will start to grow from this moment on." Mr. and Mrs. Yoji Morita left, then, on a four-day honeymoon at a rural resort. That night, the bridegroom confided to a friend, he would kiss the former Tamiko Minemura for the first time.

October 18, 1976

A Year After Marriage, 2 Japanese Find What They Call 'Love'

By ANDREW H. MALCOLM

TOKYO, Nov. 14—When Yoji Morita married Tamiko Minemura here last year, his father compared the couple's new life together to a railroad train on a long, uncharted track.

"There may be curves and dark tunnels ahead," he told them, "but we wish you a safe journey."

The first year of that journey together has provided a variety of personal discoveries about everything from dirty laundry to family finances for the newlyweds, whose courtship and Shinto marriage ceremony were chronicled at length in The New York Times last fall. As predicted, the first year also provided a handful of dark, or at least gray, tunnels, including one spat last weekend that was followed by a few hours of silence between them.

But overall, the two young Japanese, who are typical of millions of their compatriots, say their semi-arranged marriage is going well and they feel a certain closeness slowly developing between them. They call it "love."

"I feel so relaxed when I get home with him," said the 27-year-old Mrs. Morita, who has kept her job as a bank teller.

An Excursion Canceled

"She does such nice things," said her husband, a 35-year-old television film editor. "The other day when I was sick in bed she gave up an excursion to the country with her friends to stay home and care for me."

During each of their six workdays a week, they talk by phone and almost invariably meet each evening to make the one-hour train ride home together. In the street, they hold hands. In restaurants, they sometimes playfully tap each other. And shared glances, recalling some incident, can ignite chuckles.

These are subtle but significant changes in the growth of a Japanese marriage relationship, where open displays of affection have not been highly prized. It is a far cry from the day they met at an arranged tea in early 1976 after their fathers, old friends from work, exchanged snapshots and obliquely suggested the possibility of a mariage between their two "children." The prospective bride and bridegroom, who could have vetoed the match, did not even get to speak at first.

Ten days after meeting, Mr. Morita phoned Miss Minemura to propose. She decided almost immediately, but waited three days for propriety's sake. "I will make you happy," Mr. Morita promised. Then, in October, Japan's most popular marriage month, the two families were united in a wedding and reception that cost about $13,600. It was planned to be the most important day in their lives.

'An Earthquake That Night'

"But I only remember it as a hectic, confusing blur," Mrs. Morita recalls now. The two newlyweds, who had never kissed each other until that day, spent their wedding night on the 19th floor of a nearby hotel. "I remember," Mr. Morita says, "because there was an earthquake that night and we were up so high."

Then, according to the husband, they left for a quiet southern resort on a weeklong honeymoon. "No, it wasn't a week," Mrs. Morita corrected, "it was four nights and five days."

They set up housekeeping in the two upstairs rooms of the home of Mr. Morita's parents. There, they usually eat breakfast and dinner with the older couple and frequently watch an hour of television together. The mother-in-law cooks during the week and the new bride on Sundays.

In exchange, each month the young couple pays $280 of their combined after-tax income of $1,200 toward food and housing costs. They save $240 a month for the coffee shop Mr. Morita would like to open some day and the three children they plan to have.

At that time the bank may force Mrs. Morita to resign or she may choose to. "I have no intention of telling her what to do," said Mr. Morita, whose shuffling shyness is sometimes reminiscent of Dustin Hoffman movie roles. "If she wants to quit, okay. If she wants to work, okay."

A birth would also cut into the range of their shared activities, like weekend trips, movies, dinners and workaday doings. Mr. Morita does not yet spend many evenings on the town with male co-workers, as Japanese businessmen often do. Mixing socially with other couples is not common in Japan; in this the Moritas are typical.

Politically, they stand separately, with Mr. Morita remaining a staunch supporter of the conservatives in power and Mrs. Morita voting for Socialists and Communists.

"But we never fight," Mrs. Morita said, "we don't hit each other like some. If a quarrel is heating up, then we both just shut up and let it blow over. The inner anger doesn't linger. And, besides, he often apologizes to me and that solves the problem."

Tiff in a Shoe Store

The other Sunday, they traveled an hour by train to buy a new pair of shoes for Mr. Morita. (Mrs Morita buys her clothes herself without his advice.) But at the store, Mr. Morita could not decide for a long time, so his wife snapped, "Well then, let's go home." And they did—in silence. Several hours later, Mr. Morita apologized for his indecision and the issue was dropped.

But Mr. Morita has in his first 13 months of marriage sometimes been annoyed by what he regards as nagging. Typically, this happens when he leaves socks or shirts scattered about. This carelessness, combined with the burden of an evening's housework after a day's bank work, was the major unanticipated fact of married life for Mrs. Morita. "I have to tell him to pick up and tell him to pick up," she said, "and he gets sulky." But then the couple will play Japanese chess and Mr. Morita inevitably wins and is happier.

Remembers Her Knitting

There are, too, those tender private moments, often at work, when, for instance, Mr. Morita realizes suddenly that every weekend when his wife cooks a meal, it contains his favorite potatoes. Or Mrs. Morita will pause at her counter to think about the sweater she is knitting her husband "not because I have to but because I want to."

Or perhaps she will admire one more time the thin onyx ring that her husband had a jeweler secretly design and make for her recently. "I don't know why I did it," Mr. Morita insists, "it was for no reason."

Last year on her wedding day, when she was a bride of but a few minutes, Mrs. Morita said, "I think that our love will start to grow from this moment on."

The other evening, after 13 months of marriage, she was reminded of that. "I remember," she said, "it's growing."

November 15, 1977

2 Rare Salamanders Are Missing in Tokyo

TOKYO, Dec. 7 (AP)—Detectives are looking for two rare salamanders; valued at more than $40,000, that are missing from two Tokyo zoos. The search is concentrating on pet stores and gourmet shops.

The 38-inch salamanders, weighing 16 pounds and designated national monuments by the Government, have been missing since mid-November.

The lizard-like salamanders are said to be exotic food, with gourmets will-ing to pay high prices. They are also reported in demand as pets in the United States, West Germany and the Netherlands.

December 8, 1977

Where Santa Enters Through the Sliding Door

By ANDREW H. MALCOLM

TOKYO—Santa Claus, it can now be revealed, is a tall, skinny fellow as big as an adult. He is coming down to Japan this weekend. He may also stop off briefly in the United States, although that is uncertain at the moment.

These and other new details about this mysterious visitor that everybody knows but nobody sees were learned in the course of a frequently chaotic interview with eight Santa Claus experts here. The vocal authorities, all 5-or 6-year-old students at the Takanawa kindergarten, were quite certain of everything about Santa Claus, except what he eats and whether he knows any English.

They consented to the exclusive interview on the condition that their names appear in a foreign newspaper. They are Masae Kawasaki, Masako Shimizu, Katsuhiro Mori, Hideaki Saito, Kazutomo Jumonji, Shiro Nagase, So Chosay and Maiko Gokyu.

They are members of only the second generation of Japanese to be visited by Santa Claus-san. But, as does every other import into this homogeneous, insular society, Santa Claus must pass through customs and a unique Japanese cultural filter that wraps every import in a Japanese label, gives it considerable local flavor and provides a revealing insight into the Japanese outlook on the world. Thus, for instance, in Japan the names of American football teams appear on baseball hats, and on Valentine's day Japanese women give the presents.

Christmas, which is not a work holiday here, is a foreign phenomenon encouraged by department stores and celebrated when convenient. Santa Claus is not yet a member of every family because some Japanese parents do not see the point.

Portions of the interview follow. Often, several experts felt compelled to provide separate answers. In all the movement, it was not always possible to discern who said what.

Q. Isn't there some big holiday coming soon?

A. New year's

Q. No. No. I mean one with a visitor of some kind.

A. My grandfather is coming for New Year's. Oh, you mean Santa Claus. Yes, yes, Santa Claus is coming (prolonged cheering.)

Q. When does Santa Claus come?

A. He brings lots of toys. He brought me a doll last year. I got a train set with tracks. And I got a car. He brought me some cake.

Q. When does Santa Claus come?

A. At night. In August. On Mondays. No no, it's never on Monday. Is it the 23d? Where's a calendar?

You're all wrong — Santa Claus comes on the last Sunday in December, and this year it happens to fall on the 25th.

Q. How does he get here?

A. In a mysterious sleigh. And he whips the reindeer like this. Yes, and one of them has a red nose cause it's so cold. He comes down in a spiral like on an ice cream cone.

Q. What do you mean "down"? Where does Santa Claus live?

A. Up in the sky in a big white house right across the street from God.

Q. Is he fat?

A. No. Why?

Q. How does he get into your house?

A. Down the chimney. We don't have a chimney so he slides open the door; we don't lock it. And on tall apartments he uses the porch or a window.

Q. Does he go to other countries, like the United States?

A. Yes. No. Yes. No. Yes. No. He comes to Japan first and he goes to Italy. And Switzerland. China. Oh, and Burma, too.

Q. He must be a speedy person.

A. He has to be able make the morning deadline. He's the smartest man in Japan.

Q. Does he speak Japanese?

A. Yes, of course [in unison].

Q. How about English?

A. I don't think so. It's too hard.

Q. What do you eat on Christmas?

A. Bananas! Strawberries! Rice cakes! We always have curried rice. We do too.

Q. But how does he know what to bring you? Do you write him a letter?

A. No. I don't know. I do; he's up in the sky and he looks down and he hears my prayers for a toy. He's watching all the time.

Q. Have you ever seen Santa Claus?

A. Sure, lots of times. No, I've heard him; he makes a "zuni zum"

sound when he comes down the chimney. I think he looks to see if I wet the bed. He just comes quietly and leaves the gifts and goes to all the other houses. I don't think he speaks to us, but maybe he does. Maybe when I'm asleep, he comes into my room softly and puts his hand like this and prays that I'll grow up healthy and beautiful. And I don't hear him because I'm asleep.

Q. You're the only one who hasn't had much to say today.

A. Well, my parents never told me about Santa Claus. But I hear all about him from my friends. And he still comes to my house every year. He never fails to come to my house. He knows me. And he always brings me a doll.

December 24, 1977

Japan's Latest Farm Shortage: Wives

By ANDREW H. MALCOLM

OTOECHO, Japan—"Wanted: 8,000 brides for 8,000 grooms. Young women must be willing work hard in house and fields. Daily cooking. Also husband's bath preparation. Desire for many children imperative. Must be respectful of and obedient to in-laws. Taste for long winters away from town preferable. One-way airfare provided. Fluent Japanese required. Apply Hokkaido Farmland Bride Liaison Bureau."

Through want ads, posters, pamphlets and group tours, the organizations of rural Japan are seeking to solve as best they know how an increasing problem of modern-day Japanese society. That is, there simply aren't enough women in the countryside to go around.

In a society based on the extended family where each member has his or her assigned duties, many young women are choosing not to have a family, at least not on a farm. They are heading for the big cities. And the single farmboys left behind are faced with a family-less future void of heirs and free help.

It is an extremely mortifying position socially for the men in this group-conscious society and one that carries potential long-term agricultural and sociological implications for Japan, where almost 80 per cent of the 113-million citizens already live in congested, polluted urban areas. The population movement is also an indication of an increased sense of mobility among women in rural Japan, traditionally this nation's most conservative area.

In underdeveloped Hokkaido, a Maine-sized island that is generally considered Japan's last "frontier," the total population held remarkably steady in the last decade at 5.4 million. But the island's rural population dropped sharply by 600,000 to 1.6 million while Hokkaido's cities grew by the same 600,000 to 3.8 million.

Japan's urban migration began more

than 15 years ago, but the strong movement of young women away from the farms started only in recent years. Hokkaido officials estimate now there are five eligible men for every three eligible women and the gap is growing.

For centuries women have been a prominent feature of the Japanese farm scene, along with plodding oxen, straw roofs and muddy paddies. Dressed in hooded sun bonnets and baggy pants and stooped almost double at the waist from sowing, weeding and harvesting rice, the farm wives worked long hours with their husbands in the fields and

8,000 farmboys are facing a lonely future.

then put even more hours' work into housekeeping and meal preparation. By some accounts, they often slept only three or four hours a night to fulfill their duties.

Their vivid memories of these ordeals are apparently quite strong and play a crucial role in their daughters' decisions to choose another life, now that a degree of affluence has placed things like a college education—in the city—within their economic reach.

"We're trying to tell the mothers that their work is a lot easier on the farm nowadays," said one man, Yoshihide Nishimura. "Thanks to machinery, we don't need to depend on oxen anymore, either. But it's very difficult to change the women's thinking."

Many of Hokkaido's 213 communities organized committees of men to combat the local dearth of potential wives. But none could handle the problem on an island-wide scale. So the Hokkaido

Farmland Bride Liaison Bureau was formed to deal with this labor problem.

Throughout urban Japan the group places want ads and distributes posters

in a "Japanese gothic style" showing a farmer holding a pitchfork and standing by a barn. There is no wife with him, however, and the title says, "Why don't you come and sweat with us in Hokkaido?"

Recently, the committee paid all the expenses for a women's magazine reporter to travel here to write about all the eligible husbands available in one town. Some farm association officials are sent south to address large gatherings of single female textile workers in big cities. The airfares for some city women are paid to live for a month or so on a farm where they ask locally shocking questions like "What is hay?"

Large groups of unmarried women are even flown to Hokkaido in group tours to see the sights and, almost by chance, drop in on a rural campfire where a large group of unmarried farmers has happened to gather. "It is a very successful strategy," said Masao Hashimoto, the bride bureau's director, who is married.

In three years the bureau has arranged 54 marriages. Other local groups have arranged another 790. But this is just a drop in the milk bucket compared to the 8,000 farm bachelors the bureau counts on the island.

"At the moment," said Mr. Nishimura, a farm association president near this rural hamlet, "we could use at least 150 new wives here."

Not long ago his association drew up a local marriage list of single young men over the age of 21. Realizing the importance of the issue at hand, the association didn't bother initially to ask the men if they wanted to be listed or married. That is assumed here.

"The problem is due to education," said Mr. Nishimura. "The children decide they want a college education. That means they must go to the cities. Very few college graduates come back to this area. We don't have the factories or the jobs for their skills."

Suguru Ichihara, a rice farmer, signed on to the bride search list two years ago after his mother and many friends told him it was time to marry.

Japanese Society

"I know that staying unmarried at this age is close to being a crippled person," he said. " I don't care if she's beautiful or tall, but a wife would be more fun to work and talk with."

So far, Mr. Ichihara remains alone in his field, but another 30-year-old farmer, Toshiaki Kagechika, doesn't. Three years ago while working winters in a southern factory, he met a 22-year-old Tokyo school teacher named Yoshiko. Their letters built a relationship until Mr. Kagechika asked the farm association to send someone with him to Tokyo to arrange their marriage.

Married last March, they live with his parents in a modern six-room house with a freezer, console television, microwave oven and spring water. They own a truck, a car, two combines and share a tractor with six other families.

From her mother-in-law, the young bride is learning all about farm life, including the blisters. "Compared to my life in the old days," said the elder Mrs. Kagechika, "hers is a paradise." At busy times the family rises at 5 A.M. and works until 5 P.M. except for lunch, which the new wife must make.

She must also make dinner and prepare hot baths for the others. "I have a lot to learn so I expected being a farmer's wife was tough work," said the young Mrs. Kagechika, "and it is."

There will be additional demands when the baby comes next year, but there is also the slower pace and fresh clean air that comes with life in a rural valley.

And does she enjoy her new life as a farm wife? "Oh, yes," she said, "so far."

December 31, 1977

Yokohama Quietly Becoming Japan's Second Biggest City

By ANDREW H. MALCOLM

YOKOHAMA, Japan—It may occur today, tomorrow or in a few weeks. Perhaps it already happened yesterday

But one of these days a farmer will move into town, a baby will be born or two newlyweds will settle here. At that moment, quietly and without fanfare, Osaka will be displaced for the

first time in almost three centuries as Japan's second largest city.

And Yokohama, once a clump of huts around a fishing boat ramp on the shore of Tokyo Bay, will become the

A young couple pauses on a commercial street in Yokohama.

Japan ● '79

No. 2 metropolis in a crowded nation dominated by metropolises.

The historic development, which is going almost unnoticed in Japan, has significance far beyond its statistical shift. It confirms the concentration of population around Tokyo, Japan's largest city since feudal days, after years of talk about a return to city residents en masse to the countryside.

But it also heralds a new urban era, marking increased mobility between major Japanese cities and away from within the two traditionally largest cities. Because Yokohama—the name literally means "side beach"—still has room to grow and some time to plan, it offers hope too of avoiding at least partly the unzoned, uncoordinated growths that most major Japanese cities have become.

Potential for Disaster

And it also holds the potential for a historic disaster. More than 12 million people, over 10 percent of Japan's entire population, are concentrated on a plain atop one of the world's most active earthquake zones.

For generations of non-Japanese visitors, Yokohama was the first sight of these green isles. In the 1850's the fearful feudal shogun set the village of Yokohama as the site for a foreign settlement; it was not too long a horseback ride away from his capital (about 25 miles), but it was well beyond cannon range. As a result, many exotic Western items first arrived in Japan through Yokohama — strawberries, tomatoes, matches, phonographs and even Japan's first artificial leg, which was donned by Denosuke Sawamura, a kabuki actor.

Today Yokohama, which was an old village before Columbus was born, is Japan's second busiest port after Kobe, handling more than one-fifth of this trading nation's exports. Most of Yokohama's shipments are bound for the United States and a large part are the brightly colored small automobiles that last year became Japan's leading export item.

To this day in the Japanese mind Yokohama carries an exotic air associated with foreigners. Asked to name

Japan's second city, almost all Japanese would still pick Osaka, a bustling business community where many Tokyo companies keep duplicate business records for the day when Tokyo may fall to another major quake. Yokohama was never even one of Japan's major castle towns, just one of the 53 stages of the old Tokaido road, which linked Japan with Kyoto, the old capital, and Osaka.

330 New Residents a Day

Figures vary by the month and by the agency that does the counting, but an average of about 330 new residents a day move into Yokohama's 95 square miles. With about 2,689,000 residents, the former fishing village has probably slipped ahead of Osaka, whose white-collar workers are taking the trains to that city's suburbs.

Unlike many old Japanese cities with their traditional social cohesion passed from generation to generation, Yokohama today is a mixture of old port, aging heavy industries such as chemicals, and new bedrooms for 320,000 residents who commute to Tokyo daily.

"Unfortunately," said Taisuke Matsunobu, a 61-year-old bookstore owner and Yokohama native, "the sense of community is being diluted. Sometimes even here in this big city I feel lonesome."

Officials admit to a civic identity problem at times. Yokohama has no city orchestra, no city museum, no newspaper. Just one radio station, one large theater, not even its own daily UHF television outlet and a professional baseball team, the Whales, that will start playing two-thirds of its home games here this spring. And the Mayor, Ichio Asukata, has just been named head of Japan's Socialist Party.

"There's nothing special that brought me here," said Kozo Aikawa, a 30-year-old shipping company worker. "I came here from Nagasaki for school and met my wife and I guess I'll stay here for life unless the company transfers me."

Many new Yokohama residents are similar young married persons unable

or unwilling to find room among Tokyo's 8.3-million residents. Yokohama does have room. It even has some farms within the city limits. Its population density is only 28,421 people per square mile, comapared with Osaka's 34,238 and Tokyo's 38,149.

Yokohama suffered widespread destruction twice in this century, once in the great earthquake of 1923 and again during the American bombings of World War II. One reason for its belated postwar development may be that for years after the war American military forces occupied 90 percent of the port and a quarter of the city area.

But the problems of growth are severe, especially since 55 percent of the citys budget must be coaxed from the national and provincial governments. City planners estimate that they will need 54 new schools in the next five years alone. Within seven years they expect a population of 3.1 million and they are now considering growth limits. "We're going to have stringent guidance on developers," says Koichiro Yoshizawa, director of economic affairs.

New Construction Everywhere

New construction is rampant in Yokohama, both up and down. Taller, theoretically earthquake-proof office buildings are mounting while multilevel shopping malls with artificial streams and modern subway stops are being built underground.

Some officials have had second thoughts about the removal of the streetcars six years ago; streets are more clogged than ever anyway. But tiny lantern-lit alleys still lead adventurous diners past the 400 restaurants of Yokohama's well-known Chinatown.

On the waterfront in Yamashita Park, which is built on rubble landfill from the 1923 earthquake, young lovers sit on benches under giant trees at night and watch th dark forms of freighters easing through the harbor for distant ports.

"We're going to dissuade destruction," says Mr. Yoshizawa, "and we"re going to preserve our green areas. It is our heritage as a city."

January 23, 1978

Sumo Wrestling Has Judge That Never Blinks

By ANDREW H. MALCOLM

TOKYO, Jan. 22—The new year's first sumo wrestling tournament ended here Sunday, and, as usual, nine stone-faced judges presided over the matches. Eight of the judges were human: They were the ones who

blinked.

The ninth never blinked: It was a television camera.

In the United States, officials and fans of the National Football League are debating whether to videotape pro football games to help officials judge close calls, but sumo wrestling here

has routinely used this electronic aid for almost a decade. "Frankly speaking," said Uragoro Takasago, chief judge, "television is very helpful to us. I recommend it to U.S. football."

Simultaneous Thuds

During every one of the six 15-day-long sumo tournaments held annually

Television cameras help referees judge close calls in sumo wrestling.

in Japan, a television camera records the slammings, the liftings, the gruntings, the shovings, the twistings and the fallings of each day's 19 major matches.

The idea in sumo is to move an opponent out of the small ring. Most decisions are clear-cut, involving a foot out of the ring or the landing of a 300-pound combatant amid spectators sitting with crossed legs nearby.

But usually two or three times each day, the two men will step out together or land with a seemingly simulataneous thud. That is when two judges, seated unseen before a closed-circuit TV set in a nearby room, can closely study and re-study videotape of the action. Their opinions, fed unobtrusively into a tiny earphone on the head ringside judge, can determine the results.

On Wednesday in the bout between Kaiki and Kitaseumi (sumo wrestlers adopt one-word names) the television replay told ringside officials what the rest of Japan had seen instantly: The referee's victory sign to Kaiki was an error, because that wrestler's hidden elbow had touched the floor first. The reversal was then explained to the nation by the head judge.

The difference of one victory can mean considerable money and prestige in the tradition-heavy world of Japanese sumo wrestling. Like the society that pays upward of $375 for a ringside seat, sumo is hierarchical. Each member moves up and down through ranks according to his previous tournament performance.

The winner of the tournament was Kitanoumi, a Yokozuna (grand champion). He won all 15 matches and earned his 10th championship.

An Ancient Sport

If Pete Rozelle were running the sport here, this year's tournaments would have to be dubbed Super Sumo MMI, because sumo began 2,001 years ago, with the emperor in attendance. In feudal times, lords kept their own bands of wrestlers, now called "stables," for inter-royalty competition.

The sport waned in the late 1800's, as post-feudal Japan frantically mimicked and adopted Western ways. But it is now widely considered the national sport. Throughout these islands, office television sets are on every afternoon these days between 4 and 6 P.M. when the top-ranked men battle. Videotaped digests are broadcast every evening.

Towering more than six feet, with girths of seemingly equal dimension, the scantily clad sumo wrestlers dwarf the average Japanese. They are held in high esteem for their emotion-free adherence to rigid form.

Like many national sports, sumo requires that a spectator be initiated into numerous subtleties, such as the way a relatively small wrestler defeats a charging larger opponent by using the heavier man's momentum against him.

Each bout begins with an elaborate announcement and "ballet" consisting of leg liftings, slapping of buttocks, hand claps, sipping of water, crouching and tossing of salt for purification.

This goes on for many times longer than the bout itself, which can last from one or two seconds to perhaps two minutes.

A referee paces the dirt ring, and judges in black robes sit on each side. "But, as you may know," Chief Judge Takasago said in an inteview, "human eyes are not aimighty. Sometimes millions of viewers might find a judgment unfair or unusual. To persuade these viewers of our fairness, we installed a video system. It's much more practical, don't you think?"

He acknowledged that there was some opposition. There is some fear among the 23 professional judges, all of whom are former wrestlers, that the electronic gadget will sap some of the sport's human element.

What the judge did not explain was why the replay system was adopted, in 1969. The reason, which may foretell the reason for American sports' adoption of official videotaped sports replays, was a notorious official error that became page-one news nationwide.

This was in the spring tournament, when Taiho, one of history's top half-dozen sumo wrestlers, was going for his 46th consecutive victory in a last-ditch pursuit of the career record of 69, held by Futabayama.

Taiho faced Toda that day. Toda quickly drove the champion to the edge, where Taiho balanced precariously. In the struggle Toda's right foot touched the dirt outside for an instant just before Taiho fell out.

Thus, the referee gave the victory to the champion. But the judges overruled him, breaking Taiho's streak. The next day there were newspaper pictures showing the judges' error. A national uproar erupted, with taints of racism—charges that the judges had purposely and unfairly protected Futabayama's record at the expense of Taiho, who is only half Japanese.

So there was a typical compromise: The error stood, and soon afterward it was announced that videotapes would be used to help judge close calls.

January 24, 1978

Abortion Is a Major Form of Birth Control in Japan

By ANDREW H. MALCOLM

TOKYO, Feb. —Last month Dr. Shiro Sugiyama delivered 40 babies in his modern medical clinic here. During the same period he performed 80 abortions.

The two figures, which are not startling in Japan, illustrate a facet of health care here that is little known overseas. At a time when an emotional abortion controversy rages in the United States, Japan is marking the 30th anniversary of its liberal abortion law.

One result is that abortions have become an accepted, integral part of Japan's birth-control efforts, so much so that many married women have had two or three abortions while other women may have had 10 or more.

"In terms of our long abortion experience and technique," said Dr. Sugiyama, who agreed to an interview to help promote discussion of the issue, "Japan is a developed country and the United States is still a developing country."

A Growing Concern

But the widespread reliance on abortions is of growing concern among medical experts, including Dr. Sugiyama, not least because of the lowered value it seems to place on human life and the overall ignorance of modern contraceptive methods that it reveals.

The law's advantages, as cited in a series of interviews with officials, administrators, doctors and patients, are still viewed as outweighing the negative factors in terms of providing total qualified medical care and holding Japan's annual population growth to around 1 percent.

In 1976, the last year for which figures are available, Japan registered 1,832,617 live births and 664,106 reported abortions. But health experts agree that for bureaucratic and tax reasons probably only half the actual abortions are officially reported.

These developments are a result of a combination of historical, cultural, legal and administrative factors in this tradition-bound island nation of 113 million people. These factors include a lack of religious restraints against abortion, a prohibition against use of the pill for birth control purposes and, at least during the early postwar years, strong economic pressures to curb family growth.

Liberalized Law in 1948

Over the centuries economic concerns have been a powerful social deterrent to large families. During the country's feudal era, which lasted until 1868, the Japanese, especially in the poorer countryside, practiced infanticide — called "mabiki," literally "thinning out"—as a kind of ex-post-facto birth control. But under military governments in this century birth control and especially abortion were banned in the interests of producing new soldiers.

But in the social chaos of a devastated Japan after its surrender in 1945, the shortage of jobs and food combined to inhibit family growth severely. As one reflection of this need, the Eugenic Protection Law of 1948 permitted abortions under greatly broadened criteria. These included rape, mental illness, hereditary disease and leprosy. Most important, the law permits abortion through the 24th week of pregnancy for "a mother whose health may be affected seriously by the continuation of pregnancy or by delivery, from the physical or economic viewpoint."

The most frequent reason for abortions, doctors report, is the existence of two or three children already, a reason not recognized by the Health and Welfare Ministry but one that most doctors accept under a broader definition of the mother's health. Of the abortion totals reported, 99.7 percent are in this category.

The typical patient is a married woman between the ages of 24 and 35 in her second month of pregnancy. In Japan teen-agers account for only 2 percent of abortions.

Some doctors charge as little as $100 for an abortion, a small sum in this affluent, middle-class nation where students have taken collections for a pregnant classmate's abortion. If the mother's physical health is the reason for the abortion, it can be covered by national health insurance, but this requires revealing the woman's identity. There is no other government financial aid available for abortions, although a woman would qualify for child aid from the government after the birth.

February 5, 1978

In Japan, Ozawa Is Once Again 'Nakama Doshi'

By DONALD RICHIE

TOKYO

Seiji Ozawa returned to Japan with the Boston Symphony Orchestra this month and took the country by storm. "I didn't know what to expect," he said after a concert in Nagoya which was so rapturously received that the orchestra had to leave the stage before the audience would leave the hall. "I knew everyone liked the BSO, but i didn't expect this."

Mr. Ozawa's uncertainty about his Japanese homecoming was understandable. There is a Japanese prejudice against those who go out into the world, make international reputations, and then return, a feeling that they are no longer "nakama doshi"—which might be translated as "one of us." Adding to Mr. Ozawa's concern was a personal prejudice that the Japanese musical establishment, the press and most of the music critics have long harbored about him, a prejudice that dates back to the early years of his career.

At the advice of the late Hideo Saito, an extraordinary and highly individual pedagogue at the Toho School of Music (and, Mr. Ozawa now says, "The man to whom I still owe most"), the young conductor went abroad to study. "This was unheard of back then; Japanese conductors were supposed to study in Japan"— particularly one who had been officially named by the Japanese as the "outstanding talent" of 1958.

Abroad, Mr. Ozawa won various conducting prizes and was invited by Charles Munch to study at Tanglewood in 1960, thus beginning his long association with the Boston Symphony. "I remember him from back then," said one of the older woodwind players. "He used to run around on his motor scooter, always busy, always on time. He sang in the chorus—not very well— when we did the Beethoven Ninth that year."

Mr. Ozawa also won the Berkshire Music Center's highest award, the Koussevitzky Prize, then went on to study under Herbert von Karajan, and was later asked by Leonard Bernstein to accompany him as his assistant during the New York Philharmonic's 1961 tour of Japan.

After this the trouble began. Since he had achieved so much abroad and was now safely home, the Nihon Hoso Kyokai or NHK (Japan Broadcasting Corporation) Orchestra decided to take on the fledgling conductor. The NHK considered itself the best of Japanese orchestras, was largely German-trained, and usually recieved highly deferential treatment. Conflicts began at once. Here was a youngster, only 27 years old, who may have studied under Herbert von Karajan (a Japanese deity) but also seemed to have picked up some fancy American ways as well. He did not favor a repertory centered around the Beethoven symphonies and, worse, he suggested that the time-honored renderings of the classics by the older members of the orchestra were old-fashioned.

The break soon came. Mr. Ozawa was fired. Japanese opinion pointed to him as the latest example of a native son seduced by glittering foreign ways. The musical establishment lined itself firmly behind NHK, and the press, as always, followed. So the prodigal son again left his homeland—in disgrace so far as Japan was concerned. He did not, however, either feel or act like a disgraced conductor. He went on with his career, a signally successful one. Eventually, he became artistic director of the Berkshire Music Festival and, in 1973, to his complete surprise, was appointed full music director of the Boston Symphony Orchestra, the 13th since it was founded in 1881.

•

No one in the orchestra was surprised. The players had known Mr. Ozawa for almost 15 years. Indeed, it was the orchestra itself which helped appoint him, since the relatively powerful artistic advisory committee is made up of orchestra members. And they had their reasons. If Mr. Ozawa was in trouble, so was the Boston Symphony, which had lost much of its preeminence after Charles Munch retired. It was simply not playing as well as it had. An orchestra, like any other group of people, needs a sense of direction. In order for an orchestra to give of its best, it needs full and dedicated leadership. This the Boston Symphony found in Mr. Ozawa, whom most of the members had known when he was still a student.

During this period Mr. Ozawa continued to return to Japan whenever he could. (He particularly remembers how the orchestra insisted that he suddenly break their season in order to return to

Seiji Ozawa conducting.

Japan for the funeral of his father—a man to whom he was always very close.) He also returned to conduct during vacations. "After all, I am a Japanese conductor and, no matter what was thought of me, I wanted to play there."

Since NHK has to this day never invited him back, Mr. Ozawa usually led the New Japan Philharmonic orchestra on his visits back home. Here he prepared, or repeated his "foreign" triumphs—the Mahler Eighth, the Berlioz "Lelio," the concert performances of "Cosi fan tutte." In all, guest-conducting with his Japanese orchestra, he presented what the Yomiuri critic, Edmund C. Wilkes, one of Mr. Ozawa's staunchest defenders, called "some of the most interesting programming and some of the best performances in Japan."

•

Thus the Japanese critics had occasion upon which to hear, and largely ignore Mr. Ozawa's progress. Unimpressed, they awaited the arrival of the Boston orchestra with apathy. One of them told this reporter that, naturally, he was going—but merely to hear what little was left of the BSO, certainly not to hear Mr. Ozawa. Another congratulated himself that he had heard the orchestra at its best, during its "golden age" under Munch, during the 20-city tour of 1960, and he did not need to hear it now.

Amid such tepid expectations the opening concert in Fukuoka (the Brahms Third and two Ravel works, the "Valses Nobles et Sentimentales" and "La Valse") suddenly turned informed musical opinion upside down. The

critics—the major papers had sent down men as a matter of form—found themselves realizing that they had never heard the BSO play better, under Munch or anyone else.

And even more astonishing for the Japanese press, they admitted it. Even the Asahi, the paper with the largest circulation and the most conservative policies, said that *now* was the real "golden age" of the Boston Symphony Orchestra. With this accolade from the foremost opinion-maker, xenophobic prejudices were forgotten, tickets were snapped up—even for slow-selling programs featuring the two "novelties" of the tour, Barbara Kolb's "Soundings," and Gunther Schuller's "Deai," a new work composed for the occasion—and the tour turned into a triumph.

Not only was the BSO's playing immaculate, but it was also informed with that special quality which is found only when an orchestra likes what it is doing and who is conducting it. And the BSO has outdone itself in order to do Mr. Ozawa proud on his own home territory. As one of the violin players said: "Ozawa is our conductor, but he's also our friend. We've known him for a long time now. We trust him. I guess we love him."

•

The orchestra's obvious acceptance of its conductor has had much to do with Japan's sudden acceptance of Mr. Ozawa. Confronted with the evidence, and a series of splendid performances, opposition has melted. Always pragmatic, the Japanese see that when something is fully accomplished there is no longer any virtue in being against it. Consequently Mr. Ozawa is flooded with adulation, with requests to conduct (none from NHK yet), and lines of fans waiting for post-concert autographs stretch around the block. The prodigal has returned and all is forgiven.

In turn, Mr. Ozawa made sure that the orchestra enjoyed Japan. There was the trip to Kyoto. There was the grand final joint-concert with the Toho Orchestra, from the conductor's alma mater, joining in on the Tchaikowsky "Serenade for Strings" and "The Pines of Rome." There was a real demonstration of how enthusiastic the presumably unenthusiastic Japanese could be at the Tokyo

concert when Rudolf Serkin joined them for a performance of Brahms Piano Concerto No. 1. And there was the party during mid-tour when Mr. Ozawa took over Yamanaka Onsen, one of Japan's prettiest hot-spring resorts, for a real Japanese party with raw fish, geishas, hot baths, gallons of sake and the entire 105-player Boston Symphony Orchestra, together with the 50 relatives and friends who travelled with them.

It was at this party that Mr. Ozawa, awash in *nakama* and mellow feeling, remembered everything that had led up to this memorable tour. "On the night before we left Boston," he said, "I was so scared I couldn't sleep. I even started

drinking. Then I remembered what I call my 'three old men'—my father, Mr. Saito, Mr. Munch—the men who made me. Well, it seemed to me they would have favored it. You know, now I'm happy about everything that's happened to me—even the bad things. I'm a much better conductor now and a much better man for it. And just look now what the orchestra's given me. *Sugoi!* (The Japanese equivalent of "wow!") ■

Donald Richie, a 30-year resident of Japan, has written widely about Japan and the Japanese. He is best-known as an authority on Japanese cinema.

March 26, 1978

Japan Cycles Into a New Problem

By ANDREW H. MALCOLM

TOKYO, April 7—Japan is learning—the hard way—one of the burdens of being a modern, affluent urban nation: For every solution there is a new problem.

Five years ago the Government and society in general became so concerned with the problems of urban smog, automobile fumes, traffic congestion and the energy crisis that, with the Cabinet's endorsement, a movement was launched to use bicycles as a way of solving all of them.

The campaign really succeeded, so much so that the solution has become the latest problem. Every day millions of men, women and children pedal off to work, to school or on their errands. But when they arrive, having consumed no fossil fuel and emitted no fumes, they have no place to put the bikes, so they leave them anywhere—in the streets, by the tracks at stations, along fences, in front of doors, all over the sidewalks and crosswalks and on top of one another.

"It is hopeless," said Sgt. Yasushi Tanzawa of the police, surveying the sea of handlebars stretching before him.

All Sorts of Proposals

The problem, inevitably called bicycle pollution, has ignited angry editorials and speeches, lots of committee meetings and a whole new rack of solutions. These include public-relations drives, parking tickets, loudspeaker lectures, tow-away zones and, of course, new legislation. None of them have worked so far, and the situation has given the Japanese pause.

"Right after the war," said Kanari Ebihara, director of the Bicycle Association of Japan, "everybody was too poor and busy trying to make a living

The New York Times/Hirotaka Yoshizaki

A sea of bicycles stretches across the plaza outside Tokyo's busy Kamata Station. Each day, in every possible spot, thousands of bicycles are parked illegally.

to think of the bicycle as anything other than a vehicle to haul some freight. To ride them to curb pollution or for health reasons? That was nonsense.

But, Mr. Ebihara and others note, rapid economic growth and labor-saving devices, along with affluence and increased leisure, have changed attitudes and habits. For one thing, it is no longer considered unfeminine for women to ride. More important, Mr. Ebihara added in an interview, many people do not know what to do with themselves any more. "For the first time Japan has entered an era where people are looking for some purpose to their lives, as if they missed something during these hectic years of great growth," he explained. "In a sense we are now in an era of reconsideration."

Integral Part of the Search

Mr. Ebihara, who has a three-speed sport model, sees the bicycle as an integral part of the widespread search. Whatever its role, the bicycle is certainly widespread. From 10 million in 1950, the bicycle population has grown to 47 million, with 6.3 million rolling off the assembly lines annually, 16 percent of them for export.

Commuting cyclists do not yet form the whirling phalanxes that spread across streets in such places as Amsterdam. Respectful of the menacing

car and truck drivers who are claiming more and more bicycle victims, riders cling to the curbs in thin streams.

They usually center on the railroad stations that are the hub of most communities, even the sprawling new suburbs where poor public transportation almost requires bicycles if not cars. Each of the 2,179 railroad stations has a neatly marked bicycle park that some riders use. "Do you see the white line painted on the sidewalk over there?" Sergeant Tanzawa asked at the crowded Kamata station. "I guess you can't see it for all the bicycles, but it's there and it's supposed to mark the legal parking area."

Two entire sidewalks were clogged with spokes and kickstands that grab at passing ankles. A rope, put up to help pedestrians claim a part of the pathway, supported half a dozen cycles. The bushes were filled with bicycles, even tricycles. A "No bicycle parking" sign was surrounded by parked bikes chained to it. If a cyclist edging in to spot a familiar fender amid a sea of blinding reflectors inadvertently knocks over a bike, witnesses report, the resulting chain reaction can last minutes and travel a block.

Always Room for One More

For convenience's sake 17-year-old Fumi Shimada rides her bike to catch the train to school. When she returns in midafternoon she often finds it

stacked under six or seven others. She walks home, and her father drives her back to help dig it out.

"There's always room for one more," said Akemi Takahasi, a cosmetics saleswoman, as she jammed her bike among perhaps 3,000 others in the station plaza. Five belonged to policemen; two had flat tires.

"We had another roundup last month," the sergeant said, which means that six hired trucks hauled a thousand bikes to distant parking lots. The next day they all came back.

The cities seem unable to find a solution to the parking problems created by the bicycle solution. Kunihiko Ogawa, a Socialist who sees battalions of bikes lining the railroad tracks on his morning trip to Parliament, offered a railroad station parking bill. This has prompted the Government, controlled by conservatives, to subsidize a third of the cost of buying parking land and half the cost of building lots.

In Tokyo one ward launched an Abandoned Bicycles Countermeasure Committee, which meets 10 times a year but has yet to find an answer. According to Mr. Ogawa, some communities have devised a possible long-term answer: spraying illegally parked bikes with water, hoping that rust will accomplish what the police cannot.

April 8, 1978

Antismoking Drive Is Penetrating
A Thick Haze in Japan

By HIROTAKA YOSHIZAKI
Special to The New York Times

TOKYO, May 12—An antismoking campaign is catching on in Japan, where the cigarette smoke is thick indeed.

Some 34 million people, including three of five adult males, smoke almost 800 million cigarettes a day, or seven a day per person—the highest per capita consumption in the world. This means that in Japan, the second-largest bulk user of tobacco, 5,000 cigarettes go up in smoke every day per square mile, compared with 460 in the United States, where the ratio of smokers among adult males is two in five.

Not only do the Japanese smoke a lot—it is their neighbors the Chinese who consume the most tobacco—they smoke almost everywhere, any time—on the streets or on train platforms, in hospital lobbies, elevators and public halls. Smoke fills the air and butts lie everywhere despite handy receptacles at crosswalks and bus stops.

Only in recent years have efforts to reduce smoking started to gain attention. Partly as a result of the growing awareness of the impact on health and environment, tobacco sales in 1976 dropped for the first time. The decline is conspicuous among males; a recent survey indicates that 630,000 have quit in the last two years.

Trouble for Government Monopoly

This worries the Government because tobacco sales have been a stable revenue source since it monopolized the business in 1904 to raise funds for the war with Russia. In 1976 the Japan Tobacco and Salt Public Corporation sold 289 billion cigarettes through nearly 500,000 tobacco shops, coffee shops, bars and restaurants and 190,000 vending machines. Of the total revenue of $8 billion, $2.9 billion went to the central Government and $1.7 billion to local governments.

Despite any concern over sales, the monopoly started a campaign for tidier smoking in 1974. "This is because

Japanese smoking manners are still behind those in the Western nations," was the apologetic explanation of Chihiro Seki of the corporation, who consumes at least 30 cigarettes a day. A recent corporation survey shows that two out of three people who smoke do so even when walking, and among them three out of five throw their butts anywhere.

Besides putting posters and more receptacles around, the corporation has voluntarily curbed the amount of advertising on television and in newspapers and magazines. "We advertise only when we put out a new brand," Mr. Seki said.

Campaign in Subway Stations

Other efforts to reduce consumption go back as far as 1970, when a No-Smoking Time campaign began at Tokyo subway stations and major railway stations, with posters an loudspeakers urging commuters not to light up on platforms during the morning rush hour, when stations are jammed.

The rail station at Yokohama, west of Tokyo, tried a different approach two years ago. The 15th of every month was designated as No Stub-Throwing Day, when commuters may smoke but are asked to dispose of their butts properly. "The idea turned out successfully," said Kahei Inoue, assistant station master. "Till then all of us had to sweep up about 100,000 cigarette butts every day. Now the number is down by 30 percent." A high school published a comic book last year titled "Bye-Bye Smoking," illustrating its adverse effects on health.

The most recent and unique effort is an "I hate smoke" campaign started this year by Midori Nakada, a 25-year-old copywriter, and her associates. "I myself had been almost overcome in this office because most of my colleagues were chain smokers," Miss Nakada said in her tiny quarters.

"What I couldn't understand," she continued, "was that even those marching against pollution demonstrate with cigarettes in their mouth, and along the march route you could see many stubs. Also, at a meeting of pollution victims and their supporters in a closed small room, the latter often smoke callously smack in the faces of the weak."

The Right to Hate Smoke

This led her to a whole new concept,

A poster on a Japanese railway platform urges smokers not to throw cigarette butts on floor.

at least in Japan—the right to hate smoke. The emphasis of no-smoking campaigns has been that it is bad for health, to which smokers reply that they do not care. "So it was a puffers'

problem and nothing to do with nonsmokers," said Miss Nakada, who smoked in college. "If you say, 'I don't care whether you quit or not, but please don't smoke around me since I hate smoke,' that is the affair of both you and the smokers." By looking at the matter this way, she believes, the campaign can develop from an individual level to a social one.

She and her colleagues decided that the right to hate smoke was a basic human right, so they formed the Association to Protect Nonsmokers, the membership of which has increased to 2,500—all wearing "I hate smoke" badges. The group, the first of its kind in Japan, plans a nationwide rally in June. It has appealed to Parliament, where it conferred with party representatives, all nonsmokers, one of whom told them: "Polluted air produces polluted politics."

Parliament took up the subject for the first time at a committee meeting in April. A Welfare Ministry official promised to make the lobbies of the 250 national hospitals and clinics no-smoking areas and to set aside separate rooms for smokers. A committee member proposed a national No-Smoking Day and others suggested a smoking ban at Cabinet meetings. No final actions were taken, but there was one apparent improvement: The ashtrays in the usually smoke-filled committee room remained empty that day.

May 13, 1978

Even Japan Finds Poor Are Always With It

By ANDREW H. MALCOLM

TOKYO — Women in colorful kimonos attending parties in celebration of plum and cherry blossoms. Scrubbed children gambolling off to school in bonnets and pressed shorts. Well-heeled businessmen in polished cars. And well-kept lanes lined with private gardens. Affluent Japan, 1978.

Tiny rooms shared by humans and vermin. Hallways where paint peels off raw, rusting metal. Aging bodies sleeping in the warm spring sunshine. Impoverished Japan, 1978. The same nation. Two different worlds. Both are real. But one is hidden.

Poor Japanese, especially poor urban Japanese, do not fit the stereotype of an energetic, innovative people, more than 92 percent of whom consider themselves middle class, according to opinion surveys. Their presence is an embarrassment to a society with a gross national product last year of close to $700 billion and a per capita income of $6,036 — an economy so booming that last week the Governor of the Bank of Japan said he doubted Japan would be able, as hoped, to sharply reduce its huge trade surplus in fiscal 1978. But statistics do not tell the full story.

Officially, only 1.4 percent of Japan's 113 million persons are on welfare. Many other poor persons, it is believed, have not signed up out of ignorance or, more likely, pride. In the traditions of the countryside, poor people were carried along by extended families. It is the postwar decline of this traditional grouping that has marked the growth of Japan's modest welfare system. The era of rapid economic growth, roughly from 1960 to 1973, drew millions of farmers and farmers' sons to jobs in the cities.

The heady boom days ended with the energy crisis of 1973, and a time of greatly slowed growth has ensued. Industry has yet to make many of the painful, necessary adjustments, but some have reduced hiring and even laid off employees, primarily from among the less-skilled or the higher-paid older workers. This has punched holes in Japan's much-hallowed "lifetime" employment system. The future looks worse, at least for those at the bottom. Unemployment ranks are growing; the jobless rate for March was 2.12 percent, up from 1.94 percent a year earlier. The figures seem slight by United States standards, but not to the Japanese who have lost their jobs. "Of course, we can't know the precise time lag," said Takuo Suzuki, director of a city welfare center, "but we must expect that the number of poor will increase."

With the erosion of traditional ties that accompanied urbanization, the poor have nowhere to turn but to the Government, which has been dominated by conservatives for all but a few months of the last three decades. Their polices, attuned more to industrial and financial development, resulted in a grudging development of welfare that, for instance, has yet to devise a program of pensions for the elderly. Currently, welfare payments and administrative expenses cost the national Government $3.8 billion a year. Municipalities pay the remaining 20 percent of the welfare tab. But increases are hard to achieve even though the Japanese cost of living is among the world's highest.

Every day about 150 men visit Mr. Suzuki's welfare office in the heart of Sanya, a notorious Tokyo slum whose name is synonymous with street derelicts. Officials say a typical case is an unskilled man in his mid-forties; if married, he is now divorced. A few of the men obtain day construction jobs for $16 per day. Since the inns are closed by day, others lie around the streets. When younger, some of these poverty victims join gangs which make profits from illegal gambling, drugs, protection and prostitution. Experts estimate that two-thirds of this country's gangsters come from the poor homes of Korean or Burakumin families. The latter are Japan's own "untouchable" caste, but both groups still feel the heavy hand of discrimination.

A growing number of welfare recipients are elderly, handicapped or ill. Few have the college education that has been a ticket to success in Japan. While national health insurance covers most medical costs, the simple expenses of daily living are too much. One such case is the Ichiro Taniguchi family, whose name is changed here at their request. Three years ago, Mr. Taniguchi fell ill. He is not sure why, but his wife confides that he is dying of lung cancer.

Mr. Taniguchi left his father's farm in the 1950's for a construction job in Tokyo. "I was foreman of 20 men," he says. Unable to work, however, he was forced out of his home and now lives with his wife, their four children and a stray pet pigeon in a 48-square-foot room in a charity's dormitory for poor families.

Each month they receive 162,000 yen in welfare payments, the equivalent of something over $700 at today's inflated exchange rates. Of that, 14,000 goes for utilities. The city also gives them a bus pass and 180 free tickets to a public bath: that amounts to 30 baths a year for each member of the family.

Another 58,000 yen goes for for school tuition, which is required even for public schools in Japan. Other costs leave about 3,500 yen or $14 per day for their food. Mrs. Taniguchi, whose knees were crippled in a bicycle accident, buys old vegetables, shops for specials and gets discards from church dinners and bazaars. Her family doesn't know it, but to save further she eats only once or twice a day.

Her oldest son brings in some income from a newspaper route and, occasionally, Mr. Taniguchi finds an odd job sweeping floors. He must give the welfare office 40 percent of his earnings. Each month finds a growing need for more money. Mr. Taniguchi's parents and brothers say they can no longer help. Banks won't lend him money because he doesn't have a job and the city won't advance school costs unless he provides two financial references, an impossible task since all of his friends are poor.

The case is typical, say social workers, and the family's situation will worsen when the father dies, possibly next year. Then, their welfare allotments will be cut. And they will have to move. "Life in affluent Japan is fine so long as you're in the mainstream," said one slum worker, "but once you get crosswise of the rigid system, then you don't bounce back."

Andrew H. Malcolm is a correspondent for The New York Times based in Tokyo.

June 4, 1978

21 Killed as Quake Rocks Japan; Northern Coast City Severely Hit

TOKYO, June 12 (Reuters)—Japan's densely populated main island of Honshu was rocked today by the strongest earthquake to hit the country in 14 years, and at least 21 people died and 350 were injured as buildings and power lines crumbled. At least two others were reported missing.

The tremor, which lasted several seconds and set skyscrapers swaying in Tokyo, frightened millions about to go home from work and brought a tidal wave scare along Honshu's Pacific coastline. The sea, however, rose only a little.

Worst hit by the quake, which measured 7.5 on the open-ended Richter scale, was Sendai, a city of 600,000 people 180 miles northeast of Tokyo on Honshu's Pacific coast. The Japanese Meteorological Agency said the epicenter of the quake was in the Pacific off Sendai 60 miles from shore.

The agency said the quake was the strongest to hit Japan since the one that struck Niigata, a city on the Sea of Japan about 160 miles northwest of Tokyo, on June 16, 1964. That quake, which also measured 7.5 on the Richter scale, killed 26 people and injured 380.

Strongest Quake of the Year

The Uppsala Seismological Institute in Swe\n said today's quake was the most powerful recorded in the world so far this year.

All 21 deaths and nearly all the injuries occurred in Sendai.

Most of those who died were killed

The New York Times/June 13, 1978

Epicenter of quake was reported 60 miles east of Sendai.

by falling buildings. Two died when a big electric power pylon toppled on them.

Numerous landslides also occurred around Sendai, and electricity and gas supplies were cut. Two thermal power plants were reported damaged.

Most train services in the northern parts of Honshu were suspended and offi-

cials said they would not resume until at least tomorrow.

Subways stopped running in Tokyo and some high-speed intercity rail services were stopped while the tracks were checked for possible damage.

Tokyo's Haneda airport, now used mainly for domestic flights, was closed

temporarily for safety checks of runways

The Japanese have lived in constan fear of earthquakes ever since a cata strophic one killed nearly 150,000 peopl in 1923. In January of this year, 25 peopl died in a quake in the Izu Peninsula south of Tokyo.

June 13, 1978

U-Turn for Okinawa:
From Right-Hand Driving to Left

By ANDREW H. MALCOLM

NAHA, Okinawa — Japanese officials are preparing to turn this island around — or at least the roads.

On July 30, it will switch from driving on the right, American style, to driving on the left, Japanese style. After that magic — and multimillion-dollar — moment, all of Japan will be driving on the same side for the first time since the closing days of World War II, when Americans with tanks and large trucks decided that Okinawans would drive on the same side as they.

Altering hundreds of signs and carving out right-turn lanes and buying 1,000 buses and 5,000 taxis and changing the driving and pedaling and walking habits of more than a million people has been a chore of some consequence — not to mention coordinating the bureaucracies of the 12 government agencies that felt the need to be involved.

Extra Policemen Assigned

Polls indicate that two-thirds of the Okinawans are uneasy over the prospect, and the Government will be flying in an extra 2,500 policemen just in case. Kent Allen, an Air Force maintenance man stationed here, remarked: "It should be fun to watch, at least."

At 10 P.M. on July 29 all traffic must halt for eight hours. Overnight 3,000 men will scurry along the roads, taking covers off signs on the left and pulling them over signs on the right. At 5:30 A.M. on the 30th, a Sunday, sirens will sound, along with some official fireworks, and all official traffic still on the roads will creep to the left side and stop. Then at 6 A.M. the sirens will blow again, and it's off to the races.

The cost of the change, which, according to officials, is required by international treaties on road safety that forbid two driving systems in a country, will be in excess of $150 million. Some Okinawans have questioned the need for such an expensive alteration of a pattern that has sufficed for 33

years, at a time when there are acknowledged insufficiencies in such essentials as medical care and the road system throughout this 64-mile-long island 960 miles southwest of Tokyo.

The Government has devised an educational campaign that includes bilingual pamphlets, lectures and school seminars, plus a spate of slogans and symbols on signs, bumper stickers and matchbook covers, to say nothing of posters showing a bra-less woman putting on a T-shirt.

"This is a big project," said Choichi Miyagi, chief of the Okinawa Prefectural Switchover Task Force. It was delayed until 1972, when the post-World War II American military occupation of Okinawa ended; it was postponed three years more because of anticipated confusion over the resumption of Japanese control; it was again delayed by Expo 75 in Osaka, which itself was delayed until 1976. Finally the time has almost come.

While the United States will have to

Street scene from Naha City, Okinawa, as Japanese officials prepare to switch the island to left-hand driving.

Japan National Tourist Organization

pay $495,000 for road signs and other alterations at its many bases, the Government in Tokyo has agreed so far to meet $150 million of the prefectural government's costs. These include replacing the headlights on 300,000 motor vehicles so they will aim to the left instead of the right as well as the purchase of 5,000 taxis and 1,000 buses — bus stops will have to be shifted, too — plus terminal modifications, guardrail adjustments and subsidies for the purchase of private cars in some cases. Also included is the disposal of more than 600,000 perfectly good headlights, a plan to export them having been considered but rejected. Used buses are for sale overseas.

An even larger outlay is under negotiation and is likely to drag on for years. In the haste to rebuild Okinawa after the last battles of the Pacific war,

little attention was paid to whether the government owned the land under new roads. Compensation for those pieces of land, some of them just the width of a crosswalk, has been stalled in litigation handed down from father to son. Now that the government must in some cases shave off a few more feet of private land to make new turns and other modifications, the old demands for compensation are mingled with new ones.

Additionally, owners of groceries, vending machines, gasoline stations and bait shops along the roads to popular fishing spots are demanding damages for the losses they expect from the new traffic patterns. "But how," asked Susumu Sago, another official, "do you determine how much damage is being suffered by whom and why?" Added Mr. Miyagi: "If we start compensating

every little case that is filed it will be just endless. We pass them all on to the central Government."

Tokyo officials are reluctant to set costly financial precedents, so no payments have been made. The matter is complicated by prefectural demands for transportation and welfare improvements to help persuade Okinawans that the switchover will help everyone.

"This is like my Bicentennial file," said Lieut. Col. Bob Whaley, who is in charge of coordinating the switchover efforts of the American military forces with myriad Japanese agencies. "We are at this moment gaining an awful lot of very valuable information and experience that will never be of any use to anyone ever again."

July 5, 1978

Nagasaki's Magnificent Past Is About All City Still Has

By ANDREW H. MALCOLM

NAGASAKI, Japan — "A long time ago," the gardener explained, "some general named Grant — I do not know which country he was from — came here and planted that tree." The general was Ulysses Simpson Grant; 99 years ago in May the former President climbed the cobbled streets of this famous but now faltering city and planted two banyan trees.

A few years ago, when one of them died, it was quickly replaced by the city to maintain the heritage. The other tree planted by General Grant — in Japanese he is Gu-ran-toh Shogun — survives, but it requires careful tending and doctoring and remains somewhat stunted.

Indeed, the tree, with its flaking bilingual stone tablet, is an appropriate if overlooked symbol of a city that built its fame and future on people and business and things from foreign lands. Now Nagasaki, with a population of 447,000, is dying because of the past.

In the 1500's the community, which was never important enough to have its own castle, was plucked from the medieval murk as a center of foreign trade. From 1639 to 1859 it was the only city opened to foreigners by fearful feudal rulers. Through this port on Kyushu, the southernmost island, Japan was introduced to Christianity, bread, locomotives, asphalt, ginger ale and

Sofukuji Temple, known as Nankindera (Chinese Temple) in Nagasaki City.

Japan National Tourist Organization

beer and modern armaments — not necessarily in that order of importance. The departure point for trade and cultural ties to China, it was the source of school outings that often chose Shanghai before Japanese cities.

•

On Aug. 9, 1945, because it was cloudy over an alternate target, a B-29 bearing an atomic bomb blasted Nagasaki into the history books at 11:02

A.M. Over the years the vast shipyards that once turned out imperial battleships have recovered to turn out cargo vessels and giant tankers in the millions of tons. In good years 80 percent of production goes to foreign buyers; even fishermen rely on foreign fishing grounds for most of their catch.

Now the 200-mile limit threatens the fishermen; a global glut of tankers, the higher value of the yen and pricing decisions by oil producers thousands of miles away have plunged the shipyards into gloom and Nagasaki into recession. The only bright spot, a modest one, is tourism, but many of the five million visitors each year are children on excursions into their country's past. But when Nagasaki's own children graduate from high school, 40 percent move elsewhere to start careers.

●

"Traditionally," Mayuki Nishikido, a Shinto priest, explained, "Nagasaki people have been conservative, relaxed, easy-going and respectful. However, I am afraid these characteristics have been diluted in recent years."

Time was, the 71-year-old priest said, when people felt it a duty and great honor to help carry the portable shrines in the traditional fall festival, and the banks, the factories and the schools closed for the three-day holiday. These days the banks, factories and schools stay open, Mr. Nishikido said, "and people demand to be paid in yen for carrying the shrines because they say they gave up a day's work to be in the parades."

"The way people drive has changed, too," said Kenji Ihara, a taxi driver. "We used to drive a lot slower and easier. Now it's faster, more aggressive. More horns."

●

Some of Mr. Ihara's colleagues took time off recently to join several hundred teachers, students and fishermen to protest the planned transfer of Japan's only nuclear-powered ship, the crippled Mutsu, to Nagasaki waters for repairs. For years the costly ship, which developed a radiation leak on its test voyage, has been idle in northern waters. The Government has seized on the repair job as a measure to help the stricken shipyards, but officials have run aground on some citizens' powerful "nuclear allergy"—that often-ill-defined, seemingly irrational but deeply felt opposition to all things nuclear, even if they will never flash in the sky.

"I lost both of my parents and brothers that day," said Terusada Koga, a 49-year-old taxi driver who must still seek frequent checkups for radiation effects, "so right after that August I hated war very much. As time went by those feelings weakened and healed. But now this Mutsu issue reminds me of those feelings I had right after the war, and I do not like them. I do not like them one bit."

●

"The bomb exploded at an altitude of 600 meters," the guide explains, "just beyond that large fuel-storage tank. Now, over there is the Mitsubishi ship-

yards where the famous battleship Musashi was built. And behind you is the Glover House."

Madame Butterfly did not sleep there, nor did she look out over the harbor for Lieutenant Pinkerton, though, as the tourist brochures note, she could have, and that has been good enough for Nagasaki, so it has adopted Puccini's opera as local lore.

Behind the restored Glover House, at the top of the air-conditioned moving sidewalk up the hillside, is a bronze Madame Butterfly in kimono, with a plaque and a series of wall fountains arrayed like notes in the score. The only difference between the tragic Italian tale about Nagasaki and the "real life" story adopted by Nagasaki is the beginning, the middle and the end — and the parts in between.

Thomas Blake Glover wasn't named Pinkerton, wasn't an American, wasn't in the Navy and didn't leave town. He was British, he arrived in 1859 and he didn't deal in altruism but in guns, supplying some of the warring clans that were washing over a chaotic country.

Fortunately for Glover, his side won and the Emperor was restored to power. In gratitude he awarded a medal to Glover, who married his Japanese sweetheart, Tsuru. They lived happily ever after. Curtain.

July 14, 1978

---

80 Japanese Arrested To Prevent Crime War

TOKYO, July 15 (Reuters) — The police arrested more than 80 people suspected of being gangsters today in an effort to prevent an underworld war of revenge following an attempt to assassinate a leader of organized crime in Japan.

Most of the raids were on homes and offices of members of the Yamaguchi-Gumi, which is believed to have organized several "death squads" to eliminate members of rival gangs following

the attempted assassination of its boss, Kazuo Taoka, 65 years old, in a nightclub on Tuesday. Mr. Taoka suffered neck wounds.

July 16, 1978

Japanese Tangerines And Fate of Trade Talks

By HENRY SCOTT-STOKES

SHIMIZU, Japan, July 16 — Can the fate of nations and the future of what is known as the "Tokyo Round" — the most important commercial negotiation of the decade — rest on the vote of

a single small Japanese mikan farmer?

Not quite, but almost. Yasuhiro Hiraoka grows mikan, which are very like tangerines but a bit more yellow, in this part of the world not far from Mount Fuji. To save him and his fellows from extinction, the Japanese

Government is prepared virtually to wreck the Tokyo Round of continuing negotiations sponsored by the General Agreement on Tariffs and Trade.

Senior ministers say that they cannot bend an inch to an American demand for access for California and Florida oranges to the Japanese market. Both

Japanese Society

the head of Japan's Economic Planning Agency, Kiichi Miyazawa, and Nobuhiko Ushiba, External Economic Affairs Minister, made this clear in recent interviews.

Yet President Carter's trade negotiator, Robert S. Strauss, has told them that he must have a bigger Japanese orange quota — which only American producers would fill (plus perhaps a few Jaffa oranges from Israel) — or he will not be able to "sell" to Congress the Tokyo Round package that he is currently putting together with Mr. Ushiba and Wilhelm Haferkamp of the European Economic Community.

What emerges from a visit to Mr. Hiraoka's vertiginous and beautiful but extremely inefficient mikan plantation here, however, is that liberalization of orange imports to any degree would certainly kill the business of this extremely tough breed of Japanese farmer. The current orange quota is 45,000 tons a year, calculated to do minimal damage to mikan prices in the autumn season.

"I have 1.5 hectares altogether," Mr. Hiraoka said, as he stood on the shoulder of a steep mountain above this port town of 250,000 people. "But they are split up in parcels here and there."

Like so many small holders in Shizuoka province, Mr. Hiraoka has inherited scattered bits and pieces and parcels of land. He cannot work on one given spot. "Of course one of our biggest problems," he added, "is just the nature of the land here. It's steep and it's dangerous at times."

Growing Trees on Steep Slopes

In old mikan provinces like this — as distinct from the more efficient plantations in Ehime and in Kyushu provinces, which were recently planted with young, more vigorous trees — the farmers have to plant their trees on steep slopes. Planting at the valley bottom would risk severe frostbite when the trees flower in the spring.

The steepness of these mountains, however, demands great ingenuity on the farmers' part in order to collect their crops.

In the old days they were tougher, and there were more hands to do the work at harvest time. Farmers from an earlier era could carry twice their weight, up to 330 pounds, on their backs, for several miles.

These days the collection has to be mechanized. Mr. Hiraoka has built a miniature mountain railway across his land, with a small gasoline engine at the top that zigzags across his slopes and brings the fruit up the hill to a road at the top in the fall.

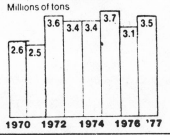

Japan's Production of Mikan (Tangerines)
Millions of tons

1970		1972		1974		1976	'77
2.6	2.5	3.6	3.4	3.4	3.7	3.1	3.5

As to the cost of such a project: "Farmers are working for years to pay off their share of the cost of building the road," explained an official from the local Seikanren, an organization of citrus farmers that serves as a cooperative and markets and cans mikan here.

Average Income Is $15,000 a Year

The average income of the smaller mikan farmers — whose holdings are typically no bigger than Mr. Hiraoka's 3.7 acres and often much smaller — rarely surpasses $15,000.

That would not be bad as take-home pay, but the farmers have to pay off an interest burden on the loans they have made these last few years because they could no longer afford to hire seasonal labor.

"Only five years ago we had about 5,000 pickers hired in the autumn," said Fujio Hiraoka, a cousin of Mr. Hiraoka, who serves as spokesman for local mikan men.

"But these days we are in a slump, ever since 1972 in fact, and that means we cannot afford more than about 500 to help us," the weatherbeaten farmer added.

On average farmers lost about $890 for every acre that they farmed last year, according to Seikanren Figurzu. On this basis, Yasuhiro Hiraoka would have lost about $3,300. Being a diligent, young farmer, he probably did better and almost broke even. He did not discuss the point, but there is no doubt that his neighbors are in trouble.

Altogether some 35,000 families work or partly work Japanese tangerine plots in Shizuoka Province, within a decade only some 2,000 will be left, according to the authorities in Shizuoka City.

Supply Outstripping Demand

The basic problem throughout Japan is that supply has vastly outstripped demand. To some extent the surplus has been mopped up by turning the mikan to juice and adding sugar before exporting to Saudi Arabia and elsewhere in the Middle East, a market

that has developed since the "oil shock" of 1973.

Still, Japan has too many mikan. Production ran about 3.6 million tons last year compared with demand of only 3 millon tons.

Importing oranges would be doubly wounding because American oranges taste much better than the mikan, which is not usually sweet, and is often dry. "The truth is that oranges taste much better than mikan," said Kenji Henmi, a professor at Tokyo University.

To make the situation more complex, mikan farmers hold key votes in rural districts that send an estimated 290 out of 763 Diet members to Tokyo, and elections are due this autumn. The estimate, made by Mr. Ushiba, is considered by some to be exaggerated.

Sympathy for Farmers Among People

In the constituencies of most of the Diet members, only a small fraction of voters are mikan farmers, but there is much sympathy for them among the people. And sure proof of the bad faith of the politicians in the eyes of many voters would be an increase in the orange import quota — at a time when the mikan industry is already threatening to fall apart.

"Liberalization is a killer," said Mr. Hiraoka, standing among his trees. "I would convert to some other crop if I could — but what could you plant up here?"

At the Agriculture Ministry in Tokyo officials argue that Japan has already liberalized grapefruit imports 160,000 tons, half of which comes from America. In addition, lemon imports have been liberalized, destroying the Japanese domestic lemon industry to the last tree. Half the 100,000 tons of imported lemons come from the United States.

And early this year the orange import was tripled from 15,000 to 45,000 tons after strong pressure on Mr. Ushiba by Mr. Strauss.

"Nintey-nine percent of these oranges come from America," said Takaharu Hatanaka of the Agriculture Ministry. "Why should we go further and put an end to our citrus industry?"

A small increase in the quota is the very maximum that the Japanese will give, whatever the consequences for the Tokyo Round as a whole.

The clinching argument in the debate over mikan for the politicians is that more than a decade ago the Government encouraged farmers, who were producing too much rice, to switch to mikan.

July 17, 1978

The trading floor of the Tokyo Stock Exchange, one of nine exchanges in Japan.

Chapter 2

The Business World

Japan has successfully incorporated many characteristics of Western life into its own social patterns. The fundamental traits of Japanese society, however, in the family or in business, rest solidly upon a bedrock of long-standing Japanese traditions. Indeed, in business, as elsewhere, the Japanese have made their mark as an industrial nation by tying homegrown talent, traditional social discipline, and harmony to a borrowed technology.

Wherein lies the secret of Japan's success story in business and international trade? How has that nation avoided many of the pitfalls which beset Western business? The answers are not simple. The traditional explanations for the Japanese business boom have centered around three major contentions: that labor in Japan is cheaper; that the Japanese manufacturing base was rebuilt from scratch after World War II; and that the Japanese government provides overt preferential treatment to its own manufacturers through complex tariffs and an abundance of import quotas serving to reduce competition at home. There are experts who contend, however, that such explanations are simplistic, and that Japanese wages, for one, are not so far below European levels as to account for Japan's almost phenomenal strides in the international market. These analysts believe that much of Japan's economic success, at least as it relates to foreign trade, can be attributed to superior marketing of products designed initially for overseas markets.

Yet there are certain features of Japanese society—basic social values and practices—that most experts regard as fundamental to Japanese business success. As is the case in Japanese society, the nation's industrial complex is organized paternalistically. When most Japanese join a company, they join for life. The massive benefits and lifetime security offered by the employer are matched by the employee through valuable long-term experience, loyalty and strong identification with the company, its objectives and its profitability. In Japan the social group is almost as important as the family, and most social groups form at the place of work. As a result, working conditions tend to be less alienating than in many countries where worker and employer maintain an adversary relationship.

While paternalism inspires devotion and allegiance, it also imposes a serious

35

burden upon management, for workers must be paid when, in fact, they are not working. In the Japanese shipbuilding industry, for example, times are tough. Once leaders in the field, Japanese shipbuilders have had to diversify into such alternative products as floating factories, floating oil tanks and floating hotels for export. Because the workers in the industry are not laid off during slump periods, large numbers of them are retrained, assigned to make-work projects, or are farmed out to more prosperous divisions of the companies.

Tradition, of course, plays an important role in determining how far women can go in the Japanese business world. Success stories relating specifically to women in business are rare. While a few women have reached executive positions or have managed to earn large salaries, the majority are relegated to secretarial positions. Almost all important executive-level positions remain closed to women.

In spite of its postwar track record, the Japanese economy also shows signs of becoming sluggish. As a result of increased fuel prices, the surging yen and high inflation, several large concerns went bankrupt last year. Principal among them was the Eidai Sangyo Company, Japan's largest plywood manufacturer. Although Edai had received financial support from five of the nation's largest banks, among them Mitsubishi Trust and Fuji Bank, by February 1978, even subsidies could no longer save the company from collapse. Several hard-pressed Japanese firms have resorted to selling wares below cost, both domestically and abroad, to keep the flow of money steady and to avoid lay-offs.

Basic to the nature of Japanese business, above and beyond its assimilation of traditional Japanese social mores and its reaction to external economic factors, is the intensely close relationship of enterprise and government. The Japanese have an unusual tolerance for blatant involvement of business in politics. Many of the members of Japan's ruling party depend on corporate support, through influence and actual finance. This close union makes it relatively easy for both worlds to act hand-in-hand, facilitating, for example, protectionist legislation.

A small island, with few natural resources, overpopulated, and threatened by terrifying natural disasters which strike year after year, Japan continues to prosper through a keen identity of interest among government, business and labor.

The Business World

Nagataka Murayama Dies in Japan; Headed Country's Biggest Paper

A page from Asahi Shimbun, Japan's largest and most presitious newspaper.

By ANDREW H. MALCOLM

TOKYO, Aug. 8—Nagataka Murayama, an owner and former president of Asahi Shimbun, Japan's largest and most prestigious newspaper, died yesterday in a hospital in a suburb of Osaka. He was 83 years old.

The immediate cause of death, as given by the family, was brain damage resulting from a stroke suffered several years ago. Mr. Murayama had been bedridden at home or in a hospital for years. He died in Kosetsu Memorial Hospital in Nishinomiya. Plans for funeral and memorial services have not yet been set.

For 41 years Mr. Murayama served as a directing chairman, or president, of Asahi—the name means "Morning Sun" —a newspaper company that became one of Japan's giant communications conglomerates with interests in newspapers, magazines, book publishing, television and radio stations.

Asahi Shimbun alone has 9,000 employees and a fleet of jet and propeller-driven aircraft. In recent years the newspaper has been in a tight circulation race with Yomiuri Shimbun, another prominent national daily. Asahi now has a total circulation of 11.4 million for its morning and afternoon editions, distributed throughout Japan.

Bitter Management Struggle

At his death Mr. Murayama was a director of the Asahi Broadcasting Company, but he resigned his directorship

Nagataka Murayama.

with the parent company in December 1965 after losing out in a bitter management struggle within the company.

The fight pitted Mr. Murayama, the adopted son of one of the paper's founders, against executives of its news and business departments. The staff said that Mr. Murayama and his wife, Ofuji, were seeking to establish domination of their personal business and editorial policies.

The Murayamas contended that senior executives of the paper had been in power too long and were thwarting necessary modernization measures.

The contest drew international attention because of Asahi's unusually powerful position in a nation with one of the world's highest literacy rates. In addition to its influential communications holdings, the company is deeply involved in cultural and charitable activities, and many members of its staff have gone on to hold powerful political positions.

Adopted Into Wife's Family

Born on March 16, 1894, to Viscount and Viscountess Okabe, Mr. Murayama was graduated from the law department of Kyoto Imperial University in 1919, after which he was married to the daughter of Ryuhei Murayama, a cofounder of Asahi in 1879 with Riichi Ueno. After the marriage the senior Mr. Murayama adopted his son-in-law, a common Japanese procedure intended to maintain the family line when there is no male heir.

Mr. Murayama resigned his positions with Asahi from 1947 until 1951 during the purge of wartime executives carried out by American occupation authorities.

He was a past chairman of the Japan Newspaper Editors and Publishers Association, chairman and later adviser to The Asahi Evening News, an English-language daily, and a director of All Nippon Airways.

Mr. Murayama is survived by his wife and two daughters, Michiko and Fumiko.

August 9, 1977

37

Japan's 'Emperor of Steel'

The New York Times/June Malcolm

Yoshihiro Inayama, the chairman of the Nippon Steel Corporation.

By TRACY DAHLBY

TOKYO—Five decades ago when Yoshihiro Inayama consulted a palm-reader for good luck, as many aspiring young Japanese businessmen still do, he was told that he was a man of iron-willed resolve who would overcome all obstacles to accomplish what he set out to do.

And, appropriately Mr. Inayama has used that iron will to help raise the Japanese steel industry from the devastation of World War II and eventually to help forge the non-Communist world's largest steel producer, the Nippon Steel Corporation, of which he is now chairman.

Nippon Steel, with 77,489 employees, is also the largest corporation in Japan, a nation of corporate giants. The company, among the most technologically advanced in the world, is involved in virtually every category of steelmaking—flat-rolled and structural steel, pipes, including seamless pipe, rails and even oil-drilling platforms.

A robust 74-year-old, Mr. Inayama, a short, slightly built man with a ready smile, is known popularly here as "the Emperor of Steel." Sitting in his executive suite at the top of Nippon Steel's new office building, Mr. Inayama surveyed the Tokyo cityscape. Thanks in no small measure to Japan's efficient steel industry, it had been transformed in 32 years from the scorched bomb-craters of World War II to a complex of grey steel and concrete high rises.

"The choice you make of anything, whether it be a wife or a career, is entirely yours to make, but once made, you must live the choice to the fullest," he said, explaining the philosophy he has followed. It has brought success to him and to the industry—Japanese steel exports to the United States jumped 34.5 percent last year over 1975 to 7.8 million tons—but ironically that was almost too much success.

In Europe and particularly the United States, the Japanese, who are also the world's leading steel exporters, have been accused of predatory pricing and other unfair trade tactics. American steelmakers are lobbying for Government restriction on low-priced steel imports, particularly from Japan.

Although the Japanese have denied American charges that they have engaged in unfair practices—the Central Intelligence Agency reportedly has forecast trade difficulties between the United States and Japan. In a report entitled "World Steel Market: Continued Trouble Ahead," the agency is reported to have said that a levelling off of growing demand combined with a need for return on its highly leveraged investment will put the Japanese under pressure to export and that with protectionism expected elsewhere in the world, those exports will be aimed at the United States.

That is not a scenario the American industry relishes, for its own production so far this year has dropped 4.5 percent to 78.1 million net tons from 81.8 million tons at the comparable time a year ago, while capacity utilization has dropped to 78.7 percent from 84.6 percent.

Indeed, steel pricing is expected to be the hottest item on the agenda next month when American and Japanese officials meet here to discuss the increasing trade frictions between the two countries. As usual, Mr. Inayama's counsel will be sought actively by the Japanese Government leaders in preparing for the official talks.

Still, he maintains that Japan "ranks second to none" in steel sales simply because of its lower production costs, primarily a result of its superior technology, which enables it to sell finished steel for less. This, the Japanese maintain, is not dumping.

Nevertheless, Mr. Inayama said, "If it's proven that Japanese steel exports are causing countries like the United States problems, then it's up to us to see if they can be eliminated perhaps by taking steps to curtail the tonnage of exports so that no market disruption will occur."

But as Mr. Inayama and his colleagues in the steel industry learned in a previous controversy over Japanese steel exports to the United States, for their own protection it's essential that the Governments be involved in negotiating any such export restraints, as they were in the Japanese agreement to limit exports of color television sets to the United States.

In that episode in 1969 the Japanese industry, united under Mr. Inayama's leadership, voluntarily agreed to restrict exports to the United States. But he was named in a suit filed by the Consumers Union contending that the policy violated antitrust laws and kept low-priced steel from American consumers. The suit forced the Japanese to abandon the restraints in 1974.

"We are bound both hand and foot" by antitrust laws of both the United States and Japan, which prevent steel producers from the two countries from reaching an agreement on orderly marketing themselves, he complained.

Despite such plaints, observers of the Japanese business scene insist that if anyone can get things done here, it's Mr. Inayama.

A part of the close-knit "old boy" network that runs Japan's political and business worlds, he is a graduate of Tokyo Imperial University—as is Prime Minister Takeo Fukuda.

Mr. Inayama began his career by passing the civil service examination and entering the then Government-owned Yawata Steel Works in 1928 on the advice of Yawata's director general who was a friend of his uncle.

He moved up the corporate ladder at Yawata and in the postwar years became "the driving force behind rebuilding the steel industry practically from scratch," according to Kunio Okabe, Nippon Steel's deputy general manager of corporate planning—international.

By 1970 Mr. Inayama as president of Yawata had become the chief architect for Yawata's merger with the Fuji Iron and Steel Company. That merger created Nippon Steel, which in the fiscal year to March 31 produced 34 million metric tons, almost one-third of Japan's total steel output of

Leading Steel Producers	
(in the non-Communist world)	
Company	**1976 Production** (millions of metric tons)
Nippon Steel	33.97
U.S. Steel	25.67
British Steel	19.07
Bethlehem Steel	17.14
Nippon Kokan	15.67
Italsider (Italy)	13.43
Sumitomo Metal Industries	13.30
Kawasaki Heavy Industries	13.30
Thyssen (West Germany)	12.82
ESTEL (Netherlands)	10.40
Source: Metal Bulletin Monthly	

NIPPON STEEL—At a Glance

Year ended March 31	1977	1976
Revenues	$9,038,000,000	$7,577,000,000
Net income	104,000,000	52,000,000
Earnings per share	—not applicable—	

Assets, March 31, 1977......$12,478,000,000
Stock price, Aug. 18, 1977
Tokyo exchange close...........................¥116
Stock price, 1977 range......¥119–¥101
Employees, March 31, 1977................77,489
Dollar figures based on March 31, 1977 exchange rate of $1 = ¥277.30.

107 million metric tons. Second-place United States Steel was just over the 25.7 million metric ton mark, while third-ranking British Steel produced 19 million tons.

The merged company was able to save substantial amounts of money by eliminating overlapping efforts in capital spending, research, sales promotion and transportation. It invested the savings in the latest production technology, which lowered costs. With less costly steel to produce and soaring world demand in the early 1970's Nippon Steel was off to a flying start.

But when the 1973-74 Arab oil embargo and quadrupling of prices dampened the worldwide economic boom, Nippon Steel, like its counterparts at home and abroad, was forced to scale down production and wait for demand to recover eventually. So far, says Ciro Arai, manager of Nippon Steel's project research office, no such upturn is in sight.

He estimated that the company was currently running at about three-quarters of production capacity, as are Japan's other major integrated steel producers—Nippon Kokan, Kawasaki Steel, Sumitomo Metals and the Kobe Steel Company. In the fiscal year to March 31 Nippon Steel reported profits of $104 million on sales of $9.04 billion, up sharply from $52 million the year before on sales of $7.58 billion.

Mr. Inayama does not expect any more such dramatic profit rises; nor does he share some observers' anxiety over a possible raw-materials shortage.

"From now on, there won't be much incentive for rapidly expanding steel-making

capacity," he says, because "the advanced economies have reached the point of growth where so-called prosperity has just about hit the ceiling. . . . Most developed countries have reached the maximum in basic human requirements and people are now turning to more nonmaterial requirements."

It is an ironic observation considering Mr. Inayama's position. A past chairman of the International Iron and Steel Institute, he is perhaps the Japanese most widely known and respected by his colleagues in the West. And he is still chairman of both Japan's Steel Materials Club and the Japan Iron and Steel Exporters' Association, president of the Japan Iron and Steel Association, vice-president of the Keidanren, Japan's Federation of Economic Organizations, and governor of the Tokyo Stock Exchange.

To help the giant steel company better cope with the long-term consequences of slower economic growth, Mr. Inayama has encouraged a thorough management reorganization in the last two months. The goal is to shift emphasis from those departments engaged directly in production to those selling the accumulated engineering skills and technology of Nippon Steel to producers in the United States, Australia, Europe, Algeria, Malaysia, Mexico, Brazil, South Korea and other markets.

At the company's annual meeting on June 29 stockholders re-elected Mr. Inayama to a two-year term as chairman and re-elected Eishiro Saito, who is in his early 60's, as president, but 10 persons were elected executive vice presidents, compared with three formerly.

But Mr. Inayama is not writing off the possibilities of expanding markets.

He has been to China many times in his role as chairman of the Japan-China Association on Economy and Trade after having pioneered economic ties with the People's Republic as early as 1957. He is still discussing the possibility of exchanging substantial amounts of Japanese steel and machinery for Chinese coal and oil.

Away from such pressures Mr. Inayama occasionally finds time for a game of golf, although he prefers such indoor sports as mahjong and Japanese chess, and business associates say, he is a noteworthy singer of traditional Japanese songs. He lives in the plush Tokyo residential area of Setagaya with his wife Tsuru. They have three sons, all businessmen, but none with Nippon Steel.

His outside interests and his views on the limited future of production growth notwithstanding, Mr. Inayama says that the essence of industry "is to fill basic human needs through a division of labor, and as long as steel fits this category, the betterment of its production will be my lifelong pursuit."

Tracy Dahlby is a Tokyo-based reporter for The Far Eastern Economic Review.

August 21, 1977

Shipbuilders, in a Slump, Float Factories

TOKYO, Sept. 2 (AP) — Some of the world's top shipbuilders, suffering from a severe business slump, are competing in a quickly developing new industry—floating factories.

Builders in Europe, Scandinavia, Japan and the United States are offering complete, ready-to-go factories of nearly all kinds that are built in big shipyards and sailed to buyers.

The floating factory idea has caught the interest of several countries impatient to develop their own natural resources. The floating factories generally cost about 10 percent less than comparable land-built plants, and a floating plant can be producing in half the time it would take to build a traditional facility, according to the builders.

At least 10 companies in seven countries are developing floating factories for fields ranging from natural gas to fertilizer. But as in shipbuilding, Japanese industries are threatening to grab the biggest share of business.

Ishikawajima-Harima Heavy Industries of Tokyo is the leader in the field so far. Last month, it began the first half of a floating paper pulp plant for Brazil, which the company said was the world's first floating plant of that kind.

IHI's factory is mounted on two huge hulls, 230 meters long, 45 meters wide and 14.5 meters deep. Each hull weighs nearly 30,000 tons.

To Be Hauled by Tugboats

In early 1978, tugboats will haul the two sections 15,600 miles through the China Sea and Indian Ocean, around the Cape of Good Hope and across the Atlantic to the Amazon River.

There they will be permanently grounded on pilings; company officials say the plant will immediately begin producing up to 750 tons of pulp a day.

The $225 million price is 10 percent to 15 percent cheaper than the price of building a comparable plant in Brazil, and the one-year construction time is only one-third of the time required for conventional construction, company officials said.

Kawasaki Heavy Industries, another major Japanese shipbuilder, is building a seawater desalination barge for Saudi Arabia, and the company says it will be the first such floating plant.

At a cost of about $5.7 million, Kawasaki officials said, it is 10 percent cheaper than a land-built plant, and has other advantages. This facility is designed to stay on the water, and can be moved to different construction sites or other areas requiring large amounts of fresh water.

The fact that the plants can be built and moved quickly and, the companies said, less expensively than conventional installations is enough to interest developing countries in the idea of floating plants.

September 3, 1977

A tanker, designed and constructed for a Brazilian company, awaits completion in one of Japan's numerous shipyards.

Japan Air Lines

The Business World

TOO MANY SHIPYARDS TROUBLING JAPANESE

Drop in Orders to World Leader Underlines Excess Capacity

By **JUNNOSUKE OFUSA**

TOKYO, Dec. 26—Japan, which has led the world in shipbuilding for 23 years in a row, now has to decide what to do with twice as many shipyards and shipbuilders as it needs to fill dwindling orders.

It is a severe problem of excess capacity, typical of many bedrock Japanese industries, including steel and aluminum.

Japanese ship companies are beset by an oversupply of ships, a sharp decline in earnings and a fall in freight rates brought about by the depressed tanker

At full strength, the recession-hit shipbuilding industry, with 400 shipyards, large and small, and 200,000 workers is capable of turning out 19 million tons of ships a year.

But the industry's ship production for fiscal 1977 ending next March 31 is expected to fall below 10 million tons, and it will further decline to 6.5 million tons in the following 12 months. After that, output will melt away to fewer than one million tons in fiscal 1979, industry spokesmen predict.

According to Hajime Yamada, executive vice president of the Japan Ship Exporters Association, "The industry is very concerned about new orders from foreign shipowners." The orders are falling off rapidly, he said, as a consequence of the mounting value of the yen, which makes Japanese products more expensive to foreign buyers.

The present backlog of orders—8.5 million tons for export—would provide only enough work to last half a year, if the shipyards were run at full time, he said

Like most Japanese industries, particularly key sectors, like steel, electronics and chemicals, shipbuilding relies heavily on export sales. Japan exports 85 percent to 90 percent of its total production, Mr. Yamada said.

The prolonged recession and the sharp appreciation in the value of the yen have already taken a certain toll in the industry. In December alone, two medium-sized shipyards, Hashihama and Watanabe, went bankrupt with debts agregating more than $1 million.

In addition, business for six major shipping companies has deteriorated. The Japan Line, which sold into a business crisis this month, asked for a moratorium on repayments of debts totaling $157.5 million. In April through September, the company sustained $35.4 million in losses.

Shipbuilding, once one of Japan's largest export industries, is beset by declining orders.

Japan Air Lines

Effect of Oil Crisis

The Japan Line's economic troubles have stemmed from its 20-million-ton fleet, of which two-thirds are tankers, one-third of them lying idle. Since the oil crisis of 1973, the world tanker business has been so poor that 100 million tons worth, one-third of the world's total oil carriers, are reported to be tied up now.

At the height of the shipbuilding boom in Japan in 1972 and 1973, orders from abroad exceeded 20 million tons a year, and orders for tankers accounted for more than 80 percent of that.

With the oil crisis at a turning point, foreign orders, particularly for tankers, began to fall steeply. When the Hitachi Shipbuilding and Engineering Company completed the construction of two 508,000-ton supertankers, the Esso Pacific and Esso Atlantic, last October, the industry had run out of orders for supertankers.

The Transport Ministry advised the industry to slow down the pace of its operation. Last year, the industry cut back operations to 80 percent of the peak rate attained in 1974. It was further cut to 70 percent this year, and shipyards predict that next year their operations will plummet further to 25 percent of the

1974 peak, far below the 65 percent recommended by the Ministry.

Edge Is Being Threatened

The industry's present backlog of 8.5 million tons for export sales represents a 50 percent drop from a year earlier. Under the present delivery schedule, 4.1 million tons are to be launched in the current fiscal year, 3.9 million tons in fiscal 1978 and the remaining half a million tons in fiscal 1979.

Meanwhile, Japan's edge as the world's largest shipbuilding nation is also being threatened by the rise of new shipbuilding countries such as South Korea, Taiwan, Brazil and some of the nations in East Europe.

Because shipbuilding is a labor-intensive industry, Japan's rising wage levels handicap it in competition with developing nations, spokesmen for the Japanese industry complained.

In recent international bidding to build 19 freighters for Nigeria valued at $375 million, shipbuilders from South Korea and Yugoslavia underbid major Japanese shipbuilders. South Korea was awarded contracts for a dozen ships and Yugoslavia for the remaining 7. Their low bids were said to be 20 percent below those of the Japanese shipbuilders.

December 27, 1977

In Japan, Women Don't Climb the Corporate Ladder

Although business in Japan is still male-dominated, some women achieve success. From the left: Atsuko Kanda, manager of the overseas division of aohan Department Store Company; Tamako Nakanishi, deputy director of the International Labor Organization's Tokyo office; Ayuchi Takita, assistant general manager of Japan Air Lines.

By TRACY DAHLBY

TOKYO—When Ayuchi Takita went looking for her first job after receiving a law degree from Tokyo University, Japan's top law school, a prospective employer asked her why on earth a woman would want to work for a big corporation. If she really had her heart set on a career, she was told, she should become an actress so that she could not be replaced by a man. But Miss Takita insisted on entering the business world, and today she is assist-ant general manager of Japan Air Lines.

At Takashimaya, one of Japan's biggest department store chains, Ichiko Ishihara rose rapidly from women's-shoe clerk to children's-wear buyer. But there her advancement suddenly stopped. By keeping a vigil at a senior executive's home, she finally persuaded him that she was ready for further promotion. Mrs. Ishihara has since become the only woman executive in her company's 146-year history.

Both of these women went to work about 25 years ago. Although times have changed, success stories like theirs are still rare in Japan's male-dominated world of big business. Virtually all executive-level positions remain closed to women—particularly in the industrial and banking conglomerates (such as Mitsubishi and Mitsui), which control the bulk of Japan's capital.

Mrs. Ishihara says, "Given the same educational qualifications, a woman competing for the same job as a man must have at least three times the ability, and it usually takes her twice as long."

The men at the top of Japan's corporate ladder, now mostly in their 50's and 60's, were reared on an ancient

Japanese maxim: danson johi—"revere the man, despise the woman."

Mariko Bando, of the Government bureau of women's affairs, explains the general attitude. "Managers of big companies," she says, "simply don't want women in positions of decision making. Women are hired only as assistants and are not trusted with important duties. And they are not expected to keep working after they get married."

While 46 percent of all Japanese women hold jobs, only 5.2 percent are considered members of management, according to the latest census, taken in 1975. And when those running boutiques, dry cleaners and other small businesses are subtracted, Mrs. Bando estimates, women occupy less than 1 percent of the executive-level jobs at Japan's larger corporations.

Japanese women with a talent for business have generally fared better outside the corporate mainstream. Some have done well on their own in female-related occupations (such as Hanae Mori, a well-known fashion designer) or in the field of private investment (such as Masako Ohya, who owns 15 restaurants in London and Paris plus golf courses, taxi fleets and parking lots in Japan).

Several women also run small and medium-size manufacturing and retail concerns. But Tomoko Shibata, director of the women's division at the Ministry of Labor, says that virtually all of these businesses are family enterprises and that the women did not take charge of them until their husbands died. She adds, "There are no women at the president or vice president level in advertising, banking or manufacturing companies that have at least 1,000 employees."

Even the few women who do hold corporate executive posts seldom rise above responsibility for operations that are not considered crucial to the company's business performance—training female office workers, for example. "This makes women like Miss Takita and Mrs. Ishihara all the more exceptional," says Mrs. Shibata. "If there are any women in higher positions, I haven't heard of them."

The typical Japanese "office lady" is in her 20's. She does dreary paperwork and takes her turn making tea for the male employees. One foreign businessman here has commented that "big Japanese companies look like medieval courts, with women doing all the fetching and carrying and opening of doors."

Another obstacle that women face is pointed out by Tamako Nakanishi, deputy director of the International Labor Organization's Tokyo office. "Women run into a structural barrier in Japan's system of lifetime, seniority-based employment," she says. Job switching is common in the United States, but in Japan a worker normally dedicates his entire career to a single company. Promotions are based as much on the number of years with the company as on ability.

"Big corporations compete in recruiting men from elite universities and then give them on-the-job training," Mrs. Ishihara explains, "but this advancement program is not open to women. Managers feel that it doesn't pay to train women who will just quit their jobs after a few years to have a family."

The women themselves have to accept part of the blame, according to Atsuko Kanda, manager of the overseas division of the Yaohan Department Store Company. "Most women college graduates want to see something of the outside world before they get married, so they view working as a social experience," she says. "They are husband hunting, and joining a big company increases their chances of making a good catch."

Marriage is still the most widely accepted goal, Mrs. Kanda observes, "so ambition in a young Japanese woman makes her an outcast, and pressure from employers and peers is hard to fight in a conformist society like Japan."

Since women in business are often given the dullest, least challenging tasks, Mrs. Ishihara says, "most young women feel that, if they can't do really interesting work, it's better to find a good husband as soon as possible and settle for supremacy in the home."

tenths of 1 percent of civil servants at management levels. Of the 760 parliamentary seats in the Diet, 25 are held by women.

Japan's Labor Standards Act prescribes equal pay for equal work, but women rarely have the opportunity to advance on a par with male colleagues. Although designed to protect women workers, the law itself constitutes a major handicap for career-minded women by sharply restricting the amount of overtime work they are allowed to do. In a country where burning the midnight oil is viewed by managers as a sign of company loyalty, "women are considered lazy since they go home at 5 o'clock," Mrs. Nakanishi says.

After Mrs. Ishihara had her first child, she resisted pressure to quit work. In Japan, she says, "the working wife faces the added burden of trying to keep a balance between office and family." As a result of postwar democratic values, she says, "younger husbands are more willing to help out around the house these days—but not too much." A Government survey shows that women spend an average of about six hours a day on housework and men about six minutes.

Once the corporate old guard hands over the reins of management to

'A woman must have three times the ability and it usually takes her twice as long.'

The Japanese man who holds a white collar job may spend 10 to 12 hours a day at the office. He usually works on Saturday, too. And he often spends his evenings with male colleagues visiting bars or playing mahjong. Consequently, the average worker's wife is left with almost complete control over household matters, including the responsibility of overseeing the children's education.

But Japanese women are beginning to break with traditional ways. Just before World War II the average woman finished school at 15, married at 20, bore five children and died at 50. Now she marries three years later at 23, becomes the mother of only two children and has a life expectancy of 76 years.

About 36 percent of all women attend college. With the advent of labor-saving devices in the home, many Japanese women (particularly in their 40's and early 50's) are now coming back into the job market. Mrs. Nakanishi says, however, that "the best these women are able to do is find unskilled work, even if they are highly qualified, since they missed their place on the company advancement ladder."

Japanese women today occupy about 40 percent of all nonbusiness professional jobs. But most of them are still teachers, nurses, pharmacists and social workers. Women account for only 9.6 percent of all doctors in Japan, 2.5 percent of lawyers and judges, 5.1 percent of research scientists and nine-

younger men and once the seniority system begins to weaken with a rapidly multiplying labor force, Miss Takita predicts that business in Japan will become more inclined to accept women in positions of responsibility. But she says, "Japanese men put so much enthusiasm into their work that women will have to prove that they can be just as effective."

The women's liberation movement, although well under way in the United States, has so far failed to catch hold in Japan. A successful business woman here tends to regard her achievement as a personal victory. Mrs. Ishihara says Japanese women do not need a liberation movement like those in Western countries because "we are already quite dominant in the home and have no real inferiority complex."

Given the Japanese emphasis on the established way of doing things, Miss Takita says that women's place in business is unlikely to improve rapidly. Her own ingrained attitudes, she concedes, show how stubborn the problem is: "In Japan, if a man calls an office and hears a woman's voice on the line, he automatically asks for a man—the assumption is that a woman cannot be competent. But when I hear a woman's voice on the phone, I do the same."

Tracy Dahlby is a reporter based in Tokyo for the Far Eastern Economic Review.

September 18, 1977

Tokyo Stock Market Losing Some of Its Foreign Listings

By JUNNOSUKE OFUSA

TOKYO, Oct. 24 — A sharp drop in turnover of foreign stocks listed on the Tokyo stock exchange and high auditing costs for their required financial reports are compelling some of the foreign companies to withdraw from the stock market here.

One American company, Borden Inc., delisted in September. Another major company, the General Telephone and Electronics Corporation, has decided to pull out by the end of this year. In stock market circles here, it is feared that the other 15 foreign concerns listed on the Tokyo Stock Exchange may follow suit, especially if trading companies to be sluggish.

Regular auditing of corporate financial reports, which is required by Japan's Finance Ministry of all stock exchange members, is a heavy financial burden on the foreign companies, company officers report. American companies must be audited twice, once by United States accounting standards and a second time, by Japanese accountants, to make the required financial reports conform to Japanese accounting standards.

Overall, Borden was said to have paid about $85,000 in listing expenses in 1976, including official listing dues, statutory inspection expenses, translation charges and postage. That contrasts with an average New York listing cost of about $30,000.

Trading Opened in 1973

The Tokyo Stock Exchange was opened for the first time to trading of foreign companies' shares in December 1973. The Government took this move under mounting external pressure to liberalize restrictions on movements of foreign capital in Japan.

Six companies, five American and one French, responded to the initial Japanese Government move and listed their shares on the stock market here. The five United States concerns were the First National City Corporation (now Citicorp), the Dow Chemical Company, the General Telephone and Electronics Corporation, the First Chicago Corporation and the iU International Corporation. The sixth pioneer was the French financial group, Paribas.

At that time businessmen and stock market experts here hailed the Government measure which, they said, would contribute to the internationalization of the Tokyo Stock Market.

Rapid Decline of Turnover

It was believed then that the foreign companies listed in Tokyo, the largest trading center in Asia, would attract a local following and thus increase their chances of expanding business activities over the whole region, including Southeast Asia. It was also said that their listing would eventually make them capable of raising capital of their own in Tokyo.

By the end of 1974, 11 more of the world's major foreign companies, including such giants as the International Business Machines Corporation and the General Motors Corporation, listed their shares on the Tokyo Stock Exchange, making the total 17 companies. Of these, 14 were American, 2 French and 1 Dutch.

However, less than two years after the trading of the foreign stocks began, the turnover began to taper off. The trading volume, which amounted to an average of 200,000 shares a month in 1974, fell to 120,000 shares a month in 1976. This year, volume has plunged below 100,000 shares a month. For the first nine months of this year, turnover totaled 518,400 shares.

The five most popular American stocks now traded on the Tokyo Stock exchange are: the IU International Corporation, with a turnover so far this year of 126,400 shares and the price as of Oct. 19 of 2,190 yen; the Dow Chemical Company, 99,400 shares, 7,320 yen; The Atlantic Richfield Company, 94,000 shares, 12,980 yen; International Telephone and Telegraph Corporation, 90,650 shares, 7,700 yen, and Citicorp, 71,950 shares, 5,870 yen.

Local investors in Japanese stocks may purchase shares in minimum blocks of 1,000. However, since the prices of foreign stocks are much higher than those of Japanese stocks—about 30 times as high, in fact—the foreign stocks are sold in much smaller blocks of 10, 50 and 100 shares for the convenience of the local investors.

The prices of American stocks listed on the Tokyo Exchange are fixed through multiplying the New York Stock Market quotations of the preceding day by the next day's exchange rate in Tokyo. Usually the range of fluctuations in price is very small about 50 yen up or down.

About 80 percent of Japanese buyers of American stocks are individuals and the rest are companies. Large institutions, such as banks and insurance companies, tend to purchase American stocks directly on the New York Stock Exchange.

Rise in Value of Yen

A spokesman for the Tokyo Stock Exchange said that a major factor in the recent poor performance of the foreign stocks is the recent sharp rise in the value of yen—and drop in the dollar's value which has discouraged Japanese investors from purchasing stocks quoted in dollars.

Experts also note that though all the foreign companies whose shares are listed here are well-established large corporations, Japanese investors have little direct knowledge about the business records and products of the foreign companies. Thus, they tend to shy away from them.

For example, local investors who are interested in the automobile industry, a spokesman said, are inclined to prefer the shares of the top Japanese makers, Toyota and Nissan, with which they are familiar, to those of General Motors. Likewise, investors interested in the computer industry are apt to choose the top local maker, Fujitsu, rather than I.B.M.

Finally, the foreign stocks' prices tend to be depressed by low demand.

Of the total of foreign shares put on sale, usually only 60 percent are bought by local investors, mostly Japanese; the remaining 40 percent are shipped back unsold to the foreign companies' home countries.

October 25, 1977

In Japan, a 57-Year-Old Upstart

By TRACY DAHLBY

OSAKA, Japan—Japanese industrialists tend to have terse sayings that sum up their personal business philosophy. That of Toshihiko Yamashita dates from his days as an air-conditioning executive: "In times of prosperity, don't overheat; in times of adversity, remain cool-headed." Mr. Yamashita's career, however, has heated up with a vengeance.

Corporate presidents here are likely to be in their 70's and graduates of elite universities. Thus, the leap of the 57-year-old high school graduate from 25th place on a 26-member board of directors to the president's seat at the Matsushita Electrical Industrial Company was considered a revolutionary event.

Matsushita is Japan's largest producer of consumer electric and electronic products sold all over the world under the National, Panasonic, Technics and Quasar brands. And Mr. Yamashita has had his hands full since his February appointment. He may need all the cool he can muster to meet the growing threat of protectionism by other nations against the sale of Japanese goods abroad and the challenges posed by slower economic growth at home.

Mr. Yamashita was the personal choice of Konosuke Matsushita, 82, the company's founder and current senior adviser. The empire had its start in a tiny workshop in Mr. Matsushita's home, where he and his wife produced two-way electric light sockets. Today, 60 years and 10,000 patent registrations later, the company employs some 100,000 workers at 118 factories in Japan and 29 overseas. Matsushita turns out a wide range of electronic gear from stereo and audio equipment, color television sets, desk-top calculators and rice cookers to generators and pollution-control devices for industry.

Such products accounted for consolidated sales for the fiscal year ended Nov. 20, 1976, equivalent to $5.79 billion, up 23.2 percent from the year before. But the gains have been tapering off. In the half-year ended last May 20, the company reported a 15 percent sales gain and in the fiscal third quarter ended Aug. 20 sales were up 8 percent. Earnings climbed 22 percent in the first nine months of fiscal 1977, and the company has predicted that earnings for the full year would be up only 14 percent. Japan is believed to be entering an era of slower economic growth—about 6 percent a year, or half the pace of the 1960's.

Mr. Yamashita has a reputation as an able, no-nonsense manager within his com-

Toshihiko Yamashita.

Jim Curry Associates, Inc.

pany, but his appointment came as a shock to Japan's rigidly hierarchical business world and to the soft-spoken Mr. Yamashita as well. Comfortably sunk into an overstuffed white-leather chair in the president's office at Matsushita's sprawling corporate complex here, he recalls: "The appointment was rather strange for a Japanese company." He turned down the offer at first, but after ample coaxing and cajoling by Mr. Matsushita and his colleagues on the board, Mr. Yamashita says impishly, "I was sort of forced to accept."

Mr. Matsushita's choice for president was clearly aimed at the future. Mr. Yamashita replaced Masaharu Matsushita, 64, the elder Matsushita's son-in-law, who became chairman of the board. By picking a relatively young and proven disciple for the post, the founder hopes to insure greater continuity for his own unconventional, democratic management philosophy. Mr. Yamashita, who went to work in Matsushita's light-bulb development division shortly after graduating from a boys' technical high school in 1938, is in some ways a product of that philosophy.

What makes Matsushita different from most other large Japanese corporations is that workers are encouraged to participate in management by submitting suggestions for the improvement of production and management policies. Such suggestions annually average about 15 per worker, and cash prizes are paid for those selected by

a labor-management committee for implementation.

While most employers here are more paternal than their Western counterparts in insuring job security and worker benefits, this is a clear break from the Japanese feudal tradition—"revere the official, despise the common man"—that has left its impact on Japanese business philosophy in creating a strict division between white- and blue-collar workers in most companies.

Mr. Yamashita says he intends to strengthen this link between executives and workers, since clear communication between "the top and the lower echelons is the kind of thing which ensures the reliability of everyone in the company." He feels this is particularly important given Japan's system of lifetime employment. In contrast to the highly mobile job market in the United States, Japanese workers usually make a career-long commitment to a single company, and employers must take the responsibility for keeping them employed. If a worker senses that the door to opportunity is closed, he will become frustrated. But "if they feel their ideas count, we can tap the fullest potential from our manpower," says Mr. Yamashita.

Masanobu Akanuma, a factory worker at Matsushita's Ibaraki television plant on the outskirts of Osaka, tells a widely circulated anecdote. In preparation for Mr Yamashita's recent inspection tour of another television assembly plant, the management had ordered a gourmet lunch readied in a private room. But when the new president arrived, he demanded that he be fed in the factory cafeteria with the regular workers.

In contrast to the Olympian remoteness of most Japanese company presidents, Mr. Akanuma says, this shows "that the average worker's feelings and opinions are reflected in management decisions." A high school graduate himself, Mr. Akanuma says he decided to go to work for Matsushita 10 years ago because, "like Mr. Yamashita's career shows, you can rise in this company by your own ability without relation to your educational background" in a society where one's job opportunities still hinge largely on having gone to the right schools.

Another aspect of Matsushita's management system that Mr. Yamashita plans to emphasize is a policy whereby each major division is responsible both for its own production plans and for profits and losses. According to Mr. Yamashita, this delegation of authority facilitates more prompt decisions than the traditional Japanese custom of top executive consensus. And in light of intensifying competition for orders in domestic and overseas markets, this is becoming increasingly important. Big Japanese companies have recently lost several major export contracts in the Middle East to foreign competitors due partly to slow decision-making here.

Mr. Yamashita is uncharacteristic of Japanese corporate leadership in yet another way. He has never been to the United States and has practically no experience abroad, although exports account for roughly half of Matsushita's sales.

In fact, it has been the very success of Japanese electronics makers' overseas sales in recent years that has brought them under fire for pursuing predatory pricing practices and other unsavory trade tactics to boost their foreign market shares.

Partly to help lessen American criticism of massive Japanese color television exports, Matsushita purchased Motorola's color television division in 1974 and also turns out black and white sets in Puerto Rico. The Motorola facility in Franklin Park, Ill., has 2,500 workers producing between 40,000 to 50,000 sets monthly, according to a company official. Matsushita also has a small Japanese managerial staff of about two dozen.

Mr. Yamashita's appointment also hints at the direction the Japanese economy will take now that it is generally acknowledged

to have entered into a long haul of slow growth.

To help maintain this export-oriented nation's international competitiveness, many Japanese say businesses need younger more energetic and innovative men at the helm. Complaints—mainly from younger management—are now being expressed over "rogai"—"old age pollution." Sign of change! Kiyoshi Kawashima, president of Honda Motor, and Norio Oga, vice president of the Sony Corporation, are still both in their 40's. And with the majority of high-ranking Japanese managers in their 60's and 70's, the outlook is bright for the advancement of younger executives.

Mr. Yamashita used to smoke two packs of cigarettes a day. He stopped cold 10 years ago. He seems to bring the same kind of determination to his views on overseas sales. The Japanese, he says, should expand their market share in countries like the United States to "reasonably permissible limits." After all, he says, "if the Americans came to Japan with better quality goods at lower prices and sold without limit, Japanese producers would raise a fuss." It is said with a smile.

The best solution to trade difficulties, the company suggests, lies in coming up with new products that do not now exist in markets like the United States or new versions of items already in production.

Matsushita is now concentrating its engineering might on such developments. "If we can come out with a television that you could carry around like a wrist watch, the future would be enormous," says a spokesman.

Mr. Yamashita, on his rare days off, enjoys climbing mountains with his wife, Kikuko. The Yamashitas live in a modern two-story home—modest by most Japanese corporate executive standards—located in Senri Newtown near Matsushita headquarters in Osaka. They have a married daughter, Keiko, who lives nearby. Their son, Kazuhiko, has a master's degree in electrical engineering from a well-known Japanese university and works for his father's company researching circuit development for the stereo division.

But when he took the mandatory hiring exam at Matsushita, Kazuhiko didn't tell his father, the president, until after he had been accepted. He didn't want people to think that his father had pulled any strings to get him the job. Mr. Yamashita says, however, "Things like that don't happen at Matsushita anyway."

Tracy Dahlby is a reporter based in Tokyo for the Far Eastern Economic Review.

November 13, 1977

Japan's Economic Invasion

By James Reston

WASHINGTON, Nov. 24—The critical problems between nations usually don't appear suddenly or dramatically —as in the Sadat Begin confrontation in Jerusalem—but develop slowly from small misunderstandings or large misjudgments while their peoples are not paying much attention.

It may be that such a creeping conflict is now developing between the United States and Japan. This year, the Japanese will sell in the United States about $7 billion worth of goods more than they will buy from us. Both sides are being very polite about this, but it is a serious economic and potentially dangerous political dilemma.

For example, the Zenith Corporation laid off a quarter of its employees a few weeks ago, and subcontracted their jobs to Mexico and Taiwan in an effort to meet the Japanese television competition. There is rising unemployment in the steel mills of Pittsburgh and Youngstown, and this is driving

George Meany of the A.F.L.-C.I.O. up the Washington Monument—an ominous sight from Capitol Hill with the 1978 elections on the horizon.

This is too complicated a problem for quick judgments or mystifying clarifications, but after spending a couple of weeks in the factories around Tokyo and Osaka, I think it's hard to avoid the conclusion that the Japanese are outselling us at least partly because they are outworking us. And also because they are working together for reasons shared by their government, their managers, planners and workers.

It has become a commonplace to make this point, but until you see the reality of this Japanese teamwork or collective will on their own ground, it is hard to understand how, with no natural resources except their own people, they have become the third most productive industrial nation in the world.

In fairness, my wife and I saw only the top Japanese leaders—Prime Minister Fukuda, and the managers of the

Nippon Kogaku, K.K., who produce Nikon cameras among other high-quality optics; and the creative minds of the Japanese electronic industry at Sony and the Matsushita Electric Industrial Company, which produce the whole range of electrical appliances in competition with General Electric, Westinghouse, R.C.A. and others in the United States.

The Japanese trade surplus with the United States is based primarily on what they call "The Three C's"—meaning color televisions, coolers (air-conditioners) and cars. Their three largest export industries are in electronics, automobiles and steel, and their success, they believe, depends on the diligence and faith of a work force that has a guaranteed job for everybody's effective working life; on cooperation between the workers and managers; coupled with an adequate supply of funds and agreement all around on the quickest possible introduction and development of the most modern technology.

The United States system, of course

The Business World

is quite different. It rejects the guarantee of a worker's job for life. It leaves the problem of work or no-work to the marketplace. Accordingly it is worried about the introduction of new machines which might threaten jobs.

The Japanese workers and managers accept the notion that they have a common interest in the success or failure of their enterprises. The American workers on the other hand, increasingly condemn the integrity of work and reject the authority of their managers.

Jerome M. Rosow, for example—former manager of employee relations for Esso in Europe, former Assistant Secretary of Labor 1969-71, and now President of the Work in America Institute—notes that the attitude of

American workers has been changed dramatically by the larger social revolution in the United States.

Workers, he observes, not only expect a better standard of living every year but insist that they are entitled to it, regardless of the success or failure of their companies; that they resist change and new technology as a "menace"; that they no longer think that "hard work" pays off, and that they increasingly resist authority in their companies, communities, churches or governments.

Maybe the Japanese, as they become more affluent and confident, will take the same permissive attitudes a generation hence, but they are clearly not doing so yet. They are putting up with very poor housing, with a physical atmosphere that is so

polluted by their factories that you can hardly see their spectacular neon advertisements for the smog.

But they *are* working, they *are* copying the industrial West but rejecting its mindless individual selfishness and cooperating with one another and with the national purpose of Japan.

This is causing us serious problems in Washington, and raising once more the old impulses of isolationism and protectionism. But the Japanese in the process may be doing us a favor. In many ways they are also making us look slack and making us wonder whether we really believe in working and competing, or whether we are trying to protect our worst rather than our best human qualities.

November 25, 1977

Japanese Sell at Below Cost In Bid to Avoid Bankruptcy

By JUNNOSUKE OFUSA

TOKYO, Dec. 8—While Japan's foreign-exchange holdings continue to snowball as a result of its successful export drive, the earnings of its export-oriented industries are rapidly falling due to the sharp appreciation of the yen.

There are exceptions, as in cars, home electric appliances and precision machines, which retain a competitive edge in international markets. But with the value of the yen up more than 20 percent since January, many are expected to ship products below cost as long as they can financially afford to in order to keep their plants operating.

It is an accepted business practice in Japan, when manufacturers are hard hit by sluggish business, to resort to selling products below cost, both domestionally and abroad just to keep the money flowing in and employment steady.

Fertile Sales Soil Abroad

But if, as is the case during the current economic doldrums, domestic buying has lagged far behind that of foreign consumers, the export instinct and the ready markets overseas make fertile sales soil.

Analysts here have said that recession-ridden small and medium-sized industries, which account for 30 percent of Japan's total exports, are particularly compelled to carry on shipments below costs, as they would go bankrupt otherwise.

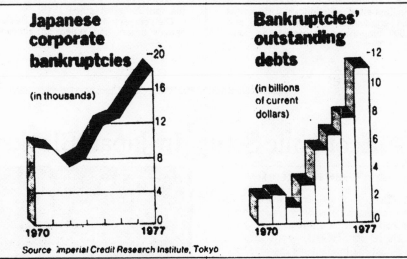

Source *Imperial Credit Research Institute*, Tokyo

Many have, in fact, gone bankrupt this year, but the special structure of Japanese industry allows companies to scrimp along on low, or no, profits for the short term while hoping for big paybacks over the longer term.

Perhaps most importantly, Japanese companies average 85 percent debt in bank loans and 15 percent in shareholder equity, versus roughly a 50-50 split in the United States. Thus dividend commitments are very low by international standards, repayment of principle is little stressed and the only major claim on a company's cash comes in the form of interest payments —and payrolls.

An Unwritten Custom

Unlike American companies that can lay off workers in slow periods, Japanese companies are governed by the unwritten custom of lifetime employment, which prevents them from dismissing workers except for prolonged illness or illegal activity.

This custom can be traced back to feudal days when it was maintained between castle lords and their "samurai" retainers and between merchants and their servants. The system has formed the foundation of the unusual management-labor relationship of this country since it set up a capitalist system a century ago.

A basic concept of the lifetime employment custom is that a company is an extension of the family—not an impersonal business corporation. It provides wages that rise with age and seniority, while the worker gives up job mobility.

Analysts agree unanimously that this paternalistic arrangment has played an important role in promoting worker diligence, encouraging a sense of loyalty to management and preventing skilled workers from moving to other rival factories.

During the 1974 recession, touched off by the oil crisis, almost all factories of major Japanese enterprises were forced to lay off surplus workers. But under the lifetime employment system, idled workers were paid 90 percent of their salaries until reinstated.

Added to Bankruptcy Rate

The lifetime employment system has been a heavy financial burden on the management of enterprises, especially in times of economic trouble, and has added much to the high bankruptcy rate already developing here. Tokyo Shoko, a private credit research agency, said that in the first 10 months this year 15,026 companies went bankrupt with debts totaling $9.9 billion and forecast that business failures would reach 18,500 concerns with total debts estimated at $11 billion by the end of this year.

Another feature of Japanese labor policy is early retirement, which has been maintained for nearly a century, and thus resulted in heavy benefit commitments.

The retirement limit of 55 years of age was set in 1885 when the first few incorporated companies were established in Japan after 300 years of national isolation. At that time, the span of an average Japanese man's life was 40 years and the action taken by the companies was considered charitable, a way of allowing the longer-lived to stop work and enjoy old age.

However, the life expectancy of the Japanese people has since grown to 72 for men and 77 for women. So, with retired persons voicing discontent, and management faced with ever-longer periods in which to pay benefits, many companies have recently extended the 55-year age limit to 58 or 60.

December 9, 1977

Assets of Hashihama Are Frozen by Court

MATSUYAMA, Japan, Dec. 12 (Reuters)—Japan's fourth-biggest business collapse since World War II occurred today when a court announced it was freezing the assets of the Hashihama shipbuilding company.

A spokesman for Hashihama, a medium-sized shipbuilder with assets the equivalent of $8.8 million and 1,000 employees, estimated the company's debs at about $204 million.

According to the Tokyo Commerce and Industry Research Company, a private concern that compiles business-failure statistics for the Government, the collapse is easily the biggest of the 16,000 recorded so far this year and the fourth-largest since 1945.

The company spokesman said Hashihama's orders had fallen off sharply because of the worldwide slump in demand for ships, and the appreciation of the yen, which had made Japan's exports less competitive.

He said the company would try to get funds to enable it to continue work on six remaining orders—three 16,000-ton freighters, two smaller freighters and a 6,200-ton container ship.

December 13, 1977

Economic Setup In Japan Blocks Sale of Imports

By ANDREW H. MALCOLM

TOKYO, Dec. 19—The Japanese customs inspector opens every crate of metal baseball bats from a foreign manufacturer. He selects one bat, saws it open and rules that the inside is not machined sufficiently. The whole shipment is rejected.

A restaurant owner importing giant pizza ovens finds the foreign products classified as "appliances" and therefore subject to much higher duties.

A supplier of veterinarian instruments wants to order some tools from abroad But he is told he must apply for an import license and then he must get approval for the import and then the import must be tested. The procedure could take a year.

Such examples of the difficulty of selling imports in Japan are legion in the foreign business community here. "It's all part of that famous two-way Japanese

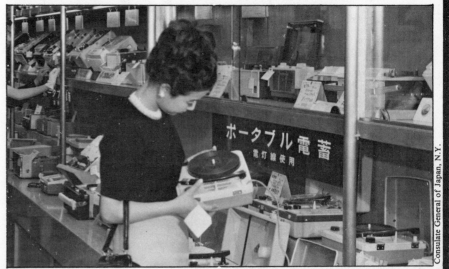

Shoppers browsing in the tape-recorder and radio section of a department store are likely to find few imported items.

street," an American banker said bitterly. "It only goes one way."

Formidable Fact of Life

And these examples also illustrate a formidable fact of life overlooked in the recent Japan-United States negotiations to defuse increasing trade tensions. The reality is that no handful of actions reached over some polished bargaining table is going to change overnight the entrenched national economic system reflecting Japan's clannish, insular structure.

"You start off with the fact that Japan has a basic protectionist policy," says Bruce Rankin, Canada's Ambassador here. "It's the natural instinct." Mr. Rankin and others believe this policy or instinct will never change without sustained intense pressure for reform from abroad.

Officially, the Japanese Government denies there is any collusion with Japanese companies to protect the hometown market for hometown concerns. But whether officially inspired or merely the outcome of historical coincidence and cultural gaps, foreign businessmen here say, the result is the same. "It's damned tough to sell here," says one.

During the immediate postwar recovery period, Japan's protectionist policies were open and designed to nurture infant industries, which in turn were designing themselves for heavy exports. "Japan is all rebuilt now," says an American banker. "They're up there in the majors. But they still want to play by Little League rules when they come to bat."

Much of Japan's statutory protectionism, such as tariffs, has been dropped or reduced over the years. But the Japanese often attach more importance in communication to what is unspoken than to what is explicit. Thus, Japan is generally considered to have more nontariff trade barriers than any other major industrialized nation.

Maple Syrup Controls Dropped

In the area of quotas, for instance, the United States has seven categories, the Benelux countries have eight and Canada, five. Japan retains 27. This fall the United States "suggested" that all of these be abolished. Japan's reply, announced here last week, was to liberalize modestly the quotas on some items and drop controls on other minor sub-items like maple syrup, not a basic commodity in Japanese homes.

But the barriers go beyond official restrictions. They include the following:

¶The simplest import procedure here requires 10 separate steps. Instead of simply inspecting invoices and perhaps spot-checking products, customs officers open every crate with a time-consuming thoroughness that is also costly. This causes delays in shipments plus storage charges for the bonded warehouse.

¶The Custom's Bureau also requires that all imported canned goods bear stickers indicating the country of origin, name and address of importer, ingredients, import date and metric weight. This requires costly hiring of workers to paste labels on every can on the pier. Under

Tokyo alone has more than 20 department stores, but foreign manufacturers find the Japanese market difficult to penetrate.

some interpretations, this also requires blacking out the weight in ounces.

¶The Government's tobacco monopoly requires that foreign tobacco products may be sold only at a limited number of outlets.

¶Ingredients in imported pharmaceuticals and cosmetics must go through renewed testing in Japan at Government-selected laboratories. Extra costly testing can be required at will.

¶Government contracts and purchases are generally negotiated or bid privately and foreign companies have been excluded.

¶Importers often are summoned to justify overseas purchases if local products are available. This is euphemistically called "administrative guidance." An importer can't be required to buy locally, but he might avoid future difficulties if he does.

¶Japanese agriculture — what one Western importer called "a fantasyland" —is also heavily protected. Beef import

quotas, for example, are controlled by a cartel that sets prices up to 10 times the world price. Medium-grade hamburger retails here for about $7 a pound. Officials say live beef can be imported without restrictions, but the lengthy required quarantine and limited facilities effectively set a quota there, too.

Language and Suspicion

But other barriers, cultural ones, may be even more resistant to negotiated settlements. There is the difficult language barrier. A basic suspicion of foreigners.

An unwritten rule against Japanese corporations selling out to a foreign takeover. A tradition of placing verbal orders subject to change compared with an inviolable Western-style written contract.

There are unique Japanese consumer tastes that, for instance, make packaged seaweeds a big holiday gift item along with a whole salmon. There is, what one foreigner calls "the 98-cent umbrella syndrome," which dictates that a cheap product, especially a foreign one, can't be any good. That results in import markups often of several hundred percent by local distributors. This limits sales.

Importantly, there are, too, structural barriers militating against change in this ancient nation of 113 million. The market is already sophisticated and quite competitive. Like Japanese society, its wholesale and distribution systems are complex, multilayered, entrenched and often based on strong personal relationships or loyalties that take years to build. Thus, for instance, a cosmetic store owner will sell the products of only one or two companies. Unless a newcomer wants to start his own chain, a market entry can be quite difficult.

And there is also a radically different management philosophy in Japan. A Japanese manufacturer, usually associated with a supportive banking institution, is prepared to endure several years of business losses in developing a market. Often, less patient Western businessmen here feel pressured to concern themselves more with quarterly profit reports.

December 20, 1977

They Try Harder

These Toyota vehicles, awaiting export in Nagoya, tell part of the story of Japan's worldwide 1977 trade surplus: $15 billion.

By Robert C. Christopher

One of the most popular American pastimes these days is belaboring the Japanese. Scarcely a day passes now without a public warning from some American politician, businessman or union leader as to the dire consequences that will ensue if Japan does not mend its ways and cease to sell so many goods in the United States.

Robert C. Christopher, a journalist who specializes in foreign affairs, has a long-standing interest in Japan.

We Americans are not alone in our taste for this particular form of activity. From time to time, the mandarins of the European Economic Commission and various European politicians also sock it to the Japanese for being so unscrupulous as to produce reliable, well-designed cars, ships and television sets more cheaply than their European competitors. In fact, this phenomenon has now become common enough in Europe that The Sunday Times of London recently felt compelled to give it a generic name: "Jap-bashing."

Still, as a participatory sport, jumping on Japan is older and more highly developed in the United States than anywhere else. It first reached major proportions back in the Nixon years when the full weight of the United States Government was thrown behind an ultimately successful drive to impoverish the Japanese textile industry for the benefit of its somewhat Neanderthal American counterpart. Since then, we have moved on to assaults upon the Japanese shoe, television and steel industries and the end is not yet in sight. Again and again, the Japanese are informed by everyone from Ambassador Mike Mansfield to Treasury Secretary Mike Blumenthal that they simply must curb their exports and vastly increase their imports. And when the Government of Prime Minister Takeo Fukuda recently offered to take some modest but potentially significant steps in that direction, chief United States trade negotiator Robert S. Strauss denounced the Japanese proposals as inadequate even before he had had a chance to read them. This bit of diplomatic poker — a game at which very few Japanese are adept —, enabled Strauss to extract still further concessions when he visited Tokyo two weeks ago, but not, so far as now appears, anything likely to alter the terms of Japanese-American trade in a radical way.

In terms of specific actions, it is not always clear what the Carter Administration wants from Japan — or even that it knows precisely what it wants. For a time, United States trade officials insisted that Japan must increase the value of the yen sharply enough to price Japanese goods out of some of the markets they now dominate. Lately, however, Administration economists have concluded that by some mysterious form of economic jujitsu, Japanese industry might actually manage to export even more goods with a higher-priced yen, and so they have shifted the focus of their attack to Japan's import restrictions. But throughout all of this, the basic United States demand upon the Japanese has remained the same: Japan, the Americans say, must undertake a drastic restructuring of its entire economy so that it can "achieve" an overall balance-of-payments deficit within the next few years. (The original American proposal was that Japan wipe out its balance-of-payments surplus — which is currently running about $10 billion a year — by the end of 1978, but now, in a burst of moderation, United States trade negotiators seem prepared to give the Japanese two or even perhaps three years in which to remake their nation.)

To the Japanese, not surprisingly, all this seems one of the most outlandish suggestions since Jonathan Swift made his modest proposal for alleviating the Irish famine by persuading Ireland's peasantry to eat babies. And, indeed, when one stops to think about it, both the nature and intensity of the American pressure on Japan do seem a little peculiar. When all the figures are in, Japan's trade surplus with the United States in 1977 will probably turn out to run between $9 billion and $10 billion. For the same period, the United States trade deficit with the OPEC nations will certainly prove to be somewhere between $25 billion and $30 billion — and no meaningful steps whatsoever are being taken to reduce that figure.

Moreover, in terms of the global economy, which the Carter Administration proclaims to be its prime concern, the situation is equally paradoxical.

There, the biggest single disruptive force is not Japan, which is expected to have a worldwide 1977 trade surplus of about $15 billion, but Saudi Arabia, whose 1977 surplus will be on the order of $25 billion. Yet no American official that I can recall has urged that Saudi Arabia export less oil or rejigger its monetary arrangements in such a way as to reduce its income from abroad. Similarly, West Germany's 1977 trade surplus of perhaps $18 billion has contributed mightily to the imbalance of world trade, yet compared with the Japanese, the Germans get off with only an occasional slap on the wrist from Washington.

One reason for this, of course, is simply that the Japanese are more vulnerable to American pressure than the Saudis or even the West Germans. With almost 25 percent of their export sales concentrated in the United States and nothing to offer in the way of essential raw materials, the Japanese have little choice but to back down whenever the United States makes a nonnegotiable demand for a specific economic concession — and, up until the present confrontation, that is what they have generally done.

But there is, I think, more to it than that. Somewhere in the recesses of their psyches, a great many Americans still regard the Japanese as inferiors — a benighted Oriental people whom, out of the goodness of our hearts, we endowed with democratic government and the sinews of modern industrial power. Among certain "progressive-minded" Americans, this kind of condescension has recently taken on new and somewhat hostile overtones, apparently because of the fact that Japan does not qualify as a bona fide impoverished member of the third world. Not long ago, I heard a well-respected American commentator on international affairs passionately denounce United States soybean sales to Japan on the grounds that Bengalis, Indians and Africans were hungrier than the Japanese and hence had a greater claim on our food crops. But even more pragmatic and responsible Americans fall victim to a kind of postoccupation psychosis when it comes to Japan. What other major nation would senior United States officials presume to instruct publicly on the proper management of its domestic ecomomy?

My point, to be blunt about it, is that there is what can only be called a strong racist component in United States thinking about Japan. And at least partly for that reason, the overwhelming majority of Americans, in-

cluding the most sophisticated and influential, remain impenetrably ignorant of how Japan really operates and what makes it tick.

As a case in point, I vividly recall the occasion in 1973 when I attended a dinner party in Tokyo at which 15 or so of the most powerful men in Japan had assembled to honor the head of a major American corporation. During the course of the dinner, one of the Japanese, an immensely successful and innovative industrialist, was asked for his opinion of the current state of Japanese-American relations, which, then as now, were strained by economic conflicts. The industrialist's reply, which unfortunately was delivered in somewhat fractured English, ran roughly as follows: "During the occupation, we Japanese suffered, but we learned from the Americans. Now it is you Americans who are suffering a little — and perhaps now you can learn something from us."

The result was pandemonium: Outraged by the notion that the Japanese could possibly have undergone any suffering under the beneficent rule of the United States, the corporate visitor and most of the other Americans present never got around to considering the accompanying suggestion that there might conceivably be things that the United States could learn from Japan.

That, I suspect, would still be the reaction of nearly all Americans. But before one dismisses out of hand the notion that Japan might have something to teach the United States, it is worth considering, in the simplistic manner of an old-fashioned grade-school geography book, the current situations of the two countries.

Japan, which is a very small island country possessed of negligible natural resources, must import all its oil, the overwhelming bulk of its industrial raw materials, and much of its food. To compound its problems, Japan is still in the throes of a prolonged economic slowdown which has resulted in slack consumer demand and a record level of corporate bankruptcies. But, despite all these handicaps, the country has an unemployment rate that remains negligible by Western standards, the country should achieve at least 6 percent economic growth in 1978, and, in compulsive pursuit of some sort of hedge against the vagaries of OPEC and protectionist trends around the world, it consistently racks up trade surpluses.

Unlike Japan, of course, the United States is blessed with almost every inherent economic advantage conceivable: It is a mammoth agricultural

Hamamatsu. Many Japanese factories are more modern than American plants because of numerous capital investment inducements.

producer, rich in raw materials, and possesses, in addition to the world's greatest industrial plant, an un-matched· pool of technology. Yet, despite all of this, the United States suffers from high unemployment and a consistently lower growth rate than Japan's, and, after running in 1977 by far the hugest trade deficit any country in the world has ever recorded, seems bent on going nearly as deep into the red in 1978.

Of course, it isn't really all that simple. For one thing, in a classic display of the perennial American piousness, the Carter Administration insists that in living so far beyond its national means the United States is only seeking to help out its neighbors. By spending so much more than it is earning, Secretary Blumenthal and other American spokesmen tirelessly repeat, the United States is helping to stimulate international trade and hence the sluggish world economy.

There are, however, a couple of flaws in this argument. One is that at bottom virtually all of the United States trade deficit is a consequence of our ever more profligate use of imported fuel — and a substantial proportion of the money that we spend on oil and gas goes to nations whose capacity to ab-

sorb imported goods is limited and which, as a result, plow much of their surpluses into comparatively sterile investments.

An even more serious drawback to the "deficits are good for you" thesis is that America's massive overspending abroad has sapped the value of the dollar vis-à-vis other major currencies to such an extent that international bankers and economists are beginning to worry about some very ugly possibilities. There is, for example, the danger that at some point the OPEC nations may decide to compensate for the dwindling purchasing power of the scores of billions of dollars they already hold and the billions more they expect to receive in the future by a significant increase in oil prices; such a development could at one stroke counteract whatever stimulative effect the United States import spree is having on the world economy.

Beyond that, there is. the concern that continued weakening of the world's key currency could undermine the international monetary system, thereby creating general financial and political turbulence — and the recent limited intervention in defense of the dollar by the Treasury Department and the Federal Reserve Bank has done little to allay that concern.

Unless one is thoroughly schooled in

the metaphysics of the new economics, it is hard to avoid concluding from all this that the most useful contribution the United States could make to the world economy would be to achieve a significant reduction in its trade deficit by significantly reducing its oil imports. Since that, however, appears to be something the United States has neither the will nor the political capacity to achieve, the most useful contribution the United States might feasibly make would seem to be to reduce its deficit by other means. And the classic prescription for achieving that — as opposed to the Carter Administration's prescription — would be for the United States to make itself vastly more competitive in world markets, including most emphatically the United States market. Or, as my Japanese industrialist friend suggested, for the United States to become more like Japan.

It would, of course, be utopian to carry this recommendation too far. There is, for example, no point to proposing that the United States raise its basic educational standards to the levels that prevail in Japan, where, despite the fact that Japanese is considerably harder to read and write than English, there is a far smaller percentage of functional illiterates than in this country. It would be even less sensible to suggest that a dose of Japanese industriousness might work wonders for the United States economy. There are, however, more modest steps which the United States might conceivably take if it wished to achieve something approaching Japanese economic effectiveness.

Perhaps the most important first step would be for private industry in the United States to abandon its cherished illusion that Japan's export successes rest on coolie wages, massive dumping of goods below cost and the stealthy trick of getting all its industrial plant destroyed in World War II and then replaced, largely at United States expense, by factories more modern than America itself has.

The fact is that industrial real wages in Japan are indeed lower than American wages — but they are higher, on average, than French, British or Italian real wages, and yet France, Britain and Italy, individually, do not sell nearly so many automobiles in the United States as Japan does. As for dumping by Japanese firms, it has undoubtedly occurred — but on a far less widespread scale than United States businessmen charge and, in any case, does not serve to explain the enthusias-

The Business World

tic acceptance by American consumers of Sony TV's, Toyota and Datsun cars or Nikon and Canon cameras, all of which, as even their bitterest competitors will admit, turn their makers a tidy profit. And the "we helped them by blowing up their old factories" charge is even more baseless: The Japanese steel industry suffered relatively little bomb damage during World War II, and many of the Japanese products that sell most briskly in the United States, such as automobiles and electronic equipment, are manufactured by industries that did not even come into existence in Japan until the postwar era.

What then does explain the extraordinary ability of Japanese manufacturers to invade the American — and Western European — market successfully? Part of the story lies in the fact that Japanese businessmen are, above all, export minded. They analyze a market before they enter it, try to determine what products consumers really want, and then give them those products with as much built-in quality and design as is consistent with a competitive price. Above all, they are prepared, where it seems sensible, to serve only a limited segment of the market — people, say, who want cars that are economical to operate but comfortably appointed, or television sets that function admirably but do not have to be bought complete with Italian Provincial cabinets, or calculators that perform only the relatively few mathematical functions acceptable to everyone but engineers and Harvard Business School graduates.

United States business, by contrast, instinctively seeks to herd all consumers into one vast mass as close to the upper end of any product line as possible. The most glaring example of this, of course, is provided by the United States automobile industry: Only now, in the wake of the oil crisis and 20 years of growing penetration of the American market by foreign manufacturers, has Detroit decided that the small-car buyer is worth serious attention.

Moreover, this United States attitude toward domestic consumers applies in spades in export markets. Most United States manufacturers are only moderately interested in export sales to begin with: They would far rather penetrate an overseas market by building or acquiring a factory in that market. As a result, relatively few United States factories produce goods consciously designed to meet the needs of a particular foreign market. And even when they have a product that is salable abroad,

American firms all too often are insufficiently aggressive about marketing it. Time and again, while traveling in Asia, I have had local businessmen regretfully inform me that they have wound up buying Japanese equipment instead of the American product they originally wanted because the Japanese were prepared to offer quicker delivery and better service.

Reinforcing these attractions is the fact that much of the time Japanese manufacturers offer export customers comparable quality at lower prices than their American competitors. One reason they are able to do this is that in all too many cases their factories are more modern and cost-efficient than American factories — and this is true primarily because, in the last 20 years, Japanese industry, relatively speaking, has invested far more heavily in

vestors, the typical Japanese business borrows up to 85 percent of its capital on terms that allow very slow repayment. This means that it pays out far less in dividends than a comparable United States firm would, and can earmark more of its earnings for reinvestment.

What really gives firms in Japan's major export industries their biggest edge in terms of reinvestment, however, is the fact that when they need capital for expansion the Japanese Government sees to it that they get it. Which brings us to the vexing question of "Japan Inc.," the interlocking directorate of Government agencies and private corporations that actually operates the Japanese economy.

When foreigners talk about Japan Inc., it is almost invariably in holier-than-thou tones, and it is true that the degree of

---

'My point, to be blunt about it, is that there is what can only be called a strong racist component in American thinking about Japan. Americans remain impenetrably ignorant of how Japan really operates.'

---

plant than American industry has. Much of the Japanese steel whose low price outrages American steel men, for example, is made in plants so heavily automated that productivity per employee is, by American standards, extraordinary.

The readiness of Japanese industrialists to plow more of their resources into new plant than their American counterparts does not simply reflect greater vision and enterprise — though that is surely a factor. The essential point is that Japanese industry finds capital easier to come by.

This is so partly because the Japanese are a thrifty people: The rate of personal savings in Japan has long been the highest in the industrialized world. But it also reflects the fact that, unlike United States firms, which raise the majority of their capital from in-

support that Japanese industry gets from the Japanese Government sometimes exceeds all decent limits: Until very recently, for example, virtually all the economic "aid" that Japan gave its poorer Asian neighbors was nothing more than a device for selling them Japanese goods and services. But the principle that underlies the operations of Japan Inc. is nonetheless one that Americans could usefully ponder: When the Japanese Government intervenes in economic affairs, its purpose is to help Japanese business to achieve greater success, not to inhibit or constrain it. Unfortunately, in the United States the underlying thrust of Government policy toward business is to a considerable degree just the opposite.

This essentially restrictive

attitude expresses itself both in the actions of the United States Government and in its failures to act. One of the most notable failures to act has been in the matter of encouraging capital formation and investment in new plant. Whatever the shortcomings of some of its managers, United States industry would surely have far more modern factories today if the tax laws had permitted faster depreciation of equipment and deductions based on replacement costs rather than historical costs. And no serious attack on this problem is yet in view: The investment tax credits which the Carter Administration proposes to give the steel industry are a step in the right direction — but an inadequate one.

Another thing that the United States Government has conspicuously failed to do has been to take adequate steps to encourage American companies to produce here for export instead of serving foreign markets by "going multinational." Much of the "export of jobs" that has occurred in the past two decades might have been avoided had there been greater inducements offered to those who manufactured for export. But instead of remedying this situation, President Carter in his latest tax-reform package proposes to vitiate such limited advantages as have been accorded United States import enterprises.

At least as destructive as these sins of omission, however, are the sins of commission attributable to every United States Administration and Congress in modern times. Can we as a nation really afford to impose on a distressed major industry like steel antipollution laws that could consume as much as a quarter of that industry's total capital investment over the next few years? And does it really make sense for Washington to seek to impose United States antitrust laws on the foreign operations of American companies and even on the operations of their foreign subsidiaries? To most foreigners, it looks like an out-

The workers on this assembly line are manufacturing some of the more than 3 million cameras made in Japan each year.

Japan Air Lines

and-out case of economic imperialism when the United States — as happened recently with Gulf Minerals Canada — badgers the Canadian subsidiary of an American firm for participating in a cartel which it was explicitly ordered to join by the Government of Canada. And imperialism or not, such actions obviously inhibit the ability of United States firms to adapt to foreign business environments.

Much the same applies to the pending legislation which would make "illegal payments" by United States firms abroad an offense punishable by fines of up to $1 million. In the current American climate, it is far more acceptable to express unalloyed enthusiasm for sadomasochism than it is to express reluctant tolerance for bribery under special circumstances, and I do not propose for a moment to depart from the moral norms. It may, however, be permissible to note that no other major industrial country shows any sign of following the United States' lead in this matter, and that in certain of the more lucrative markets of Asia, Africa and the Middle East — not to speak of some parts of Europe — a corporation that cannot pay bribes will find it virtually impossible to do serious business.

What I am suggesting is that it might be both diplomatically wise and commercially useful if the United States Government, like most other governments, refrained from trying to impose its own economic morality outside the areas over which it holds political sovereignty. I am not suggesting that within the United States itself we give public sanction to bribery or engage in wholesale scrapping of the antitrust laws. Equally, I do not mean to suggest that we should emulate Japan's economic *modus operandi* in every respect.

Indeed, there are aspects of the Japanese approach to economic life which the United States should resolutely reject. One of these is the Japanese tolerance for overt business involvement in politics;

The Business World

the fact that so many members of Japan's ruling party depend entirely on corporate or trade-association patrons for their financing far too often resulted in special interests taking precedence over the public good in Japan.

This, in fact, is one of the primary explanations of the persistence of another Japanese practice which the United States emphatically should not emulate: rampant protectionism. Beef, oranges and whisky, to name just three of the most egregious examples, all cost Japanese consumers

riers. But it is scarcely kosher for the United States to do so at a time when it is seeking to bar Japanese goods from its own market. And, unhappily, a penchant for protectionism is one of the few elements in the Japanese economic model that the United States currently seems inclined to adopt. To re-establish protectionism in America, moreover, it is not necessary that we heed A.F.L.-C.I.O. President George Meany's recent demand that the United States treat international trade as "the guerrilla warfare of eco-

fire in a most destructive way. It is almost certainly unrealistic to insist that Japan vastly increase its purchase of foreign manufactured goods: There is, as Nobuhiko Ushiba, Japan's Minister for External Economic Affairs, recently pointed out, no evidence of any greater consumer demands for such goods in Japan. And it is even more unrealistic to suggest, as United States trade officials have, that there must be a restructuring of the giant trading companies that dominate Japan's marketing and distribution system.

cans, ranging from ordinary citizens to Cabinet officers, could bring themselves to look at the world, at least briefly, through Japanese eyes. When Japan first set out to become a modern state, its leaders looked around and noticed that all the powers which then dominated the world had colonial empires. So Japan set out to build an empire of its own — only to be bloodily instructed by the United States in World War II that the rules of the great-power game had changed and that imperialism, at least when practiced by Asians, had become unacceptable.

Having dutifully absorbed that lesson, the Japanese decided to change course and build a strong democratic society based on industrial power and capitalist enterprise. And in so doing they quite consciously chose as their model that citadel of free competition, the United States.

A surprising amount of that postwar admiration for the United States still persists in Japan — or did when I was last there. In Tokyo, six months ago, I had a long conversation with Kiichi Miyazawa, the able and attractive man who recently became director of Japan's Economic Planning Agency and who is sometimes touted as a future Prime Minister. During the course of our talk, Miyazawa remarked that, while he certainly could not say as much for Western Europeans, he believed that "Americans as a whole are still competition oriented and free-market oriented."

For public consumption, I presume that Miyazawa would still say the same thing. I cannot help wonder, though, what he would say on the subject these days in a purely private conversation. Would he perhaps complain that, once again, alarmed by Japan's extraordinary success, the United States is trying to change the rules of the international game? And, if he did, could any dispassionate observer assure him that he was totally wrong? ■

Mass production lines of TV sets are shown at the Ibarari Plant of Matsushita Electric Industrial Co., Ltd.

horrifying sums simply because Japan's inherently uneconomic farmers and distillers have succeeded in bulldozing the Japanese Government into maintaining outrageously high duties and restrictive quotas on American citrus fruit, American and Australian beef, and Scotch whisky.

It is entirely right and proper for the United States to demand that Japan permit a natural increase in its imports, particularly its agricultural imports, by dismantling most if not all of its trade bar-

nomics" and throw up a host of new barriers against imports; the policies the United States is currently seeking to foist upon Japan can, if they are carried far enough, achieve precisely the same end. For these policies, in essence, amount to what a French economist has described as the perfect crime in the field of international trade: persuading the victim voluntarily to renounce his ability to compete in your market.

In this case, however, the perfect crime could well back-

But these demands are worse than unrealistic: They are overbearing. Already there are signs of resentment at the relentless United States pressure in Japan and it is not inconceivable that, if that pressure continues long enough, what is now only a sense of grievance on the part of the Japanese could grow into a full-fledged xenophobia that would gravely threaten Japanese-American relations.

It might help matters considerably if, just for once, a reasonable number of Ameri-

January 22, 1978

The Japanese Are Tough Customers

By TRACY DAHLBY

TOKYO—The antique mural in the office of Cornilis Bossers, president of the Japanese subsidiary of Philips Industries N.V., shows Dutch traders arriving in Japan more than three centuries ago in the hope of opening trade with this island nation. In those days, Japan's feudal authorities strictly controlled foreigners trying to do business here. Today, Western businessmen bitterly grumble that not much has changed over the years since Mr. Bossers's countrymen first tried to get a toehold in Japan.

Charges and countercharges revolve around Japan's import quotas and high tariffs, which are the focus of negotiations now going on between Japanese and American officials. Should these trade barriers be removed, however, much formidable barbed wire will remain: the cultural and linguistic differences that have long baffled old Asia hands such as Philips, the Netherlands-based electrical-products giant.

"Windfalls never happen in Japan," says Mr. Bossers. "It's a matter of choosing a few good products and doggedly working along."

After five years of trying to penetrate the consumer market in Japan, Philips is only now beginning to make a profit on the line of electric coffee makers, shavers and other small appliances it introduced with high hopes in the early 1970's.

In its search for profitability, the company found it had a lot to learn about a lot of things in Japan. The quality and maintenance characteristics had to be lifted above standards demanded in the West. And there were special design requirements.

The size of the coffee maker, for example, had to be reduced to blend with the small scale of Japanese homes. The shaver also had to be shrunk— from three rotary heads to two. The original model, says Mr. Bossers, was "just too large for the male Japanese hand." And there was another reason for making the shaver compact enough to be easily tucked into a coat pocket or a briefcase: "The Japanese don't like to waste time shaving at home," he explains. "They shave on the subway or at traffic lights on their way to work."

Tracy Dahlby is a reporter in Tokyo for the Far Eastern Economic Review.

Philips got off to a faster start selling some of its other items—particularly electric components and medical equipment such as X-ray and laser machines. With sophisticated products of this kind, the Dutch company still has a technological edge over its Japanese competitors. But in the small-appliance field, in Japan as in the United States, competitors are quick to copy any hot-selling item.

When Philips introduced its coffee maker in Japan, for instance, it had only three competitors. Now it has 19, mostly Japanese companies. Their innovative flair and familiarity with the nation's bureaucratic quirks and creaky distribution structure give them a big edge over foreign companies.

Sharp rivalry from such internationally known Japanese industrial giants as Matsushita, Sony and Toshiba has whittled Philips's share of the coffee-maker market to about 35 percent today. Four years ago Philips had 85 percent of what was a considerably smaller market.

"How to fight your way in is the problem," says Mr. Bossers. "For starters you need easily salable and easily serviceable products, and it always helps to be the first in the field."

Philips saw an opportunity for the coffee maker when fresh coffee beans started to appear on grocers' shelves here in the early 1970's. In Japan, where green-tea sipping is traditional, many housewives choose instant coffee because they are not familiar with the freshly brewed kind. Their businessmen husbands, however, have acquired a taste for the real thing from the coffee shops that have become something of a cultural institution. Businessmen like to talk shop with clients or chat with friends over a demitasse. What Philips did was to appeal to a rising demand for quality in coffee by providing a cheap and easy way to make the freshly brewed beverage at home.

Philips had to back this appeal with higher levels of quality control and maintenance than Western markets would have demanded. According to P. J. van den Bergh, general manager of the Nihon Philips Corporation, Japanese consumers put a premium on quality that "exceeds Western standards." And social custom in Japan demands a high degree of after-sale maintenance, he says, "because of the value placed on loyalty and duty."

Japanese consumers are particularly critical of a product's appearance. Mr. Bossers says: "Product packaging must be done more carefully than for items marketed in Europe or the United States. So the whole process has to be upgraded to insure that there are no finger spots or scratches—everything has to be 100 percent."

In addition, Mr. Bossers says, instruction manuals for Japanese users must be much more detailed than those supplied to consumers elsewhere, including elaborate technical explanations of how the product works. "This doesn't mean that the Japanese are less intelligent—only that they have a greater curiosity," he explains.

"In the West," continues Mr. Bossers, "after-service is much slower and more impersonal than in Japan. Here our staff, which is predominantly Japanese, must satisfy their personal obligations to their Japanese customers to insure against any disturbance in relations. This involves an element of apology for any inconvenience caused, which is rooted in the Japanese psychology."

Sometimes the psychology takes an odd turn. "The Japanese know they know how to make good tea, but they think that only a foreigner can make good coffee," says Mr. Bossers. To help overcome this notion, which retards coffee-maker sales, Philips relies on television. It uses Kyosen Ohashi, the host of a popular late-night talk show, to help persuade his countrymen that they can brew as good a cup of coffee as anyone. The TV commercials are designed to reach businessmen after they have returned home from the late hours at the office still required by many Japanese companies.

"For the average white-collar worker, Ohashi is the ideal man. He's good at golf, horses, mah-jongg and girls, and he's the dazzling wit most of them would like to be," says Maxakazu Shibaoka, the advertising executive in charge of the Philips account at Hakuhodo Inc., one of Japan's biggest ad agencies.

Philips has benefited from its well-known brand name. The company first tried to get into Japan's consumer market in the mid-1960's, when it began importing standard European models of audio and stereo equipment. That effort collapsed with the dramatic rise of Sony and other big domestic manufacturers of home electronic products.

So Philips decided to concentrate on a few items that were potentially more

The Business World

profitable. Shavers and coffee makers headed the list, partly because Philips (unlike several of its Western competitors) was building its own distribution system here. The company saw little future in asking the big Japanese trading companies to move its goods. Some importers who did rely on the Japanese for distribution, observes one knowledgeable source, "never got off the ground."

Japanese manufacturers who do their own wholesaling have also established exclusive retail outlets. About 55,000 of these small electric appliance shops are scattered throughout Japanese cities. But a rising demand for variety and quality at lower prices is driving many consumers to the larger discount and department stores. As a result, even the "mom and pop" appliance shops have begun to drop their traditionally close ties with a single major producer and to sell a variety of brands.

This trend has helped Philips because it sells to large and small outlets alike. Mr. Bossers says, "Cracks are starting to appear in the old system of captive markets, and this is where we have a chance to break in."

Talking about "a chance to break in" at this late date! Another sign of how difficult it is to penetrate the Japanese market.

Mr. Bossers says that foreign companies thinking of doing business in Japan must forget about hoping to turn a profit after only a year or two. Even in the long run, he adds, "you must be satsified with lower profit margins than one would expect in American and European markets—sometimes only a fraction of 1 percent."

The most important step of all, foreign businessmen agree, is hiring a local staff. The cultural and language barrier is bolstered by the traditional Japanese suspicion of foreigners. That makes it vital to have a well-trained staff able to walk a cultural tightrope in a country where business and personal relationships are closely intertwined.

Mr. Bossers, after 27 years of business experience in Asia, including a decade in Japan, says, "The chances of miscommunication are such that you have to be constantly on your toes so that your relations with everyone are excellent." He tells about a fuse on one of the first Philips coffee makers marketed in Japan. The fuse did its job so well that it actually exceeded the specifications set by a Government ministry. "But the newspapers got wind of a story to the effect that Philips products were no good—they didn't match the specifications," says Mr. Bossers.

"You visit your customer, bow deeply and be patient," says Mr. van den Bergh, the Nihon Philips general manager. "Of course business will follow only if your product is good and if the proper rebates are offered." Rebates are paid to Japanese wholesalers, who demand much higher discounts on foreign products than domestic ones. They maintain that an extra reward is necessary because handling imports involves "risks," such as uncertainty of supply.

Now, after all these centuries, Dutch businessmen have a toehold in Japan. But Mr. Bossers is wary of letting success go to his company's head. "We've always been especially careful," he says. "Product cycles are much shorter in Japan because copies—good copies—proliferate here faster than anywhere else in the world. If you want to survive, you must be convinced of your own continuity in the long run and keep pace with the technological competition."

January 29, 1978

Japanese consumers seem to want more detailed operating manuals than consumers elsewhere.

6 More Politicians In Japan
Are Linked To Lockheed Payoff

TOKYO, Jan. 30 (UPI)—Six more Japanese politicians were implicated today in the $12 million Lockheed payoff scandal that rocked Japan's Government last year.

Toshiharu Okubo, former managing director of the Marubeni Trading Company, testified in court that he was instructed by All-Nippon Airways to deliver a total of $123,967 to the six politicians as "rewards" for their efforts in introducing Lockheed TriStar jetliners to Japan

Mr. Okubo at first refused to disclose in the trial stemming from the scandal, said he did not know if the money was delivered because "I did not witness the actual transfer of money."

Mr. Okubo at first refused to disclose

the names of the six but on order from the presiding judge, he identified them as former-Transport Minister Tomisaburo Hashimoto; former Vice Transport Minister Takayuki Sato; Susumu Nikaido, former state minister and chief Cabinet Minister; Kazuomi Fukunaga, former chairman of the ruling Liberal-Democratic Party's special committee on aviation affairs, and Hideyo Sasaki and Mutsuki Kato, party members in Parliament.

Mr. Hashimoto and Mr. Sato are already on trial on bribery charges in another facet of the scandal. Mr. Hashimoto was accused of receiving $16,666, and Mr. Sato $6,666 from Lockheed.

The giant American aircraft maker was alleged to have spent $12 million in questionable payments to promote the sale

of its aircraft in Japan between 1972 and 1975.

The scandal, which broke out in February 1977, led to the arrest of former Prime Minister Kakuei Tanaka, Mr. Hashimoto, Mr. Sato and about a dozen top executives of Marubeni and All-Nippon.

Marubeni is the former Japanese sales agent of Lockheed, and All-Nippon, a major domestic airline, is Japan's sole operator of the TriStar.

Mr. Okubo, testifying as a prosecution witness in the 39th session of the trial, said he was asked by All-Nippon to deliver kickbacks to the politicians in the name of the airline the night before the company decided to purchase the Lockheed jetliner over its rival, the McDonnell Douglas DC10, on Oct. 29, 1972.

January 31, 1978

Japanese Lumber Giant Bankrupt
As 5 Big Banks Remove Support

By ANDREW H. MALCOLM

TOKYO, Feb. 20—The Eidai Sangyo Company, Japan's largest plywood manufacturer and a major homebuilder, declared bankruptcy today in what is believed to be this nation's second largest corporate insolvency since World War II.

Today's step, which rocked business, financial and Government circles here, ended a five-year struggle by five major banks to save the company and its four subsidiaries, which left an estimated total of $750 million in debts. It also dramatized the growing number of corporate bankruptcies in selected Japanese industries these days as the nation's economy painfully adjusts to an era of slower growth.

The Government of Prime Minister Takeo Fukuda immediately began a concerted drive to minimize the economic and psychological effects of the Eidai Sangyo collapse, especially in overseas financial circles which had purchased $10 million worth of the company's bonds. Nonetheless, the domestic impact is expected to be considerable—not the least among Japan's powerful banking institutions whose sympathetic support until now have been propping up many ailing enterprises. While some corporations here have sought in recent years to reduce their outstanding loans in preparation for leaner times, operating with 70

to 80 percent borrowed capital is not unusual in Japan. And there was speculation here tonight that the fall of Eidai Sangyo might mark the start of a tougher attitude toward some wobbling clients by increasingly cautious banks.

Eidai Sangyo's banks decided, in meetings over the weekend and early this morning, that further private rehabilitation efforts were futile. It was this decision that prompted today's collapse. The announcement that Eidai Sangyo (literally, "eternal big industries") was technically filing for rehabilitation in Osaka district court was made by Ryuzo Kawakami, the company's president. He was

installed a year ago by the Daiwa bank, the company's largest creditor. If the court decides a recovery is feasible, it can appoint a receiver.

A similar process was applied following the 1975 bankruptcy of the Kohjin Company, a leading textile and real estate concern, with liabilities estimated at upwards of $800 million. That rehabilitation process is still incomplete, Finance Ministry officials said today, so no exact debt ranking is available.

Eidai Sangyo was founded in Osaka in 1946 by Shigeru Fukao. Within 10 years it became Japan's largest plywood maker. In 1960 it expanded into the prefabricated-housing field, where it quickly became one of the top five companies. Shortly before the 1973 oil crisis, Eidai Sangyo was selling 10,000 units of

prefab housing annually. In 1976 the company's sales totaled about $350 million. Estimated sales for the current fiscal year, ending March 31, are $322 million.

Part of Eidai Sangyo's problems were attributed to overhiring and excess investment, even after the oil crisis and its accompanying inflation, which touched off a stubborn recession that has yet to wane for some Japanese industries.

Uncertain consumers in Japan have cut their spending, especially on big-ticket items such as housing. As a result, last year Eidai Sangyo put up only 3,000 units and its overall rate of operation was only 40 percent. Additionally, Japan's plywood sector, like many older Japanese industries, is encountering increasingly stiff competition overseas as well as price difficulties because of the increasing value of the yen, which has appreciated about 20 percent in the last year.

Other hard-pressed industries include pulp, steel, shipping, shipbuilding and textiles. A survey of 377 major companies published today by Nihon Keizai Shimbun, the economic daily newspaper, showed that their six-month pretax profits are expected to fall 6 percent while one out of five companies expects a deficit in the same period.

After almost 15 years of an economic climate in which annual growth of 10 percent was common, the number of bankruptcies in Japan has been increasing since 1973 and now averages about

The Business World

1,500 a month. Companies are taking a variety of steps to deal wtih their problems. They include production cutbacks, slower hiring, encouragement of early retirement, shifting of some production workers into sales and the lending of workers to more prosperous affiliated companies.

In addition to a myriad of existing assistance programs for hard-hit industries, the Government is said to be designing new ways of helping smaller and medium-sized companies that do not have the strong financial resources of the larger corporate groups.

About 300 such companies are affected by today's bankruptcy. They are suppliers that relied almost totally on Eidai Sangyo's business to stay afloat. Government officials began aid efforts this morning, concentrating on credit assistance to avoid so-called chain bankruptcies. About 4,200 workers are directly affected by the declaration of the Eidai Sangyo and its subsidiaries—Eidai Housing, Eidai Mokuzai Kogyo, Mpahama Plywood and Daiichi Plywood.

The five banks involved are Daiwa, Tokyo, Mitsubishi Trust, Dai-ichi Kangyo and Fuji, with Daiwa alone carrying almost half of the debt.

February 21, 1978

Asahi, World's Largest Paper, Girds for Battle

By ANDREW H. MALCOLM

TOKYO — The squeak of a bicycle's hand brakes, the crackle of paper being folded, then a light thunk. It happens 62 million times a day in Japan. And behind the rickety bicycles, their rusting handlebar baskets stuffed with a perishable commodity, looms a vast computerized industry: the Japanese newspaper business — a clannish but competitive group of commercial fiefdoms whose total number of employees equals the population of Buffalo.

Twice a day these legions of reporters, printers and newsboys — augmented by truck convoys, mobile news rooms, radio relay networks and private airplane squadrons — bring the news of Japan and the world (in 24 pages or less) into the cramped homes of this nation of

Standing tallest among the dailies, for the moment at least, is Asahi Shimbun (literally, the "rising sun newspaper"). Its combined morning and afternoon circulation of 11.7 million makes it the world's largest newspaper. (America's circulation champion is The Daily News of New York, which sells 1.9 million copies on weekday mornings, 2.6 million on Sundays.)

Asahi Shimbun has a new chairman at its helm, a new headquarters under construction and a new price increase swelling its coffers. This publishing giant is beginning a fresh and fierce round of competition with its archrival, Yomiuri Shimbun (the "read and sell newspaper") and the financially weak Mainichi Shimbun (the "daily newspaper"). Together, these three national newspapers, all publishing both morn-

These Japanese-language tele-typewriters receive news stories for the Japanese press.

Consulate General of Japan, N.Y.

59

ing and afternoon issues, control almost half of Japan's total daily circulation. The rest is divided among the nation's 110 other dailies (13 are devoted to sports).

Japan's newspapers had total 1976 earnings of more than $4.78 billion, at today's foreign-exchange rate. Their income is expected to jump sharply this year. On March 1 Asahi Shimbun became the first big newspaper to raise its package subscription rate (both morning and afternoon every day) by 18 percent to $8.33 a month. The other major papers, also pinched by inflation amid only moderate advertising growth in the recent recession, are expected to raise their subscription rates, too — but not before a scramble to pick up circulation among bargain-hunting readers.

Circulation battles in Japan have always been spirited, involving shaded statistics and bonus gifts of towels and soap. In the last price war, Tokyo Shimbun scooped up nearly a half million new subscribers by delaying its rate increase.

This time Yomiuri is likely to seize first place in circulation from Asahi, at least temporarily. Mainichi will probably limp far behind in third place with a circulation of "only" 7 million. Mainichi had to be financially reorganized in December because of its massive debt load. Interest was costing it $64,000 a day.

Asahi's revenues, already largest, in the Japanese newspaper industry, will

undoubtedly expand as a result of the paper's subscription-rate increase. Asahi's revenues were $372.3 million in the six months ended March 31, 1977, the latest period for which figures have been disclosed. Asahi reported a profit of $9.3 million for those six months — a 2.5 percent rate of return, slightly higher than that of the industry as a whole.

But such figures do not convey Asahi's influence or the scope of its operations. The parent Asahi publishing company has 9,069 employees (who are paid an average of $18,000 a year) scattered in five major Japanese cities, 23 overseas offices and 281 local news bureaus, where young reporters get their start. Available for use in covering the news are 125 cars, 82 motorcycles, 53 radio-

The Japanese have one of the freest and most vigorous newspaper industries in the world today.

The Asahi Shimbun

The Business World

equipped jeeps, 13 vans equipped for radiophoto transmission, three jet aircraft and four helicopters, not to mention the 300-bed dormitory and giant bath at the company's Tokyo headquarters.

Articles written by reporters are sent by telephone and punched tape to a third-floor Tokyo newsroom that is just as cluttered as any in Chicago's hallowed "Front Page" days. But there are at least two major differences: The clutter here includes disposable wooden chopsticks, and there are no typewriters. Because of the mechanical difficulty of reproducing up to 4,000 of the Japanese language's more common characters with a typewriter, news items are written by hand. At Asahi this daily process consumes 122,000 sheets of paper and 1,450 pencils.

Elsewhere in the Asahi empire, however, modern technology reigns — neat, precise and swift. Most of the type is machine-set from punched tape. A pioneering project called Nelson provides computerized page makeup for 30 of the 150 pages composed daily for Asahi's many regional editions. From a special room, radio technicians transmit pages to printing plants miles away.

Asahi has 18 major morning editions, 10 in the afternoon and 105 more that vary with the locality where they appear. The newspaper's high-speed presses, some of them using the offset printing process, devour enough rolls of newsprint every day to stretch from Tokyo to Kansas City. Hundreds of trucks, some of them almost as wide as the cramped alleys of Japan's cities, then haul the bundles wrapped in plastic to 70,000 Asahi delivery workers.

And that's just the Asahi Shimbun operation. In addition, the company publishes an English-language afternoon newspaper, three weeklies, three monthlies and 10 yearbooks. It also holds interests in 60 other enterprises, including radio and television stations, travel agencies, real estate firms and an airline — All Nippon Airways, Japan's largest passenger carrier. Like other newspapers, Asahi sponsors a variety of cultural activities and exhibitions. One of its annual projects is a nationally televised high school baseball tournament, which transfixes the whole country for two weeks in August.

Basically, there is not much difference in the news content of Japan's big dailies. Because reporters cooperate in covering the main categories of news, scoops are rare. But there is a difference in the way the papers present the news. Both Yomiuri and Asahi carry serious political and financial stories. But Asahi appeals more to the country's intellectuals with its somber approach and conservative gray makeup, while Yomiuri has drawn a growing number of readers by carrying more human interest stories in splashier makeup with larger pictures.

Competition is sharpest in the streets.

Door-to-door circulation workers decry opposition papers while praising their own, and they offer tiny pocket calculators as subscription incentives. These days representatives of Yomiuri are distributing thousands of handbills stating that, unlike another major newspaper, theirs has not raised the subscription rate.

True to Japanese business tradition, at neither Asahi nor Yomiuri does the top management contain colorful leaders boldly proposing dynamic moves. A system of corporate consensus blurs personality differences and emphasizes the company's overall image. If anything, Asahi's leaders may be considered even more conservative than their peers.

Asahi was founded 99 years ago by the Ueno and Murayama families in Osaka as Japan was emerging from its feudal age. Like other Japanese newspapers then, it needed a Government license to publish. Over the decades Asahi developed a reputation as Japan's opinion leader, a reputation that did it no good under the military regime of the 1930's. Today some critics assert that Asahi is smug and too liberal and that its news is overly emotional. Some also say it is not critical enough in certain areas of coverage such as mainland China.

A feud between descendants of the founding families centers on alleged attempts by the Murayama family, which owns about 35 percent of Asahi's stock, to influence the paper's news content unduly. Opposing them are members of the Ueno family, which owns about 20 percent of the stock, and the paper's executives, who control Asahi's 10-member board of directors. The rest of the stock is owned by former and present Asahi employees, who trade the shares between themselves.

Last December the board elected Seiki Watanabe, 63 years old, a former editorial writer, as Asahi's new president, and elevated Tomoo Hirooka, 70, former managing editor, to the powerful post of chairman. He will preside over Asahi's further diversification efforts and its struggle with a variety of business problems.

Labor is about to begin its spring wage offensive throughout industrial Japan. Unlike American newspapers, Asahi has only one "house" union to deal with. Many costs are rising, including those of vital technological equipment and newsprint, which in Japan is now $507 per metric ton of 2,200 pounds. (In the United States, papers in the Northeast pay $336 for an equal amount of newsprint.)

One stabilizing financial factor enjoyed by Japanese newspapers is their immense home delivery system, with personnel totaling 373,000, which assures them of a steady flow of sales by the month. Ninety-eight percent of Asahi's vast circulation is thunked onto readers' doorsteps.

Before World War II, subscriptions accounted for 60 percent of Asahi's revenues and advertising 40 percent. During the booming 1960's the proportion was reversed. After the 1973 energy crisis touched off Japan's still-lingering recession, the advertising share of income fell but has since increased to about 45 percent.

Mr. Hirooka, who is also president of the Japan Newspaper Publishers and Editors Association, says a 50-50 split is financially the soundest. He sees strong demand for newspaper advertising space now that advertisements on Japanese television seem to have reached the saturation point. A full-page ad in Asahi costs $89,300.

Despite the growing competition for people's leisure time, Mr. Hirooka maintains that the Japanese remain a people addicted to reading. Much of the advertising in Japanese newspapers is for books and magazines. "Before the war," Mr. Hirooka said in an interview, "newspapers had chapters from two or three novels every day. But today we find readers' tastes much more mature. They are seeking more serious articles, interpretive articles, that contribute to their daily lives and don't just entertain them as spectators."

Asahi's plans for diversification, considered quite conservative in past years, will almost certainly involve the general area of communications. "As times change," Mr. Hirooka said, "it has become less easy to live solely on newspaper income." Stockholders generally apply only mild pressure on business in Japan, so Asahi is free to choose new ventures not only on the basis of profit potential but also for the strength they add to the "mother ship," the newspaper.

Through a research division, Asahi is experimenting in a Tokyo suburb with facsimile transmission — a system that "delivers" a newspaper automatically by printing it on a machine in the subscriber's home.

Although Japanese journalism is dominated by the nationwide dailies, prefectural newspapers are strong in their own markets, thanks in part to the official encouragement they received during the years of American occupation. Newspaper executives generally do not see a Japanese trend toward smaller papers' combining into large newspaper chains, as in the United States.

"We need competition," Mr. Hirooka said, "It's good for Japanese journalism and Japan.

"Our democracy is still new and weak. If a dictator like the military in the 1930's ever showed up again, one good newspaper might be easy to handle. But if there are many, then the people and their freedoms are stronger."

Andrew H. Malcolm is a correspondent in the Tokyo bureau of The New York Times.

March 19, 1978

Japan Acts to Revive Depressed Shipyards

Airport, Hotels At Sea Studied

By ANDREW H. MALCOLM

NAGASAKI, Japan — The huge Japanese shipbuilding industry, once the world's leader but now run aground on the rocks of recession, is turning to a variety of new — and unusual — ways to keep afloat. The immediate outlook, however, is for more rough seas.

The new corporate projects include mammoth floating platforms carrying power-generating stations, factories, sprawling oil storage tanks, farms, even hotels and an airport at sea.

Surplus workers, whose numbers grow as orders dwindle, are encouraged to retire, or are retrained, assigned to make-work maintenance or even sent elsewhere to assemble automobiles for more prosperous corporate divisions.

Rise in Defense Spending Sought

Costly unused capacity for heavy machinery and continuing high overhead costs for labor — workers traditionally cannot be laid off here — have prompted calls by Japanese businessmen for increased defense spending, a sensitive subject in this region that once experienced Japanese militarism.

On the success of these ambitious — some call them farfetched — efforts hangs the economic fortunes of thousands of Japanese workers, hundreds of supplier companies and three dozen communities throughout this island nation, where building seaworthy craft was illegal until feudal rulers were overthrown 110 years ago.

Since then, here in Nagasaki, for instance, shipbuilding has come to dominate the local economy, and Mitsubishi Heavy Industries has come to dominate shipbuilding. In 1976 Nagasaki's

100,800-DWT Tanker "Oigawamaru" on the building berth of Innoshima Shipyard of the Hitachi Shipbuilding Company.

Consulate General of Japan, N.Y.

manufacturers produced $960 million worth of goods, 68 percent of which were ships. Of the manufactured goods, Mitsubishi (literally, "three diamonds," which is the company's symbol) produced two-thirds.

There are 11 other shipbuilders here, many of which concentrate on coastal or commercial fishing craft. Their orders have not sunk like those for the big ships, but the large Sasebo Shipyards near here are teetering on bankruptcy, and the Government is involved in rescue efforts.

Mitsubishi Cutting Back

In Nagasaki, Mitsubishi is not going bankrupt. The yard here is but one of the giant conglomerate's five major yards in Japan. But it is cutting back its Nagasaki operations. And when one company employs half a city's manufacturing labor force and supports 178 other suppliers, that can hurt.

Four years ago in the peak shipbuilding years, the Mitsubishi yard employed 16,716 workers who turned out 19 supertankers totaling 5.07 million deadweight tons. The company was booked solid for 36 months. This year the company has fewer than 14,000 workers. They will produce 14 cargo ships (no tankers) totaling 500,000 tons. In 180 days the orders will run out. Company officials say they are operating at 60 percent of capacity now, and they expect the figure to fall to 50 percent in coming months. In three or four years, they estimate, the global tanker surplus — one-third of the world supply — will be largely absorbed, and new orders will arrive.

"Still," said Yamanouchi Shigeaki, director of the company's planning department here, "We won't get the big orders we did before. Those days are gone now forever."

Salaries Affected

Through hiring cutbacks and attrition, Mitsubishi here will pare its work force closer to 13,000 employees. They are hired for life in Japan and receive full pay even in hard times. Overtime, however, is virtually gone. And for an average worker, such as Nobuhiro Yanagidani, that means a pay cut of 30,000 yen, or $133, from his monthly gross pay of 250,000 yen, or $1,111.

Mr. Yanagidani, who once helped to assemble vast 150-ton ship sections, now works on car carriers like the 3,900-vehicle Jupiter Diamond that will be delivered to its Singapore owners and Japanese lessees late this month. He will also be trained in a variety of tasks and management skills that may be useful in future years. Some colleagues have been transferred to Mitsubishi operations that make cars, turbines, aircraft, armaments and engines for Chrysler.

Other workers spend time on equipment maintenance chores. Recently three dozen of them shoveled dirt from the cavernous interior of an idled 300,000-ton drydock. While an 80-ton crane daintily lifted the tiny bins of dust, some men played pogo on their shovels.

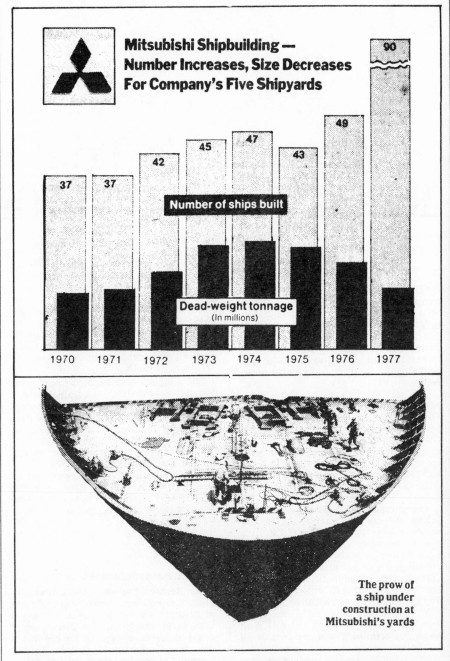

Mitsubishi Shipbuilding — Number Increases, Size Decreases For Company's Five Shipyards

Number of ships built

Dead-weight tonnage (In millions)

	1970	1971	1972	1973	1974	1975	1976	1977
Number of ships built	37	37	42	45	47	43	49	90

The prow of a ship under construction at Mitsubishi's yards

Offshore Airport Considered

Salesmen, who once simply processed the flood of orders, must now scour the world for leads. One proposal is for a vast floating oil storage terminal, which would help shipbuilders and steelmakers, both in difficult times, at nearby Kamigoto Island. Osaka is studying an offshore airport on giant barges. A floating pulp plant sailed for Brazil last fall. And other builders are mapping plans for floating hotels.

However, export sales, which have comprised 80 percent of Mitsubishi's business, are jeopardized by the rising value of the yen, which makes Japanese goods more expensive for foreigners, and by the rising competitiveness of newer shipbuilders in South Korea, Singapore, Taiwan, Yugoslavia, Brazil and Singapore, which unlike Japan still have low wages. One plant sign here urges: "Let's Boost Exports by Lowering Our Costs."

Acknowledging the structural economic changes under way, city officials say they can no longer rely so heavily on shipbuilding. They are inviting other industries to town and seeking low-interest Government loans to help existing companies finance diversification. "However," said Kingo Shinozaki, Nagasaki's planning department director, "the prospects are not bright. Given the sluggish business sectors, new investments are not so easy to find."

June 20, 1978

American's Trial in Japan Raises Trade and Ethical Issues

By HENRY SCOTT-STOKES

YOKOHAMA, Japan, July 9 — The atmosphere in the Yokohama district court on a hot summer day was sleepy. The judge had bustled back from a quick "curry-rice" lunch. He wore a black gown, without a wig. The prosecuting attorney came in late, carrying a huge purple furoshiki wrapper full of legal documents.

This was the 47th session of the Rempell case, which has lasted four years. The defendant, Steven Rempell of Long Beach, a town on Long Island, who is charged with customs fraud, stood up briefly with his back to the public gallery, his shoulders a little stooped now. A near-sighted defense attorney held a document close to his eyeglasses, as if smelling the paper.

The somnolent atmosphere of this trial belied the controversial issues that it raises, especially regarding trade. At a time when Japan's trade surplus with the United States is soaring above last year's record figure of $8.9 billion, this case, involving the attempt by an American small-business man to import liquor into Japan, is attracting much attention here.

Mr. Rempell was arrested four years ago, put into a crowded jail cell with hardened criminals, and deprived of all his belongings without any proof of his guilt having been established. As his saga illustrates, efforts to compete with big business in Japan can be hazardous.

Charged With Defrauding Customs

The affair began early in 1974 when Mr. Rempell, then 31 years old, a Cornell graduate in mathematics and a former executive for the International Business Machines Corporation, was charged with defrauding customs by under-invoicing, and thus evading taxes of over $250,000. He had started out in business on his own only 18 months before.

Having observed the steep consumer prices in Japan, particularly on imported goods, he had decided to start his own small business importing liquor and other items bought on the free market in Hong Kong, avoiding the clumsy Japa-

nese distribution system and going directly to the customer.

Mr. Rempell was importing Rémy Martin, one of the best brand names in foreign liquor in Japan, at a cost, after payment of duties and taxes, of well under $5 a bottle. By so doing, he was able to retail it at about $30 a bottle, compared with the $50 a bottle charged by Dodwell & Company, the Hong Kong-based British concern that is the established agent for the French brandy.

Mr. Rempell also handled other good brands: He imported Jack Daniels black label, in direct competition with Suntory, the Japanese giant that holds over 70 percent of the Japanese whisky market. He brought in Steinhager gin in competition with Mitsubishi Corporation, one of the largest trading companies in the world. And he imported Chivas Regal, the license for which is held by Kirin beer, the largest beer concern in Japan and, like Suntory, a virtual monopolist. all these vastly bigger rivals have since testified against Mr. Rempell, their tiny competitor.

Essentially Simple Strategy

Mr. Rempell's strategy was essentially simple. Goods were being sold in Japan at 10 times their import cost, leaving a very large margin that a direct seller could undercut. He put up $50,000 of his own money, borrowed another $50,000 from his father, and opened a tiny office in his Tokyo home with three helpers. He also set up a similar, even smaller operation in Hong Kong to purchase the liquor.

As soon as the first shipments hit the Japanese market, following early test-and-trial shipments, Mr. Rempell began to be noticed. And it was only a few months later that he found himself in a detention center here, with his business destroyed and his inventory and bank balance, a total of about $200,000, confiscated and unrecoverable. The authorities made five examinations of Mr. Rempell's accounts in the Tokyo branch of his bank, the Algemene Bank Nederland, and 12 members of the bank's staff have been summoned to Yokohama to testify.

The most dramatic episode in the case was Mr. Rempell's initial period of incar-

ceration, during which customs and police officials attempted to extract a confession from him. "I was detained for the first two months," he asserted in written testimony at the trial, "in a cage which was just large enough for three men" to lie down on mattresses.

"However," he said, "there were often five in the cage. The walls were cold stone and the floor wood, and there was no heat, although it was March. We were allowed two threadbare and filthy blankets during the day to keep us warm."

Later Sent to a Prison

Later he was sent to a prison, where he found conditions "like a country club" by comparison, he testified. There he learned to play shogi, or Japanese chess. But, he asserted, the food was bad — usually soggy rice three times a day, and soup in the morning.

During this time, the United States Embassy reportedly took no steps to assist him, and he received only one visit by a junior consular official.

Four years later, Mr. Rempell's trial is nearing an end. On July 18 the defense counsel, Haruo Abe, who is occasionally compared here to Ralph Nader, will sum up, and the court will return a verdict in the fall.

One striking aspect of the case, which has legal, human rights a d commercial aspects, is the sharpness with which it illustrates the difficulty of importing goods into Japan, despite the extremely high prices here. A minister told a recent visitor, in fact, that Japan had the highest prices for all major food items in the world.

By all accounts, the reason for this difficulty can be found in the nature of big business in Japan. The large companies dominate society, and pay politicians to help them. When someone breaks the unwritten code, as did Mr. Rempell, signals are given and the interloper is put down.

Competitors Are Suspected

Both Mr. Rempell and his attorney suspect that he was denounced to customs officials by one of his competitors — Dodwell, Suntory, Mitsubishi or Kirin. But given the nature of Mr. Rempell's ven-

The Business World

ture, and the desperate atmosphere of early 1974, just after the oil embargo by Middle Eastern states against Western-oriented consumers, Japan suddenly found itself with a huge trade deficit, and the authorities may indeed have been looking for a scapegoat.

Mr. Rempell is not sure. But meanwhile, there is no doubt about the facts. "Imported goods cannot get into the marketplace at reasonable prices," he asserted. "I was breaking through the distribution system and selling products at way below the prices" that had been estab-lished for retail. "I was too early," he said, "and I made a lot of enemies."

As a recent example of dealings on the consumer front in Japan, Mr. Rempell related that for the first time since World War II, Japan is importing cherries from Washington state. "I see they have a C.I.F. price of 300 to 400 yen a kilo," he said, referring to the price to the importer after having paid the item's cost, insurance and freight. A kilo is 2.2 pounds, and at the current exchange rate of about 200 yen to the dollar, the cherries would cost a little less than $1 a pound.

"But then the landed cost," or cost to the importer after payment of duties and taxes, Mr. Rempell said, "is about 1,200 yen a kilo, and I would like to know where that extra 800 yen comes from. Something"s going on."

"The fact is," he said, "they've got to sell far higher than Yamagata cherries," a domestic variety, "and so you have them on the market at 400 yen for 100 grams," or one-tenth of a kilo, "and that's a lot of money for cherries." Thus, the Washington cherries end up at 10 times their C.I.F. price, as did the Remy Martin brandy before Mr. Rempell's importing efforts.

July 10, 1978

Tony Yamada holding a striped bass used in the preparation of sushi, at his store in Fort Lee, New Jersey.

Chapter 3

The Japanese Abroad

In California there is a factory that produces frozen noodles for Japanese residents. Another plant manufactures tatami mats to furnish Japanese homes. There are several hotels that provide Japanese-style facilities for visiting businessmen. New York's Nippon Club on posh 57th Street is just one center of Japanese social life in a city considered the "plum" of foreign assignments by Japanese sent abroad by their companies. Japanese bankers have established a European center in Dusseldorf which now abounds with Japanese schools, restaurants and even a hotel.

The increasingly large Japanese presence abroad is an astounding phenomenon if one realizes that little more than one hundred years ago, under the Tokugawa Shogunate (1603-1868), Japan was virtually cut off from the rest of the world. For a native to leave Japan was more than unthinkable—it was punishable by death.

Today there are approximately 1.6 million people of Japanese origin living outside of Japan. On the average, 17 Japanese leave the motherland each day with no intention of returning. Their reasons for leaving are much the same as those of any emigrant group and boil down to the search for a better life. In recent years these emigrants have been young, urban, and, in some cases, affluent and well-educated. Because of its chronic population problem, Japan does not impede citizens who wish to leave. On the contrary, the Japanese government offers them unusually lavish assistance. It briefs them, trains them, and often pays the airfare to their new homes.

Thousands of Japanese abroad are industrial and business transients. They have been sent by their companies for a three- or five-year period. Both permanent immigrants and businessmen tend to gather in artificial community centers with a distinct Japanese flavor. Some areas of Southern California are a slice of Japan in America. Nearly every major Japanese company, for example, maintains a branch in the vicinity of Gardena, California, where Japanese restaurants and food shops are everywhere evident and two Japanese-language daily newspapers are published.

In New York, Japanese restaurants, business hotels, bookshops, food stores, fashion outlets, clubs and a wide variety of cultural institutions are appearing in increasing numbers. Japanese communities are springing up in Riverdale, an upper middle-class section of the Bronx, in Fort Lee, New Jersey, and throughout Queens and Westchester County. At present, about 20,000 Japanese citizens work in Manhattan alone. There are nearly 450 Japanese corporations with branches in New York City.

Most Japanese businessmen assigned to overseas positions have studied either the native tongue of the foreign country or English, the international language of the business community. Often, they precede their families by six months to accustom themselves to the new land. America, particularly New York, has been a difficult place of resettlement for the wives of Japanese businessmen. Isolated from family and friends left behind and with husbands working between 12 and 16 hours daily, they often find life in the United States overwhelmingly strange and depressing. Yet, rather than making new friends, most Japanese wives tend to remain at home and to blame themselves for the emptiness they feel.

The most difficult problem facing the Japanese overseas is the education of their children. In Japan, mothers generally begin to prepare their children for college at age five or six. Expectations that their children will be accepted by the best schools cause great anxieties for Japanese parents, and for the children. To meet this pressure, weekend schools for Japanese children abroad have been established. These schools emphasize Japanese language skills and the type of training needed to fulfill the rigorous Japanese university requirements. There are also several Japanese day schools with long waiting lists. Some businessmen resolve these problems but create more agonizing ones by leaving their families in Japan when they are sent abroad.

America is the most popular, but not the only, area of Japanese business colonization in the West. Latin America is filled with branches of Japanese concerns, and the local Japanese enclaves in France and Germany are rapidly growing. A visit to Montmartre will reveal a Japanese fast food shop, several Japanese painters, and probably a dozen or more Japanese tour buses.

Whether they are on a tour, on business, or have left Japan for good, the Japanese abroad face difficult periods of adjustment to their new lives.

Foreign-Controlled Coast Banks
Are Charged With Discrimination

By LES LEDBETTER

SAN FRANCISCO, Aug. 9—A coalition of 10 activist organizations today filed a class action antitrust complaint with state officials here against 39 foreign-controlled banks, each with more than $100 million in assets in California.

The complaint, charging discrimination in hiring, promotion and community service policies, was filed with the State Superintendent of Banking and the California Secretary of Business and Transportation by Public Advocates Inc., in behalf of groups representing minorities, women, veterans and consumers.

Specific action was brought against the Sumitomo Bank Ltd. of Japan, and its subsidiary, the Sumitomo Bank of California. The action seeks to block or revise the $19.9 million acquisition of 19 Bank of California branches by Sumitomo, already the 10th largest bank in the state with 23 offices.

Donald Parachimi, a Sumitomo Bank board member and counsel to the bank, said he was unable to comment on specifics in the complaint, which he had not yet seen.

He said, however, that the complaint was "not something we foresee at major stumbling black" to the branch acquisitions, and he questioned why a complaint was filed with banking officials rather than with the courts or with agencies dealng with discrimination.

Sue Hersham of Public Advocates said that the complaint action was taken because state officials, unlike courts, can establish general guidelines for all the foreign-controlled banks as well as a "code of multinational social responsibility" for such businesses. A one-year moratorium on expansion by such banks is also sought.

The antitrust complaint, believed to be the first filed in the "public interest" in the United States, charges that Sumitomo and other foreign-controlled banks have exclusionary policies in violation of the Cartwright and Clayton Antitrust Acts, the (National) Bank Merger Act of 1966 and a number of California statutes and code sections, because they operate in an "unsound and unsafe manner" by being vulnerable to discrimination lawsuits.

Mr. Parachimi acknowledged that Sumitomo employed only **Japanese** in major policy positions in the bank, explaining that "basically it is a minority bank" that has historically served the Japanese community in California and trade between Japan and the United States.

"That is not our policy, however," said Mr. Parachini of the predominance of Japanese and Japanese-Americans at the bank. "The pattern developed in relationship to the amount of business with Japanese customers."

"Very few Americans can handle" the language and cultural barriers in dealing with Japanese customers, he added. The pattern would change, he said, with the acquisition of the Bank of California branches and of more employees and customers who were non-Japanese.

Groups seeking the state action against Sumitomo in particular and the 38 other banks in general were Chinese for Affirmative Action, the National Association for the Advancement of Colored People (Western Region), the National Organization for Women, the United Latin American Citizens, Women Organized for Employment, San Francisco Consumer Action, the American G.I. Forum, the Filipino Community of San Francisco, the California Filipino Certified Public Accountants and the Mexican-American Political Association.

August 10, 1977

Japanese Beachhead
in California

By ROBERT LINDSEY

GARDENA, Calif.—A motorist could get lost in this southern California city of 4,500 and think he had wandered into Japan. The tallest building in town is the Mitsubishi Bank. At the Pacific Square shopping center there are 40 shops, and it is unusual in any of them to see a face that is not Japanese.

At the big new Meji supermarket, the best-selling items include octopus, squid and gallon cans of soy sauce. In the sushi bars and restaurants nearby, the lights glow until late at night, illuminating groups of Japanese businessmen in dark suits with bottles of Asahi, Sapparo and Kirin beer in front of them. Meanwhile, at home, when their wives turn on the television set they have a choice of two channels that broadcast only programs imported from Japan.

Within a 20-mile radius of Gardena, there are hundreds of Japanese companies—Datsun, Toyota, Honda, Seiko, Hitachi, Kawasaki, the Y.U.K.K. zipper plant, and many others.

Without much notice, Japan has built a sizable economic beachhead in southern California. In the last five years the number of Japanese companies with offices, plants or other facilities in the Los Angeles area has more than doubled, to 435.

More significantly, the number of Japanese facilities with some kind of assembly or manufacturing function

BEER, WINE & SAKE

A scene outside the Meji Supermarket in Gardena, Calif.

has increased from nine in 1972 to 53.

But there has been growing concern among Japanese businessmen. They assert that California, which became the first step for Japanese companies largely because of geography, could lose some of its edge because of what they assert is an antibusiness climate in the state capital of Sacramento.

City officials say they believe almost 20 percent of the families who live in Gardena are connected to the Japanese trading companies, manufacturers, banks and other concerns that have come here to attempt to tap the American market. Gardena is one of several communities with substantial concentrations of Japanese. In all, the Japanese consul general estimates, there are at least 24,000 Japanese nationals in the region.

And they have brought with them a piece of Japan. "You could get into some parts of Gardena and think you're in Yokohama," says George Yoshinaga, an editor of The Japan Daily News. It is one of two daily Japanese language newspapers that were established, like the four Japanese language schools and scores of restaurants and shops, largely to serve the community of Japanese business emigrés.

There is a factory that produces frozen noodles for the Japanese. One plant makes tatami mats so they can provide Japanese-style living quarters. And there are several hotels that provide Japanese-style rooms for Japanese businessmen.

Typically, the Japanese come to this country for three to five years. Theodore Tsukahara, a professor at Claremont College, said a study of Japanese banks showed that "they were using their American subsidiaries for training their people. They would send them here for three years and then bring them back to Japan, where they would

The Japanese Abroad

get top jobs on the foreign-exchange desk.''

Compared with Japan, the Japanese businessmen say, the cost of living is cheaper here, so this is another reason why an American assignment is desirable.

California, being on the West Coast, was a natural first stop for the initial Japanese traders who reopened American offices following the signing of the 1952 treaty that formally ended World War II and resumed trade relations. When Toyota and Nissan Motors, which market Datsun cars, made their first tentative steps to penetrate the American auto market during the 1950's, they established marketing offices here. Since then virtually all of the major Japanese export companies and trading companies have established offices in this region.

Expansion of the offshore activities, for the most part, has paralleled the rapid growth of Japanese exports to the United States, which soared from $5.9 billion in 1970 to $15.5 billion last year, according to the Commerce Department.

Most of the Japanese offices here have been sales, administrative and distribution headquarters. Recently there has been a significant increase in Japanese banking activity as well as a modest increase in manufacturing by Japanese companies using American labor.

There were only two Japanese-owned state-chartered banks in the area in 1970. Now there are seven. There are also 15 other Japanese banks that have agencies or other representation here.

Last month Japanese interest moved to expand their involvement in banking when the Sumitomo Bank of California announced an agreement to buy 19 branches of the Bank of California for $19.9 million.

Behind the slow increase in manufacturing are political rumblings in Washington and with organized labor about the growing Japanese exports to this country—especially automobiles, television sets and steel—as well as increasing labor costs in Japan and currency fluctuations that have narrowed the advantage of manufacturing in Japan.

The 53 Japanese manufacturers turn out products ranging from soy sauce and zippers to truck bodies, toys, tea bags and fishing tackle. In many cases there is relatively little manufacturing of components; instead there is assembly of parts imported from Japan.

Yoshikazu Takeuchi, a Japanese vice consul here, says it "appears that there may be a trend toward establishing manufacturing operations in the United States, although it is difficult to project."

Four years ago the Sony Corporation established in San Diego a plant to manufacture television picture tubes and assemble TV sets. The plant now employs about 1,100 people, and only about 40 of them are Japanese.

Melco Sales, a United States subsidiary of the Matsushita Electric Corporation, opened its first plant in this country early this summer at Irvine, between Los Angeles and San Diego. The plant, which assembles television sets from parts imported from Japan, apparently represents an effort to dampen criticism of Japanese TV imports.

In a similar move, the Tomy Corporation, a subsidiary of Tomy Kogyo of Japan, announced last week that it had signed a 20-year lease for a 246,000-square-foot plant in Carson, a city near here. The company now assembles toys at two much smaller facilities. It says it intends not only to consolidate this operation at the new plant but also to begin on-site manufacture of components as well as assembly.

Political leaders in California hope their state's role as offshore port for so many Japanese companies will give it an edge in winning a prize that is sought by virtually every other state in the union: the long talked-about but still uncertain construction of an American assembly plant by one or all of the three big Japanese auto makers —Toyota, Datsun and Honda.

State officials say California, where people buy more Japanese cars than in any other state, is a logical place to build the plant. But California in general, Gov. Edmund G. Brown Jr. and one of his closest aides, Thomas Quinn, director of the Smog-Fighting State Air Resources Board, have acquired an antibusiness reputation.

Mr. Brown and Mr. Quinn, who have had a number of widely publicized confrontations with business over pollution control, have made trips to Japan in recent weeks in hopes of countering this reputation and of persuading the Japanese car builders to build their facilities in California.

"Japanese businessmen find it difficult to build manufacturing plants in California," Tatsumi Iwata, chairman of the Japan California Bank, said. "If a company comes to California to manufacture rather than export, it has a big problem because of the high taxes in the state. Many companies would like to come here, but they cannot because they would find themselves in the same predicament as Dow Chemical."

This was a reference to a decision earlier this year by the big chemical company to abandon plans for a projected facility near San Francisco. Dow said it did so because of a multiplicity of permits required and other delays.

"California has some problems in this area," Richard G. Kjeldsen, a vice president and senior economist of the Security Pacific National Bank, said. "Many Japanese firms look at California's environmental laws, its complex zoning regulations and its tax structure and decide it would be cheaper and easier to go elsewhere. So far, the fact that California has a large Japanese population and is the gateway to the Pacific outweighs these disadvantages, but this may not always be true."

American wage costs, he said, are also a deterrent to expanding Japanese manufacturing here. Japanese businessmen have looked "very carefully" at the cost of manufacturing in the United States, he added. Although the balance has improved somewhat, low-wage areas such as Taiwan and South Korea may still look more favorable to Japanese businessmen when they ponder their decisions back in Tokyo.

August 21, 1977

Adjusting to Life in America

By FRED M. H. GREGORY

LOS ANGELES—Takeo Mukasa and his family have been living in the United States for seven years. Except for a brief period of residence in New York City, that time has been spent in the Los Angeles area. Mr. Mukasa is West Coast regional manager for the Leader Instruments Corporation, a Tokyo-based electronics concern.

Mr. Mukasa, 32 years old; his wife Sumiko, 28, and their 3-year-old son live in a modest but comfortable two-bedroom bungalow in Northridge, one of the many suburban residential communities that surround Los Angeles.

The Mukasa home is on a quiet street lined by palm trees. The house adjoins a neat lawn with well-trimmed shrubbery. Mrs. Mukasa's Pinto station wagon is often seen parked in the driveway. Mr. Mukasa's Pontiac Fire-bird Trans-Am is housed in their two-car garage next to a dismantled Harley-Davidson motorcycle and a partly opened parachute. (Until the birth of their son, Mr. Mukasa was an avid sky diver. Now he has become a golfer instead.) To all appearances, the Mukasas are a typical southern California family.

It is an adjustment they made easily. Their biggest difficulty upon arriving from Japan was the English language. "When I came here, I almost couldn't speak at all," Mr. Mukasa says in accented but competent English. His first assignment was in New York, where he worked as a service technician with other Japanese-speaking employees. When he was elevated to a sales position and transferred to Los Angeles, most of his co-workers were American. So, through contact with them, Mr. Mukasa's English improved.

Still, the Mukasas found that a command of the language was not an absolute necessity in the Los Angeles area. "If you don't go farther than some areas or certain zones, you don't need English to live," Mr. Mukasa says. He points out that Japanese food is carried by many supermarket chains. There is Japanese-language television, and there are several areas close to his home where almost nothing but Japanese is spoken. Though the Mukasas chose to live in an English-speaking neighborhood and have many English-speaking friends, they maintain close relationships with other Japanese whose employment requires them to live in the United States. And Mr. Mukasa follows events in Japan on his short-wave radio.

Not all Japanese adjust as easily, at home with her son, she says, it is "hard to find people to converse with in order to improve my English." Mr. Mukasa is also concerned with their son's education. He is learning to speak both English and Japanese. But his mother fears that, when he reaches school age, he will not be able to get a proper academic grounding in Japanese. Though there is a Japanese school

One difference a newcomer finds: 'Our company's president has about the same size house in Tokyo as we do here.'

however, Mr. Mukasa says. "Some miss Japan every day, every hour."

For those who can make the transition, residence in the United States can be pleasant. "It's much easier to live, and the ratio between pay and the cost of living is not so bad," Mr. Mukasa says. To illustrate the difference between life in Japan and in this country, Mr. Mukasa says, "Our company's president has about the same size house in Tokyo as we do here."

Mrs. Mukasa says, "I love the weather—not too cold, not too hot." But, because she spends most of her time in Los Angeles, it operates only one day a week. Consequently, Mrs. Mukasa intends to teach her son at home, using textbooks from Japan.

In spite of this, the Mukasas intend to stay in the United States at least three more years. Mr. Mukasa is not sure whether he and his family will return to Japan. "It all depends on the company's decision," he says.

Fred M. H. Gregory writes on business topics from Los Angeles.

August 21, 1977

The Sun Also Rises in New York

By PAMELA G. HOLLIE

The contest is over, and the winning entry in Hitachi America Ltd.'s employee song-writing competition has been chosen. It will be performed for the first time at the Manhattan sales company's Christmas party. One of the verses and the chorus:

"Standing together, holding hands.
Working together in a foreign land.
Striving together in every way,
Looking ahead toward a bright new day.
(Chorus)
Hitachi America in the U.S.A.
Hitachi America is here to stay . . . ."

Hitachi America, sales arm of a giant electrical manufacturing organization, is among the 450 Japanese companies operating in New York City, part of a wave of direct Japanese investment in the United States that now approaches $1 billion, a fourfold increase since 1973.

Some 20,000 Japanese nationals now labor in Manhattan's canyons. In his dark suit, white shirt and modest tie, briefcase in one hand, calling card in the other, the Japanese businessman has become a familiar figure in New York. Yet in essential ways he lives a life apart, holding to his sense of identity with the land to which he will return, worrying about his children's "Americanization," settling his family in enclaves in New Jersey or Westchester—and working 12-hour days trying to accommodate Japanese business practices and philosophy to the American scene.

Japanese trade operations began in the United States a century ago, but their activity was mostly limited to sales offices. As Japanese products gained increased American acceptance in the 1970's, Japanese companies began setting up offices in the States to tap American technology and study American markets firsthand. And with the yen growing ever stronger against the dollar, Japanese investment here has burgeoned.

Manufacturing and assembly facilities have been added to the list of banks and sales offices. And the process has been encouraged by the Japanese Government, under international pressures to reduce the nation's balance-of-payments surpluses.

The Japanese success in capturing major markets in electronics and automobiles is well known: Sony, Sanyo,

The Japanese Abroad

Japanese children at play.

Honda, Toyota and Datsun are household words. But the Japanese have also made inroads in such areas as chemicals and sewing machines. YKK Zipper (U.S.A.), the American subsidiary of the world's largest zipper company, has captured 20 percent of the $1 billion American zipper market. Fuji Photo Film U.S.A. is taking on Kodak on its own turf with expectations of wresting away up to 10 percent of the United States market.

The Japanese executive who comes to New York to serve in these companies finds a very different way of doing business. In Japan, for example, businessmen seldom make definite appointments to see one another. When a visitor arrives, they take time. Japanese workers leave the office when the day's work is finished, not before. More than one Japanese executive has been astonished to see his American staff march out at 5 P.M.

The quantity of correspondence in the United States is another surprise. "Americans send too many letters," said Toshitaka Okazawa, a representative here for the Kirin Brewery. "It is like a contractual society," the legally trained executive said. "In Japan, we trust each other." There is no need to put things in writing because a verbal commitment is enough. "There is no need to confirm and reconfirm."

Meanwhile, the trading companies have continued to proliferate, with more than 90 of them in New York.

They cluster in midtown where Mitsui & Company (U.S.A.), for example, with annual contract sales of $4.3 billion, is within snarling distance of the Mitsubishi International Corporation, with 1976 trading transactions of $6.8 billion.

With the trading and manufacturing companies have arrived a host of Japanese banks, most of which do almost 80 percent of their business with Japanese companies.

"Twenty years ago," said Tanehiko Kamiura, executive vice president of the Fuji Bank and Trust Company, a subsidiary of the Fuji Bank, "there were fewer than five Japanese banks in New York. Now there are about 30." The Bank of Tokyo Trust Company, the largest, had assets of $150 million a decade ago. As of last June, assets exceeded $2.4 billion.

The Japanese who have come to work in these companies and banks have found, basically, a very different society. Japanese spend their lives with a single company, and they are expected to be steady performers rather than superstars, interested in gradual growth in sales and earnings; flashy results are not encouraged. The policy of Sumitomo Shoji America, a trading company, is typical: "To look for speculative profit is, in no case, allowed."

Said Mr. Kamiura of Fuji Bank and Trust: "We are not brought up to act as individuals. So Japanese tend to think in terms of a group. We work for the benefit of all, not just ourselves."

The businessman works long hours —routinely, from 9 A.M. to 11 P.M.— and spends much of that time in discussions.

"Japanese work by consensus," said an executive at Hitachi America. Everyone must contribute to the decision so there will be no dissension later. "It sometimes takes a long time for everyone to agree, but once they agree, then we work fast."

Americans tend to take this team philosophy for clannishness and the Japanese dedication and loyalty to the job as ambition. But to the Japanese their companies are more than a place to work—they are very much an extension of the family.

Hiroyuki Sato, vice president and general manager of Mitsui & Company (U.S.A.), considers the assistance of new employees one of his major responsibilities. Among other services, he often greets them at the airport on their arrival and helps them find homes—he estimates he's arranged for housing for 200 employees during his 11 years in New York.

Many executives—Mr. Sato is one— go back and forth, Tokyo to New York, several times during their careers. The first time, though, is apt to be the toughest.

When Yoshio Amura, a 32-year-old engineer, arrived in New York from Japan last month, he came without his wife and children. It is his company's policy, typical for Japanese concerns here, to give employees a three-month adjustment period to buy a car, find a house and take care of other necessary arrangements before their families join them.

For most Japanese executives, the adjustment period includes intensive study of English. Like many of his compatriots, Mr. Amura is worried about that. "I can do a good job here," he said falteringly, "if I can learn to speak English."

Yet Japanese companies here are structured so that Japanese employees spend most of their time with other Japanese, who comprise at least 10 percent of the workforce.

Typically, working hours include the evening sessions that are an integral part of Japanese business practice. Colleagues and clients meet in leisurely fashion over dinner or drinks. Some 200 Japanese restaurants in New York cater to this trade, many with upstairs piano bars where the nostalgic newcomer can find solace.

Much of the businessman's New York life centers on such organizations as the Japanese Chamber of Commerce and the Japan Society. The Nippon Club at 145 West 57th Street, with a membership of 2,800, is at the center of social activity. It has dining facilities, banquet and meeting rooms, a beauty shop, a baseball league, group excursions and classes of all kinds. Dignitaries and visitors are ushered through the club's elegant red-carpeted lobby, complete with rock garden and a pond for live carp, on their way to meet Japanese society in New York.

Japanese businessmen consider the New York assignment a plum. It usually means a promotion and a higher salary, with a life-style more luxurious than they had enjoyed in Tokyo. Middle-management executives here can afford more appliances and better homes than they ever could in Japan.

Most live in five metropolitan sites: Manhattan; Flushing, Queens; Riverdale, the Bronx; Westchester County, and Fort Lee, N. J. More than 1,500 Japanese have moved into the Fort Lee area in the last two years; many stores have Japanese-speaking clerks to cater to them.

The greatest fear among the Japanese is that their children will be handicapped by having lived in the United States. All Japanese executives, no matter how long they spend here, expect to return to Japan. And they know that, without fluency in Japanese, it is impossible for a child to succeed in the gruellingly competitive Japanese system, which requires long hours of preparation for shiken jigoku, or "examination hell." These tests select a limited number of the best and the brightest who will go through the narrow gates—or semaki-mon—to a Japanese university.

The businessmen worry about their children's vocational chances should they not be selected, and about their daughters' chances of finding Japanese husbands when their language and education are inadequate. Rather than expose their children to such danger, some businessmen who come to the States leave their wives and families in Japan.

The Japanese have established Saturday morning schools to try to help their 2,000 school-age children stay up to back-home standards. And an all-day Japanese school with tuition of $1,400 a year has been set up in Queens, but it can accommodate only 223 students, and there are hundreds on the waiting list.

The problem was described feelingly by Masahiro Yoshida, an executive vice president of a zipper company, who has been in the United States for eight years. His children have never lived in Japan, and they speak English 70 percent of the time, Japanese about 30 percent. "They are Americans," he said. "Someday they must make a home in a land they know nothing about."

October 23, 1977

Rising Number Of Emigrants: Asset for Japan

By ANDREW H. MALCOLM

TOKYO, Nov. 6—Tomoyoshi Nakajima is a member of an unusual, growing, yet little-known group of Japanese. He wants to leave his country permanently.

And he is leaving. In a few days Mr. Nakajima and 57 other Japanese citizens will board a jet plane here to join the steady stream moving to lives and careers in other countries.

Of course, the crowded, urbanized islands of Japan are not likely to be depopulated in the future by any gigantic exodus. But since 1868, when Japan began allowing emigration, one million Japanese have left to seek their fortunes abroad.

Today, with their descendants born overseas, about 1.6 million ethnic Japanese are scattered throughout the world.

And on the average, 17 now leave here every day, almost all of them for North or South America.

Their reasons are basically the same as for emigrants anywhere—the possibility of occupational or social advancement, personal or financial difficulties, a simple desire for change or extended travel abroad and the lure of adventure in Western lands, which to many Japanese often appear romantic and exotic.

Additionally, emigrants speak of the danger of future energy shortages, economic hard times and unemployment in Japan, a resource-poor country dependent on other lands for 99 percent of its oil and substantial amounts of most other raw materials and food.

Implicit in Japan's liberal emigration policy is the hope that the accomplishments and cultural and family ties of Japanese abroad will help improve relations with the emigrants' new homelands, and enhance access to their resources and markets.

More Young Emigrating

In recent years the characteristics of the Japanese emigrants, and the Japanese population as a whole, have been changing. The number of emigrating farm families has decreased while the ranks of young, unmarried skilled workers from the cities has grown. Some of them say they are seeking a challenge overseas that they cannot find in the comfortable confines of modern Japan.

But if the thought of 6,000 well-educated citizens fleeing an affluent, middleclass life each year does not match the usual image of a refugee, then neither does the Japanese Government's attitude seem to fit that of a nation spurned.

Japan may be the only country that presses lavish assistance on its outgoing emigrants, briefing them, training them and even paying the air fare to their new prices from the local Japanese aid agency. homeland, where the settlers can borrow money or buy good land at reasonable

This policy, which is seen officially as an integral part of Japan's foreign aid efforts to help developing countries, is in marked contrast to the policy toward immigrants to Japan.

That policy is basically that there should be no immigrants, not even temporary ones such as Vietnamese refugees with no confirmed acceptance by other countries. Overlooking the possible element of racial hostility toward outsiders in this homogeneous society, Foreign Ministry officials attribute the policy to Japan's small size, about the area of California, and its large population, 113 million.

It is the same immigration policy followed by Japanese governments for centuries, even when the population was considerably smaller. As for emigration, until the overthrow of feudalism in Japan in 1868 it was impossible, since it was illegal to own a boat large enough to be seaworthy.

The first Japanese emigrants left in 1868 for Hawaii. The movement was largest during the Depression, with Brazil then the most popular destination, at times drawing 20,000 a year. World War II interrupted the flow until 1952, when it resumed to average 10,000 a year until

the mid 1960's, a period of rapid economic growth. The numbers fell to about 4,000 then, but they have risen again to 6,000 a year. Some officials expect the number to grow if further economic hard times fall on Japan.

U.S. Is Most Popular

The United States remains the most popular destination, drawing almost half the annual total, or 2,684 last year. An estimated 620,000 Japanese and their descendants live there. Latin America takes the next largest total, as a result of emigration treaties with Japan and the ties of family members already there.

For the recipient countries, the emigrants produce the opposite of the brain drain, a brain gain. For Japan they are a minimal manpower loss that may have valuable side effects in foreign policy and trade, especially with countries rich in natural resources.

"Emigration is a spontaneous act of each individual seeking happiness for his own reasons," said Katsuhiko Tsunoda, director of the Foreign Ministry's emigration division. "These people are useful to developing areas, and they help promote international understanding, so we consider it useful to help them."

His division, together with the Japan International Cooperation Agency, a government body, help negotiate openings

for emigrants, broaden their trade and linguistic skills before departure and help match workers here with work there.

In the case of Mr. Nakajima, a motor technician, the agency placed a job-wanted advertisement in a Brazilian newspaper, relayed the responses, gave him six months of additional mechanical training plus some Portuguese lessons and will pay 80 percent of his plane fare.

"For years I've been thinking of getting out of this country to build my life in a foreign land," said the 29-year-old Mr. Nakajima. "Japan is too stuffy and formal, and everybody's life runs on a preset rail. Overseas, you get paid according to your ability, not your seniority. And I think my money will go farther there."

The emigration decision was easy for Kogo Saito but difficult for his wife and three children. His small plastics company has had hard times since the 1973 oil crisis. Last winter he visited Paraguay at his own expense to study the setting. As a result, the family will leave Nov. 26 to start a farm and then a cattle ranch.

Almost all the emigrants speak of the severe wrenches their moves cause families. Mr. Nakajima's mother said, "I thought he was joking at first. But he was serious. And now I ask him, "Why must you go to such a remote land?'"

November 7, 1977

The Japanese Presence Inobtrusively Makes Itself Felt

By MICHAEL GOODWIN

Hideo Kitayama has been in this country since 1923, when he was 20 years old. He has lived in New York since he was released from a Japanese "relocation" camp after World War II. One of his fondest memories is of West 65th Street. He remembers it as a place where, in the days before Lincoln Center, many of his countrymen lived and worked, giving the area the makings of a very little Little Japan.

"There was a restaurant, a rooming house and all kinds of food stores," Mr. Kitayama recalled. "Of course, some Caucasians lived there, too, but almost

every house was occupied by Japanese. They all scattered when Lincoln Center came."

Scatter is the correct word, for now there are Japanese communities in Flushing and Forest Hills, Queens, in Manhattan, in Riverdale, the Bronx, and in Westchester County and Fort Lee, N.J.

The influx of Japanese in recent years has quietly left an imprint on the metropolitan region, spawning not only residential communities but also any number of such small businesses as Japanese bookshops, restaurants and clothing stores. In midtown Manhattan there is a Japanese hotel, the Kitano, which is owned by the Kitano Arms Company, a

subsidiary of one of Japan's major construction concerns. And on television, there are even special Japanese-language programs.

Depending on where one goes for estimates, the Japanese here now number anywhere from 18,000 (the Japanese Consulate) to 40,000 (the Overseas Courier Service, newspaper importers and publishers). Nearly everyone agrees, however, that about 75 percent of the total, any total, are here on business assignments lasting three to five years.

While those planning to stay have increasingly adopted American ways, much as immigrants from other nations have, those here on business are keenly

75

aware that too much Americanization would make re-entry into Japanese society difficult, and they accordingly tend to be more Japanese.

"There is no friction between us," said Mr. Kitayama, who works with the Japanese-American Association of New York. "We don't bother them and they don't bother us."

●

Shigemi Morita, who has been here since 1954 and who says he is the only real estate broker in the city who speaks Japanese, has benefited handsomely from the influx of the nearly 500 Japanese companies that now have offices here. He has been involved in nearly 50 real estate deals and has some observations about his countrymen's difficulties.

"Language is the biggest problem, especially when dealing with real estate matters," Mr. Morita said in almost flawless English. "They can't read the lease, so it's hard to sign."

But reading the lease is only part of their problem, Mr. Morita added. "There are so many restrictons on remodeling and that kind of thing," he said. "And once you sign, it's very difficult to back out. The leases here are mostly prepared for the benefit of the landlord. I have to explain to them this is the way we do business in the United States."

His Japanese clients often mistake gross space for net space, he said, and sometimes wind up with 25 percent less usable space than they need.

He cited as a further difficulty, a minor one, that some Japanese try to avoid the fourth floor in much the same manner that Americans try to avoid the 13th. It seems that the pronunciation of the character "four" is the same as that for "death."

●

The postwar trickle of Japanese immigration to New York became a flow during and after the 1964-65 World's Fair in Flushing. Many Japanese companies set up exhibitions there, and their employees and families found housing in the surrounding neighborhoods.

And while the suburbs are popular among those Japanese who can afford them, Flushing remains the heart of the Japanese community. Perhaps some 4,000 or so live there, with others not far off in Forest Hills.

On a recent Saturday afternoon, families from New Jersey, Manhattan, Riverdale and Westchester could be found at 41-54 Main Street in Flushing, site of Main Street Foods Inc. Seaweed, dried mushrooms, squid and other salted and dried fish were only some of the edible reasons business was booming.

"Our way of life is American, but as you can see, food—we prefer Japanese

Hotel Kitano, New York, has a distinctively Japanese flavor.

food," said Toshiyuki Okamoto, who lives in Hartsdale and works in Manhattan for Mitsui Trust. "Fortunately, we can get the food we want here."

To be sure, Japanese food is no problem in New York. There were, at last count, some 200 Japanese restaurants in and around the city, in addition to a number of mini-supermarkets, of which Main Street Foods is the largest.

According to Minoru Hirano, who owns the Tenryu Restaurant on West 46th Street and parts of four grocery stores in New Jersey, 90 percent of these restaurants are owned and operated by investors in Japan.

●

Kaoru Tsukamoto came to New York five years ago, carrying a photograph of the man her father had arranged for her to marry. In somewhat of a break with tradition, though, she came early so she could meet her finace before the wedding. She liked him, and now she and

Mamoru Tsukamoto live on the top floor of a Flushing high-rise. It had to be the top floor, she said, because "my husband is crazy about ham radios."

Keeping in character with her desire for an advance peek of her then husband-to-be, Mrs. Tsukamoto also has broken with the custom of most Japanese women here by getting a job in an American company. She studied nights at the Fashion Institute of Technology and is now a weaver. Mr. Tsukamoto works with a Japanese electronics concern. They are not sure when they will be sent back to Japan, but Mrs. Tsukamoto is in no hurry.

"I was very lonely at first, but I wanted to know American people and American ways," she said. "It's really been a good experience, and we have a good life now. I'm really satisfied."

Satisfied. It is a word one hears often when talking with the Japanese. Those here on business often live partially at company expense, and their executives, some of whom live in company-owned or -rented homes in such places as Scarsdale and have chauffeurs, can afford to live in a well-heeled fashion—the opera, the theater and weekends in the country.

In addition, the Nippon Club and the Japan Society offer back-home settings and most of the women have the opportunity to join one or more wonmen's groups.

●

The 500 companies and 200 restau-

rants, not to mention the need for employes' housing, has had what industry observers say is a substantial impact on the real estate market, especially office space in Manhattan. Sylvan Lawrence, probably the major owner in Lower Manhattan, has several Japanese clients, including the Bank of Tokyo and the Bank of Tokyo Trust, which jointly lease 16 of the 23 floors in Mr. Lawrence's building at 100 Broadway.

"I find them very honorable people," he said.

Howard P. Malloy, a vice president of Helmsley-Spear Inc., has negotiated deals for a number of Japanese companies in Manhattan, including four financial institutions now leasing space at 140 Broadway. He, too, says he enjoys working with the Japanese and finds them excellent tenants, even if some of their business habits are a bit unorthodox by American standards.

"Usually, they want the top floor," Mr. Malloy said. "Some firms even send people over to take pictures out of every window so they can judge the view. They would not usually consider a floor below another Japanese firm."

●

Prestige, it seems, is as Japanese as raw fish. Several brokers noted that Japanese clients go first for "name" buildings, regardless of price. Even better is the top floor of a name building. And even better yet is to have the deal for the top floor of a name building negotiated by a name broker.

The desire for things prestigious, however, does not end at the office. Everything from dark business suits to whisky are bought according to their brands, just as playing golf and mahjong are the required social graces.

One woman declined to be interviewed for this article until after her husband's bosses' wives had had their turn. In the end, all three requested anonymity so as not to embarrass their husbands or their husbands' company.

The Japanese, whether here permanently or temporarily, still seem to feel that America is the land of opportunity and that it is good to be here. At least, that is the impression of Michael Rubin, an American who is bilingual coordinator for three public elementary schools in Riverdale, one of which has 200 Japanese students.

Mr. Rubin, who speaks Japanese, works closely with both children and parents. He says that Japanese parents are very active in school affairs, and notes that the teachers in Riverdale are very glad that the Japanese are here, one reason being the Gucci and Mark Cross gifts they receive on proper occassions.

"Things are going well here in Riverdale," Mr. Rubin said. "The Japanese have a way of taking an American custom, like giving gifts at Christmas, and observing it more religiously than Americans. They've adapted quite well."

November 27, 1977

Japanese Brokers Cultivate an American Image on Wall St.

By HENRY SCOTT-STOKES

Yoshitoki Chino, deputy president of Daiwa Securities, one of Japan's Big Four brokerage houses, has a superb 17th century gold screen in his Tokyo office—inherited from his samurai ancestors of the Tokugawa era.

The same man has decreed that no Japanese works of art, nor scrolls, nor paintings shall be on view in the front offices of Daiwa's American subsidiary on Wall Street.

It's part of a move to Americanization—by which the Japanese mean anything from changing the office decor and hiring Americans for top jobs—a strategy used by the Big Four in efforts to improve their dismal profits here.

The Big Four of Japan—Daiwa, Nikko, Nomura and Yamaichi Securities—make huge profits in Tokyo, where they dominate the world's second largest stock market as brokers, dealers and underwriters.

Nomura Securities recently announced net profits for the year ending September 1977 of $140 million, the highest figure ever recorded by a broker anywhere in the world. Merrill Lynch's last net figure was $107 million, a record, in 1976.

But in America the Japanese have lost money for much of the last 25 years. Why are the Big Four here?

The reasons include the following:

¶They provide Wall Street information to their head offices in Japan, which greatly influences the Kabutucho, the Tokyo stock market.

¶They train their Japanese staffs to speak English and to use American business methods.

¶They sell Japanese securities to Americans, American stocks to Japanese, and underwrite United States domestic bond and Japanese share issues in America.

The Big Four do not make money directly in America by collecting information. "But it is very, very useful to our people in Tokyo," said Taro Yamada, executive vice president at Yamaichi International America.

"We learned here such basic concepts as those of growth stocks and price/earnings ratios, which were the key to the development of the Tokyo stock market in the golden age, the 1960's, when the Japanese economy

Keisuke Egashira
Nomura Securities Int.

Haruzo Hayakawa
Nikko Securities Co., Int.

A free adaptation of the characters above this bond salesman' drawing
in an advertisement is "Grab it now."

Hisashi Kawahara
Yamaichi Int. (America)

Jiro Yamana
Daiwa Securities America

was growing at more than 10 percent a year in real terms."

These concepts have since died on Wall Street. And they are no longer winners in Tokyo. But in the 1960's and early 1970's the Big Four used them to revolutionize the Kabutucho, while the market shot from little over 1,000 to more than 5,000 on the Dow Jones index.

Teaching Japanese executives to speak English was also essential because the boom in foreign buying of Japanese stocks, which started in the early 1960's, dictated that the Big Four have scores of people who were fluent in English.

The presidents of the Big Four's American subsidiaries, including Hisashi Kawahara at Yamaichi, all speak excellent English after decades of international experience. "But it took us many years of painful effort to learn," said Jiro Yamana, president of Daiwa Securities America.

The hardest task is just to do business here, however. "In the early 1960's we began to do well and make money," said Ryozo Kobayashi, executive vice president at Nikko Securities International, "but then came the interest equalization tax, and that wiped us out for most of a decade—we are starting again from zero."

The tax, which started in 1963, imposed a 15 percent charge on purchases by Americans of foreign stocks and brought American buying of Japanese securities to a halt. After it was lifted three years ago, the attractions of the

Tokyo market, hit by the oil crisis, had diminished. Sales of American stock to Japanese investors also went very slowly.

Because profits were hard to make, the Big Four kept their offices here small. The number of employees ranges in size from 27 (Nikko) to 105 (Nomura) on annual revenues ranging from $3 million or less up to $5 million.

About half of the Big Four's American revenues come from brokers' commissions. But they make little profit on stock transactions while volume remains low—American investors have actually been selling Japanese stocks since March, taking profits as the yen rose against the dollar—and they must share commissions with American houses such as Merrill Lynch because they are not members of the New York Stock Exchange.

Expansion of Underwriting

Their strategy is to expand underwriting, on which profits are much higher. The Big Four join underwriting syndicates and have participated in about 500 bond issues this year, lead by Nomura with over 150 participations.

"What we have to do is to push up our underwriting bracket," said Toshio Mori, former president of Nikko's United States subsidiary, who has just been replaced by Haruzo Hayakawa. The underwriting bracket of a house determines the amount of bonds a syndicate gives it to sell.

"This is a tough business," said Mr. Yamada of Yamaichi, "because we sell United States domestic bonds to American clients. Few Japanese investors

will touch them." The competition of American underwriters is severe, and the Europeans often outdo the Japanese, too.

"Recently the Swedes came in and set up Scandinavian Securities," said Keisuke Egashira, president of Nomura Securities International, "and they immediately jumped to a higher bracket than Nomura by establishing the right connections and hiring Americans."

Scandinavian Securities, which was set up by the Skandinaviska Enskilda Banken last year, invited Eugene Black, former president of the World Bank, to be chairman, hired top flight American executives and obtained the support of Citibank and Morgan Stanley in underwriting.

"We have to ask ourselves," said Mr. Egashira, "whether this is an example that Nomura can follow, whether we can become truly American, too—or are we doomed to remain largely as liaison offices?"

Mr. Egashira, whose office is decorated with a huge picture of Mt. Fuji, is in favor of "Americanization" and has hired several American vice presidents since he came here two years ago.

But head offices in Tokyo are extremely reluctant to give local autonomy to their foreign subsidiaries and run their world-wide networks of offices on a taut rein.

And Mr. Egashira acknowledged in an interview that progrfess would be slow and that "the changes which we want to implement could take 20 or even 50 years to yield a major result," he said.

December 5, 1977

YKK Zipper
Finds Success in the South

By WAYNE KING

MACON, Ga.—At the YKK Zipper Company here, cautionary signs around the plant read: "Safety First, Quality Second, Production Third." This is an attitude that would seem rare in the highly competitive Southern textile industry.

But the situation here is something different inasmuch as YKK is a Japanese company with a Japanese business philosophy, set down in the middle of southern Georgia.

At the four-year-old installation here, the traditional Japanese company song is seldom heard, except when a supervisor returns home, and then it is only the Japanese who sing it. But if Macon workers do not know the words, they do appear to know the tune, and the transplant of the paternalistic Japanese management techniques to this superficially very foreign climate appears to have been a success, although a qualified one.

After four years in Georgia, YKK (U.S.A.) Incorporated, which produces 850-miles of zippers a day (enough in a year to unzip the globe around the equator) is undergong an expansion that will add another 165,000 square feet of manufacturing space to the 330,000 already here. The company employs 300 people, and projects 500 in two years.

Both sales and company profits have increased each year since the plant opened, said a company spokesman, with 1977 "a banner year."

The decision to expand here rather than at any one of the giant company's 31 other plants around the world, including three others in the United States, at Chicago, New Jersey and Los Angeles, was related in part to market, but a major factor was the favorable employe climate.

'Very Productive' Worker

"We have found that the southern worker was very productive," said Marvin Cooperberg, a transplanted New Yorker who has worked for YKK for 11 years and is now vice president of the Macon plant. "In some cases southern workers exceeded what was expected. I guess it's good training and good feeling."

The Japanese management technique and corporate attitude differ substantially from that of American industry. Primarily, there is greater cooperation, an effort to generate intense company loyalty, to make the worker feel he or she is a member of a family that holds the worker interest on par with that of the company.

At the same time, caution in parts of the plants, possibly hazardous with unfenced roller-bearing conveyers and oil-slick concrete floors, would seem a necessity.

The company operates on what its founder and president, Tadao Yoshido calls "the cycle of goodness." If productivity increases, for example, the savings in cost per item produced is distributed in thirds: one third to the buyer in the form of a price reduction, one third to the company for expansion or profit, and one-third to the worker as a bonus or wage increase. Too, operating on the thesis that "wages alone are not sufficient to insure our employees of a stable life and a rising standard of living," employees can invest at least 10 percent of their salaries in the company and 50 percent of bonuses. "The savings of all YKK employees, Mr. Yoshido writes in a company brochure, "are used to improve production facilities, and contribute directly to the prosperity of the company. Superior production facilities improve the quality of the good produced. Lower prices increase demand."

This accelerated economic climate, with attendant spinoffs in income, investment, tax payments, and so forth, Mr. Yoshido writes, creates a cycle which "enriches our free society and contributes to the happiness of those who work within it. The perpetual working of this cycle produces perpetual prosperity for all. This is the cycle of goodness."

Hand in hand, with such business principles—a kind of Puritanism overlayed with something vaguely mystical—YKK encourages total immersion in company affairs.

Each supervisor—about half our Japanese, slowly being phased out in favor of home grown types—holds meetings daily with his employees, and even the top company brass, such as Ken Kitano, the plant president, makes daily tours and speak personally to as many employes as possible.

Mr. Kitano, who wears a grey poplin company jacket, similar to a golf jacket, with a corporate monogram, instead of a grey flannel suit, shows none of the aloofness characteristic of American corporate executives.

"I go out and listen, I listen how to make an idea," said Mr. Kitano, who is almost never in his small, spare office. "Marvin (Cooperberg), he does this also, and this way we improve, we improve."

The system is at base a highly democratic one, with management lines of authority far more blurred than in an American plant. All management personnel are encouraged to listen, not simply to give orders.

"You know, it is your frontier system," said Mr. Kitano. "Your father, your grandfather, did this—but now you forget. But in the south, you understand."

February 18, 1978

New York a Strain
for Wives of Japanese Businessmen

By EDWIN McDOWELL

Every morning after her husband leaves for work in Manhattan, Sachiko Watanabe begins another long, lonely day in her apartment in Hartsdale in Westchester County. With luck she might see her husband around midnight. Meanwhile, she will spend a good part of the day confined to her modern apartment, staring at the Japanese scrolls on the wall and dreaming of home.

"Sachiko Watanabe" is not her real name but she is a real person. Moreover, she is typical of many wives of Japanese businessmen in the New York area, a growing number of whom are having serious problems adjusting to their new surroundings.

Their problems go beyond the usual difficulties of Japanese assigned to New York in coping with a vastly different culture.

Although most Japanese wives in New York, like their husbands and children, appear to survive the usual three-to-five year assignment without incident, serious maladjustment cases seem to be on the rise, manifested in psychological disorientation, depression, and, in some cases, suicide.

Considering a Hot Line

Indeed, the difficulties are regarded as so serious that the Union of Protestant Churches in Japan (Kyodan) recently sent a minister to New York to assist primarily the wives of Japanese businessmen.

Other ministers and doctors concerned about the problems, including the Rev. Justin Haruyama of the Japanese American United Church of Christ in Manhattan, are considering a hot-line telephone program with counselors fluent in Japanese.

The Japanese now represent the largest foreign business colony in New York City. From fewer than 300 businesses and 4,000 nationals here in 1964, the Japanese presence has grown to almost 450 companies and approximately 20,000 businessmen and their families.

Contributing to the normal strains are the work habits, particularly the long hours, of Japanese husbands, inadequate preparation for life in the United States, and a widespread belief that seeking professional help would signify personal weakness and perhaps bring shame to the family and the husband's employer.

Accurate statistics about the problems are not available, in part because the Japanese colony is dispersed throughout the metropolitan area. Moreover, Japanese companies here and the Japanese Consulate say they are not aware of the problem.

'Nobody Gives a Damn'

"Japan is a close-knit society, where there are many relatives to discuss problems with and who give support," said Dr. Yori Kumasaka, a psychiatrist who has treated a number of Japanese housewives suffering from several maladjustment problems. "Traditionally Japanese culture itself has built-in psychological help and support.

"But in New York, it's exactly the other way around—nobody gives a damn, you're left alone," said Dr. Kumasaka.

Hiroshi Suzuki, a pastoral psychothera-

pist from Japan who has heard of "a substantial number of serious breakdowns and suicides" among Japanese wives here, said: "The Japanese businessman's workday in New York is 7 A.M. to 11 P.M. Even the healthiest housewife would have trouble coping with that."

"The more devoted Japanese wives are to their husband's career, the worse the problem," said Dr. Norike Lippit, Japanese-born, Yale-educated assistant professor of comparative literature at the University of Southern California. "When Japanese women have problems, they tend to blame themselves and they suffer tremendous guilt, and serious psychological problems."

Moonray Kojima, a New York lawyer, said that six years ago, when he was president of the Japanese American Citizens League, "we tried to help these wives, because we knew how serious the problem was." "But we ran up against a brick wall everywhere we turned—the Nippon Club, the Consulate," he said. "It must be part of the mentality that Japanese wives are expected to be strong."

'Snobbiness' a Problem

In interviews, a number of psysicians agreed that the wives were strong, perhaps more tolerant of isolation than most other women. But the psychological conditions under which they live in New York, said Dr. Kumasaka, who is on the faculty of New York University Medical Center, are sometimes too much even for women raised in a society that puts a premium on stoicism.

The principal problem of loneliness is exacerbated by the "hierarchical" residential system common to Japanese. "There's a certain snobbiness among Japanese companies, between the élite and nonélite," said George Yamaoka, the first Japanese-American admitted to the New York State Bar. "It sometimes causes tension."

"In the U.S., wives don't usually choose friends thinking of their husbands' careers," said Professor Lippit. "But Japanese wives have to be careful not to be mixed up with wives not of their social status."

Another matter of concern is children's education, for which Japanese wives are traditionally responsible.

The three to five years that a Japanese child spends in the American school system, at least beyond the earliest years, just about precludes his admission to a prestige university. And in Japan, more than most places, career prospects are closely tied to the college one attends.

Fear that their children will lose out in the educational race causes considerable anxiety among Japanese wives in America, and there is no doubt that Japanese wives sent to America are woefully unprepared to cope with their new surroundings.

Afraid to Answer Phone

Some women, said Katsuya Abe, Japanese-born publisher of the "JOP Journal," aimed at Japanese nationals in the metropolitan area, "are afraid to answer the telephone because they don't know the language." "Some who did, later wound up with a room full of furniture they never ordered, sent C.O.D.," he said.

After several Japanese families in Westchester County telephoned relatives in New York City and asked them to report fires in their Westchester dwellings, Fire Chief Walter Schoonmaker of Hartsdale (where many Japanese families live) ordered distribution of a newsletter in Japanese giving directions for reporting fires.

Critics accuse the companies, some of them multibillion-dollar enterprises, of indifference to the problem and of being primarily interested in protecting their corporate image.

Others, however, criticize the Japanese Consulate. Mr. Abe said: "Every January our JOP Journal prints the Consulate's address, but we skipped it this year when it was clear they didn't care about anything."

Masao Kawai, a spokesman for the Consulate, said: "We have too many Japanese here to have special programs. We cannot take care of husbands and wives."

March 14, 1978

Study Finds Japanese Presence In City Causes No Loss of Jobs

By EMERSON CHAPIN

Has the growth of the Japanese business community in New York taken jobs away from American citizens here?

Evidently not, according to a study conducted for the Japan Society by the Conservation of Human Resources Project of Columbia University, a 28-

year-old organization that has carried out an extensive series of studies on utilization of manpower amid social and technological change. The study produced estimates that for every Japanese worker brought here by a Japanese company, 2.1 local residents are provided jobs in those companies.

Payrolls and other business expenses of the Japanese companies amounted to an estimated $758 million a year, representing more than 1 percent of all

personal income in New York City. And the Japanese companies—there were 436 in the New York area in 1976—pay an estimated total of $95 million in taxes to the local, state and Federal Governments.

Theater Contribution Exceeded

The amount contributed by the Japanese business community to the local economy is seven times that of New York's theater industry, the report says.

The Japanese Abroad

According to Eli Ginzberg, director of the Conservation Project,
study was requested by the Japan Society, as a means of assessing "the legitimacy of the periodic criticisms that
were being raised about the loss of
employment to United States citizens
as a result of the expansion of Japanese business in New York."

The report did not address itself to
complaints from Americans working in
Japanese companies here that they felt
discriminated against and few opportunities for advancement. Japanese employers have acknowledged that there
are difficulties in this area, explaining
that unfamiliarity with Japanese customs, business practices and the difficult Japanese language is at the root
of the problem.

And it acknowledges that "clearly
to some extent the growth" of the
Japanese presence, whether in banking
or restaurants, resulted in the slower
growth or even decline of American
competitors.

Questionnaires Circulated

The survey was conducted through
questionnaires circulated to all companies listed in 1977 as members of the
Japanese Chamber of Commerce of
New York, 115 of which provided "usable information" in response.

Dr. Ginzberg, who is also a professor
at the Graduate School of Business at
Columbia, noted that responses came
from "several companies in each of
the major areas in which the Japanese

business community is well represented—in manufacturing, trading, banking."

But as David MacEachron, executive
director of the private, nonprofit Japan
Society, put it, the study also 'proves
the extensive economic contribution
that the Japanese have made to New
York."

The report notes that "after more
than a decade of rapid growth, the
Japanese business community in New
York has reached a significant size and
is stabilizing." The 436 Japanese corporations with offices here in 1976 had
11,383 employees, with an average salary of $24,000, of whom 3,657 were
Japanese while 7,726 were local personnel. The report did not provide a
breakdown of pay by nationality.

More than 5,200 of the employees
work in offices of manufacturing companies while 3,200 are employed by
the 87 trading companies that had offices here, including the nine largest
of these companies in Japan. About
1,700 people work in Japanese financial institutions here and 1,200 in a
variety of other service companies.

Through the 1960's, trading companies, which carry on a large proportion
of Japan's international trade, accounted for the largest number of employees
here, the statistics showed, but as
Japanese brand names became more
familiar to Americans, individual
manufacturers increasingly set up their
own service networks in the United
States.

"Entering the market in this fashion
generally requires the manufacturer to

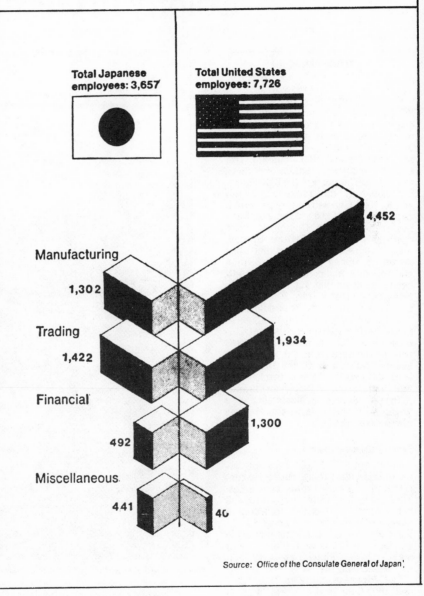

Employment Patterns in Japanese Companies in New York

Total Japanese employees: 3,657

Total United States employees: 7,726

Manufacturing — 1,302 / 4,452

Trading — 1,422 / 1,934

Financial — 492 / 1,300

Miscellaneous — 441 / 40

Source: Office of the Consulate General of Japan.

establish his own office in the United
States rather than relying on a trading
company," it notes.

Among the other findings of the survey are these:

¶"Research in urban economies suggests that the multiplier for employment in metropolitan areas ranges between four and five," meaning that the
12,500 jobs directly traced to Japanese
companies probably support a total of
57,500 local workers.

¶Japanese employees here have 7,262
dependents in the New York area with
them who are estimated to spend well
over $88 million in the area.

¶Japanese corporations are large
users of commercial space, largely in
New York, with total occupancy costs
of $29.8 million."

¶Japanese corporations are large
purchasers of various business services
from advertising, legal, accounting,
financial and other companies based
in New York City, spending more than
$328 million annually on such.

¶The Japanese presence also inspires
tourism and an estimated 162,000 Japanese visit New York annually, spending
about $51 million.

April 6, 1978

Japanese Banking Colony in Germany

By JOHN VINOCUR

Special to The New York Times

DUSSELDORF, West Germany — At the end of the Königsallee, one of the country's most elegant streets, is a neon enclave with signs that read Toshiba, Bank of Tokyo and Asahi Pentax. Thyssen and Klöcknerstahl, two German industrial giants, are there too, but with bit parts in the light show.

Although the city ranks only eighth among West Germany's largest, with a population of 615,000, Japanese businesses have made Düsseldorf their operations center in Central Europe. Now, aggressive competition has grown up among American, German and Japanese banks for a chance to finance the deals that Japanese traders bring back largely from East Europe and occasionally from the Middle East.

The most vigorous competitors have their own Japanese specialists. At Citibank he is Yutaka Amano, who was transferred here from Tokyo, as were Susumu Nakada of Chase and Hidetsugu Yoshikoshi of the Deutschebank. Morgan Guaranty's Düsseldorf branch manager, Steven Schlossstein, is a Texan with fluent Japanese who has also served in Tokyo.

Seven Japanese Banks

There are about 4,000 Japanese living in Düsseldorf representing 192 concerns, 42 of them trading companies. They are backed up by seven Japanese banks whose total assets, according to most recent figures, are about 4.3 billion deutschemarks. The total of loans on their books — and this is what makes business interesting — is 2.3 billion deutschemarks.

The Japanese came to Düsseldorf and the Ruhr after World War II mainly to buy equipment and know-how. They stayed, setting up their own schools, restaurants, bookshops and, this August, a hotel, but became sellers rather than buyers. With the European Common Market's tightened attitudes on the import of Japanese steel and ships, the trading companies here have focused increasingly on Eastern Europe as a market for heavy machinery, ready-built factories and oil refineries. Japanese exports to the Warsaw Pact countries grew 21.5 percent last year, compared with export growth of 8.6 percent to the Common Market.

Downtown Dusseldorf, where 4,000 Japanese represent 192 concerns.

German Information Center

A leading German exporter of heavy equipment concedes that the Japanese constitute very tough competition in the Middle East. "Their strength comes not only from the relatively low wages in Japan, but also because the Japanese companies can often offer their customers lower interest rates through the Export-Import Bank of Japan than German and American companies can offer," he said.

Help Sought from U.S. Banks

Because financing deals with countries in Eastern Europe and the Mediterranean basin is more difficult for the

Japanese — Poland, Turkey and Algeria are examples of countries that have trouble in getting cash — there is more help sought from the big American banks here.

"Personal contact is everything with the Japanese," said Mr. Schlossstein, whose bank has had to turn down some Japanese-Eastern European business this spring because of exposure considerations. "It is really a case where the banker who drinks sake with a client" — Mr. Schlossstein is the only Western member of the local Japanese club — "or can talk about the sumo wrestling scores with him, is more likely to get a call than someone with whom a Japanese businessman might not feel as comfortable."

According to the American banks themselves, their advantages in Düsseldorf are the ability to move quickly and very good access to international money markets. Their Japanese specialists also understand that it is not a Japanese custom for a bank to charge a fee, as it might elsewhere, for consultation on a merger or an acquistion.

Extremely Close Relations

The American banks' disadvantage is that their Japanese competitors have extremely close relations with the trading companies and manufacturers, contacts so narrow that an executive of an American bank said, "The man from Fuji Bank and Mitsubishi almost go out prospecting holding hands."

The basic pattern of Japanese sales involves a representative going out from Düsseldorf to Warsaw or Ankara, for example, seeing ministerial, bank

ing and industry people, and then returning here with an idea of what kind of business can be done. The financing problems are turned over to the banks and they move as quickly as they can to get into the business.

"Very often we'll be offered the worst pickings," an official of one of the non-Japanese banks said. "For example, handling a 12-year North Vietnamese heavy-industry loan, which, frankly is pushing it. That kind of stuff has to be turned down."

Mr. Nakada, who has been with Chase for 25 years, neatly skirted the problem by saying: "Part of our job is really showing that we can handle the Japanese companies' business anywhere and that they're dealing with a genuinely worldwide operation. Much of our work involves counseling and just listening well. The direct rewards are not always visible there."

Most direct business between Japan and West Germany is handled by banks from the two countries, but the Ameri-

cans are increasingly interested, staying close to a trend that has developed over the last two to three years for more direct Japanese investment in West Germany.

Wega, the Sony sister company, Toyota, NTN Roller Bearings, the Canon camera company and Kawasaki are among concerns that have recently set up facilities in West Germany.

Mr. Schlossstein, who was having a sake with Toshio Takeuchi, deputy general manager of the Bank of Tokyo, the other night, said that "it's pretty interesting what you can hear in the space of an evening."

"You hear a lot about the Tokyo giants, first of all, but then there's so-and-so's last trip here or there," he said. "I suppose it's the country club school of doing business, but with the Japanese, and particularly in this town, if you don't do it, you can be sure the competition will."

July 5, 1978

The Marunouchi section of Tokyo, with many of the country's leading banks, is the economic heart of Japan.

Chapter 4

Japan's Economy

All signs contribute to the impression that the Japanese economy is booming. Large trade surpluses, omnipresent wealth at home, unprecedented tourism around the world, profitable economic invasions into all continents and the soaring exchange value of the yen all characterize Japan's economy. Yet the nation's leaders claim the economy is flagging, even stagnating. The problem appears to be one of perspective.

While the large Japanese conglomerates like Mitsubishi and Mitsui were recording new highs in profits, smaller firms went bankrupt at the rate of more than 1,500 a month. Japan has a huge trade surplus, but it is complemented by a sluggish home economy where government restrictions on imports and a high rate of inflation have impeded growth. Thus, the economy produces for export. Trade soars while domestic business founders.

Over the past few years the United States has been encouraging Japan to stimulate her economy and last year threatened exchange rate manipulations to underscore its concern. Prime Minister Fukuda proposed a plan in August 1977 to raise the domestic rate by cutting foreign reserve holdings. Even he, however, raised doubts about the feasibility of immediate sharp changes.

In October 1977 the Japanese government announced plans to spend $7.6 billion to shore up its economy and to reduce Japan's foreign trade imbalance. By the end of 1977, the government was speaking of increased purchases of foreign goods to cut surpluses in the 1978 budget.

Early in 1978 the Japanese minister of finance, Michiya Matsukawa, detailed a plan whereby imports would rise 13% while exports would rise only 7%. A $9 billion package in public works and plans to import aircraft, uranium and crude oil from abroad were the principal stimulative elements in the government's new economic policy. The results have proved disappointing. Imports continued to lag and the national growth rate dropped far below even the most pessimistic projections.

By August 1978, the exchange value of the yen had risen to an unprecedented level, under 200 to the U.S. dollar. On several occasions the Bank of Japan has bought up billions of U.S. dollars in an effort to reverse this trend, but without any apparent success. An extremely high exchange value for the yen might be regarded as crippling to the economy because Japanese goods would be priced out of the export market. But as the yen rises, the cost of imported raw materials drops. This diminution has a moderating effect on retail prices. By late July 1978 there were still calls for the government to take action upon public works spending and a 2-trillion yen ($10 billion) income tax cut.

In general, the large industrial conglomerates in Japan are able to change with the demands of the times, diversify when necessary and shift their revenues among the various branches of their companies. Smaller businesses, unable to adapt effectively, are folding by the dozen, falling prey to their larger compatriots.

Some municipalities, too, are struggling—a phenomenon of striking familiarity to American observers. In February 1978 Tokyo Mayor Ryokichi Minobe, a Socialist-supported independent, announced that his city was on the brink of fiscal insolvency and faced central government takeover. Ten other smaller cities have already gone into bankruptcy and are under state control.

Japanese Preparing Plan To Cut Holdings of Foreign Reserves

By JUNNOSUKE OFUSA

TOKYO, Aug. 4—Japan's Ministry of Finance and other Government bureaus, under instructions from Prime Minister Takeo Fukuda, are drawing up plans to reduce that country's foreign exchange holdings, which have been spiraling since the beginning of this year.

The nation's foreign exchange reserves reached $17.64 billion at the end of July, up $251 million from the preceding month. The holdings increased $1.16 billion in the first seven months of this year. As a result, the current reserves are the largest in four years and four months.

Also, the ruling Liberal Democratic Party yesterday adopted a new package of economic stimulation measures to spur sagging domestic consumption that would promote imports.

The Government appears to be increasingly sensitive to criticism rising in the United States and Europe over Japan's expanding exports, a major cause for the marked climb in its foreign exchange holdings. While Japan's exports to the United States rose 20 percent in the first six months of this year over a year earlier, its imports from America increased by only 13 percent.

Mansfield Issues Warning

The United States Ambassador, Mike Mansfield, warned Japan in a recent speech that the $5 billion American trade deficit with Japan last year was a "disturbing figure" and "provides much ammunition to the advocates of protectionism" in the United States.

The ministries concerned here have not yet drafted a final plan for a marked

Takeo Fukuda.

reduction in the nation's foreign exchange holdings. Though the pace of growth in exports has slowed in recent months, partly because of external pressure on Japan's shipments and partly because of the appreciation of the Japanese yen, exports still maintain a high level, while imports continue very low due mainly to the depressed domestic economy.

Mr. Fukuda has pledged internationally that Japan will achieve an economic growth of 6.7 percent in fiscal 1977, which ends March 31 next year. He says that in order to attain this objective the Government has to enforce reflationary

measures to stimulate the faltering domestic economy, thereby accelerating a marked increase in imports.

Despite this optimistic view, however, Mr. Fukuda told a parliamentary session last week that although the Japanese economy was showing "a tendency of gradual recovery," domestic business remains stagnant.

1,500 Companies in Bankruptcy

Since the beginning of this year more than 1,500 companies have been declared bankrupt every month. In June, business failures totaled 1,526, up 29 percent from a year earlier, and their combined debts amounted to $790 million, up 46 percent. In the first six months of the current year there were 9,117 corporate bankruptcies, up 30 percent over a year earlier.

Because of the existing feeble domestic economy, industrial production and shipments are dropping, while inventories are rising.

Japan also is reportedly considering another discount rate reduction to support a package of additional reflationary measures, including a further easing of credit, to shore up the flagging economy. The central bank lowered the official discount rate by 1 percent to 5 percent in April shortly after it had carried out a reduction of 0.5 percent.

The mainstay of the proposed reflationary measures is another large supplementary budget calling for massive public works spending. The Government is planning to introduce that budget to an extraordinary session of the Diet, which will be convened in late September or early October. Other similar spending plans have so far not been successful in stimulating consumer buying.

August 5, 1977

Japan to Spend $7.6 Billion More To Shore Up Flagging Economy

By JUNNOSUKE OFUSA

TOKYO, Oct. 3—Prime Minister Takeo Fukuda, under severe pressure from other nations to stimulate Japan's economy and thus ease strains in world trade, said today that the Government would spend an additional $7.6 billion to shore up the country's flagging economy in the fiscal year ending March 31, 1978.

"Although the Japanese economy has entered a moderate expansionary phrase, its resurgeance is proceeding only slowly, the employment situation is inactive, and there are differences in economic performance among industries," Mr. Fukuda told the Diet, or parliament.

Mr. Fukuda also said that Japan's growing trade surplus would be reduced through measures being planned by the Government, including a positive approach to the multilateral trade negotiations, steps to promote imports and increased economic cooperation with developing countries.

The Prime Minister said that despite the sluggishness of the economy, Japan would achieve its promised target of 6.7 percent real economic growth in the current fiscal year.

The Government submitted to the Diet today a $1 billion supplementary budget to finance its stimulus package, which calls for public works projects, additional Government loans for 100,000 houses, extra spending on local government public works and encouragement for private investment in plants and equipment.

The supplementary budget would bring total Government expenditure in fiscal 1977 to $109.8 billion, up 16.8 percent over the previous fiscal year.

The Government plans to issue $737 million worth of bonds to make up deficits in revenues for the supplementary budget, which would mean total borrowing accounts for 29.7 percent of the total budgeted revenue in fiscal 1977.

Meanwhile, the Government's economic planning agency made public a revised economic outlook for the current fiscal year after getting approval at a special Cabinet session today.

The revised outlook envisages a marked increase in Japan's trade balance to $14 billion from the original estimate of $7.3 billion. The balance of payments on current account — including merchandise trade, services and transfers — is expected to register a surplus of $6.5 billion compared with an original estimate of a $700 million deficit.

Foreign Exchange Holdings Up

The Finance Ministry said that Japan's foreign exchange holdings increased by $101 million in September to reach $17.9 billion at the end of the month. The fourth straight monthly increase brought Japan's foreign currency reserves to the highest level since they stood at $18.1 billion at the end of March 1973.

In the foreign exchange market here, the yen rose today to its highest value in more than four years.

In heavy trading, the yen rose to 261.75 arainst the dollar, then eased a bit to close the day at 262.08, highest since July 10, 1973.

A rush of dollar selling sent the American currency plummetting and turnover totaled $524 million, up from Friday's $512 million.

Banking sources here note that upward pressure on the yen has increased since the United States Secretary of the Treasury, W. Michael Blumenthal, urged Japan to reduce its soaring trade surplus at a joint meeting of the International Monetary Fund and World Bank in Washington last week.

Foreign exchange market sources said that despite the rising selling pressure, the Bank of Japan apparently did not step in to bolster the dollar, letting the exchange rate find its own market level.

October 4, 1977

Foreign Loan Surge Expected in Tokyo

PARIS, Oct. 27—A major increase in foreign borrowing in Tokyo is in prospect, according to a wide-ranging survey of international capital markets published here today.

Foreign bond issues in Japan will rise above a record third-quarter level of $245 million, according to a report by the Organization for Economic Cooperation and Development, the Paris-based grouping of industrial nations.

The O.E.C.D. view, arrived at in consultation with Japan, which is a member of the organization, is that "foreign isues are expected to rise substantially towards the end of the year."

Next year, such yen bond issues could double or triple to reach a total in excess of $1 billion dollars, experts said, following a total of $360 million in the first nine months of 1977.

Pressure to Cut Payments Surplus

They add that Japan has been under pressure to find ways of reducing its payments surplus, and that opening the Japanese capital market to foreigners would be one way to diminish criticism in the West of Japan's financial policy and rising exports.

Japanese securities companies here said that recent borrowers on the Tokyo foreign bond market had been the European Investment Bank and Mexico, while issues by Brazil, New Zealand, Venezuela and the World Bank were scheduled before the end of the year.

October 28, 1977

Japan Holds $7 Billion
Not Counted in Its Reserves

TOKYO, Nov. 4 (AP)—The Ministry of Finance has about $7 billion in deposits and loans outstanding to Japanese commercial banks that are not counted in the country's overflowing foreign currency reserves, a Bank of Japan official said today.

The money is in the form of foreign currency deposits from the Finance Ministry account and loans to the banks in a "swap" arrangement with the ministry to promote imports, the official said.

If added to the record total for foreign reserves as of Oct. 31 of $19.577 billion, Japan's foreign currency holdings would top $26 billion.

"These aren't secret deposits and they aren't anything new," the central bank official said.

Deposits Started 5 Years Ago

The deposits from the Finance Ministry at one-month term market interest rates began about five years ago when the collapse of the Herstatt bank of West Germany caused monetary chaos and Japanese banks were in effect barred from easy borrowing overseas.

The swap arrangement for import financing was started at the same time also to make it easier for Japanese banks to get money. Since then the arrangement has become an unwanted burden for some banks, the official said.

Meanwhile, a Japanese plan to reduce foreign reserves by importing and stockpiling strategic raw materials could result in some of the biggest spot purchases ever on international commodities markets, according to published reports here.

The immediate object of the "emergency imports," as Ministry of International Trade and Industry officials are calling them, is to hold down Japan's fast-rising foreign exchange reserves and to ease speculative pressures on the yen.

The Government's plans are attracting wide attention because of their possible effects on world commodity prices and the potential profits that could be made on the spot transactions, whose combined value could total $2 billion.

Prospects for commodity purchases include natural uranium. The Japanese Government is interested in buying almost 10,000 tons of uranium oxide from the United States, partly on an emergency-import basis.

Japan will first try to buy part of the reserves held by the new United States Department of Energy, which is absorbing the former Energy Research and Development Administration, but it is still unclear whether the United States Government is willing to sell.

Tokyo Bonds Draw Investors

By JUNNOSUKE OFUSA
Special to The New York Times

TOKYO, Nov. 4—The sharp appreciation of the yen and the marked decline in interest rates in recent days here have made the Tokyo capital market extraordinarily attractive to large foreign borrowers and investors.

An increasing number of foreign governments and international organizations are floating yen-denominated bonds on the Tokyo money market to satisfy their domestically needed funds.

Sixteen yen-quoted foreign bond issues, amounting to $1.2 billion, are scheduled to be floated by the end of this year, a record. The previous record of six yen-denominated issues worth $344 million was registered in 1972.

A spokesman for the Finance Ministry said that the ministry welcomed the rapid growth in the issuance of yen-denominated foreign bonds and tried to encourage the new trend because it reduced Japan's large international balance-of-payments surplus and promoted the internationalization of the Tokyo capital market.

Foreign Holdings at Peak

The ministry also believes that the new trend may help mitigate international criticism of Japan's growing foreign-exchange reserves and of its continuing substantial trade surpluses.

Japan's foreign currency holdings, announced this week, reached a record $19.58 billion at the end of October, up $1.71 billion from September.

The first yen-denominated foreign bond, amounting to $25 million, was issued in Tokyo by the Asian Development Bank in December 1970.

In 1974, the Japanese Government disapproved all foreign applications because of the sharp decline in Japan's balance-of-payments position after the 1973 oil crisis.

The successive drop in long-term interest rates here in the current year, which was accompanied by three cuts in the official discount rate to 4.25 percent and the subsequent easing of the domestic money market, has brought about the resumption of yen-quoted foreign bond issues.

In the first 10 months of 1977 foreign governments and large institutions, including the Governments of Ireland, Spain, Mexico as well as the World Bank and the European Investment Bank, floated $672 million worth of national bonds here.

November 5, 1977

Japan's '78 Budget Seeks Surplus Cut

By ANDREW H. MALCOLM

TOKYO, Dec. 22—Spurred by the demands of its major trading partners, Japan has drafted an expansionary fiscal 1978 budget designed to increase its purchases overseas and reduce its multi-billion dollar trade surplus.

The proposed budget, which is still subject to change during upcoming deliberations in parliament, where the Government's numerical control is slim, totals about $142 billion on the basis of 240 yen to the dollar. That represents an increase of 20.3 percent over the Government budget for the current fiscal year, which began last April 1. And it includes $30 billion in public-works spending, a favored fiscal tool of Japan's postwar conservative governments.

But the budget proposals, which are to be formally released tomorrow, were received with considerable skepticism in financial, business and diplomatic circles here today. The general feeling was that they reflected an overly optimistic view and were perhaps designed more to dampen current international criticism of Japan than to reflect realistic economic goals.

There were also signs that Japanese officials were backing away from the ambitious 7 percent 1978 annual growth rate they promised during negotiations with American authorities in Washington last week.

United States officials had found Japan's slim package of tariff cuts and quota increases "insufficient" to balance Japan's mounting trade surpluses, but they said the 7 percent figure was "a step in the right direction." If achieved, it would be by far the best of any industrialized nation.

But in the week since the Washington talks ended Japanese officials have begun stressing how "difficult" a seven percent growth will be to achieve. In Japanese the word "difficult" or "mooskashi" means "nearly impossible."

And at a news conference today Hiroshi Sawano, a top official of the Economic Planning Agency, corrected an interpreter when she translated a sentence of his as, "the Government is determined to attain a growth rate of seven percent."

"That should be "around" seven percent," Mr. Sawano emphasized.

Among Japan's trading partners, and especially the United States, the percentage figure has become an important indicator of Japan's determination to stimulate domestic growth and assume greater international economic responsibility by buying more abroad to aid the economies of other lands.

Unemployment on Increase

Through November this year Japan's trade surplus totaled $14.4 billion while its current-account surplus, which includes other costs such as insurance and freight, totaled $9.84 billion.

Originally, the Government of Prime Minister Takeo Fukuda predicted a 1977 deficit of $700 million and an economic growth rate of 6.7 percent. Now, the 72-year-old Mr. Fukuda himself admits that growth will be more like 5.3 percent.

These have been embarrassing miscalculations. Before becoming Prime Minister last December Mr. Fukuda had earned a domestic reputation as an economic wizard for his successful anti-inflation work in previous cabinets.

But now unemployment, unheard of for years in this affluent, crowded land, totals more than one million with millions more under-employed or furloughed on partial pay. Manufacturing production hovers around 70 percent of capacity while consumer buying, which comprises more than half of Japan's gross national product, remains virtually stagnant.

The result has been declining imports, although job-providing exports, notably cars and electric appliances, have grown steadily. Local businessmen now fear that the rising value of the yen will make exports more expensive and slash orders from overseas.

December 23, 1977

An Expression of Confidence In Economic Growth for Japan

The Economic Scene

After outlining some complex actions in taxing and spending areas that the Japanese Government has drafted for the fiscal year starting April 1, Michiya Matsukawa, Vice Minister of Finance, expressed confidence here earlier this week that Japan would achieve one of the key objectives in its recent trade agreement with the United States—an economic growth, in real terms, of 7 percent in the coming year.

Some prominent American and Japanese analysts have been quite skeptical that such an increase could be attained following the disappointing 5.3 percent growth now expected for the current fiscal year. According to the 54-year-old Japanese finance official, however, the skeptical outsiders were "looking at outdated data and were not well informed about the magnitude and the content of our budget."

Washington and Tokyo agree that the effort to reduce Japan's huge global trade surplus (about $16.5 billion this year) will hinge on increased imports by Japan in an expanding economy. That, in turn, could be facilitated by lower tariffs and more liberal trade regulations by Japan, which are also promised.

The New York Times

Michiya Matsukawa at the Pierre Hotel before leaving for Japan.

"At this time, we have done our best," Mr. Matsukawa declared in an interview at the Japanese Ministry of Finance's New York office in the Wall Street district. "We are asking all other governments to make the same sort of efforts. We know our expansionary policies will soon be showing benefits in shifting our balance of payments—in diminishing our surplus and moving us toward equilibrium."

● ● ●

Mr. Matsukawa glanced at a recent issue of International Finance, published by the Chase Manhattan Bank, which contained a front-page article headline: The Fiscal Revolution in Japan. "I couldn't describe it as a 'fiscal revolution,'" Mr. Matsukawa commented, "but that is really what we have done."

He had in mind the breakthrough his Government intends in raising total Government debt in the coming fiscal year beyond the traditional ceiling of 30 percent of Government expenditures. The plan is to push Government borrowing to about 32 percent of outlays as a stimulus measure, thereby crossing a threshold of "such symbolic importance that it had sometimes been described as an unwritten part of the Japanese Constitution," the Chase publication said.

Mr. Matsukawa, who has spent more

than three decades in top Government financial posts, after service as a naval officer during World War II, also mentioned an innovative tax policy intended to provide substantially greater resources for expanding public-works spending in the year ahead. The plan, still subject to approval by the Japanese Parliament, would allocate corporate tax payments of about $8.3 billion expected in May 1979, to the coming fiscal year, and thus permit larger Government spending in that period, instead of raising the amount of the already enlarged Government borrowing operations.

• • •

"By planning this one-time tax adjustment," he said, "we have arranged to increase our tax revenues available for spending without increasing the tax burden. We will have to float an enormous amount of Government bonds at the same time—about $83 billion, or 10 percent of our gross national product."

Mr. Matsukawa, who received his master's degree in economics from the University of Illinois in 1951 and spent five years during the 1960's in New York and Washington as a Japanese Government financial representative, came to the United States this week, he said, "for good will purposes and to deepen the mutual understanding of our countries on economic matters." He met with top American monetary officials in Washington and with leading bankers and businessmen in New York.

He said the "real problem" on the Japanese trade surplus was "on the import side, not the volume of exports," and expressed confidence that

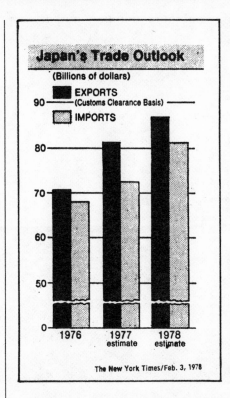

Japan's Trade Outlook

(Billions of dollars)

■ EXPORTS
(Customs Clearance Basis)
□ IMPORTS

The New York Times/Feb. 3, 1978

higher imports by Japan would develop this year. The goal is an increase of about 13 percent in Japanese imports from all countries and a rise of about 7 percent in Japanese exports in dollar terms. In the past year, the figures were virtually reversed, leading to a gain of more than $5 billion in Japan's

net trade balance with the world, compared with the 1976 fiscal year.

• • •

Mr. Matsukawa, like all monetary officials, was cautious about discussing current foreign exchange rates for the dollar, the yen and other currencies and the scope of Japan's intervention activities to prevent further increases in the value of the yen.

He indicated, however, that the appreciation of the yen over the last year or so had caused "difficulties for business and labor" in Japan, and said his nation was "pleased" with the recent decision of the United States to intervene more actively in the foreign exchange markets to support the value of the dollar.

He also reported that Japan was taking a number of steps to liberalize and simplify foreign exchange controls there by the end of April, and that the nation was pursuing "a most expansionary monetary policy now, with the level of the discount rate [4¼ percent] the lowest since 1972."

On the international scene, Mr. Matsukawa said he feared that the economic picture overall "will be a little bit worse in 1978 than last year," if all governments "do not take courageous actions to cope with economic problems."

While peace and quiet now seem to have settled over the tense economic relations between the United States and Japan, intensive discussions are continuing behind the scenes to assure that agreements reached last December are implemented and are successful.

February 3, 1978

Tokyo, on the Brink of Bankruptcy, Facing Central Government Rule

By ANDREW H. MALCOLM

TOKYO, Feb. 3—Tokyo, one of the world's largest cities, is on the brink of bankruptcy and a financial takeover by the central Government.

In negotiations reminiscent of New York City's recent fiscal crises, city and central Government officials have opened talks on necessary spending cutbacks as well as proposals to issue new bonds to help cover the city's $979 million deficit.

The fiscal dispute, which underlines a

wide philosophical gap between central Government leaders belonging to the conservative party and Tokyo's Socialist officials, also reflects the new political realities in Japan where no single party holds firm legislative control any longer.

Like New York's fund shortage, Tokyo's has been coming for years. City authorities have encouraged talk of their fiscal difficulties as part of their annual bargaining with the central Government, which provides 10 percent of the city's income through subsidies and must approve another 10 percent obtained

through bond sales. Thirty percent comes from corporate taxes, 20 percent from personal taxes, 20 percent from special fees and 10 percent from property taxes.

"We realize that like New York we have been criticized for crying 'wolf,'" said Masaaki Yoshida, a senior Tokyo finance officer, "but I can tell you that this year is the worst ever."

Unlike New York's revenue difficulties, however, Tokyo's do not stem from a fleeing middle class. If anything, there are too many people (11,688,100) packed into the 840 square miles of Tokyo, which

Tokyo, a metropolis of over 11 million people, is on the brink of bankruptcy.

Consulate General of Japan, N.Y.

is a prefecture as well as a city and includes more than 20 satellite cities as well as a string of islands stretching 300 miles south into the Pacific.

For years the rising costs of providing services for this population and paying the city's 188,000 employees have steadily increased the general account budget until it totaled $10.9 billion for the current Japanese fiscal year, which ends March 31. The proposed 1978 fiscal budget announced this week totals $12.6 billion.

But since the 1973 energy crisis set off a recession here, the crucial corporate tax revenues of Japanese cities in general and Tokyo in particular have been even more sharply pinched. The result has been mounting municipal deficits. According to Japanese law, debt ceilings vary according to a city's size. In Tokyo's case this year the ceiling is about $416 million.

By contrast, New York City, though not so large as Tokyo, has a long-term-debt ceiling of $8.027 billion and a short-term one of $7.920 billion.

In the case of Tokyo, exceeding the $416 million at the end of the fiscal year would require a formal declaration of bankruptcy and assumption by the Home Affairs Ministry of financial control of the city, probably for two or three years. Ten smaller Japanese cities and towns are now under such control, but the bankruptcy of a prefecture, let alone the capital, would be unprecedented in modern-day Japan.

A legal takeover could presage a fierce political struggle here and carries a potential for sharp cutbacks in services and for severe labor strife. This is because the central Government is controlled by the conservative Liberal-Democratic Party while Tokyo is run by an opposition party administration headed by Governor-Mayor Ryokichi Minobe, a Socialist-supported independent.

In recent days Mr. Minobe and other city officials held a series of meetings with central Government authorities, including Prime Minister Takeo Fukuda and Home Minister Takenori Kato. The focus is a plea by the city for permission to issue additional bonds to cover its deficit.

Tokyo has a self-imposed bond limit under which the annual interest payments may total no more than 8 percent of that year's annual budget, a policy that gives its standard 10-year bonds a very high rating in the financial community. Banks buy about half of Tokyo's bonds, which are now paying about 7 percent, while the central Government buys 10 percent and large corporate investors take the rest. There are few individual purchasers, in part because a new law permits a maximum tax-free holding of only $12,500 in combined bank accounts and municipal securities.

So far, the central Government has refused Tokyo's latest bond sales request. It says that the city must cut much spending and redirect other expenditures.

Traditionally, the central Government has favored heavy public spending on such large-scale projects as expressways, railroads, bridges and airports, which tend to have a great stimulative impact on the national economy. This would be especially helpful this year for the Fukuda Government, which promised in a recent trade agreement with the United States to take action to stimulate its domestic economy to a 7 percent growth rate.

But Governor Minobe's administration, which has been supported by the Buddhist Komeito, or Clean Government Party, and the Communists, favors more people-oriented bond projects concerned with welfare, schools and hospitals.

Conservatives Have Majority

In local elections last summer, the Liberal-Democrats gained a further edge on Mr. Minobe by capturing, in conjunction with other conservative-oriented parties, 69 of the 126 seats in Tokyo's metropolitan assembly. The body meets next month to pass on the 1978 fiscal budget.

To show his sincerity in the bond talks with the central Government, which has demanded more self-help efforts before stepping in with assistance, Mr. Minobe announced an increase in some school tuitions, abolition of anual pay raises for city employees, an end to chauffeured limousine service for some city officials, a cutback in hiring and the sale of $221 million worth of city-owned land.

"If the central Government takes over," said Mr. Yoshida, "we expect sharp cuts in employees and welfare spending. Until now, they could only make these suggestions. But then they could order them. And we will lose our civic autonomy."

"We understand how hard the Tokyo government is trying right now," a Home Affairs Ministry spokesman said, "but it is already two years too late. They should have adjusted their spending policies to their revenue realities a long time ago."

February 4, 1978

Tokyo Selling Off Land As Its Latest Expedient To Prevent Bankruptcy

By HIROTAKA YOSHIZAKI

TOKYO, April 8—For sale: 4,058 pieces of land. Asking price: $451 million.

The seller is not a wealthy realtor but one of the world's largest cities, Tokyo, which like many urban governments is strapped for money.

As in the case of New York, Tokyo's financial problems have been growing for years, and each year the city teeters on the brink of bankruptcy. For example, in the last fiscal year, which ended March 31, Tokyo incurred a deficit of $448 million despite the last-minute sale of municipal bonds worth $24.7 million. As a result, the municipal government will have to sell at least $238 million worth of the real estate it owns in order to cover the deficit that is expected for the new fiscal year.

To avoid bankruptcy and the taking over of its finances by the central Government, Tokyo had earlier announced that it would cut $278 million from its expenditures for this fiscal year. The economy measures included a temporary suspension of annual pay raises for its 220,000 employees, an end to special allowances for those in managerial posts, abolition of chauffeured limousine service for directors and other high-ranking officials, a 300 percent increase in school tuition, and other cuts.

205 Acres to Be Sold

However, since these measures were not enough to balance the budget, the metropolitan government, for the first time in its history, set in motion on March 1 plans to sell 205 acres of its land.

"I feel guilty for having to do this," said Michio Ishida, who heads the 76-man task force that will sell the land, "be-cause Tokyo originally bought the land with its citizens' tax money. But there was no other way to bail out the city from its financial crisis."

There are two types of land on sale: vacant lots and property that is already leased to corporations and individuals. The vacant land will be sold through public bidding, while the occupied property will be offered to the present tenants, which include the giant Marubeni trading company and the Mitsukoshi department store. The task force has already determined that nearly half of the 4,013 tenants want to buy the land.

The vacant lots, however, are either small—in most cases less than one acre—or in poor locations for business.

"So, it might be difficult to sell them," Mr. Ishida noted, "but we've got to do it."

April 9, 1978

The Sting In Japan: A Backlash Of Success

By ANDREW H. MALCOLM

TOKYO

It might be something of an overstatement to say that the economy of Japan hangs on the sales of men's suits and the quality of new calendars. But if the global army of statisticians, economists and politicians who daily monitor tons of computer readouts on the vital affairs of Japan, the world's third largest economic power, had checked the department stores that sell men's wear and the sidewalk stalls that peddle calendars last winter, they could have predicted what would happen the rest of the year.

And if they took another stroll these chilly winter days, they would get a pretty good reading of the prospects for Japan's 1978 economic performance. Suit sales are down. Calendars are plain. And in Japan that spells, trouble.

Japan's difficulties are likely to come on a broad economic and political front at home and abroad. They include an appreciating yen—it rose almost 20 percent during 1977—that threatens the price competitiveness of Japan's all-important exports, stagnant domestic consumer demand, substantial overcapacity in key industries, rising unemployment, a continuing wide culture gap with the rest of the world, strong new competition in certain sectors from developing countries such as South Korea and mounting tensions between an aggressive Japan and its increasingly impatient trading partners.

To confront these difficulties, Japan is equipped, as always, with its fabled diligence. But its aging, conservative political leadership has been slow to move with authority and corrective fiscal measures. Its control in parliament has been cut to a handful of votes. Because of Japan's global economic clout—its gross national product in 1978 is expected to be $878 billion—its problems have ramifications far beyond the island nation's rocky shores.

In Japan's export picture: static.

Basically, Japan's problems appear structural, despite all the publicized negotiating over such details as steel dumping, beef quotas, tariffs and nontariff trade barriers, which abound. Ironically, Japan's 1978 problems stem from its past successes.

Exports fuel the economy for Japan's 113 million people. If domestic demand is sluggish, as it has been the last two years, then businesses— which are saddled with high overhead because of Japan's tradition of lifetime employment—instinctively turn to foreign sales to take up the slack. With lower prices (even below cost in some cases) and quality goods, exports have mushroomed since 1975. Last year Japanese color television sets flooded the United States market until an orderly marketing agreement stemmed the downpour. Now the TV flood is directed at the Middle East, and Japanese manufacturers are starting massive exports of microwave ovens to the United States.

Automobiles, now Japan's largest single export item, are a prime example. The industry here turned out 8.52 million vehicles in 1977. With domestic sales slipping, they shipped cars abroad in great quantities. As a result, 51 percent of Japan's motor vehicle production in 1977 was sold in other countries.

These successes, combined with Japan's lagging purchases abroad, led to a trade surplus last year about $16 billion and a current-accounts surplus close to $10 billion. Prime Minister Takeo Fukuda had promised President Carter that Japan would have a deficit of $700 million. This stirred a storm of criticism against Japan, led by the United States, its chief trading partner, for failing to assume a role of economic leadership commensurate with its economic power by, for instance, buying more foreign products.

New Zealand's Prime Minister Robert Muldoon, among others, said it was time that an insular Japan was "dragged, kicking and screaming," into a responsible role in the international community.

Japan's usual strategy in such situations is to draft a special package of minor trade concessions to placate the loudest critics. Its December package, described as the "maximum possible," included some tariff cuts and liberalized import rules on items such as smoked herring and maple syrup. The United States, citing growing protectionist pressure in Congress, rejected the concessions as "insufficient" and urged a more basic economic restructuring of Japan's trade.

A series of American emissaries carried the message across the Pacific. In mid-January officials of both nations agreed on a communiqué that called for Japan to reduce its surplus markedly, increase foreign aid and take steps to ease foreigners' access to Japanese markets. A keystone of the agreement was an expansionist budget for fiscal 1978, beginning April 1, of about $143 billion, including $22 billion for stimulative public works projects, a favorite fiscal tool of Japan's Liberal Democratic Party, which is actually conservative.

The goal, Japanese officials said, was a domestic economic growth rate of 7 percent. This, they said, would draw in imports and perhaps by yearend help reduce the surplus to $6 billion.

President Carter's Special Trade Representative, Robert S. Strauss, called the 7 percent promise a "step in the right direction." In Tokyo economists, businessmen and bankers called it impossible, since it would have to come on the heels of Mr. Fukuda's promised 1977 growth rate of 6.7 percent and the real 5.3 percent growth that occurred.

"Anyone who believes that 7 percent solution," said an American banker here, "will believe anything." Many suggested that 4.3 percent would be more realistic.

Japan's Economic Planning Agency said that Japan had managed only a "very slow recovery" in 1977 and that it would continue to be slow this year. "Private enterprise has very little confidence in the economy," said Tatsuo Ueno, the agency's director of research. Competition from Taiwan, South Korea and other developing nations with low-cost labor has forced a "restructuring of the economy" away from labor-intensive industries, he said. The textile industry, in particular, has been hard-hit.

The situation has led to substantial inventories and large overcapacity. Corporate bankruptcies averaged a record 1,500 a month last year, and at year's end manufacturing industries were producing at only about three-quarters capacity. And, with the fabled conservatism of Japanese consumers in times of economic uncertainty, the outlook was for a continuing decline in the popularity of the 73-year-old Mr. Fukuda, once considered an economic troubleshooter.

With the United States Congress, which has three dozen protectionst measures before it, taking an increasingly assertive role in foreign policy, the 1978 outlook for bilateral trade relations matched the grim forebodings of the meager sales of men's suits here.

Diplomats of both Washington and Tokyo planned new talks to ease the trade tensions. Any American envoys making the trip to Japan might well recall another United States emissary. He, too, came to Japan to open these islands to foreign business. His name was Matthew Perry, and the year was 1853. □

February 5, 1978

Japan Sops Up
Billions of Dollars to Protect Yen

Fewer and fewer Americans, it appears, will know the medieval charms of Kyoto, the mists over Mt. Fuji, or the glories of the Ginza. These wonders, and a tempting array of Japanese cars, television sets, stereo equipment, and cameras are steadily receding beyond the reach of American consumers, as the value of the dollar against the Japanese yen continues to drop dramatically.

Last week the decline, which began in earnest last September, turned into a rout, as the dollar fell to a postwar low, forcing the Bank of Japan, the nation's central bank, to intervene in the market at near-record levels to prevent the yen from rising any higher.

The dollar had stabilized by the end of the week, but at the market's close on Friday, one dollar was still worth only 223.4 yen, compared with just over 230 yen the preceding week. Since December 1971, when the current floating exchange rate system came into existence, the dollar had lost almost 40 percent of its value vis-a-vis the Japanese currency.

This was still not as severe a decline as the dollar has suffered against the two Samsons of the international currency markets, the West German mark and the Swiss franc. The mark has risen by about 58 percent over the so-called Smithsonian rate (after the agreement that initiated the current system) while the Swiss franc has soared by more than 100 percent.

The yen has not risen higher in large part because of massive intervention by the Bank of Japan. Bankers in Tokyo estimate that since September the monetary institution has purchased an estimated $11 billion worth of American currency on the Tokyo money market, in a lonely struggle to prop up its value. On one day last week the bank purchased more than $1 billion in its support efforts.

Japanese policymakers are loathe to allow a significant appreciation of the

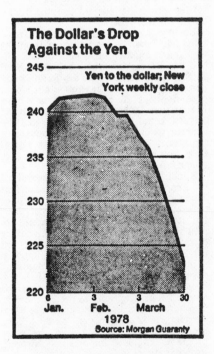

The Dollar's Drop Against the Yen

Yen to the dollar; New York weekly close

245
240
235
230
225
220

6   3   3   30
Jan.   Feb.   March
1978
Source: Morgan Guaranty

yen because of the effect it has on the prices of Japanese goods in the American market. Simply put, the higher the yen rises, the costlier Japanese exports become to foreign buyers. As a result, the heavily export-oriented Japanese manufacturers in Japan lose sales, threatening to add to the nation's already relatively high unemployment.

The alternative, trying to slow the yen's rise by sopping up dollars in the currency market, has a number of drawbacks as well, however. When the central bank buys up huge quantities of the American currency with yen, the Japanese money supply is swollen with this new injection of funds. Bankers estimate that the money released by the central bank in the last six months amounts to about 2.3 trillion yen. The

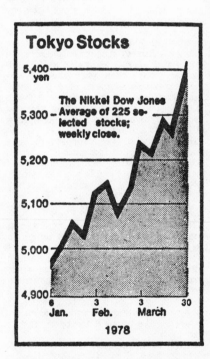

Tokyo Stocks

5,400 yen

The Nikkei Dow Jones Average of 225 selected stocks; weekly close.

5,300
5,200
5,100
5,000
4,900

6   3   3   30
Jan.   Feb.   March
1978

bulk of these funds have gone into the free yen bank accounts of foreigners or to Japanese trading companies and export enterprises.

This enormous amount of liquidity has the potential of creating a severe burst of inflation in Japan, although at the moment, that possibility is still only a threat. Partly because of restrictions on bond buying by nonresidents and low interest rates on bonds and deposits, much of the money has flowed into the Tokyo stock market.

Last week the market was booming along at record levels, and the Nikkei Dow Jones average hit a high of 5,400 yen, up from less than 5,000 yen at the beginning of the year.

ANN CRITTENDEN
April 2, 1978

Japan in Plight as Exports Expand, Contrary to Trade Commitments

By JUNNOSUKE OFUSA

Special to The New York Times

TOKYO, April 7—As Japan began its new 1978 fiscal year this month, it found itself in a serious predicament. Contrary to international commitments, its exports continue to expand vigorously while its imports grow only slightly.

Despite growing pressure from other nations to trim its balance-of-payments surplus, Japan's foreign-exchange holdings have reached an all-time high of $29.2 billion. It has gained $12.3 billion in the last 12 months alone, thereby becoming the world's third largest foreign-exchange holder after only West Germany and Saudi Arabia.

Japan's current account surplus for the 1977 fiscal year is estimated at $14 billion, far more than even the Government's revised estimate of $10 billion. One year ago, Prime Minister Takeo Fukuda assured Japan's trading partners his country would have a $700 million deficit in its current account.

How did what was supposed to be a modest deficit turn into such a substantial surplus, creating embarrassment and questions for Mr. Fukuda just four weeks before his scheduled summit meeting with President Carter?

Monthly Rate of $3 Billion

Japan's dollar surplus has increased at a monthly average rate of $3 billion in the last three months. Half of the excess has stemmed from the influx of foreign capital and the other half from the trade surplus. It has also been augmented through dollar payments from overseas move up by a "leads and lags" business policy that trading concerns and manufacturers have adopted to cope with the higher yen.

In the 1977 calendar year, Japan's exports to the United States rose sharply, by 25 percent, to $19.7 billion, while its purchases from the United States registered only a growth of 5 percent, amounting to $12.4 billion.

Mike Mansfield, the American Ambassador, in a speech before top Japanese bankers, businessmen and industrialists in Osaka this week, warned that Congress might lose patience if Japan's trade surplus continued to grow.

The Government's optimistic estimate for trade in the 1978 fiscal year puts the nation's export growth at 7 percent and import growth at 13 percent, thereby cutting down its current surplus to $6 billion for this year.

However, experts in business circles said that Japan''s current surplus might well reach another huge sum of $15 billion this fiscal year, which began on April 1. They pointed out that the nation's exports might not gain in volume but would expand about 10 percent because of a rise in yen exchange rates whose basic upward trend remains unchanged. The imports would increase only about half the export growth because Japan's flagging internal economic conditions are seen as likely to linger.

Kiichi Miyazawa, director general of the Economic Planning Agency, said that Japan's exports might become stagnant to some extent in the 1978 fiscal year, but its imports would not step up immediately because of the huge inventory of raw materials on hand, which account for 80 percent of Japan's total imports.

In an attempt to stimulate the domestic economy and trim its mounting balance-of-payments surplus, the Government has adopted four programs in recent months. The initial program called for huge fiscal spending of 2 trillion yen, or $9 billion, in public works. Measures in the other programs include imports of aircraft, uranium and crude oil.

The Government maintains that these measures have not produced satisfactory results as yet chiefly because the yen's sharp appreciation has brought about a deflationary impact on the economy, slowing down the nation's economic recovery.

In coping with the higher yen, Japanese export industries have raised the prices of their products. At the same time, the industries have compelled their subcontractors to lower their delivery prices.

Banking circles here said that a large reduction in bank interest rates following a series of cuts in the official discount rate has greatly eased the heavy financial burden of export enterprises. This has helped them keep the costs of their products relatively low.

The banking circles added that there is a parallel today to a strong potential for inflation that existed in 1972. The huge excessive liquidity created in 1972 by the central bank's release of yen, amounting to 1.5 trillion yen, as a result of its massive purchase of dollars on the Tokyo money market, was seen as a major cause for the inflation from which Japan suffered in 1974.

The Finance Ministry said that the money released by the Bank of Japan because of its dollar purchases amounted to 1.3 trillion yen, or $6 billion, last month.

Despite a denial by financial authorities, there is an indication that a move to change money into commodities has begun among some consumers. Michiyo Nakane, chief of the jewelry section of a major department store, Takashimaya, in Tokyo, said that sales of gold had doubled since the end of last year. Popular demand for art objects, jewelry and immovable property is also said to be slowly rising.

April 8, 1978

Growing Japanese Concern Over Worldwide Depression

The danger of a world depression—and the political and military disasters to which it might give rise—are very much on the minds of Japanese leaders today. Nobuhiko Ushiba, Japan's Minister of External Economic Affairs, says he sees an alarming parallel between world economic conditions today and those at the start of the Depression of the 1930's.

The Economic Scene

He is particularly worried about the threat of protectionism and the fragility of the world monetary system with an unstable dollar.

"There is no question," he said, "that the Depression led to World War II."

Japan's Economy

How to prevent a recurrence of that tragic sequence of events is the dominant worry of Japan's Government.

"There is little room for optimism on the part of either developed or de Takeo Fukuda recently told the Japan Society here. "I am deeply concerned that unless we find a way out a situation may develop where world stability and peace are endangered."

Mr. Ushiba, in an interview here a few days ago, said that Japan's worry was that, in the present disordered state of the world economy, country after country might be driven to take protectionist measures, with a ruinous impact on world trade.

Did he think the United States was moving in that direction?

"There is much protectionist talk in Congress," he said, "but the present Carter Administration is not protectionist." Mr. Ushiba has worked closely with Robert S. Strauss, President Carter's trade negotiator, and feels that his aim is to contain protectionist pressures by giving ground when necessary but not surrendering liberal trade principles.

Mr. Ushiba acknowledged that he faced strong protectionist pressures from troubled industries in his own country. The most severe of these, he said, were from Japan's farm lobby.

"So far," he said, "the Government has been successful, I think, in containing those pressures."

But as a small island nation he says

Japan is at a disadvantage in agriculture. "We are not competitive," he said. "Nevertheless, we must maintain some amount of agricultural production as a basis for the security of the nation."

• • •

Only 10 percent of the Japanese population is engaged in agriculture, and many members of farm families, Mr. Ushiba said, also work in industry.

He was cautious in saying how much Japan would reduce its balance-of-payments surplus this year. "We will slash it as much as possible," he said.

However, he noted that the target figure of a $6 billion surplus in Japan's current-account balance of payments—including trade and services—might be too low. The $6 billion figure had been "mentioned before" and was the basis of the budget for the fiscal year 1978, which began April 1. But it was then thought that the preceding year's payments surplus was only $10 billion. It has since developed that Japan ran a $14 billion surplus last year.

"For that reason," Mr. Ushiba said, "a $6 billion surplus this year may not be realizable, but there is still a chance."

• • •

Japan's surplus in trade alone last year was $20 billion. Mr. Ushiba suggested that hi country would be doing well to get the figure down to $12 billion or $13 billion this year.

What is the most important thing Japan can do to reduce its trade surplus?

"More rapid expansion of our domestic economy," he said. He stated his confidence that Japan could achieve 7 percent growth this year after adjusting for inflation.

Industrial production has been moving up faster during the winter and spring than was expected—at an annual rate of 14 percent from October to March.

Japan means to reach its growth goal with the help of fiscal stimulus, mainly in the form of public-works spending. This approach has been criticized by outside economists as likely to do little for Japanese import demand, compared with what tax cuts for consumers would do.

But Mr. Ushiba said the Japanese savings rate was "very high—more than 25 percent—and even if we gave a break to consumers by tax cuts, the money would go into savings, not into consumption." He contended that public-works investment would have both direct and indirect effects in increasing purchasing power "perhaps over a longer period of time."

As in his own country, Mr. Ushiba thinks protectionist pressures and disintegrative tendencies throughout the world economy can be checked only if all the industrial countries—including West Germany, he said—"upgrade their rate of growth."

This would also be essential to help the less-developed countries, who need "a bigger flow of resources" and "more purchasing power for their goods," he said. But Japan is uneasy about granting special trade concessions to all so-called developing countries.

"Some are much stronger than others, such as Korea, Mexico and Singapore," Mr. Ushiba said, "and need to be treated like equals."

Worried about the weakness of the dollar, he gave the standard prescription that the United States should curb its inflation and its appetite for energy. But when asked whether he would rather see this country curb its inflation or curb its growth, he said, "Continue growth." Yet he hastily added that "so long as the dollar is unstable, there will be no end to trouble in money and trade all over the world."

May 9, 1978

Japan's Planning Chief On Growth and Tariffs

TOKYO, May 19—As head of Japan's Economic Planning Agency, Kiichi Miyazawa is the country's spokesman on domestic economic affairs. Last December he predicted—against the advice of the great majority of Japanese Government economists—that the economy would leap forward early this year.

The official figure for growth in January will be announced in two weeks. But in an interview here, Mr. Miyazawa disclosed for the first time that the economy had recovered sharply in the first quarter of this year and predicted that gross national product would rise in the current fiscal year, which began April 1, to nearly half the size of the G.N.P. of the United States.

Mr. Miyazawa is a former foreign minister and minister of international trade and industry. He was appointed to his present post last year.

• • •

QUESTION: What was Japan's growth rate in the January-March quarter?

It was better than 2.1 percent in real terms, and at 2.1 percent we will have made 5.3 percent in fiscal 1977, exactly as I predicted. We will know the numbers in about two weeks. This means that our gross national product this fiscal year, assuming a 7 percent real growth rate, will be close to $1 trillion, depending on the exact exchange rate you use—nearly half the size of the United States [G.N.P].

97

QUESTION: Does this [recovery], still accompanied by massive trade surpluses, mean that Japan''s ability to make concessions in the Tokyo Round of GATT tariff cuts is increased?

· The G.N.P. is a flow of money, not a stock. The size of flow is one thing, the standard of living another. Our stock of wealth is not that of America nor of the European democracies. In the coming negotiations in the Tokyo Round we shall do fairly well in manufactures. But we may do less well in farm products. Our Achilles heel is still in agriculture. The hardest tariff rates for us to cut are on computers and color film. We made general tariff cuts in March already, in advance, across the board, but the United States still has lower tariffs. Probably on computers and color film we will make further efforts to live with much lower tariffs. As for autos, we have zero tariffs.

● ● ●

QUESTION: And what about agricultural items?

There you have meat and citrus products. The extent to which we can go is rather limited. If Japanese concessions on meat are going to be the final requirement for the success of the whole Tokyo Round, then I think we must consider some formula whereby Japan raises the import quota on beef under some carefully devised formula. But this shouldn't really be a United States concern. Some Texas cattle-raisers are concerned about Japan [in this field] but the primary beneficiaries of liberalization would be Australia and New Zealand.

● ● ●

QUESTION: What about the other item, citrus products?

There we are in an almost impossible situation. In 1977 our production of Japanese mandarin oranges was 3.6 million tons, as compared with maximum consumption of 3 million tons. The excess production is the result of the Japanese Government suggesting 10 years ago that farmers switch from rice to mandarin oranges. The Government can probably ask the farmers to cut down trees, about 20 percent of them. But here we have a domestic problem. I am not sure how far we can go.

● ● ●

QUESTION: Wouldn't it be in the interest of the great majority of Japanese people to have much lower food prices?

Here we are on tenuous moral ground as a Government. The Government is at least partially responsible for getting farmers into their present situation, and we feel guilty about that. The farmers account for 10 percent of the population and there is a strong feeling that rural farmers should be the foundation of a sound, healthy Japanese race. We should maintain a minimum population in rural districts. So coming

Kiichi Miyazawa.

Consulate General of Japan, N.Y.

back to the Tokyo Round I don't see how we can get out [of our difficult situation] on citrus items.

QUESTION? What is Japan's economic diplomatic strategy, looking ahead to the Bonn summit in July?

By Bonn we should have put the Tokyo Round virtually behind us. We won't have crossed every "t" and dotted every "i" but the fundamentals should be complete. There may be some divergence on the safeguard clause [to protect national industries] but government heads at Bonn should be able to resolve whatever issues remain. We've got just two months. And if you can't solve the problems in two months then you can't do so in two years either. Is there enough will? Two months should be enough.

● ● ●

QUESTION: Japan will go to the Bonn meeting with huge trade surpluses and a current-account surplus that could be as big as last year, $14 billion? Would it not be wise to abandon your official forecast of $6 billion for fiscal 1978? ·

We are doing our utmost on exports. This year's total steel export tonnage will be down 10 or 15 per cent. Color TV sales to America will be [down from] 1976. Exports of cars to America will be held below the 1977 figure. To what extent can we reduce our current-

account surplus? That depends mainly on the inflationary trend in importing countries. At the moment we just go on raising prices, as in the case of car exports to America, where prices went up six times in 16 months, up 20 percent. If that trend continues. . . .

● ● ●

QUESTION: And on the import side?

Imports are just beginning to go up. We are making sizable purchases of raw materials and oil. We are trying to make "emergency imports" to cut down our current-account surplus. We sent a mission to America in March to raise imports. On import finance, we have made a 180-degree turn away from the traditional policy of limiting official lending to three months. We have opened up our foreign exchange account and lend at 5 to 6 percent for 10 years. We will buy uranium, helicopters for the Marine Self-Defense Forces and we will advance purchases of jet aircraft.

● ● ●

QUESTION: How far can emergency imports go?

The Government will store up to 5 million tons of oil in 1978 worth $500 million. But there is no storage available. We are starting to build a floating storage tank in Kyushu but that will take over a year. In the meantime we can take 20 tankers of 250,000 deadweight tons each and moor them. That would account for 5 million tons. But then fishermen in the area demand an indemnity. Should we send the tankers down to Iwo Jima, to moor there? We are pretty close to our wits' end.

● ● ●

QUESTION: So Premier [Takeo] Fukuda will still go to Bonn with huge trade surpluses?

I am not able to form a judgment. The yen is between 220 and 230 to the dollar as against 290 in early 1977. Seventy yen should make a difference. It's bound to affect our exports if textbooks on economics are any guide.

● ● ●

QUESTION: But don''t such textbooks often ignore the dynamics of trade?

They shouldn't do so. But there is a strong body of opinion that says that the 70 yen [drop against the dollar] does not make that much difference. I simply don't know, but I still tend to believe the textbooks. Really there's too much emphasis on the current account [of the balance of payments]. Japan, if it wishes to export capital, should earn that much, and spend whatever surplus we have abroad. The fact is, we shall spend more on capital transfer. We are doubling foreign aid in three years, too. The Americans are very insistent on the current-account approach. But we should look at the basic balance of payments.

Henry Scott Stokes

May 20, 1978

Exports Aid
G.N.P. Rise For Japan

TOKYO, June 2—Japan's economy grew at an annual rate of almost 10 percent in the final quarter of the 1978 fiscal year, lending credence to the Government's target of 7 percent growth for the current fiscal year, but still showing a dependence on exports for producing the gain.

A report released by the Economic Planning Agency today said that the nation's gross national product rose 2.4 percent in real terms in the January-March quarter, the largest increase since a 3.4 percent rise in the January-March period of 1973. This put the growth for the full 1978 fiscal year at 5.4 percent, above the official Government goal of 5.3 percent.

Japan would be able to attain its 7 percent growth target in the 1979 fiscal year, which started April 1, if the G.N.P. rose just 1.8 percent in each of the upcoming four quarters, a spokesman for the agency said.

The growth report may prove an important prop for Japan's position at the economic summit meeting in Bonn

scheduled for mid-July. Japan has been under heavy pressure from major industrial nations to adopt more stimulatory policies this year to help raise the industrial world's economic growth rate.

Just last week, when the secretariat of the Organization for Economic Cooperation and Development, a group of 24 major industrial countries, presented its latest economic recovery plan, it urged that Japan and West Germany take the lead in a coordinated economic stimulation plan.

The idea is that the two, along with other nations, to a lesser degree, take local stimulative actions that would tend to increase their imports from the rest of the world, step up international trade and lower their current large surpluses in international payments.

The plan was designed to be the basis for an agreement on how to bolster the area's economies at the July summit meeting. However, senior economic officials from a significant number of countries generally rejected the plan, leaving open the question of whether any important agreement would be reached in Bonn.

Other earlier recovery plans also were dependent on stimulatory economic action by Japan and West Germany. Thus fr, however, the two countries have refused to take steps, despite the calls from their trading partners in the last couple of years.

Today's Japanese report, then, may take the edge off criticism of Tokyo, showing as it does that the country's economic growth is already running at a rapid rate. On the other hand, the importance of exports in the gain was seen as a negative factor in the upcoming discussion.

The agency figures showed that the G.N.P. totaled the equivalent of $820 billion in the latest period.

Major items responsible for the expansion were consumer spending, public works and exports. Consumer spending, which accounts for about 54 percent of the G.N.P., rose 2.1 percent, while exports surged 7.5 percent. Government spending rose 2.4 percent, mirroring its huge investment in public works.

June 3, 1978

Rising Yen No Problem
For Japanese Exports

By HENRY SCOTT-STOKES

TOKYO, June 22 — For a nation whose very existence is based on trade, common wisdom has it that a sharply rising currency is anathema — as it prices exports out of reach of customers and thus casts a pall on the economy generally. Not so in present-day Japan.

While the yen has soared in recent weeks, many industries, notably oil and steel, have seen the costs of raw materials drop dramatically. Other industries, autos among them, have found they can raise prices in export markets with impunity, thanks in large part to the generally inflationary state of the world economy.

Steel Is Helped

In fact, as the yen jumped to a rate of less than 210 to the dollar this week, closing today at 209.85, most industry sources displayed complacency. With marketing strategies already largely based on a 200-yen-to-the-dollar rate, many were doing better than expected.

"Japanese industry, including exporters, were prepared for the continued rise of the yen," said a spokesman for the Japan External Trade Organization. "There has not been any expression of deep concern over the surge."

The rise of the yen, which stood at more than 270 to the dollar a year ago, and at 230 just a few weeks ago, is a positive boon to such ailing industries as steel, which is cur-

rently operating at only 70 percent of capacity.

Imports of ore and coking coal, priced in dollars, have fallen by more than 20 percent in value in the last year, constituting quite a shot in the arm for such companies as Nippon Steel, the world's biggest steel company.

Oil refiners, whose imports are also priced in dollars, have benefited equally as the cost of their raw material has dropped in terms of the yen, with which their Japanese customers buy finished products.

There are, of course, areas in which the yen's climb has been a hardship.

Textiles and shipbuilding, already in a severe slump and without much hope for recovery within the Japanese market, face an additional hurdle in declining export markets.

But there is limited official concern about these industries, as Japan is revamping its industrial structure in favor of more sophisticated, particularly high-technology products.

Such corporate giants as Sony have long been prepared for the currency appreciation. A spokesman for the electronics company said planning had been based on reaching a rate of 200 yen to the dollar sometime in 1979, but industry sources said that Sony and other major exporting companies had already adjusted export prices on the basis of 200 yen to the dollar.

As long as the exchange rate remained above the 200-yen level, the sources pointed out, the exporters' profit margins would be bigger than planned.

At Toyota, a spokesman said that if the yen persisted at present levels the company simply would raise prices in

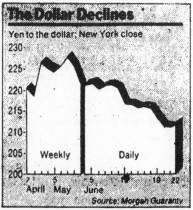

The Dollar Declines

Yen to the dollar; New York close

Weekly   Daily

Source: Morgan Guaranty

The New York Times/June 23, 1978

Assembly line at the Toyota Motor Company. Export sales continue to be brisk in spite of the rising yen.

Consulate General of Japan, N.Y.

the United States. Such an increase would be the seventh in less than 18 months — the cumulative price increase is about 20 percent — but as American competitors have also been raising prices, such increases have had little impact on export sales.

Komatsu, a maker of bulldozers, also said that raising prices abroad would not hamper its exports.

Sale of Dollar Continues

Hitachi, the big electrical concern,

acknowledged that the higher yen was causing some difficulties, but that cost-cutting was helping it to remain competitive.

Behind the sharp appreciation of the yen are heavy sales of dollars, largely by foreign banks, that have depressed the American currency's value.

Citibank alone is said by market sources to have sold $50 million here yesterday, though the bank, following standard practice, would not confirm that figure.

Other active sellers of the dollar, according to market sources, include the Bankers Trust Company and the First National Bank of Chicago among American institutions, Barclays Bank

Ltd. of Britain and the Swiss Bank Corporation and Union Bank of Switzerland, and the Hongkong & Shanghai Banking Corporation.

Japanese banks, restrained by the Government, sold much smaller amounts, according to Japanese bankers. Only the Bank of Tokyo, the top foreign exchange bank here, was prominent in the market, they said.

Japanese trading companies, given greater latitude by the authorities, were more active in currency markets. The Mitsubishi Corporation reportedly sold dollars heavily as did many other exporters.

June 23, 1978

U.S. Economists Study Japan Surplus

By HENRY SCOTT-STOKES

TOKYO, July 2 — Four academic economists from the United States are to arrive here tomorrow to examine the

reasons for Japan's huge balance-of-payments surpluses, the United States Embassy said today.

The four economists, whose visit is organized by the Nomura Research Institute, are: Robert Baldwin of the University of Wisconsin, William Parker of

Yale University, David Bradford of Princeton University and George Ease of the Land Institution.

They are here to take part in a Nomura seminar and also to visit leading export companies, including the Toyota Motor Company, Japan's number-one auto exporter; the Matsushita Electric Industrial Company, the top exporter of light electrical goods; the Hitachi Shipbuilding and Engineering Company; the Sumitomo Chemical Company; Showa Denko K.K., a nonferrous metals firm; Toray Industries Inc.; the Nippon Steel Corporation; Nippon Kokan K.K.; the Kawasaki Steel Corporation, and others.

Their visit was suggested by Jiro Tokuyama, head of the Nomura Research Institute, an arm of Japan's top brokerage house. The Japanese, it is said, wish to impress upon their American visitors that Japan's trade surpluses are gained by fair competitive methods, rather than by any special factors.

According to one official forecast, Japan will have a trade account surplus this fiscal year of $23 billion, despite the recent sharp rise in the value of the yen.

Last week the Japan Economic Research Center forecast that the balance on current account, including service items such as insurance and dividend payments, might reach nearly $18 billion, compared with last year's record $14 billion.

So far the rise in the yen appears not to have troubled Japanese exporters. Their confidence that they will continue to do brilliantly overseas is reflected in the Tokyo stock market, which Saturday closed at 5,529, as measured on the Dow Jones index, not far short of the all-time high of 5,555 recorded in April.

Inflation Abroad Blamed

Japanese officials generally blame inflation in other countries for the rise in exports. The Finance Ministry here yesterday welcomed the news that the United States Federal Reserve raised its discount rate as a sign that it is trying to beat inflation.

The question here is whether the Japanese Government will bring in a supplementary budget this autumn to boost the economy and hopefully to raise imports.

Prime Minister Takeo Fukuda said today that the Diet might be called into special session after mid-September to approve an additional budget.

He said he was confident that Japan's growth rate would reach 7 percent this fiscal year, but added that the rise of the yen might undermine business confidence, thus increasing the need for a supplementary budget.

July 3, 1978

Spending Dollars in Japan
Americans Find Goods Cost 20% More

By HENRY SCOTT-STOKES

TOKYO, July 24 — The middle-aged American woman was wandering around the streets of central Tokyo near the Karasumori shrine carrying a heavy laundry bag and looking puzzled.

"I'm searching for some soap," she said when a passer-by asked if he could help. "I want to go the laundromat but I can't find anyone to tell me where to buy the soap; there's none there."

Could she not inquire in the big Western-style hotel close by? "Oh, that," she said and laughed, looking back at the Dai-Ichi Hotel, "That's where I am staying." The laundry charges were just too high.

In years past a scene like this would have been unimaginable, but with the yen having soared in valure by 20 percent this year alone, to the point where a dollar will buy barely 200 yen, the American currency just will not go very far here.

Tourism Still Rising

That fact has turned the lives of Americans in Japan — tourists, military personnel, businessmen and diplomats alike — upside down. It has had a huge impact on business, making Tokyo an international financial center, and it is transforming United States defense arrangements here.

The number of Americans visiting Japan as tourists is still rising. It was 276,000 in 1975, 313,000 the next year and 345,000 in 1977. But the rate of increase — about 10 percent a year — began to fall off in April, according to the Japan National Tourist Organization.

Tourist habits have changed radically. Japan is no longer a place to shop. "Many of them told us that they would wait and shop in Singapore and Hong Kong," said Shintaro Amita, chairman of a group of 50 souvenir stalls in Kyoto. "They are in no mood to shop here."

"Our sales in dollar terms might not have fallen, but in yen terms, ah.. . . Many of us have dropped 20 percent, though we are still selling watches and cameras."

Shift in Armed Forces Salaries

The financial position of the United States armed forces in Japan is woeful. The collapse of the dollar means that wage scales have been revolutionized to the point where a Japanese guard at an American military base gets paid more than a lieutenant colonel in the United States Army.

Spokesmen for Japan's defense agency and the United States forces in Japan in Tokyo said that a senior guard working since 1952 at an American base received $28,625 before tax, including bonus, compared with an estimated pretax annual income of $28,000 for a lieutenant colonel with 16 years' service.

Japanese diplomats working with the American Embassy on support payments reported that the pay of 22,000 Japanese personnel here amounted to about $400 million, which is what the United States paid for twice as many Japanese five years ago. The Americans have pruned back their local staff to zero effect in dollar terms.

American businessmen based here are also unhappy about the plunge in the dollar. "It hurts," said James Abegglen, president of the Japanese subsidiary of the Boston Consulting Group in Tokyo. "My income is dropping like a rock."

Cost of U.S. Executives

The cost of a United States executive here is about three times his base pay in the United States. "A $25,000 or $30,000 man becomes a $100,000 man here," Mr. Abegglen said. "The cost of entry to the Japanese market gets higher and higher."

As the price of the man in Japan goes

Although the dollar buys less in Japan, the number of American tourists is rising.

Japan Air Lines

up, American companies are cutting back on representation and promoting Japanese staff at a fraction of the original cost. Last year the number of foreign businessmen on three-year visas stayed constant at just over 16,000. But within that total, Americans accounted for only 8,188 last year, down from 8,858 in 1976.

Americans are leaving and more Europeans are coming, including Germans and Swiss from hard-currency countries. The International Business Machines Corporation has switched Americans based in the Far East to Hong Kong and United States membership in the American Club has fallen in the last year although total membership has risen by 470.

Every American visitor is affected. "Our per-diem allowances are up by 30 percent," said Albert K. Webster, managing director of the New York Philharmonic, which visited here this month, "And we can't lay that on the Japanese; our contract was fixed when the dollar was 30 percent higher."

Advantages of Local Ventures

There are some advantages. American companies with local ventures are doing extremely well.

"For companies that are already here, it swings both ways for them," Mr. Abegglen said. "They have cheaper imports and higher earnings in yen."

Companies that benefit include I.B.M. Japan, Caterpillar Mitsubishi,

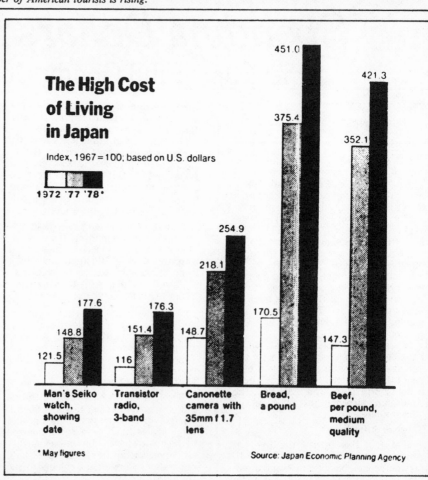

The High Cost of Living in Japan

Index, 1967 = 100; based on U.S. dollars

1972 '77 '78*

	Man's Seiko watch, showing date	Transistor radio, 3-band	Canonette camera with 35mm f 1.7 lens	Bread, a pound	Beef, per pound, medium quality
1972	121.5	116	148.7	170.5	147.3
'77	148.8	151.4	218.1	375.4	352.1
'78*	177.6	176.3	254.9	451.0	421.3

* May figures

Source: Japan Economic Planning Agency

The New York Times / July 25, 1978

Toa Nenryo Kogyo (in which the Exxon Corporation and the Mobil Corporation have 25 percent each), Mobil Sekiyu, N.C.R. Japan, Coca-Cola (Japan), Burroughs, Nippon Univac, Ebara-Infilco (a Westinghouse Corporation affiliate), Pfizer Taito, Shinko Pfaudler and Japan Upjohn.

The Japanese are not disturbed by the rising yen. "The economy has great elasticity," said Toshio Kimura, Japan's former Foreign Minister and a leader of the ruling conservative party, who comes from Mie prefecture.

"We have a big pottery industry in my area, and they export 70 percent of their products," he said in an interview. "When the dollar was at 230 yen there was a lot of howling, but now they turn out to be fully prepared for the 200-yen level — there have been some small bankruptcies and mergers, nothing more."

Japan has emerged this year as a West Germany or a Switzerland. This is a new, stable Japan with abundant capital and much steadier finances. "Gone are the days of 15 percent growth and 9 percent inflation," said a foreign banker here. "Instead you have 7 percent growth and zero or negative inflation."

July 25, 1978

Dollar Plunges Below 200-Yen Level in Tokyo

Bank of Japan Support Totals $300 Million

By JUNNOSUKE OFUSA

TOKYO, July 24—The rate of exchange for the United States dollar plunged today below the psychologically significant barrier of 200 yen for the first time since World War II.

In heavy trading, the dollar closed at 199.10 yen, down 2.15 from Friday's finish. The previous low of 200.50 yen was registered on July 5.

[In early trading on Tuesday, the dollar continued to slide, opening at 197.95 yen on the Tokyo foreign exchange market, The Associated Press reported.]

The plunge of the dollar reflects world concern over the expected record United States trade deficit this year and a record Japanese trade surplus. Because of these trends, holders of dollars exchange American money for yen, driving up the value of the yen relative to the dollar.

Reacting to the dollar's fall today, the price of gold in both London and Zurich rose sharply, approaching record levels. In London, bullion climbed $3.25 an ounce to close at $195.00 and in Zurich, it rose $3.75 an ounce to $195.375. Gold's record high of $197.50 an ounce was set on Dec. 30, 1974, in London.

The dollar suffered a further blow at the end of last week when the Oil Minister of Kuwait said that currency experts of the Organization of Petroleum Exporting Countries had agreed at a London meeting that the dollar should be replaced by a "basket" of currencies in computing oil prices.

Dollar Opens at 201.10 Yen

Reflecting a sharp overnight fall in overseas money markets, the dollar opened lower at 201.10. Immediately after foreign and Japanese banks rushed to sell dollars, the Bank of Japan stepped into the market and absorbed the unloaded dollars in an attempt to keep the yen from breaking the 200 barrier.

However, the Bank of Japan was forced to withdraw in half an hour under strong dollar selling pressure. The central bank's purchases of dollars amounted to $300 million.

Total turnover amounted to $900 million, the third highest on record for the Tokyo currency market and the second highest since the former international monetary system based on the fixed rates was abandoned under the Smithsonian Agreement of 1971. On March 29, the central bank purchased more than $1 billion from the Tokyo market.

A spokesman for the Bank of Japan said that the central bank had discontinued its intervention today because it realized the extent of the huge purchases of dollars from the market in order to maintain the 200-yen level in the face of the strong American currency selling pressure.

The central bank was worried about the huge liquidity that would be created by its additional release of yen as a result of the large purchase of dollars from the money market, thereby providing a major cause for inflation, such as the nation experienced in 1974, the spokesman said.

Both the Government and Bank of Japan apparently expected the yen's further climb as did many Japanese and foreign banks. However, Government and central bank authorities tried to play down the yen's fresh upsurge, saying that the Japanese currency had apparently peaked out.

Market sources said reports from overseas that the currency experts of the Organization of Petroleum Exporting Countries had agreed that the dollar should be replaced with a "basket" of currencies in fixing oil prices were a major factor that fueled speculative currency dealings. However, whether OPEC would pursue such a course was not known.

Business leaders expressed concern that the yen's steep appreciation would dampen Japan's economic upswing. They said they believed that, externally, the Government would come under pressure to do something about cutting the huge Japanese payments surplus promptly, as was promised at the recent Bonn conference.

Top business leaders called on the Government today to take additional business-stimulating measures such as the adoption of a supplementary budget for greater fiscal spending in public works and implementation of a large-scale income tax cut to stir up consumer spending.

Shigeno Nagano, president of the Japan Chamber of Commerce and Industry, said that the Government should consider an income tax cut of about 2 trillion yen, or $10 billion, to stimulate demand in the private sector of the economy.

July 25, 1978

Rotor for a turbine produced by Hitachi, Ltd. being assembled at Miboro Power Station of the Electric Power Development Company

Chapter 5
The Energy Crisis

Japan's energy problem has always been critical. The nation must import virtually all the atomic and fossil fuel it uses. When the price of Middle Eastern oil began to soar in 1974, Japan diversified its petroleum sources and increased its reliance upon atomic power. In October 1977 a joint Soviet-Japanese drilling project reportedly discovered large oil deposits off the coast of the Soviet island of Sakhalin. These may prove to be the largest deposits in Asia. In February 1978 Russia's hostile neighbor, the People's Republic of China, signed a trade accord with Japan which could be worth as much as $20 billion. Under the terms, Japan reportedly was provided with 49.6 billion barrels of crude oil in 1978 and will receive more than twice that amount by 1982. Such figures tempt the Japanese to ignore Russia's warnings against close alignments with China. In June 1978, overcoming Socialist and Communist party opposition, the Japanese Diet ratified a treaty with South Korea to drill for oil and natural gas on the continental shelf off the East China Sea. Preliminary reports show the deposit could contain as much as 6.3 billion barrels. The Japanese have also contracted for 100 million tons of coal from Siberian fields. This coal, which will be purchased for $459 million, is essential to Japan's extensive steel industry.

For long-term needs, Japan places its greatest reliance upon atomic energy. Atomic fuel has a special significance for the Japanese who are the only people ever to have experienced its destructive capacities. Because the United States is currently Japan's sole supplier of uranium, it can exert control over Japan's nuclear policy. The Carter Administration initially opposed the spread of nuclear power under any terms, but the Japanese insisted and, in September 1977, Tokai Mura, Japan's first nuclear reprocessing plant, opened for a two-year trial.

Reprocessing is a procedure used to convert uranium into atomic fuel. A by-product of reprocessing, however, is plutonium, the vital element in the production of atomic weapons. The plutonium produced at Tokai Mura will be carefully monitored and stored under strict safeguards. Shortly before the opening of Tokai Mura, Japanese negotiators signed an accord with the French government to allow Japan to reprocess American uranium in French installations. In November 1977, the Soviets offered, and the Japanese quickly accepted, a plan to exchange Russian uranium for Japanese industrial goods. If the agreement is implemented, the U.S. would lose its status as the only supplier of Japan's uranium and, with it, its control over Japanese nuclear policy.

In May 1978 Prime Minister Fukuda proposed a $1 billion joint U.S.-Japanese fund for the development of nuclear fusion as a source of energy. Later that month, Japan urged the Carter Administration to sanction further reprocessing of nuclear fuel in Europe; including a long-term accord with Great Britain for the reprocessing of nuclear fuel in that country.

Carter's Nuclear Test in Japan

President Carter must soon make a decision that will reveal whether there is substance or only bluster in his efforts to restrict the spread of dangerous nuclear technologies. Japan seeks permission to "reprocess" nuclear fuel supplied by the United States in a pilot plant at Tokai Mura, northeast of Tokyo. Mr. Carter has rightly tried to minimize such reprocessing because it typically produces plutonium, which can be used as fuel in nuclear reactors—or as the explosive force in nuclear bombs. No responsible American official believes the Japanese intend to make bombs; they could have done so long ago had they desired. But the Administration's response to the Japanese request could determine whether Mr. Carter's general campaign against proliferation will succeed or fail.

There have been disturbing hints that the American resolve is softening under a barrage of complaints from Japan. Some officials believe the Administration has given up hope of blocking the Tokai Mura plant and is seeking a fallback formula to allow reprocessing under restricting conditions. We urge Mr. Carter to stand firm. A decision to let Japan proceed would make it all the more difficult to persuade others to forego reprocessing.

Japan's desire to push ahead with reprocessing is understandable but challengeable. The country has few energy resources and must import the bulk of its nuclear and fossil fuels. The Japanese believe that reprocessing would let them extract additional energy, economically, from the fuel rods used in the present generation of nuclear reactors. That estimate is considered too sanguine by American experts. The Japanese also see reprocessing as a source of plutonium fuel for the breeder reactors of the future. But the day of the breeder is far off, and plutonium for experimental breeders could be obtained elsewhere. Japan's further belief that reprocessing would reduce the problems of nuclear waste disposal is disputed by American experts. And although Japan rightly fears the loss of technological and commercial experience, the disadvantage would presumably diminish if all nations restrain their reprocessing.

Tokai Mura has become a hot political issue in Japan —a test of whether the Japanese will let the Carter Administration dictate their energy future. Mr. Carter's position is weakened by the fact that for many years the United States advocated reprocessing and the use of plutonium. The Tokai Mura plant would not have been built without at least tacit American approval. Now that Washington has belatedly recognized the proliferation danger, it is asking Tokyo to reverse direction as well. Understandably, the Japanese demur.

Is there a way out of the impasse? The Administration seems bent on finding technical solutions that would make reprocessing less vulnerable to misuse. One option would be to allow coprocessing, a procedure that leaves the feared plutonium in a mixture with uranium and possibly other substances. That would make it more difficult—though by no means impossible—to extract the plutonium and make a bomb. But coprocessing should not be enshrined as an acceptable alternative until other, potentially safer, methods have been investigated.

At the Administration's behest, an international study has begun to explore ways of insuring that nuclear technologies and fuels are not misused to make weapons. Reprocessing at Tokai Mura should be delayed until that study is completed in two years. How ironic, and sad, if the only nation ever to suffer the horrors of the bomb, and the most vociferous in proclaiming its nuclear weapons "allergy" should set a precedent that further spreads the nuclear contagion.

August 15, 1977

U.S. AND JAPAN AGREE ON TOKYO'S OPENING OF ATOM FUEL PLANT

2-YEAR EXEMPTION FROM BAN

Pact on Reprocessing Station Now Satisfies Carter Policy to Bar Ability to Make Weapons

By ANDREW H. MALCOLM

TOKYO, Sept. 1—The United States and Japan today announced basic agreement on plans to allow the Japanese to open a nuclear fuel reprocessing plant that the Carter Administration had originally opposed as part of its policy to curb the spread of nuclear weapons.

The agreement, which is expected to be signed in Washington Sept. 12 or 13, would permit the Japanese to open their newly built Tokai Mura reprocessing plant just north of here on a controlled experimental basis for two years while conducting intensive research into alternative recycling methods.

The problem is to develop a system for reprocessing spent power plant fuel in such a way as not to produce pure plutonium, which could be used in amounts as small as 15 pounds to build atomic weapons.

U.S. Supplies Uranium

Because the United States provides the enriched uranium that is used in Japanese nuclear power plants, it has reserved the right to rule on the use of the spent fuel and so has had a virtual veto over the reprocessing plant.

United States officials had viewed the problem of how to allow the Japanese to open a plant that could produce plutonium as setting a vital precedent for the Carter Administration's nuclear dealings around the world, and it has caused high-level political concern in Japan as well. It was the subject of three rounds of talks and, according to one source familiar with the negotiations, a recent telephone talk between President Carter and Prime Minister Takeo Fukuda.

The Japanese, who must import virtually all their fossil fuels, have planned on using Tokai Mura and similar facilities to help them gain more self-sufficiency in energy by producing plutonium for the next generation of nuclear reactors, known as "breeders."

But the completion of the five-year Tokai Mura construction project coincided with President Carter's tough new policy, announced April 7, to discourage the spread of nuclear weapons. As an example, Mr. Carter ordered the suspension of the costly American commercial reprocessing facility in Barnwell, S. C., and took a tough initial stand against approval of Japan's plant.

'A Major Milestone'

Gerard Smith, who led the American negotiating team, emphasized at a joint news conference today that no one feared that Japan, the only nation to suffer the effects of nuclear attack, would develop such weapons. Japan last year ratified the treaty intended to halt the spread of nuclear arms.

Mr. Smith described the new agreement as "a major milestone" that was "very equitable" and the result of "a good deal of hard bargaining." He and his counterpart, Sosuke Uno, director general of Japan's Science and Technology Agency, refused to discuss the pact's details, pending its formal signing.

But officials cited the "very limited" nature of the plant's opening and provided these other details of the agreement:

¶The Japanese will open the Tokai Mura facility in "an experimental mode," probably later this fall, and within the next 24 months will be allowed to produce a limited amount of plutonium nitrate and uranium nitrate, as originally planned. These solutions are to be stored separately under strict safeguards.

¶Emphasis at Tokai Mura will shift to research on alternate methods of fuel reprocessing that do not permit production of weapons-grade material. One prominent method is "co-processing," which produces not pure plutonium but a mixture of plutonium and uranium unsuitable for weapons. The results of this costly research are to be discussed by technical experts of both nations in two years and are to determine the future of the Tokai Mura project.

¶The Japanese offered and the Americans accepted an indefinite postponement of a planned $15 million nuclear conversion facility, which would have turned the plutonium nitrate into plutonium oxide, the next step in the production of nuclear fuel and weapons.

This postponement is expected to set back by several years Japan's ambitious nuclear energy development program, and apparently it means that Tokai Mura, in effect, may be turning out a nuclear product without the ability to make practical use of it.

But American officials said privately that the postponement move was "a key factor" in the agreement and was strong evidence of Japan's intention to investigate seriously alternate reprocessing methods. The Americans also described the decision as a useful symbol to other nations of the importance attached to nonproliferation by two major nuclear energy powers.

September 2, 1977

Japanese Town Gets Atom Plant And a New Life

By ANDREW H. MALCOLM

TOKAI MURA, Japan, Sept. 12—Chuzo Akuzawa doesn't know much about nuclear energy. But he does know one thing: the hard-won agreement to open Japan's first nuclear fuel reprocessing plant here, which was formally signed by the United States and Japan in Washington today, is good for Japan, this little town and him, not necessarily in that order.

The agreement, following a confrontation between Japan and President Carter's policy against the spread of nuclear weapons, also means that Tokai Mura, the town that once lived only for sweet potatoes and peanuts, will remain the hub of Japan's vast nuclear energy development program.

Already 10 major nuclear facilities stand inside the town's limits, with one more on the drawing boards. At this rate, officials here figure that some day they may even have to build a police station.

In recent months, the name Tokai Mura (literally, East Sea Village) has become internationally synonymous with the problem of developing peaceful uses for nuclear energy without simultaneously promoting the spread of nuclear-weapons material.

Long Costly Effort

Japan, which has few fossil fuels of its own, had spent more than five years and $200 million on its newest plant here, which was intended to reprocess spent nuclear fuel into plutonium for the next generation of nuclear-power reactors. But the Carter Administration, which can control Japan's use of spent American fuel, suggested that there were other ways to reprocess the fuel without producing pure plutonium, which can be used in amounts as small as 15 pounds to build atomic weapons.

After three rounds of talks, much emotional news coverage here and a phone conversation between Mr. Carter and Prime Minister Takeo Fukuda, the two sides announced basic agreement on Sept. 1. The facility would open for a two-year trial period, they said, while beginning research into alternate reprocessing methods.

Today, the sprawling plant, all but its candy-striped smokestack hidden behind a grove of lush pines, began "warm-up" procedures for a scheduled start-up Sept. 22. And some of Tokai Mura's citizens reflected on the advantages, changes and problems that the atom has brought to their community, 63 miles northeast of Tokyo.

"Without nuclear energy," said Mr. Akuzawa, "I'm sure Tokai Mura would go bankrupt." So, likely, would he. Mr. Akuzawa holds three jobs, all nuclear-related. He is director general of the Nuclear Conference, which seeks to teach residents about atomic energy. He is general manager of the only local hotel, which houses visiting foreign technicians. And he is the chief of the general-affairs bureau of the Nuclear Souvenir Shop, which offers earrings, ashtrays and vases that, according to the sign, have been exposed to cobalt rays.

Tourists Showing Up

The recent publicity and the new nuclear museum here have drawn many tourists in recent days and Mr. Akuzawa was so busy this morning that he did not have time to use an electric shaver, which is run on current produced in a nuclear plant across the street.

A few statistics illustrate the dramatic changes since the Government chose Tokai Mura, a 1,500-year-old farming community, as the focus of its nuclear energy research.

In 1955, the year the towns of Muramatsu and Ishigami merged to form Tokai Mura, the population here was 11,583 humans, 1,526 horses, and 88 goats. Today the same 14-square mile area has 26,609 humans, no horses and no goats.

About two-thirds of the town's economy and almost half the labor force is built around atomic energy. Many farmers were able to retire early on the profits of land sold to the Government. And the

annual taxes from nuclear facilities have financed a new firehouse and a modern town hall, complete with color television.

One new school has been built. Another hinged on today's agreement with the United States. "For a farmer," said Tomio Sudo, a city hall spokesman, "his investment is in his land. Engineers and scientists invest instead in their children's education."

But a local economy run on nuclear energy has not come to Tokai Mura without opposition and fears of atomic accidents. There are also the usual frictions between old residents and new.

Major Election Issue

The size of the nuclear development was a major issue in yesterday's elections for town chief. Saichiro Kotsuchi, a 48-year-old farmer and political unknown, garnered 6,100 votes by suggesting that nuclear development here was going too fast. Thanks in part to the last-minute settlement with the United States, the incumbent, 63-year-old Yoshihiko Kawasaki, who invited the nuclear plants here in the mid-50's, won his sixth term with 8,200 votes.

But the long campaign took its toll, and Mr. Kawasaki was too busy resting today to receive visitors. However, a former mayor, 77-year-old Tokinosuke Nemoto, told of his doubts.

"Maybe all this is good for Japan," he said. "But it's not necessarily good for this village. We used to live here quietly, simply and honestly. The people were friendly. The rivers were clean. And the streets were quiet. But now everyone is more calculating. They must earn more and more money. Life is more like a city, with no sense of duty or humanity. People talk about 'progress,' always 'progress,' and their hearts seem hard."

Soon now, because of the mushrooming nuclear growth of Tokai Mura, city engineers will come to tear up Mr. Nemoto's mossy garden and move his old home with the tiled roof back a bit. They told him they must do this to make room for a new traffic circle.

Shift in U.S. Stand Denied

WASHINGTON, Sept. 13 (Reuters)— The United States Government said today that the agreement to let Japan open its Tokai Mura nuclear-reprocessing plant did not reflect any change in the policy of discouraging a spread of nuclear weapon-making capacity.

The agreement, signed here yesterday, defers for two years a decision on whether the United States would permit fuel supplies to be reprocessed in the Japanese plant.

September 14, 1977

The Silver Lining of a Nuclear Cloud

President Carter's campaign to restrict the spread of dangerous nuclear technologies emerged from its first major test, in Japan, battered but not beaten. A new United States-Japanese agreement will allow Japan to begin operating an experimental nuclear reprocessing facility at Tokai Mura—just the kind of facility that Mr. Carter has focused on as dangerous because it produces plutonium that can be used to make bombs.

The agreement is being characterized by some observers as a surrender to Japanese pressure. There is no denying that the cause of anti-proliferation would have been better served if Japan had been willing to forgo any reprocessing. We had urged that operation of the plant be delayed at least until completion of an international study of ways to prevent the diversion of nuclear fuels to weapons use. But American negotiators, whose approval was necessary before Japan could reprocess fuel supplied by the United States, concluded that delay was impracticable: The Japanese public had been aroused against American meddling in its energy affairs and the Tokyo Government wanted to operate the $200-million French-built plant while its warranty was still in effect.

So the American negotiators got the best deal they could. Japan will reprocess a limited amount of fuel for a limited time—essentially operating the facility as originally planned for a two-year period. Some fuel will be used for experimental purposes, but most of it will simply be stored and guarded and will not be used in existing uranium-fueled reactors. The agreement is provisional

and will have to be renegotiated at the end of the two-year international study.

The decision to allow even limited reprocessing in Japan could set an unfortunate precedent. It has already increased pressures to allow reprocessing elsewhere. And it will further undercut the Administration's efforts to persuade the French and West Germans to break contracts to supply reprocessing facilities to Pakistan and Brazil.

But in some ways the agreement with Japan could give a boost to Mr. Carter's efforts to slow nuclear proliferation. The joint communiqué carries a Japanese endorsement of the American view that plutonium poses "a serious proliferation danger" and should not yet be used commercially in the present generation of reactors. Japan is the first major nuclear-industrial power to join the United States in a firm stand against the rush toward plutonium-based energy systems. As a nation with enormous energy needs and a strong commitment to nuclear power, Japan's avowed concern about plutonium is apt to carry weight in international deliberations. Japan backed up its words by agreeing to delay construction of a conversion plant needed to complete the processing of the fuel at Tokai, and by deferring a large reprocessing plant that would have been used to produce plutonium in commercial quantities. If Japan, which seemed committed to plutonium only a few months ago, has really undergone a radical change of attitude, it could prove a strong ally in Mr. Carter's efforts to pull the world back from the plutonium precipice.

September 16, 1977

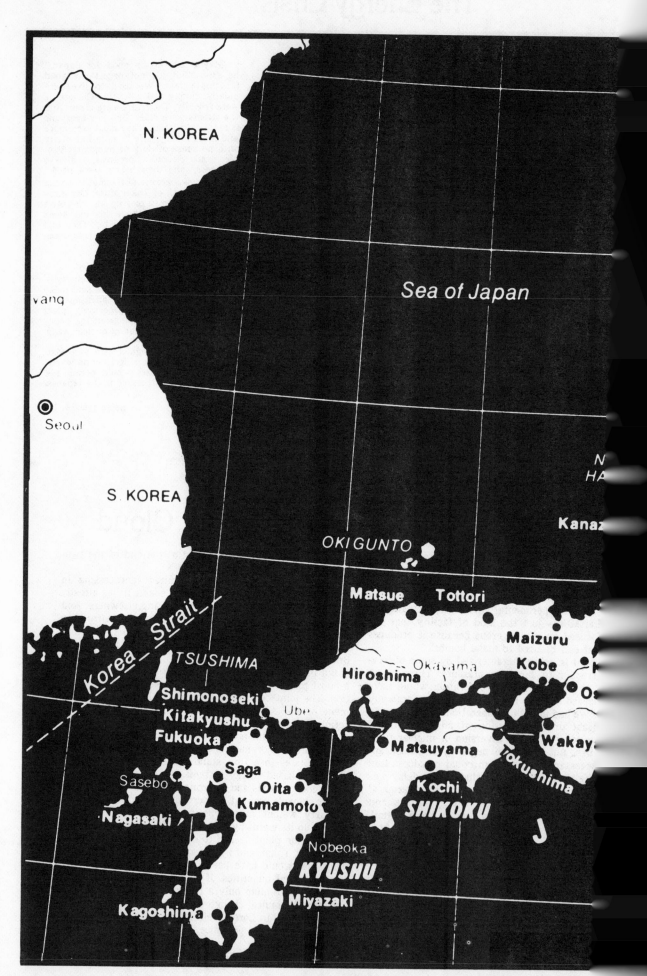

Muroran

Hakodate

Aomori

Hirosaki

Hachinohe

Noshiro

Akita

Morioka

Sakata

Sendai

Fukushima

HONSHU

Utsunomiya

Mito

Tokyo

Yokohama

Yokosuka

OSHIMA

MIYAKEJIMA

MIKURAJIMA

HACHIJOJIMA

ADGASHIMA

SUMISU

Wakkanai

Kitami

Asahigawa

Sapporo

Kushiro

HOKKAIDO

Muroran

Hakodate

Aomori

Hachinohe

Hirosaki

Noshiro

44

42

40

36

32

JAPAN TODAY

miles

0   100   200

Paris-Tokyo Nuclear Reprocessing Pact
Is Viewed as a Blow to Carter

By JONATHAN KANDELL

PARIS, Oct. 6—An accord signed by Japan to have its used nuclear fuel reprocessed in a French installation appears to be another major challenge to President Carter's uphill campaign against the use of plutonium as a reactor fuel.

Under the agreement, signed in Tokyo last week, the Japanese will be able to reprocess up to 1,600 tons of their spent uranium fuel each year when the French installations at La Hague begin operation in 1985.

The reprocessing produces plutonium, which the Japanese can use as a fuel. Plutonium can also be used in making nuclear explosives, which is the main reason that the Carter Administration has opposed its spread as a fuel for atomic plants.

Some officials, who have been following the French-Japanese accord, have minimized the challenge it poses to Mr. Carter's antiplutonium campaign.

Must Have U.S. Permission

These officials point out that the United States would have a measure of control over the agreement because the United States provides Japan with its enriched nuclear fuel and would have to give the Japanese permission for every shipment made to the French reprocessing plant.

The officials also noted that the accord will not go into effect before 1985—by which time international agreements will have been reached either banning plutonium or permitting its widespread use as a fuel. On the other hand, the French-Japanese agreement is the latest step taken by American allies towards plutonium-based energy sources.

France has been at the forefront of those countries who believe that reprocessing plants and plutonium-fueled fast breeder reactors will inevitably play a major role in meeting energy needs.

Must Import Uranium

Officials here emphasize that Western Europe and Japan are far more vulnerable than the United States because they must import their uranium, along with oil and coal.

As an alternative to breeder reactors and other plutonium-fueled plants, President Carter has asserted that the United States and other countries, such as Australia, could meet the world's needs for uranium.

But French officials point out that there is great uncertainty that the United States will be able to expand its uranium enrichment capacity in the face of mounting public disenchantment with nuclear energy. Australia, the other great source of uranium with about 20 percent of the Western world's deposits, has been having a bitter public debate over whether or not to exploit its ore.

Uranium prices have soared from $8 a pound to over $40 a pound over the last four years. So the French have moved ahead with their plans for commercial uranium-enrichment plants despite their expense.

French Lead in Breeder Reactors

France also says it has a lead over the rest of the world in breeder reactors, which in theory produce more plutonium fuel than they consume. A 250-megawatt breeder reactor is already in operation, and a commercial 1,200-megawatt breeder is under construction.

The French are by no means alone in their drive toward plutonium-based energy sources.

Last July, France, West Germany and several other European nations signed agreements for further research and development of plutonium-fueled fast breeder reactors and their eventual sale abroad.

Despite some strenuous diplomatic maneuvering by President Carter, the West Germans are proceeding with their multibillion dollar agreement to supply

Brazil with nuclear facilities—including a reprocessing plant that will produce plutonium, thus giving the Brazilians the potential to build an atomic bomb.

The French Government has also publicly pledged that it will carry out a similar controversial sale of a nuclear-fuel reprocessing plant to Pakistan.

Japan to Operate Plant

Last month, after drawn out negotiations, the United States signed an agreement with Tokyo, allowing the Japanese to begin operating an experimental nuclear reprocessing facility at Tokai Mura. The $200 million French-built plant will use fuel supplied by the United States.

The West Europeans and the Japanese have not completely closed the door to President Carter's initiative. As a compromise, they have agreed in principle to join a two-year study to devise ways of insuring that the increasing use of nuclear reactors will not lead to further proliferation of nuclear arms.

But the Europeans and Japanese have insisted that in the meantime they will

continue research and development of breeder reactors and the use of plutonium as a nuclear fuel.

This dual strategy of investigating safeguards while pursuing development of plutonium energy sources was repeatedly voiced at the annual general conference of the International Atomic Energy Agency in Vienna last week.

"Let us remember that in the long run there is no way of stopping the spread of nuclear technology among the nations, and we must face the proliferation problems that result," said Sigvard Eklund, director general of the agency, in the opening address of the Vienna conference. "The question is, therefore, not how to stop nuclear development but how best to make use of it and how to apply effective safeguards."

October 8, 1977

Russia and Japan
Report Discovering Sakhalin Oilfield

TOKYO, Oct. 12 (UPI)—A Soviet-Japanese oil drilling venture said today that it had located a significant oilfield off the Soviet island of Sakhalin. Sado Kobay-ashi, president of the Sakhalin Oil Company, said oil deposits there could be the largest in Asia, surpassing those of Indonesia.

Four test wells sunk about four miles off the coast of northwest Sakhalin are now producing a combined daily flow of 7,000 barrels of crude, he said. The oil

The Energy Crisis

has a sulfur content of about 25 one-hundredths of 1 percent and a 1.26 percent paraffin content.

The joint drilling program will continue until the autumn of 1978, and assessment of the field's commercial potential will require four to five years, Mr. Kobayashi said.

1972 Development Accord

Japan, which imports virtually all of its oil, mostly from the Middle East, signed an accord in 1972 with the Soviet Union to develop oil and natural gas off Sakhalin's continental shelf. The island is north of Japan's uppermost island, Hokkaido.

Under the agreement with the Soviet Union, Japan would receive 50 percent of the crude oil produced over a 10-year period. The cost of development, estimated at nearly $1 billion, is to be shared equally.

The Soviet Union has been eager to develop offshore resources for Pacific markets, particularly Japan. The Chinese have been making progress in developing oilfields in Manchuria and on the Yellow Sea, relatively close to Japan, and have been exporting oil to Japan at a growing rate.   October 13, 1977

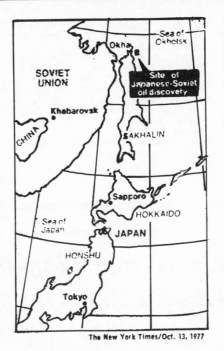

The New York Times/Oct. 13, 1977

SOVIET OFFERS URANIUM FOR JAPANESE IMPORTS

TOKYO, Nov. 10—The Soviet Union informed Japan today that it was keenly interested in selling enriched uranium in exchange for imports of Japanese industrial plants.

Moscow's overture was conveyed by A.M. Petrosyants, chairman of the Soviet State Atomic Energy Committee, in a 45-minute meeting with Sosuke Uno, director general of the Science and Technology Agency.

At present, Japan is importing all enriched uranium fuel from the United States for its 13 light water reactors, and is shipping spent radioactive fuel to Britain and France for reprocessing.

The Soviet official arrived in Tokyo yesterday and is to sign this week a five-year atomic energy cooperation agreement between Moscow and the semi-governmental Japan Atomic Industrial Forum Inc.

The new agreement provides joint study and cooperation on power reactors and fusion. It also stipulates the exchange of results of experiments on them as well as of nuclear technicians.

November 11, 1977

Soviet Rails Reach Coal for Japan

By THEODORE SHABAD

Soviet rail-laying crews, keeping 14 months ahead of schedule in their northward advance through Siberian virgin forest, have reached a coal basin that is expected to supply a significant part of the fuel needs of the Japanese steel industry in the 1980's.

The Japanese have invested $450 million in the big strip mine under a 1974 accord, granting credits for the purchase of equipment abroad. The investment is to be paid back with 100 million tons of coal, of which the newly developed South Yakutian basin will provide more than 80 million.

Prompted by rising world prices, the Russians appear eager to expand their resource exports to the West in return for advanced technology. The coal project, situated at Neryungri, is the first of several mineral sites to be developed for export over the 2,000-mile-long Baikal-Amur Mainline system, probably the biggest current rail project in the world.

Line Compared to Trans-Siberian

Prof. Victor L. Mote of the University of Houston, an expert on the project, says in a new book, "Gateway to Sibe-

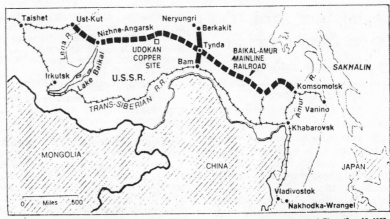

The New York Times/Dec. 17, 1977

Soviet rail crews have completed a line to Neryungri in the heart of the Siberian coalfields, about 14 months ahead of schedule.

rian Resources," that the Baikal-Amur line "should have at least as much influence on the development of Pacific Siberia in the last quarter of the 20th century as the Trans-Siberian had on Western Siberia in the first quarter."

According to some forecasts, the rail system, scheduled for completion in

1983, may enhance the Soviet export potential by making available more Siberian resources to the world market. Much of the mineral wealth and timberlands of the Siberian land mass have remained unexploited because they lie beyond existing transportation lines.

A settlement of 4,000 people has grown up at the railhead, known as Berkakit, which serves the Neryungri mine being developed 15 miles away. When it reaches an annual capacity of 13 million tons of coal, planned for 1983, the mine will begin shipping 5 million tons of high-grade coking coal a year to Japan. Coking coal is suitable for making coke, which is used in steel smelting.

The coal will move by rail to Nakhodka, on the Pacific coast, where a specialized coal-loading terminal is under construction at the new port complex of Wrangel, designed to become the Soviet Union's largest bulk-cargo export harbor. Japan has also been involved in construction of the port facilities, which are expected to handle much of the raw-material export trade to be generated by the Baikal-Amur Mainline.

The east-west mainline will pass near a variety of mineral deposits that represent a potential for development. They include the copper of Udokan, the asbestos of Molodezhny, the iron ore of the Tokko-Chara watershed as well as commercial timber stands suitable for forest-products industries.

The South Yakutian coal basin now reached by the north-south transverse line is the first export-oriented mineral project to be reached by the railroad development program.

December 17, 1977

Mitsubishi Group Signs Contract For 2 Desalination Units in Iran

TEHERAN, Iran, Jan. 4 (AP)—Iran has signed a contract to exchange $270 million worth of crude oil for two Japanese water desalination units, it was disclosed today.

A Japanese consortium, headed by Sassakura Engineering and including Mitsubishi Heavy Industries, signed the contract with Iran's atomic energy organization.

The desalination units will be constructed next to two West German nuclear reactors being built close to the city of Bushehr. Heat from the 1,200-megawatt reactors will be used to help take the salt from about 200,000 cubic meters of seawater a day.

The Government is attempting to turn Bushehr into a major industrial and commercial center. The desalination units are expected to alleviate acute water shortages in southwestern Iran.

January 5, 1978

JAPAN AND CHINA SET TO SIGN TRADE PACT

Major Long-Term Accord, First Between Countries, Calls for $20 Billion Exchange

By FOX BUTTERFIELD

HONG KONG, Feb. 13—Japanese businessmen and China are set to sign a major long-term trade agreement in Peking this week that provides for an exchange of $20 billion worth of goods over the next eight years.

Under the accord, the first between China and Japan, China will supply crude oil and coal in return for Japanese exports of steel, industrial plants and technology. The benefits of the deal will be divided equally, with each country selling $10 billion of selected products between 1978 and 1985.

Japanese sources say the pact is expected to be signed in Peking on Thursday by China's Vice Minister of Foreign Trade, Liu Hsi-wen, and Yoshihiro Inayama, chairman of the Japan-China Association on Economy and Trade as well as vice chairman of Keidanren, or federation of economic organizations. While technically a private venture by Japanese businessmen, the trade agreement has the clear support of the Japanese Government.

A Significant Breakthrough

The agreement is considered a significant breakthrough in trade between the two countries because it commits both to purchase specified quantities of goods within a given period of time, something they had been reluctant to do before.

From Japan's point of view, the pact assures its steelmakers of a steady and perhaps growing market for their exports at a time when the country's sales of steel to America and Western Europe have come under increasing attack from local producers.

From Peking's side, the trade agreement guarantees a regular source of foreign exchange to help finance imports of advanced foreign equipment and technology as Peking seeks to meet its proclaimed goal of modernizing itself by the year 2000.

The trade accord is seen by analysts here as one of the strongest indications yet of the new development-minded policies being pursued by China's post-Mao leadership.

Last week China also signed a five-year trade agreement with the European Economic Community. However, because it merely provided a legal framework for trade between the Common Market and China, rather than setting up actual commercial exchanges as the accord with Japan does, its significance was considered more political than economic.

Over the last year China has been increasingly stressing its relations with Western Europe in an effort to bolster European unity and resolve against the Soviet Union.

Oil Purchase Plans Outlined

The precise figures for China's oil and coal exports to Japan have not yet been released. But well-informed Japanese sources say Japan will buy 49.6 million barrels of oil from China in 1978, with the amount rising to 109.5 million barrels in 1982.

The 49.6 million barrels is the amount Japan bought from China in 1976 and 1977. Oil represented nearly 50 percent of China's exports to Japan last year. Even without the formal trade agreement, trade between the countries has been on the increase. According to figures just published by the Japan external trade organization, the volume reached $3.49

The Energy Crisis

billion last year, up 14.9 percent over 1976.

Japan had a trade surplus with China of $391 million, up 34 percent. Steel accounted for about 40 percent of Japan's overall sales to China. Japan is China's largest trading partner, with the Common Market second.

Much of the momentum for the long-term trade agreement had come from Japan's steelmakers, who wished to step up sales to China. The idea for the pact was initially broached in 1974, but the downturn in Japan's economy and reluctance to commit itself to large purchases of Chinese oil, which has a high wax content, held up the discussions.

February 14, 1978

Foes of Nuclear Energy Lose a Battle in Japan

TOKYO, April 25—Japanese groups opposed to the widespread construction of nuclear power plants lost a significant legal battle today with a precedent-making court decision.

The ruling, the result of a five-year court struggle begun by local residents, said that the Japanese Government did have the legal authority to build such plants and was adequately assuring safe operations.

The suit, the first ever here to challenge the safety of nuclear power plants, was specifically directed against the No. 1 nuclear power plant of the Shikoku Electric Power Company in the city of Ikata, 450 miles southwest of here. But the ruling, which was handed down by the Matsuyama district court, is expected to be a severe blow to efforts, by environmental and other groups to block such facilities.

The decision gives the Government "a green light" to vigorously promote the peaceful uses of nuclear power, according to Katsuomi Kodama, the Justice Ministry attorney who represented the Government side.

April 26, 1978

Fukuda Proposes Joint Financing on Fusion.

Prime Minister Takeo Fukuda of Japan said yesterday that he had proposed to President Carter that the United States and Japan set up a joint fund of up to $1 billion to develop nuclear fusion as a source of energy.

At a luncheon at the New York Hilton, Mr. Fukuda said that even though his country had "experienced untold suffering" from nuclear weapons, this should not preclude an intensive joint effort to develop nuclear fusion, particularly since both nations are heavily dependent on foreign oil.

Nuclear plants already in operation around the world are based on fission, or the splitting of heavy atoms. Fusion, the process of the hydrogen bomb, involves the joining of light atoms and has not yet been controlled sufficiently for the production of useful energy.

Mr. Fukuda said nuclear fusion and solar energy were suited to joint development "since both are considered to be ultimate energy sources for the future" and require enormously expensive research to make them practical.

Proposed to President

The Prime Minister said he had made his proposal during a three-hour meeting with the President on Wednesday.

An aide to the Prime Minister said in an interview that the President's reaction

The New York Times/Garx Settle

Prime Minister Takeo Fukuda of Japan enjoying a light moment at the Japan Society luncheon in New York. With him was an interpreter.

had been favorable, but he said the idea had been discussed only in broad terms. The aide said that in past discussions of the proposal, Mr. Fukuda had said that each nation could put up $250 million to $500 million, and that Japan's share would be primarily government money.

Mr. Fukuda's speech was read to the 1,300 guests by an interpreter at the luncheon, which was sponsored by the Japan Society and the Foreign Policy Association.

The 73-year-old Prime Minister came to the United States to reassure Congressional leaders and the Administration that Japan is determined to reduce its growing trade surplus which is aggravating the American trade deficit and is a prime cause of the weakening of the dollar.

The Japanese Economy

United States officials have been pressing Mr. Fukuda to stimulate his country's economy to divert exports to domestic consumption and increase the demand for imports.

Mr. Fukuda said Japan's economy was now growing 7 percent a year. He vowed that if growth falls below that, "I will be ready to choose additional measures to achieve 7 percent growth."

The Prime Minister has been critical of the Carter Administration's policy of letting the dollar find its own level in relation to other currencies, but he appeared, in a question-and-answer session, to approve of recent American action.

He said he was pleased that the President had ordered the sale of gold to support the dollar and that the Federal Reserve Board had raised interest rates in the money market.

May 5, 1978

Japanese Urge U.S. To Allow Processing Of A-Fuel in Europe

By DAVID BURNHAM

WASHINGTON, May 20—A group of Japanese utility executives have told United States officials they hope the Carter Administration will approve a long-term Japanese plan to reprocess American-supplied uranium in Britain and France.

Officials in the State Department, the Department of Energy and the Nuclear Regulatory Commission said today that the businessmen had indicated that Japan planned to invest about $1 billion over the next 10 years in construction of reprocessing facilities in France and Britain that can be used to extract plutonium from the radioactive waste from conventional reactors. Washington's permission is necessary for transfer to Britain and France of spent fuel from American-supplied uranium.

Japan, France and Britain have long planned to extract plutonium from the spent fuel of uranium-powered reactors and use the plutonium in fast breeder reactors.

The United States had similar plans until recently, but the Carter Administration has sought to halt construction of an experimental breeder reactor on the Clinch River in Tennessee and to persuade other nations not to develop this type of technology.

Use in Weapons Possible

President Carter has opposed the construction of the experimental reactor at Clinch River because plutonium, unlike the uranium used in conventional reactors, can be used to make nuclear weapons with relative ease.

The Administration has contended that the widespread use of plutonium would almost inevitably lead to an expansion in the number of nations that have nuclear weapons and would greatly increase the chances that a group of terrorists one day might be able to obtain or make such a bomb.

However, Japan and France, which are heavily dependent on other nations for oil, view plutonium-powered reactors as beneficial because they would reduce dependence on outside sources of energy.

May 21, 1978

Japan and Britain Sign Pact on Nuclear Fuel

By JUNNOSUKE OFUSA

TOKYO, May 24—Japan signed a long-term contract here today with Britain for the transport and reprocessing of spent nuclear fuel from 1982 through 1990.

Sir John Hill, chairman of British Nuclear Fuel Ltd. and also president of the British Atomic Energy Authority, signed the contract with representatives of 10 major Japanese power companies.

Under the contract, a total of 1,600 tons of spent nuclear fuel will be delivered to Britain for reprocessing over the eight years. The cost of the reprocessing is put at $1.02 billion.

Britain plans to build new reprocessing facilities under its controversial Windscale project for a nuclear-fuel-reprocessing complex. The project, which brought on strong public criticism, was finally approved by Parliament on May 15 of this year.

Reprocessing Set for 1987

According to a spokesman for the Japanese power companies, although the agreement will become effective in 1982, the work to reprocess spent fuel from American-supplied uranium to be transported to Britain is expected to begin in 1987 after the completion of new reprocessing facilities that meet Japanese requirements.

In September 1977, the 10 Japanese power companies signed another contract with a French nuclear fuel company, Cogem, for transfer and reprocessing a total of 1,600 tons of spent fuel. The cost to transport a total of 3,200 tons of spent fuel to Britain and France is estimated at $578 million.

Japan is the third-largest producer of nuclear power after the United States and Britain. It is currently importing all enriched uranium from the United States.

Under the existing United States-Japanese nuclear power agreement, Washington's approval is necessary for transport overseas of spent fuel from American-supplied uranium. Both the Tokyo Electric Power Company and the Kansai Electric Power Company shipped to Britain and France spent fuel from American-supplied uranium for reprocessing after obtaining Washington's permission in 1975.

The spokesman for the Japanese power companies said that they had not yet received the Carter Administration's sanction for transfer of nuclear spent fuel as provided for in the new contract.

"The Japanese companies will carry on their endeavor to get Washington's approval in the next four years before the contract takes effect in 1982," the spokesman said.

A group of Japanese utility executives visited Washington recently in the hope that they could get the Administration's approval of the long-term contracts concluded with Britain and France.

May 25, 1978

Japan-South Korea Oil Treaty Ratified

By JUNNOSUKE OFUSA

TOKYO, June 14 — The Japanese Parliament today ratified the controversial treaty signed by Japan and South Korea in 1974 on the joint development of continental shelf oil and natural gas resources lying between their shores and the East China Sea.

Although the South Korean National Assembly ratified the accord in 1974, action by the Japanese Parliament had been blocked for four years by strong objections by the opposition parties headed by the Socialists and Communists.

The continental shelf, under the treaty, covers a 30,880-square-mile zone and both nations started exploration there, following the release of a 1968 United Nations geological survey indicating the existence of hydrocarbons in the area.

Oil Presence Confirmed

The Japanese Government maintains that an authoritative survey has confirmed the presence of an oil reserve totaling 6.3 billion barrels in the Japan-South Korean joint development zone, west of Kyushu.

Japan imports 99 percent of its oil requirements, which amounted to 1.8 billion barrrels in the 1977 fiscal year, according to the Petroleum Association of Japan. Those imports, valued at $26.9 billion, accounted for 40.03 percent of Japan's total imports in value in the last fiscal year.

Terms of The Agreement

Under the agreement, the explorationn and development costs are to be equally shared by Japan and South Korea.

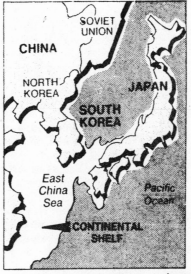

The New York Times/June 15, 1978

Before the pact was signed in 1974, three Japanese companies had filed applications with the Japanese Government for exploitation rights in the continental shelf.

Four other oil companies — Korean-American Oil, Caltex, Shell and Gulf — also had applied for the same right to the South Korean Government.

The seven are expected to go ahead with exploration now that the treaty has been ratified.

One problem with the area is that part of the Japan-South Korean continental shelf is in the East China Sea and geologically attached to the Chinese continent. A month after the signing of the pact, Peking's Foreign Ministry issued a statement that called the treaty an infringement on Chinese sovereignty.

In April 1977, the Chinese Embassy here filed a protest with the Foreign Ministry that said that Tokyo and Seoul had divided the continental shelf in the East China Sea without Peking's consent. The embassy warned that if Tokyo and Seoul arbitrarily developed the area under the 1974 accord, both must bear responsibility for any consequence.

Violation Is Charged

This year, Han Nien-lung, Peking's Vice Foreign Minister, in a meeting on May 10 with Heishiro Ogawa, Japanese Ambassador to Peking, charged that the the Japanese Government was acting along with South Korea in violation of China's sovereign rights.

Reports from Peking reaching here today indicated that the Chinese Government would renew its protest against the continental shelf agreement. However, China has not shown any intention of taking retaliatory action against Japan immediately or linking the issue with the projected Japan-China peace treaty.

The Japanese opposition parties, which blocked the ratification of the treaty for four years, contended that the Government should have discussed the joint development issue with China and North Korea before the agreement was concluded.

The Government, however, maintained that the pact was necessary to secure the nation's energy resources.

June 15, 1978

2 Nuclear Reactors to Be Built
in Japan If Subsidy Is Approved

TOKYO, June 16 (Reuters)—Japan's Electric Power Development Company said today that it was planning to build two Canadian heavy-water nuclear reactors, subject to approval by the Government.

The company will seek public funds to help finance the project because of the high cost of building the "Candu" reactors. It is not known whether the Government will approve such a plan, industry sources said.

Japan now operates light water reactors. The proposed ones will operate on 600,000 kilowatts.   June 18, 1978

How to Get Oil by Selling Oil

Imports now account for about 40 percent of the oil consumed in the United States. That is slightly less than last year, but enough to put our international trade balance deeply in the red and — more important — leave us vulnerable to another Arab embargo. A tough energy program to reduce consumption remains the only long-term response to this dependence. However, as recent reports of the disappointing oil production in Alaska suggest, minor changes in Federal regulations could sharply increase domestic production and reduce the trade deficit within a few years. A shrewd program for greater self-sufficiency begins, paradoxically, with oil exports.

●

The key to the paradox lies in the West Coast's current oil glut. Completion of the Alaska pipeline last year greatly increased the amount of domestic oil available, but there is no market for much of it on the West Coast and no pipeline to send the excess to needy refineries in the Midwest. Instead of paying the exorbitant cost of shipping excess supplies eastward through the Panama Canal, producers are leaving it in the ground. At the present rate, oil production in Alaska and California by the early 1980's will be at least a million barrels a day below capacity.

The quickest, most effective means of stimulating that production would be to offer the oil companies a lucrative new market: the Far East. By changing the law to allow oil *exports*, the United States could sell its extra oil to Japan, then turn around and use the foreign currency thus earned to pay for some of the necessary imports to the East Coast. Japan, which is now heavily dependent on Middle East oil supplies, would be delighted, not only by the alternate source of supply but also by the opportunity to even out its trade accounts with the United States. The United States would not only reduce a huge trade deficit with Japan through the next decade or two but would also reduce its dependence on the oil of the Middle East. The total American oil imports would not be affected, but the available domestic supply in case of emergency would have been enlarged. In the event of an Arab embargo, Japan-bound oil could, if necessary, be diverted to higher-priority use.

If exporting oil is so desirable, why has the White House been reluctant to ask Congress for permission? Primarily because the President expects opposition from House members who suspect the motives of the oil companies. A ban on exports was written into the Alaska pipeline law to allay Congressional fears that the new oil would be diverted to more profitable markets overseas. The export plan would indeed induce production precisely because foreign sales would be profitable. But the oil comnpanies' gains are not, in this case, the consumer's loss. We all stand to benefit from a reduced trade deficit and a greater capacity to withstand an embargo.

There is always the danger that O.P.E.C. would reduce production to offset the added flow of Alaskan oil. In this sense, however, Alaskan oil is no different than oil from the North Sea or the coast off New Jersey. Every move toward stimulating greater production among O.P.E.C.'s customers can be interpreted as a threat to the cartel. Considering the alternatives, we have little choice but to strive to reduce our dependence on O.P.E.C. while also using political and economic influence to contain its power.

A more significant objection has been that exports

might discourage pipeline construction to the Midwest. It is not clear that a brand new pipeline should in fact be built; the national interest is well served by selling oil to Japan. But if we did choose this expensive project, it would be easy enough to guarantee the pipeline a good supply of oil by limiting the exports to surpluses beyond its capacity.

Self-sufficiency in energy is going to be hard to achieve with the best of efforts. With real sacrifices still to be made, it would be folly to bypass so simple and painless a step toward that goal.

July 10, 1978

The National Diet Building in Tokyo which houses Japan's national legislature.

Chapter 6

The Political World

Through alliances with smaller parties, Japan's governing Liberal-Democratic Party (LDP) has continued to control Japan's parliament by a slim majority. Although it has dominated the federal government since 1945, the LDP faced a number of crucial tests during 1977-78.

Plagued by a domestic economic recession and sharp criticism from abroad for his nation's huge trade surplus, Prime Minister Takeo Fukuda shuffled his cabinet in November 1977, a reliable technique to allay criticism. Out of this cabinet shift emerged Nobuhiko Ushiba, ambassador to the United States from 1970 to 1973 and now Japan's chief negotiator in the crucial trade talks with the U.S. Other key position changes included the transfer of Kiichi Miyazawa, a former foreign minister. In addition, Tatsuo Murayama, a little known official in the finance ministry, was made finance minister. Toshio Komoto, a prominent economist and businessman, was named Minister of International Trade and Industry. It was hoped that such a sudden change in the cabinet would help to check the rising exchange value of the Japanese yen against the American dollar.

Japan was also rocked by two political crises of a more sensational character: the Red Army hijacking of a Japan Air Lines jet and the violent police-demonstrator clashes over the opening of Narita Airport.

On September 28, 1977, a Paris to Tokyo Japan Air Lines DC-8 jet with 156 passengers was reported hijacked soon after a stopover in Bombay, and was forced to land in Dacca, Bangladesh. The hijackers, five members of the ultra-leftist Japanese Red Army, revealed their demands the following day: freedom for six comrades jailed in Japan and $6 million in ransom. For failure to comply, they threatened to slaughter the hostages. The Red Army was responsible for the Tel Aviv airport massacre of 1972 which left 24 dead and 76 wounded, as well as several diplomatic kidnappings, numerous hijackings and the torture and murder of at least fourteen of its own members, the result of internal divisions. Aware of the Red Army's notorious history and convinced it would carry out its threat, the Japanese government acquiesced to the demands. The airliner next flew to Damascus where ten hostages were released and then to Kuwait where another seven were freed. On October 5 the plane arrived in Algeria where money and hijackers quickly vanished, despite the Japanese government's request that the terrorists be remanded to Japanese agents. The Japanese government was criticized at home and abroad for its rapid capitulation to the demands of the hijackers. When the West German government accomplished a daring military rescue of a Lufthansa plane hijacked to Somalia two weeks later, the contrast between responses was not overlooked by the world press.

In March 1978 international attention focused upon the scheduled opening of Tokyo's new international airport at Narita, for 13 years a *cause célèbre* for both the local farming population and Japan's militant leftists who have embraced the issue. Japan's postwar economic boom brought with it the expansion of Tokyo, which, in turn, engendered the need for a second metropolitan airport to relieve traffic at the over-extended Haneda facility. Narita, an agricultural site 46 miles northeast of Tokyo, was selected by the government then headed by Prime Minister Eisaku Sato, to the dismay of local farmers whose land was to be expropriated to construct the airport. At first local populace, aroused by the government's apparent indifference to their lot, petitioned peacefully. By the late 1960s, having tried all legal means to defend their property, the farmers turned to violence, with the support of the Japanese Red Army. As the farmers saw it, the traditional political process and the various political parties, even those on the left, had failed them. In the struggle that ensued over the past decade, hundreds of police and demonstrators were injured and five were killed.

There is a deep reserve of sympathy among the Japanese for the farmers. They are considered to be victims of the ever-expanding middle-class. At first only a localized quarrel over the appropriation of farmland, Narita soon became a seething cauldron of grievances, including air and noise pollution and the potentially dangerous transportation of large amounts of fuel over the poor road network to the new airport. Also at issue is the claim that Narita might someday serve as a take-off point for airborne action against East or Southeast Asia in case of trouble. Opening ceremonies were planned for March 30th; the airport was to receive its first plane on April 2nd, just in time for an expected horde of tourists. On March 26th, protestors hurling firebombs attacked Narita and demolished the control tower. Postponement of the airport opening for over a month was regarded by some as a victory for the farmer and student coalition and an embarrassment for the government of Takeo Fukuda, the fourth Prime Minister to be confronted by this issue. On the morning of May 20th, Narita Airport was officially inaugurated with 13,000 riot guards on hand and thousands of demonstrators nearby. The first flight, to Peking, took off as scheduled. Landings began on the 21st with only minor disruption.

J.A.L. Jet With 156 Abroad Hijacked

TOKYO, Wednesday, Sept. 28 (Reuters) —A Japan Air Lines DC8 jetliner was hijacked today as it left Bombay and was forced to fly to Dacca, Bangladesh, the airline reported.

The aircraft, hijacked shortly after take off on a scheduled flight to Bangkok and Tokyo, was carrying 142 passengers and 14 crewmembers.

The spokesman said there had been only one conversation between the pilot and traffic controllers at Bombay airport, and the airline had no information on any demands from the hijackers.

The National Police Agency here quoted the pilot as saying the aircraft had been hijacked by the Japanese Red Army as an act of "resistance" to the Japanese Government. But it gave no details of how many hijackers there were, or what they were demanding.

The Red Army, which advocates world revolution, has been involved in a succession of bloody incidents around the world, including a massacre a Tel Aviv airport in May 1972, when three guerrillas killed 27 people and injured more than 80 others.

In March 1970, nine Red Army members hijacked a domestic flight in Japan. They permitted the passengers to disembark and then flew to North Korea with a deputy transport minister who offered himself as a hostage.

In July 1973, a Japan Air Lines jumbo jet carrying 145 people was taken over by three Palestinian guerrillas and a Japanese on its way from Paris to Tokyo. The hijackers eventually released the passengers and crew and blew up the aircraft at Benghazi.

Other operations included an abortive attack on an oil refinery in Singapore in 1974, an attack on the French Embassy in The Hague later that year, and a raid on the American consulate in Kuala Lumpur in 1975.

September 28, 1977

Japanese Willing To Meet Terms Of Air Hijackers

DACCÁ, Bangladesh, Thursday, Sept. 29 — The Japanese Government agreed early today to meet the demands of Japanese guerrillas holding about 150 hostages aboard a hijacked airliner here that it free nine imprisoned "comrades" and pay $6 million in ransom.

But the Japanese, who communicated their decision to the guerrillas through Bangladesh officials, said it was impossible to meet the additional demand that they deliver the prisoners to Dacca within 18 hours.

The guerrillas, who seized the Japan Air Lines plane over India early yesterday and diverted it here, said they would kill the hostages one by one unless all demands were met.

Five Hostages Freed

But less than two hours after the Tokyo Government's decision was relayed to the hijackers, they freed two of five Americans reported aboard the plane, as well as an Indian couple and their infant son, the airline announced.

The Americans were identified as Carole Karabian, the pregnant wife of Walter Karabian of Monterey Park, Calif., and a man named Krueger, who was ill. Mr. Karabian, who was also aboard the plane, is a former member of the California Assembly and was its Democratic floor leader in 1971.

The two other Americans aboard the plane were John Gabriel of Montebello, Calif., and his wife. The hijackers had said that if their demands were not met they would execute the hostages, one by one, starting with Mr. Gabriel, president of the Garfield Bank.

Dacca authorities indicated the hijackers believed Mr. Gabriel is Jewish and for that reason they placed him first on the death list..

[Representative George E. Danielson, Democrat of California, said Mr. Gabriel is a native-born American of Armenian-Christian ancestry who had been in Soviet Armenia visiting relatives. Mr. Danielson, contacted in Washington, said he was a personal friend of Mr. Gabriel.]

The hijackers, on hearing the Japanese

decision, insisted that the prisoners and ransom money be delivered before midnight tinight (2 P.M. Thursday New York time) and said they would then free Indians, Pakistanis, women and children among the 142 passengers at Dacca, take off again and release the remaining hostages at various airports. Most of those aboard are Japanese. Also aboard is the jetliner's 14-member crew.

Dacca airport sources said Japan had agreed to meet the demands shortly before the expiration of a deadline set by the hijackers for 3 A.M. today.

Number of Hijackers Unknown

The four-engine DC-8 sat isolated on the Dacca airport, with the hijackers threatening to shoot at anyone or anything moving within 500 yards. It was not known how many hijackers were aboard or what kind of arms or explosives they had.

Japan Air Lines officials said the DC-8 was on a flight from Paris to Tokyo and had just finished a stop in Bombay yesterday morning when it was commandeered. The hijackers were believed to have been among a group of Japanese who boarded the jet in Bombay.

The jet flew to Dacca, and after several hours negotiations began by radio with Bangladesh officials. Throughout the day the plane stood in heavy heat and humidity.

Two Hijackers Seen

The negotiations in Dacca were led by Air Vice Marshal Abdul Gaffar Mahmoud, chief of staff of the Bangladesh Air Force, with Japanese diplomats standing by in the airport tower. The Indian national

The New York Times/Sept. 29, 1977

Hijackers of plane from Bombay to Dacca demanded that prisoners be flown there from Tokyo.

news agency quoted Marshal Mahmoud as having said that he had seen at least two hijackers on the plane, one wearing a red bandana over his face.

The DC8, commandeered 13 minutes after leaving Bombay for Bangkok, Thailand, was at first refused permission to land at Dacca, but with fuel running low it headed for the runway. It narrowly missed a Bangladesh airliner that was taking off.

There were unconfirmed reports that three passengers had collapsed from heat aboard the jet. But air travelers arriving in Calcutta from Dacca were quoted by the Indian news agency as having said

generators had been plugged into the plane to provide power for air conditioning and electricity.

Japan Explains Position

TOKYO, Thursday, Sept. 29 (AP)—Chief Cabinet Secretary Sunao Sonoda said today that the Bangladesh Government had taken responsibility for handling the direct negotiations with the hijackers of the Japanese airliner since the plane was in its territory.

He said the Japanese Government had asked only that Bangladesh not let the plane leave Dacca unless another country agreed to receive it.

A Foreign Ministry spokesman in Tokyo said the hijackers demanded they be addressed as the "Hidaka commando unit." Authorities believed this was a reference to a Red Army leader, Toshihiko Hidaka, who reportedly committed suicide after being arrested in Jordan in October 1975 for allegedly using a forged passport.

The Red Army is the best known of Japan's ultraleftist terrorist organizations. Its avowed goal is to foment revolution in Japan, but most of its operations have been outside the country. In 1972 three Red Army members sprayed gunfire through a lounge at Israel's international airport. Twenty-six persons were killed, including two of the guerrillas. The third is serving a life term in Israel.

The Japanese police estimate the Red Army has 20 to 30 active members.

September 29, 1977

Japanese Red Army's Hijacking
and Its Demands Said to Reflect
Political and Financial Desperation

By ANDREW H. MALCOLM
Special to The New York Times

TOKYO, Friday, Sept. 30—The hijacking of a Japan Air Lines DC-8 to Bangladesh by five persons believed to be members of the Japanese Red Army is the latest in a series of destructive and often bloody international incidents initiated by left-wing extremists.

The current hijacking, which has imperiled more than 151 passengers and crew, breaks a two-year lull in extremist activities, which included a grenade and machine-gun attack on the Tel Aviv airport in May 1972 by three Japanese, who killed 24 persons and wounded 76 others.

Over the years militants have also occupied embassies and consular offices in The Hague, Kuwait and Kuala Lumpur, attacked an oil refinery in Singapore, blown up a Boeing 747 jet in Libya, ignited several fatal bomb explosions in Japan and killed at least 14 of their members in bitter internal feuds.

The ostensible cause of the terrorism has been furtherance of the "people"'s revolution" and denunciation of capitalism, imperialism and Emperor Hirohito, whom they hold responsible for the World War II deaths of millions. The actual effort has been more to free captured fellow "revolutionary commandoes" than anything else.

Signs of Desperation Discerned

While it appeared to some that the Japanese Government's acceptance of a $6 million ransom demand and the release of nine prisoners was somewhat quick, Washington authorities and experts here saw elements of financial and political desperation among the terrorists.

They also saw the firm revolutionary hand of a mysterious underground leader named Fusako Shigenobu whose 32d birthday coincided with the hijacking. She is believed to have been working out of Lebanon, where the Red Army has trained, produced false passports and established close ties with the Marxist Popular Front for the Liberation of Palestine. The ties were so close that Miss Shigenobu's husband, Takeshi Okudaira, was one of the gunmen who died in the Tel Aviv attack, and her brother-in-law, Junzo Okudaira, is among the prisoners in Japan whose release is being demanded now.

They are part of an ultraleftist movement that has perhaps half a dozen or more factions encompassing a few score hard-core members and sympathizers. The 20 or so believed to be Japanese Red Army members come from a tradition of violence and rebellion rooted in alienation from the conservative mainstream of Japanese life.

The members' backgrounds are similar —well-educated, middle class, small town and rural—and they swung to a radical ideology, and eventually to violence,

when they entered the crowded universities in the large cities.

Miss Shigenobu began her radical career by smuggling oak staves hidden in golf bags past police lines into her comrades in embattled university buildings. That was in the late 1960's, when the vital issue was the speedy return of American-occupied Okinawa. A previous generation of leftist students coalesced around the 1960 extension of the United States-Japanese security treaty.

Factional disputes, a mark of everyday politics here, also produced new splits and new alliances. One prominent domestic group that emerged was the United Red Army, which gained worldwide notoriety in February 1972 during a long nationally televised gunfight with policemen surrounding a mountain villa. The same month the police found shallow graves containing the bodies of 14 United Red Army members, men and women, who had been tortured on the ground of ideological deviations.

While on overseas assignment Miss Shigenobu resigned from that group and formed her own, concentrating on nations believed more fertile for violent revolution than economically prosperous Japan. The ideological goal, though never fully defined publicly, was to promote a simultaneous worldwide leftist revolution through an active alliance with guerrilla groups abroad. The link with the Palestinians in 1971 was the first step.

Miss Shigenobu reportedly was a successful recruiter for the cause. She had her countrymen take circuitous sightseeing routes to the Middle Eastern training grounds. She married Mr. Okudaira to use his name and list "honeymooning" as the reason for travel.

The group snared headlines in 1973 for blowing up a Japan Air Lines 747 on the runway at Benghazi, Libya, in January 1974, for attacking a Shell refinery in Singapore and in September 1974 for seizing the French Embassy in The Hague to obtain the release of a colleague in a French prison. In August 1975 the group

seized Swedish and American Embassy offices in Kuala Lumpur to force the Japanese Government to release five imprisoned radicals.

Times have been more difficult for the Japanese Red Army since then. Several members were arrested in Jordan, Sweden and Canada and returned to Japanese jails; funds apparently ran short while the Lebanese civil war made operations there difficult.

The group's revolutionary writings, smuggled back here through a complex mail relay, seemed to speak increasingly of the need for "solidarity" and "unity" with other leftist units, an apparent bid for more manpower. This might also account for the inclusion of seven nonmembers of the Japanese Red Army on the list of nine to be exchanged for the airplane passengers.

Of course, another prime reason for the hijacking is the ransom money, which the police said would be the largest amount ever "robbed" in Japan. The terrorists apparently knew their nation's psychology well; in group-conscious Japan the doings of Japanese overseas cannot be dismissed as the acts of individuals; everyone feels a responsibility, and many felt they were on an international stage today.

In predawn Cabinet meetings the Government readily assented to the hijackers' demands, but during the day some opposition to the prisoner releases, especially among public prosecutors, became apparent. "For a country governed by law," said Sunao Sonoda, Chief Cabinet Secretary, "it is unbearable to release the criminals who bombed or murdered people and whom the police risked their lives to arrest. But we cannot ignore the lives of the passengers either."

Speaking of the prisoners, Kitotaro Asanuma, national police director, said: "If we have to release on a political basis, I feel my heart torn to pieces because it means we yield to lawlessness."

September 30, 1977

Hijackers Free 7 Hostages in Kuwait and 10 in Syria

DAMASCUS, Syria, Monday, Oct. 3 (UPI)—Japanese terrorists aboard a hijacked jetliner landed here early today and traded 10 hostages for enough fuel to take them and 19 remaining hostages to an undisclosed destination.

An official Syrian source said two of the 10 hostages released here were Americans, leaving only one American still a prisoner.

The plane touched down at Damascus Airport at 5:30 A.M. (11:30 P.M. Sunday New York time) after a 700-mile flight from Kuwait, where seven ailing hostages had been released.

After initially withholding permission to land, Syrian officials said they had relented "for humanitarian reasons." Syrian policemen and soldiers ringed the airport.

Syrian Government and Japanese em-

bassy officials were on hand when the plane landed. Negotiations were started and a Syrian source said the hijackers had agreed to trade 10 hostages for fuel and supplies.

Kuwait's Minister of Defense and Interior, Sheik Saad al-abdullah al-Sabah, said four of the hostages released in Kuwait were from Japan, two from Australia and one from Singapore. An airline spokesman said a total of 40 persons were aboard when the plane left Kewait 22 passengers, a crew of seven, the five original hijackers and six comrades released by Japanese authorities.

The plane originally was refused permission to land, but Sheik Abdullah said he had relented after receiving what he called "a last message" from the pilot, Capt. Kumitetsu Sakuraba.

The plane had left Dacca, Bangladesh, yesterday with about 10 hours of fuel aboard and had been in the air nearly eight hours when given permission to land, a spokesman for the airline said.

The plane, which also carried six pri-soners freed from jails in Japan and $6 million in ransom, took off from Bangladesh after four and a half days of negotiations.

Airline spokesmen identified one of the three Americans still aboard the plane as Eric Weiss, believed to be from the San Francisco area. The other two American hostages, both men, were identified only as Phalen and McLean.

The Japanese Government earlier yesterday urged the Bangladesh Government not to allow the plane to take off, but officials in Dacca, under pressure from a coup attempt, ordered the plane to leave.

The hijackers, all thought to be under 30 years of age, seized the plane carrying 156 passengers and crew members last Wednesday after it left Bombay during a flight from Paris to Tokyo. They were armed with pistols, hand grenades and plastic explosives.

They demanded the release of comrades held in Japanese jails and a ransom of $6 million in American $100 bills return for the lives of the hostages.

The Japanese Government agreed to meet the hijackers' demands and flew six prisoners and the ransom money to Dacca.

October 3, 1977

ALGERIANS REFUSE TO YIELD HIJACKERS

Japan Rebuffed in Its Request That 5 Who Seized Airliner Be Returned

ALGIERS, Oct. 5 (UPI)—Algeria today refused Japan's indirect request for the return of five hijackers and a $6 million ransom paid for 151 hostages, saying it "will not tolerate that its good faith and good will be exploited."

The Tokyo Government had earlier expressed the "hope" that Algeria would send back the terrorists who seized a Japanese airliner over India — held it for five days in Bangladesh, and then forced it to fly to Algiers.

But the Japanese refrained from demanding outright the extradition of the leftist guerrillas because a Foreign Ministry official had waived the right to do so during the negotiations.

Algeria said it would abide by the conditions agreed upon with Japan under which the five, members of the extreme leftist Japanese Red Army, were allowed to land Monday.

Algerian sources said that the hyjackers surrendered on the understanding that they would not be sent back to Japan.

Algeria's Good Faith Noted

"In all its action in this affair, Algeria faithfully put into action measures and modalities which were decided in common" with Japan, a statement issued by the Algerian press agency.

"Algeria will not tolerate that its good faith and good will be exploited to distort its action and attack its prestige."

The statement pointed out that "Algeria intervened in this affair only at the official demand of the Japanese Government and in conditions laid down in common."

The Japanese request for the return of the hijackers was relayed to the Algerian Ambassador in Tokyo, Brahim Ghafa.

Algeria may keep the terrorists under police surveillance, informed sources said, but is unlikely to keep the ransom. In the past it has confiscated ransom money and returned it to the authorities who paid it.

In a two-hour interview in a Middle Eastern capital, the Japanese identified himself as a member of the Red Army's leadership of "less than a dozen members" and said he has been using the name Yano Kenichi. He said he was high on the wanted list of both the Japanese and Israeli Governments.

Stepped-Up Attacks Vowed

NICOSIA, Cyprus, Oct. 5 (Reuters)—The man who says he had planned the hijacking of a Japanese airliner says the Japanese Red Army will use the $6 million ransom money to step up attacks on "world imperialism," with Japan and Israel as prime targets.

In a two-hour interview in a Middle Eastern capital, the Japanese identified himself as a member of the Red Army leadership of "less than a dozen members" and said he has been using the name Yano Kenichi. He said he was high on the wanted list of both the Japanese and Israeli Governments.

October 6, 1977

Two Japanese Gunmen Hijack Commuter Bus

NAGASAKI, Japan, Saturday, Oct. 15 (Reuters) — Two masked men, one armed with a sawed-off shotgun, took over a commuter bus with about five or six passengers aboard here today, the police said.

From slogans scrawled on the gunmen's masks, the police said they believed the men to be members of the Japanese Red Army—the leftist group that hijacked a Japan Airlines DC-8 over India last month, and extracted a $6 million ransom from the Japanese Government.

About 100 policemen were deployed around the bus, but authorities said no demands had been immediately received.

October 15, 1977

JAPAN'S SOCIALISTS FAIL TO PICK LEADERS

Party Parley Ends in Discord as Factional Feuds Continue—New Effort Set in December

By ANDREW H. MALCOLM

TOKYO, Oct. 1—Japan's troubled Socialist Party, the largest single opposition group in Parliament, held a convention here this week to pick new leaders. But about all that the disputing delegates could agree on was that they could not agree on new leaders.

Another convention was set for December to try again.

The bitter stalemate, the result of fierce factional feuds within the leftist umbrella party, continued a long tradition of intraparty rankling that dates backs a quarter century from a fight over the party's stand on Japan's 1951 peace treaty with the United States. The latest fighting also provided further evidence for Japanese editorial writers to question the Socialists' ability ever to replace the conservative Liberal Democrats effectively.

The conservative party's 22-year grip on the political majority here appears to have been slipping significantly in recent elections. It now holds only 258 of the lower house's 511 seats and 125 of the upper house's 252 seats, often requiring the help of conservative independents to enact legislation.

Voter Support Slipping

Few independent observers expect the Socialists to supplant the conservatives as the single dominant party in Japan, an affluent, heavily middle class nation of 113 million. The Socialists have shown moderate to disappointing gains in the last two elections and now control only 53 seats in the House of Councillors, the upper chamber, and 121 in the House of Representatives, the lower house. The remaining seats are divided between the Buddhist-oriented Komeito, or Clean Government Party, the Democratic Socialists, the Communists, independents and the New Liberal Club, a conservative splinter group.

In terms of votes, the Socialists attracted 11.7 million ballots in the lower house election last December; a drop from 22 percent of the total to nearly 20 percent.

Basically, the internal dispute pits the party's more powerful, well-organized, Marxist-oriented left wing, which prizes rigid ideological purity, against the fragmented remainder of the more moderate right wing, which is open to compromise and the continuation of some democratic institutions if a Socialist government should ever come into existence.

Party Split in 1960

In 1960 a band of these moderates left the party to form the Democratic Socialists, a more conservative grouping that has in recent months cooperated at times in Parliament with the governing Liberal Democrats. Last spring Saburo Eda, a deputy chairman of the party, who has since died, left the party in a similar dispute. And this week three more prominent Socialist members of Parliament seceded from the party, saying it was not capable of necessary internal reforms. They are Hideo Den, the top vote-getter in the upper house election last July, Yanosuke Narazaki and Yutaka Hata.

The catalyst for this week's fight was the selection of replacements for the party chairman, Tomomi Narita, and the secretary general, Masashi Ishibashi, both of whom had resigned in the wake of their party's poor election showings. But the traditional arguments of the secretive and Soviet-oriented left wing for continued class party struggles clashed with the moderates' assertions that staunch Marxism-Leninism could not sustain the Socialists in the necessary democratic alliance with other opposition parties to overthrow the conservatives.

Then Ichio Asukata, the Socialist Mayor of Yokohama and heir-apparent to the party chairmanship, withdrew his name, saying he was "disgusted" with the continued feuding.

The two-day convention was extended 24 hours but no resolution could be hammered out. So Mr. Narita and Mr. Ishibashi will stay on as caretakers of Japan's No. 2 party until another Socialist convention is convened in December.

October 2, 1977

Japan Cabinet Changed by Fukuda

TOKYO, Monday, Nov. 28 (AP)—Prime Minister Takeo Fukuda, plagued by a recession at home and criticism of Japan's trade policy abroad, shuffled his Cabinet today, naming a specialist in economic diplomacy to a newly created position in his Government.

The changes, the first by Mr. Fukuda since he took office 11 months ago, were announced by Shintaro Abe, the new chief Cabinet secretary. He said the new Cabinet would tackle "crucial international and domestic" problems.

Kiichi Miyazawa, a former Foreign Minister, was appointed to the new post of State Minister in Charge of External Economic Relations. He also will head the Economic Planning Agency.

A Huge Trade Imbalance

The Government has been criticized in recent weeks by Japanese exporters for failing to prevent the sharp rise of the yen. This has made Japanese products more expensive abroad, reducing earnings from exports and leading to economic stagnation. The yen was quoted at slightly over 240 to the dollar in early trading today. It was 267 to the dollar two months ago.

The yen's rise has pleased Japan's trading partners, but they have become increasingly critical of Japan's huge trade imbalance. This surplus with the United States alone reached $5.9 billion in the first nine months of this year; the total for 1977 is expected to be $8 billion.

A recent series of talks with American officials in Tokyo resulted in no solution to the trade problem, and the Americans reportedly told Japan it must set a specific date for turning the surplus situation around to give "a clear-cut picture of cooperation."

Mr. Fukuda appointed Tatsuo Murayama, a Finance Ministry official, to be the new Finance Minister. Toshio Komoto, chief of the ruling Liberal Democratic Party's policy board, was named Minister of International Trade and Industry.

Sunao Sonoda, former chief Cabinet secretary, was named Foreign Minister, replacing Iichiro Hatoyama. One of Mr. Sonoda's main goals will be to promote the stalemated negotiations with China on a treaty of peace and friendship.

Opposition leaders have accused the Fukuda Government of dragging its feet in the talks, which bogged down nearly three years ago over the issue of whether to include a clause condemning hegemony. The Japanese fear such a clause, sought by Peking, would anger the Soviet Union.

November 28, 1977

REACTION POSITIVE
TO FUKUDA'S SHIFT FOR CABINET POSTS

TOKYO STOCK MARKET SOARS

Dollar Up Sharply Against Yen in Early Trading Today — No Evidence of Support Seen

By JUNNOSUKE OFUSA
Special to The New York Times

TOKYO, Nov. 28—Prime Minister Takeo Fukuda carried out a sweeping reorganization of his cabinet today in an effort to deal with Japan's mounting trade surplus and the steady rise in the value of the Japanese yen.

In the business community, reaction to Mr. Fukuda's moves was positive and the Tokyo stock market shot higher. While the foreign exchange market initially appeared unaffected by the shuffle, the dollar did hold firm against the yen as the bank of Japan continued its support operations for the American currency.

[In early trading Tuesday, the dollar rose sharply, however, to 241.20 yen from 240 at Monday's close, Reuters reported, with no evidence that the Government was intervening to support the American currency.]

The Prime Minister, deeply concerned over the state of Japan's relations with the United States and Europe, created a new cabinet position, Minister for External Economic Affairs, and named Nobuhiko Ushiba, former Ambassador to Washington, to the post.

Mr. Fukuda also reshuffled nearly all of his other cabinet ministers. In key moves, Kiichi Miyazawa was named director general for economic planning, Toshio Komoto, was named Minister of International Trade and Industry, Tatsuo Murayama was named Finance Minister and Sunao Sonoda was named Foreign Minister.

In announcing plans for the reshuffling on Saturday, the Prime Minister said Japan faced "the gravest situation" since World War II. In installing the new team today, he said its goals would be to stabilize the national economy and "make renewed efforts toward insuring the cooperation and development of the international community of nations."

Ushiba's Main Task

The choice of Mr. Ushiba for the new cabinet post underscored the extreme importance the Japanese Government attaches to the existing strained economic relations with other industrial countries, particularly the United States, the new chief cabinet secretary, Shintaro Abe, said.

Mr. Ushiba's main task, Mr. Abe said, would be to deal with the current crucial economic problems with which Japan is confronted. He will travel abroad whenever necessary to handle troubles that may arise with Japan's trading partners.

Some observers said, however, that the cabinet reshuffle was merely a cosmetic change. It remains to be seen what achievements the new cabinet will accomplish in the grave trade issues existing between the United States and Japan.

The new Finance Minister, Mr. Murayama, 62 years old, is little known to the public. He is a former bureacrat from the Finance Ministry and is regarded as a top economic expert.

Mr. Miyazawa, an outstanding expert in diplomatic and international affairs and now in charge of the Economic Planning Agency, has participted in most of the major negotiations with the United States since Japan regained independence in 1952.

Reaction Is Favorable

Mr. Komoto, the new Minister of International Trade and Industry, was formerly a businessman and a leading economist. It is the second time he will head the Trade Ministry. The reaction to the new cabinet generally was favorable.

Following last week's rebound, the Tokyo stock market surged higher today. Analysts said that investors were given a strong psychological lift by the promise Prime Minister Fukuda made last weekend to take further reflationary measures under his new administration.

The local Dow Jones average, which gained a record of 172.90 yen on Saturday, closed today at 4,822.50, up 52.34 yen from Saturday. In expectation of increased spending in public works construction projects, public works issues led the advance. Also firm were export-oriented issues like electricals, autos and cameras.

The Tokyo foreign exchange market was initially unaffected by the cabinet reshuffle. The dollar edged higher to 240 yen temporarily but remained unchanged at 240 yen most of the day. The Bank of Japan absorbed an estimated 70 million yen, turnover amounted to $260 million, down $27 million from Friday's volume.

Market sources said that speculative pressure remained low as a result of the central bank's new policy of actively intervening in the market.

According to Government sources, the recent sharp appreciation of the yen has brought about deflationary effects, offsetting the impact of a 2,000 billion yen, or $8 billion, business stimulative package the Government has enforced for this year.

As a result, the Finance Ministry is drafting a second supplementary budget to stimulate the stagnant economy. The budget, which is for fiscal 1977 ending March 31, 1978, will amount to about 1,500 billion yen, or $6 billion.

The second supplementary budget will be spent mainly on public works construction projects such as roads.

Officials of the Finance Ministry said that without the second supplementary budget Japan's economic growth in fiscal 1977 would fall 0.4 or 0.5 points short of the Government target of 6.7 percent.

November 29, 1977

Fukuda's Leadership Under Fire in Japan

Prime Minister Called Ineffective on Government Reform, Party Unity and Economic Issues

By ANDREW H. MALCOLM

TOKYO, Dec. 10—Prime Minister Takeo Fukuda, who entered office almost a year ago on a pledge to reform the government, unite his party and forge new economic progress, now finds himself in trouble on all three fronts.

Today, as the 72-year-old Mr. Fukuda and his economic ministers put the finishing touches on a 1978 budget and a package of economic proposals to negotiate in Washington this week, he came under continuing domestic attack, especially from farmers, for even the scant trade liberalization that his Cabinet has approved.

Tomorrow Nobuhiko Ushiba, Minister for External Economic Affairs, will leave for Washington for five days of talks on Japan's economic structure and huge trade surplus. Back here Mr. Fukuda is under mounting criticism, especially for his economic leadership—or lack of it, according to critics.

This week Mr. Fukuda, who has promised Western leaders that Japan would show a 6.7 percent growth rate this year, admitted that the rate probably would be more like 5.7 or 5.8 percent when the fiscal year ends March 31. Earlier, his administration's estimate of a $70 million current-account deficit with Japan's trading partners had to be revised to a $6.5 billion surplus, a figure now already surpassed. Experts believe the final total will be more like $10 billion. This has ignited blunt criticism among Japan's trading partners.

Yen Rises in Value

The rise in value of the yen from around 290 to the dollar a year ago to 242.05 at yesterday's close of the exchange market has also drawn fire from export-oriented industries because it makes Japanese products more expensive overseas. Exports have been responsible for much of Japan's economic recovery from the effects of the 1973 oil shock while domestic consumption remains sluggish. Unemployment hovers at more than 2 percent by the Japanese calculation, much higher than recent years, while many industrial facilities, plagued with overcapacity, stand idle.

In Parliament, where Mr. Fukuda's Liberal Democrats hold a thin edge, a long extraordinary session ended two weeks ago without approval of any of the Government's key measures. A special four-day session had to be convened this week to handle items such as fare increases for the deficit-ridden national railway.

The legislative inaction is a measure of the Liberal Democrats' weakness. Having dominated Japanese politics since 1955, Mr. Fukuda's conservative party now controls only 125 of the upper chamber's 252 seats, with two vacancies, and 257 of the more powerful lower house's 511 seats, with three vacancies. It is virtually impossible now for the Liberal Democrats to enact major legislation without the assistance of one of the five major opposition parties.

Mr. Fukuda need not call lower house elections for three years, and his term as party president, and thus Prime Minister, has another year left. But behind-the-scenes maneuvering for the succession, if Mr. Fukuda does not run again, has already begun, and Masayoshi Ohira, the party's secretary general, is the prime contender.

'Abolished' Factions Reappear

Last spring Mr. Fukuda "reformed" the party by encouraging all of the factions to abolish themselves. They did, but they have reappeared as "study groups."

Twelve days ago in an effort to tune the shifting factional power alignments and pay political debts, Mr. Fukuda reshuffled his Cabinet. This brought Yasuhiro Nakasone, a powerful leader who had been in eclipse, back into the spotlight as a party executive along with Kiichi Miyazawa, a former foreign minister who some observers see as a future candidate for prime minister.

The Cabinet moves provided a brief psychological boost and gave the impression overseas of determination to act on economic problems. But it has produced no new policies. It prompted one local newspaper columnist, Hideo Matsuoka, to comment: "If a prime minister thinks a cabinet reshuffle changes and refreshes the political situation, he is under a grand delusion."

Criticism From a Stronghold

This week it was the groups from the agricultural areas, the Liberal Democrats' traditional stronghold, that took aim at Mr. Fukuda's Government. In heated sessions before party executives and groups of legislators, farmers' organizations threatened sucession from the party and demanded strong stands against the American demands for trade liberalization.

A prominent theme was that the small and declining agricultural interests should not see their competition from abroad increase to meet foreign criticism of Japanese industrial exports. "Why should expansion of beef imports be the first task of the reshuffled Cabinet?" said one speaker, Sadanori Yamanaka.

Another, Noboru Minowa, said increased agricultural imports would not help much to reduce Japan's trade surplus. "We should think of importing more arms and planes from the United States," he said.

At lunches and over drinks Japanese officials told diplomats, primarily the Americans, that this kind of fierce domestic opposition showed how impossible it was for Japan to make any major trade concessions now.

December 11, 1977

Farmers in Japan Also Can Harvest Many Votes

Their Power Was Evident in Last Week's Talks

By ANDREW H. MALCOLM

TAKASAKI, Japan — When Toshiji Matsumoto, a Japanese farmer here, sent his daughter Michiko off to a distant place called California the other day, he made her take along a parasol because he had heard that it never rains there. Mr. Matsumoto, who raises rice, vegetables and dairycows, was simply protecting his teenage daughter's future. In Japan, suntans on women are still generally considered disfiguring, especially by farm folk and especially before a marriage can be arranged. Such thinking provides a peek into the seemingly mysterious perceptions that dominate much of life in Japan, particularly in the dwindling rural areas. These populated pockets, which seem much farther from Japan's sprawling cities than the maps indicate, have become the focus of international attention during the dispute between Japan and its trading partners, primarily the United States.

On Friday the thirteenth, Robert Strauss, President Carter's special trade representative, and Nobuhiko Ushiba, Japan's Minister for External Economic Affairs, announced in Tokyo a "settlement," at least for the moment, of their six-month-old trade dispute. Designed to liberalize Japan's economic involvement with the world and reduce its

Japan's farmers traditionally vote for the conservative Liberal Democratic Party.

whopping $17 billion trade surplus ($8 billion of it with the United States). The Japanese package includes tariff cuts, promises of increased market access here for foreign firms, some liberalized quotas and economic stimulation to boost growth by 7 percent this year to draw in more imports. Mr. Strauss hailed the agreement but Administration officials, it was clear, believed they had wrung maximum concessions and would ease the pressure for now.

Over the years Japan's conservative politicians now presided over by Prime Minister Takeo Fukuda, have proved unable or unwilling to instigate important domestic reforms and change, which have come instead only after periodic pressures from abroad. "One of the most important things a Japanese politician must learn," one high-ranking Japanese politician admitted the other day, "is to skillfully exploit foreign criticism within Japan."

Thus, the "settlement" is likely to be but one more pause in the trade tensions with an aggressively-exporting Japan. Moreover, the agreement does not address a fundamental difficulty in Japan's international relations: the nation's entrenched insularity and insecurity that greatly limit its vision and understanding of an increasingly interdependent world. Nowhere is this more apparent than in the world of Japanese agriculture, what one Westerner calls "Fantasyland."

Japan is a latecomer to the industrial age. Traditionally, its life was based on agriculture, and a strong identity with the land still exists among many Japanese, even the millions who forsook smaller cities such as Takasaki for the coastal metroplexes that now house 80 percent of Japan's 113 million citizens. About 22 million Japanese reside in rural areas now, but many of them work at least parttime in nearby factories. Only 643,000 households depend entirely on farming, a three percent decline in the last year.

Operating on farms that may total ten acres, for a large holding, they produce a plethora of plants and animals on an arable area only slightly larger than West Virginia. But Japan is self-sufficient in only two important crops, rice and oranges. It must import 30 percent of its foods, $3.6 billion worth from the United States alone in 1976. In fact, United States officials claim there are more Americans producing food for Japan than there are Japanese producing food for Japan.

Utilizing every family member in every corner of land, along with a growing number of machines, farmers labor over their tiny plots from dawn to dusk in a time-consuming manner that would shock an Iowa farmer atop his efficient tractor on mile-square fields. But in Japan, farmers hold the same social and political standing as apple pie and motherhood in the United States. Legislative districts, drawn up before the urban migration, give parliamentary over-representation to rural areas, where the conservative Liberal Democratic Party has maintained its stronghold for 23 years. The farmers are well-organized (unlike Japan's consumers) through a network of neighborhood, prefectural, national and crop-affinity groups that plan discount tourist trips to Hawaii and monitor agricultural developments. At the drop of a bucket, they can mobilize thousands of chanting demonstrators, as they did before the United States Embassy recently, or, more importantly, move party members to protect some local interest from perceived foreign threats. As one result, 22 of the 27 categories limited by import quotas involve agricultural products.

Rice is a prime example. Last year Japanese farmers

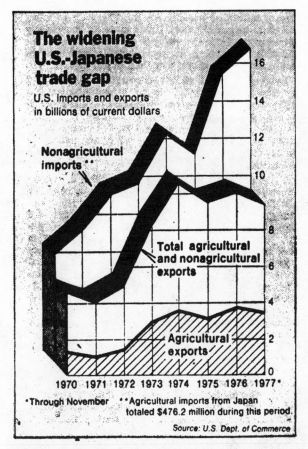

The widening U.S.-Japanese trade gap
U.S. imports and exports in billions of current dollars

Nonagricultural imports

Total agricultural and nonagricultural exports

Agricultural exports

1970 1971 1972 1973 1974 1975 1976 1977*

*Through November   *Agricultural imports from Japan totaled $476.2 million during this period.

Source: U.S. Dept. of Commerce

produced 1.85 million tons more rice than the country could eat. By next fall the surplus, purchased and stored by the Government at high support prices, may top 5 million tons. Because of the profitable support price, farmers are reluctant to give up a sure thing, despite government incentives to switch crops. And to many, rice-growing is less a business than a way of life.

Now, Japan's farmers say they should not have to pay the "penalty" in imports for the export successes of Japan's mighty industries. Mr. Fukuda's aging conservatives, who nervously watch increases in the city votes of Socialists and others, have been unwilling to significantly shake anybody's tree. But the time for a belated decision may be fast approaching. Japan's trading partners, who last year bought over $70 billion worth of goods here, increasingly view Japan's agriculture as a stark symbol of this country's basic protectionist stance in many areas.

"Japan is behaving like an undeveloped nation, screaming about a few tons of oranges or beef imports," one visiting American official said last week at a press conference not far from farmer Matsumoto's fields. "Japan isn't Bangladesh or Lesotho," the visitor said, "it's a great, great nation, and it ought to act accordingly." The speaker was S.I. Hayakawa, a Republican Senator from that distant —and sunny—place called California.

Andrew H. Malcolm is a correspondent for The New York Times, based in Tokyo.

January 15, 1978

Disputed New Tokyo Airport Now Set to Open on March 30

Consulate General of Japan, N.Y.

Tokyo's new Narita Airport, the focus of intense controversy.

By ANDREW H. MALCOLM

NARITA, Japan, March 3—Everything is just about set now—probably—for the opening of Japan's newest airport on March 30.

All that government and airline officials have to do is to move 32 airline operations, 16,000 people, 1,120 airport vehicles, a few jumbo jets, 1,500 truckloads of equipment, 800,000 computer cards and 90 million pounds of jet fuel to the new airport under the threat of guerrilla attack by farmers and radical students.

Once that is accomplished and the airlines resolve their problems over high landing fees, a costly downtown terminal and growing union grievances, passengers can begin their two-hour, $50 cab rides to the new terminals behind the electrified barbed-wire fences, where all plane movements will be prohibited late at night.

While cracks in the single runway and jet-fighter traffic nearby are not considered serious difficulties, trouble is foreseen from unexpected and violent air turbulence at low altitude that caused at least one test pilot to become ill on an approach.

Just in Time for Spring Flow

The first plane will not land at the New Tokyo International Airport on April 1—some people saw symbolic significance in the date—but the next day, which is just in time because spring is the peak tourist period. This year Japan is attracting, among others, 72,000 Rotarians for their global convention.

The $2.9 billion facility was completed five years ago and has tried repeatedly to begin service. The story of the airport, sometimes called Narita for the farm town nearby, began 16 years ago when planners foresaw the obsoles-

cence of crowded 47-year-old Haneda, which is on the south side of the capital and reachable in 20 minutes by monorail or car. Now handling 400 daily overseas and domestic flights.

Haneda will have only domestic flights except for those carrying arriving dignitaries.

The new four-square-mile site, 46 miles northeast of downtown Tokyo, was chosen in part because the Government owned some of the land as the imperial horse farm. Getting the project off on the wrong foot, the planners neglected to consult local residents first—a cardinal sin in this consensus-based society. The result has been bitter confrontation. Over the years there have been hundreds of violent demonstrations involving at least five deaths. They show no signs of abating; not long ago a burning radio-controlled van crashed into the airport gate.

Expropriation and Pollution

Originally the protests centered on expropriation of ancestral farmlands—peanut and vegetable fields that have been handed down for generations. With the participation of the radical students, some now approaching middle age, the focus broadened to include noise and air pollution and ill-defined grievances of Marxist-oriented groups.

Residents of the area thwarted construction of a pipeline for jet fuel, so the volatile fuel is being moved in tank cars, a more dangerous method that instigated strikes by railroad workers. On Wednesday night 20 firebombs were lobbed onto a road near the airport and yesterday riot policemen were stationed every hundred yards along the fuel train's 30-mile route.

Transportation of people to the airport was to have been by high-speed train, but angry residents prevented the railroad from acquiring a route, so it has built only an arrival platform. Two other lines that are close by require shuttle buses, which must merge with taxis and private cars and trucks on the single narrow road to the airport. Walking is out of the question because the planners forgot sidewalks. A bus that will run from central Tokyo will require checking in four hours before flight time. Japan Air Lines applied to schedule six DC-8 flights a day from Haneda to the new airport, but the Government vetoed the plan.

28 Gates, 114 Shops, $1.25 Coffee

While the concourses leading to the 28 departure gates are temporary dormitories for riot policemen, the terminals are occupied by workmen scurrying to finish the 114 shops and 9 banks. A cup of coffee will be $1.25, and it will cost airlines almost $6,000 per plane to land on the lone 13,124-foot northwest-southeast runway (two more are planned).

To meet farmers' demands for restraints on noise pollution, the landing approaches will be sharply reduced at 9 P.M., which is a peak takeoff time, and the airport will close at 11 P.M. for seven hours. To airline officials this raises the specter of fully loaded planes prepared for takeoff being ordered back for the night with resulting schedule snarls at distant points.

The start of what officials expect will be 150 flights a day, with more than 20,000 passengers, is good news for hotels that stand in the midst of brown fields and thatched roofs and that have struggled along on wedding parties and luncheons. Managers expect many guests to be travelers familiar with Japanese traffic jams who leave for the airport a day early.

March 7, 1978

PROTESTERS IN JAPAN STORM NEW AIRPORT, RAVAGE CONTROL UNIT

Radicals Seize Tower and Smash Vital Equipment Despite Regime's Mobilization of 14,000 Police

By ANDREW H. MALCOLM

TOKYO, March 26—More than 300 radicals, hurling firebombs and wielding lengths of steel pipe, crashed a truck through a fence and seized the control tower of the New Tokyo International Airport today.

Before riot policemen firing tear-gas guns at point-blank range could evict them three hours later, a half-dozen helmeted leftist youths had destroyed vital equipment in the control tower of the $2.9-billion facility that had been scheduled to open later this week.

The attack came during a protest demonstration by more than 6,000 people outside the airfield. Complaints about the new airport originated with local farmers, who felt that their interests had not been taken into consideration sufficiently by officials, despite compensation for land that was taken over. Radical students, many of them no longer in school, broadened the protest to include ill-defined Marxist-oriented grievances as well as concerns over air pollution and noise and the dangers of transporting large fuel loads over an inadequate road system.

Extent of Damage Uncertain

Embarrassed government officials, who had mobilized 14,000 riot policemen to stop any attack, worked late into the night to assess the damage to the 12-story heart of the new airfield, situated 46 miles east of the capital.

But there was widespread doubt that the necessary repairs could be made before the opening ceremonies, which were scheduled for Thursday, and the arrival of the first commercial flight, which was scheduled for next Sunday.

"It's almost hopeless," said a Transport Ministry official.

Privately, some international airline officials were also expressing growing fears that the controversial new airfield, which is already five years late in opening because of the continuing demonstrations, will be unsafe as Japan's principal international gateway because of the activities of the protesters.

For decades both overseas and domestic passengers have used the overcrowded Haneda Airfield just nine miles south of central Tokyo. Planning for the new airport began 12 years ago, but from the beginning the airport—a four-square mile facility sometimes called Narita after a nearby farm town—has been the focus of hundreds of demonstrations, arson attempts, sabotage and clashes with the police. Four policemen and one other person have died in the fighting.

Today's crippling attack, intended to begin a week-long "antiairport offensive" by opponents of the field, is a substantial political embarrassment for the conservative Government of Prime Minister Takeo Fukuda.

The Tokyo International Airport Authority had drawn the 14,000 riot policemen from all over the country to deal with the demonstrations planned for this week.

Police Act to Remove Barrier

The confrontation began late last night when policemen began removing another tower, 55-feet high, that the opposition forces were building on privately owned land to block the airplanes' flight path.

Late this morning a large crowd of protesters began gathering near the airport. There were scattered outbreaks of violence with the authorities. One police kiosk was firebombed.

And then just before noon about 350 youths wearing red helmets and carrying banners marched or rode in trucks toward the airport's north gate.

Suddenly, a large open-backed truck sped and crashed through the fence.

Some protesters ran through the opening while others rode in the back of the truck as it made its way, virtually unmolested, through the airport grounds.

From the rear of the moving truck youths hurled firebomb after firebomb at clusters of policemen and parked vehicles, several of which were engulfed in flames, sending large columns of oily black smoke into the bright sunny air.

At the control tower building, which also houses the airport's main offices, the truck smashed another barrier and six of the youths, carrying pipes and sledgehammers, entered the building and made their way toward the top. By late tonight authorities had offered no explanation as to why there had been no guards in sight at the tower.

Four workers in the control tower had locked their door, so the youths climbed the last few floors on parapets outside the modern building. They smashed the windows, sending showers of glass shards to the street below, climbed inside and could be seen ripping out wires, and scattering thousands of pages of technical data out of the windows.

The four airport workers, meanwhile, had climbed to the roof, where a police helicopter lowered a rope to lift them to safety one by one. The air blast from the helicopter's rotors, and those of other craft hovering nearby that belonged to news organizations, sent the thrown documents hurtling high into the air.

Authorities said at least 20 people, including 17 policemen, were injured. Several thousand people who had participated in the demonstrations at the airpo did not become involved in the violence.

At least 108 people were arrested, including the six who climbed to the control tower, who were seized when a team of riot policemen crawled outside and fired tear-gas cannisters through the shattered windows.

March 27, 1978

Associated Press

At Tokyo's new airport in Narita, Japan, demonstrator caught fire as he threw gasoline bomb at policemen. He was reported in critical condition.

JAPANESE POSTPONE OPENING OF AIRPORT IN FACE OF PROTESTS

Riot Police Arrest Another 51 at Site — Fukuda Calls Attack 'Challenge to Social Order'

By ANDREW H. MALCOLM

TOKYO, Tuesday, March 28 — The Japanese Government, confronted with the threat of mounting radical violence that has crippled the control tower of the New Tokyo International Airport, today formally decided to postpone the opening of the new facility indefinitely.

Transportation Minister Kenji Fukunaga said it would take at least two weeks, and probably longer, to repair and replace the array of control tower radio, radar, guidance and lighting equipment that was destroyed by six radical students during clashes with police on Sunday.

Early this morning another 51 persons were arrested, including 41 in a secret underground escape tunnel, in fighting at a home-made cement fortress overlooking the controversial new airport. Fourteen thousand riot police continued Japan's most extensive police mobilization in almost two decades since the anti-American disturbances of 1960.

Calling the radicals' attacks "a challenge to social order and democracy," Prime Minister Takeo Fukuda, who had staked his administration's prestige on formally opening the airport Thursday, bowed to the urgent advice of aviation advisers and assented to the postponement.

'The Situation Is Grave'

Another Cabinet meeting later this week is expected to set a new opening date for the $2.9-billion, four-square-mile facility. Its opening has been delayed five years by protests in which five persons have died.

An air of expectancy hung over this island nation as the public watched the latest flare-up over the airport, sometimes called Narita for a nearby farm town. "The Narita issue is approaching its climax," the influential Asahi Shimbun said in an editorial yesterday, "and the situation is grave."

Policemen, clad in helmets and silvery asbestos coats and firing teargas canisters, launched their latest offensive at dusk yesterday, using powerful water sprays, tall steel ladders and cement drills to dislodge one group of radicals from an impromptu fort and a 50-foot-tall steel tower near the airport. Other towers that actually blocked airplane approach paths were removed last year.

Sunday's battle, which saw 56 persons injured and 115 arrested in a three-hour melee of club-swinging and firebombing was called a victory by protest leaders.

The protesters' attack on the airport and their running firebomb battles with the police diverted the attention of the authorities, allowing six youths to slip into the unprotected control tower, where most of the damage was caused.

"Guerrilla activities are not our main objective," said Issaku Tomura, a protest leader who returned last week from consultations in Beirut, Lebanon, with the Palestine Liberation Organization. "Our victory may be the grave of the Fukuda Government. For us, things are looking good." Mr. Tomura, speaking in a telephone interview, added, "We shall resort to any tactics or any means."

Such statements, against the background of the airport battle, raised concern among airline representatives for the safety of travelers.

"If the opposition can walk into the control tower and destroy it before the opening when the airport is an armed camp, what can these people do once the gates are open?" said one airline official. "The potential for disaster is terrifying," added another.

The confrontation appears to leave no room for compromise on either side. Mr. Fukuda, who is being accused by fellow conservatives of ineffective economic policies, is the fourth Prime Minister to commit himself to opening the new airport. In Parliament, opposition parties demanded yesterday that the airport remain closed as long as any danger existed. But the danger of overcrowded air traffic at Tokyo's present Haneda airport, south of the city, is also growing.

The opponents of the Narita airport say there is no room for negotiation short of demolition and returning the lands to their farm owners. At first, the farmers in their straw hats and rubber boots dominated the opposition, but they appear to have given way in recent years to a coalition of radical youths.

The protest groups, which sometimes battle among themselves, include the Proletariat Youth League, the Battle Flag faction of the Young Communist League, and Inter-Guerrilla Group No. 4, whose members were said to have seized the tower. Their grievances against the airport range from noise and air pollution and "capitalist exploitation" of farm workers' lands to avowed concern that the field will be used in the future for military purposes.

Focus of Various Grievances

Some experts believe that with the end of the Vietnam War, the airport struggle has become a convenient focus for the expression of grievances by radical youths. A survey several years ago found youths in Japan to be more dissatisfied with their lives than in other affluent societies. Haruo Matsubara, a Tokyo University sociology professor, noted yesterday that the specific grievances were not clearly articulated and were often expressed through the medium of other issues, such as the controversial airport.

This fertile ground for protest was further compounded, in the view of academics, businessmen and journalists, by government errors and oversights, including poor consultation with local residents. This can partly be attributed to the bureaucrtic makeup of the Tokyo International Airport Authority, a hybrid semigovernmental body that drew its employees, some of them about to be retired, from a number of other agencies.

"If you're tapped to contribute a quota of workers for a new agency," one official said, "do you think you'd give away your best men?"

In addition, the authority of the airport agency was limited to building the airport and did not encompass other aspects like access highways, railroads or fuel pipelines, which often fell between the planning floorboards. As a result the new airport was served by only one highway, with taxi fares to Tokyo ranging as high as $50 or more, one runway, dangerous crosswinds, no sidewalks, no fuel line and a bitter local confrontation that shows no signs of waning.

March 28, 1978

NEW AIRPORT'S DELAY EMBARRASSES FUKUDA

Japanese Radicals Jubilant · Over Postponement of Its Opening for at Least a Month

By ANDREW H. MALCOLM

TOKYO, March 28—Opponents of the New Tokyo International Airport reacted with jubilation to the Japanese Government decision today to postpone indefinitely the formal opening of the controversial $2.9-billion facility.

The postponement, which came after two days of violent clashes in which more than 165 protesters were arrested, scores more injured and the control tower's instruments destroyed, has greatly embarrassed the conservative Government of Prime Minister Takeo Fukuda. He had assured the nation and other governments that the new airport would finally open this week, five years after its completion.

The Government's decision, which was accompanied by a tough policy statement on radical agitation, came at a Cabinet session that had been delayed because of the incident.

The latest postponement is expected to last at least one month and more likely six weeks, meaning that the new facility, situated on farmland 46 miles northeast of here, would go into service at the height of Japan's tourist season. Radical opponents of the airport have vowed to continue their protests.

Travel Plans Disrupted

The postponement left airlines with employees and equipment divided between the new airfield and the old Haneda Airport and disrupted the transportation plans of thousands of travelers. Travel agencies and airlines here were swamped with calls from people who were not sure which airport to go to starting Sunday, when the new field was to have become operational.

In addition, thousands of tickets had been sold on extra domestic flights from the old Haneda Airport starting in April when, it was believed, all internaitonal flights would use the new airport. Now, traffic controllers face the prospect of even greater crowding at Haneda, especially during the hectic week that starts April 29, a peak travel time here because it contains three national holidays.

Meanwhile, the radicals announced plans for a "mass victory rally" on Thursday that threatened to develop into another confrontation with the authorities. About 14,000 riot policemen have been mobilized, the largest number in Japan in 18 years.

"It's a giant victory for us and a serious wound for the Fukuda Cabinet," Issaku Tomura, one of the leaders of the demonstrations, declared today. "The credibility of the Japanese Government has been seriously undermined."

"Everybody here is crushed," Gennojo Itch, an official at the new airport, said this afternoon. "Planning anything here is impossible," added one airport shop owner.

Customs officials, who were in the process of moving to the new airport near the farm town of Narita, have now started moving back to Tokyo. About 800 employees of Japan Air Lines and their families have already resettled near Narita and now face a three-hour daily trip to work in each direction.

'We're Happy to Wait'

Airline officials faced the difficult task of convincing prospective travelers that they would not be caught in new violence at the airport when it does open. "These protesters don't seem to have any fears at all," said one airline spokesman. "It's terrifying. But until passengers' security is guaranteed, we're happy to wait. We could never go in there right now."

Law enforcement authorites have promised to tighten airport security. They admitted today that the six radicals who wrecked the control tower Sunday were able to sneak under security lines through sewage pipes because, unlike the police, they had maps showing the pipe routes and manhole locations.

Transport Minister Kenji Fukunaga acknowledged today that one of the Government's most difficult tasks was to deal with "a loss of confidence abroad."

The 74-year-old Prime Minister said today that he was "very sorry" and that he would assume full responsiblity for failing to fulfill his international commitment.

New Strains on Cabinet

One consequence may be the deepening of divisions within Mr. Fukuda's Cabinet. Like all Japanese cabinets since the Liberal Democratic Party took control in 1955, it is carefully constructed to reflect the current political balance within the party.

It was apparent even to television viewers Sunday afternoon that due to the damage to the control tower, the formal opening of the airport could not take place Thursday. Yet it took the Government almost 48 hours to acknowledge this.

According to well-informed political sources, this delay was due not to the need to assess the damage, as the Government had explained publicly, but instead to Mr. Fukuda's difficulties in persuading some party leaders, such as the 67-year-old Mr. Fukunaga, to accept at least a temporary defeat at the hands of the radicals.

The delay was considered a sign that Mr. Fukuda's control of the party was slipping. He is already under attack for his economic policies, and there are rumors that his health is frail. His two-year term as president of the party expires in December.

Today's tough policy statement by the Cabinet indicated at least a nod to the conservative faction. It denounced the "destructive actions of exteme leftist groups." called them "outrages" that differed from the protests of local farmers against the airport and pledged to prevent future violence. The short statement did not spell out any specific steps, however.

March 29, 1978

Foes of New Tokyo Airport Vow to Keep Protesting

By ANDREW H. MALCOLM

NARITA, Japan, March 29—"We will continue our struggle forever," said a farmer who opposes construction here of the New Tokyo International Airport. "We will never stop fighting."

He was standing in spring mud near a wooden hut that he and others who are resisting the Government's plans to build the second runway of the air facility have built on the runway site.

Farmers and young leftist radicals have been protesting the airport for 12 years, and the latest demonstration, a dramatic raid last Sunday in which sensitive equipment in the control tower was destroyed, forced an indefinite delay in the airport's opening. Official attention is now focused not so much on new construction as on simply trying to keep the existing facilities secure.

The complex is now guarded by 14,000 riot policemen who man roadblocks and monitor highway traffic from camouflaged roadside positions. But today, while embarrassed authorities continued to review oversights that allowed protesters to break into the airport on Sunday, 10 youths drove up to the new Hotel Nikko near the airport, broke the front windows, lobbed gasoline bombs inside and drove off. The fires were extinguished without injury.

A few hours later several farmers, youths and townspeople paused in their preparations for tomorrow's "victory rally" here to talk about their land, their struggle and the reasons behind the "war." "Twelve years ago," said a farmer, "the Japanese Government simply decided to build an airport here, completely ignoring us. We turned on the television one night and there is the news, and we learn that the Government has decided to build this new airport right here on our land. We were astonished. They figured that somehow we could manage to survive. We can never forgive this kind of attitude."

Like most of the protesters around this farming center 46 miles northeast of Tokyo, the speaker was reluctant to reveal his name, because the police are believed to be quietly arresting protest leaders.

During these days of confrontation and much publicity, the protest movement here is believed to have swelled to perhaps 6,000 people, most of them students and former students in their 20's and 30's. The rest are local farmers, their families and sympathizers from elsewhere in Japan.

Refuse to Identify Leaders

The young people are divided into

about half a dozen leftist factions, which, members acknowledge, frequently struggle among themselves for dramatic moves in a kind of radical one-upmanship.

They refuse to identify their leaders, because, one youth said today, "We are at war here, and that is classified information." But one overall leader has emerged. He is Issaku Tomura, a 63-year-old sculptor and farmer who is referred to respectfully as "the Chairman," but his real influence in the movement other than as a spokesman is not known.

Like all the protesters interviewed in recent weeks, he lists as the principal reason for his group's opposition the Government's "high-handed attitude" toward farmers, and the farmers' ancestral attachment to their lands.

Mr. Tomura believes that the new airport is facilitating what he called Japan's economic aggression against the developing countries, and sees its construction as a further step toward the country's militarization, because it could be used by the military in any future hostilities in the region, especially in Korea. He cites as evidence of such an intention the extra-thick runways here, which would be needed for heavily loaded military aircraft, and the American desire to place a military post office on the airfield for its forces in Japan.

The protesters reject charges that they have initiated the violence through their airport assaults and firebombings. Such moves, they say, came only in response to "Government violence" in taking farmers' lands, forcibly evicting them and stationing thousands of policemen here in riot gear.

"There is no room for compromise," said one youth. "The airport must be abandoned. We will resort to any means."

March 30, 1978

TOKYO PLANS TO OPEN NEW AIRPORT IN MAY

Government Decision Sets Scene for Another Confrontation With Leftist Protesters

By ANDREW H. MALCOLM

TOKYO, March 31—The Japanese Government decided today to try to open the controversial New Tokyo International Airport in the latter half of May.

The decision, made at a somber Cabinet meeting, set the scene for another full-scale confrontation with several thousand radical youths and farmers similar to the one last Sunday during which the protesters wrecked the control tower. The violent assault caused postponement of the scheduled opening yesterday of the airport. The newest date for the opening will be decided at meetings early next week, but it is expected to be May 20.

Protesters called the Government decision a direct challenge and said they would respond accordingly. They have scheduled a "victory rally" for Sunday to celebrate the latest delay.

The $2.9 billion airfield was to have opened five years ago when construction was completed. But continuing protests, legal snarls and bureaucratic oversights have forced frequent postponements.

Delay Embarrassing for Government

The delay is an embarrassing one for the Government of Prime Minister Takeo Fukuda, which must now decide on the new opening day. The $578,000 in damage from Sunday's raid can be repaired by mid-April and improved perimeter fencing erected by late April, officials said, and some ministers want the opening as soon as possible to minimize the impact of the leftist attack. Another factor is the $300,000 a day cost of maintaining the facility while it is not in use.

But the unions of airport workers, transportation employees and airline pilots have demanded that the opening be delayed until total security can be guaranteed.

But April 29, Emperor Hirohito's birthday, begins a week of three national holidays when travel facilities are always strained. And Prime Minister Fukuda will be abroad from April 30 to May 7 for a meeting with President Carter in Washington.

A delay until May 20, which is a good luck day on the lunar calendar, would also provide additional time for the organization of a new airport security unit.

The seven-week delay also would allow more time for efforts to reach a compromise with the airport's opponents, who are bitter over expropriation of farmlands and oppose what they say is the field's potential military value. One compromise being considered in some Government circles is to offer a promise not to expand the existing runway and not to build the two others originally planned, eliminating the need to obtain more land. While this might not satisfy the ardent bands of leftist youth, some officials hope the offer might split them from the farmers.

In addition to costly moves of airline equipment, the Government's chagrin and the uncertainty caused for travelers, the delay has brought some other inconveniences.

The Government had to postpone issuing a special airport commemorative stamp. The airport will have to change the date on the gift cases of the 6,000 liquid-crystal thermometers it bought for ceremony guests at a cost of $22 each.

And the airport authority decided to send out thousands of formal cards announcing the postponement. The trouble was, however, that the cards announcing the delay were themselves delayed and did not reach their addresses until today, a day after the scheduled date for the festivities.

April 2, 1978

---

4 Accused of Attempted Murder In Rioting Over Tokyo Airport

CHIBA, Japan, April 18 (Reuters)—Four left-wing opponents of Tokyo's new airport were charged today with attempted murder for their part in a three-day battle against the police last month. The Chiba district prosecutor's office said the four had hurled cement blocks at riot policemen and struck them on the head with steel pipes, injuring five officers.

Forty-five other people who barricaded themselves in a three-story bunker outside the airport and held off security forces were charged with lesser offenses.

Because of damage to vital control-tower equipment, the Government postponed opening of the airport from March 30 until May 20.

May 20, 1978

New Tokyo Airport Finally Opens With 13,000 Policemen on Hand

By HENRY SCOTT-STOKES

NARITA, Japan, Saturday, May 20— Shortly before 10:30 A.M. this morning, a Shinto priest in a white kimono and wooden shoes entered a fourth-floor room in the north wing of the new airport terminal here. Surrounded by dark-suited officials from the Transport Ministry, the Narita Airport Authority and Customs and Immigration, the priest waved a wand, chanted a prayer and ceremonially purified this $2.9 billion facility.

Emperor Hirohito was not there, nor was Prime Minister Takeo Fukuda. In their absence, Transport Minister Kenji Fukunaga presided over the opening of the New Tokyo International Airport.

The presence of all three was once planned. But it was no longer appropriate. The opening had been delayed for seven years by opposition from left-wing radicals and local farmers, and the final ceremony, postponed a dozen times, was low-key.

Some 13,000 riot policemen were on hand—with shields, stout poles, pistols (never issued to riot policemen normally), helmets and walkie-talkies—to protect the 50 officials and the priest. Nearby, thousands of demonstrators prepared for what the authorities regard as an inevitable confrontation sometimes today.

Narita Airport had finally been opened —but not before one more alarm. Early this morning airport opponents of the left-wing Chukaku-ha, or Core Faction, cut an air-traffic-control cable at Tokorozawa, 20 miles from Tokyo.

Air traffic in Japan was briefly disrupted by the cutting of the cable, which is part of a system linking pilots in the air with ground control. But a Transport Ministry official said that "80 to 90 percent of the flights are going through."

A plane carrying Zbigniew Brzezinski, President Carter's adviser for national security, who stopped in Tokyo overnight on his way to China, was the first to leave Tokyo's Haneda Airport this morning.

The New York Times/Hirotaka Yoshizaki
Masaji Ishibashi is a spokesman for the farmers who oppose the opening of airport at Narita.

International flights are to be shitfed from Haneda to Narita this weekend, and by next week almost all international flights are to pass through Narita.

At 6:10 A.M. tomorrow the first plane will land, Japan Air Lines Flight 45, a cargo jet; it will be followed by JAL Flight 446, the first passenger jet, at 11:25.

Hundreds of Leftists Gather

Near the airport's terminal here, ready for a centerpiece battle in front of television cameras and several hundred reporters and cameramen, 6,000 Chukaku-ha members had gathered.

"The Chukaku-ha will deploy their entire strength from across the nation in front of the airport on May 20," a police official had said. "They will make one of their straightforward, concentrated, rather massive violent attacks."

"They will fail," the policeman continued, "but what worries me are the other factions. They are prepared for a marathon, not a frontal clash." They include the Fourth International, the Battle Flag and the Proletarian Youth League, small groups that use weapons like homemade bombs and that, according to the police, whose information comes from informers, are preparing hijacking sallies and the taking of hostages.

The police also fear that the exiled Red Army, which they think now has only about two dozen members, will make a reappearance from overseas. Last year its members hijacked a JAL plane to Bangladesh, and obtained the release of half a dozen leaders from prison in Japan plus a $6 million ransom from the Japanese Government. "The silence of the Red Army overseas is very strange," a police official remarked.

Three Aims of Ultraleftists

The ultraleftists have three aims, according to the police: the attacks on Narita, attacks on the Japanese imperial family and the release from prison of 19-year-old Kazuo Ishikawa. A member of the "untouchable" lower caste of Burakumin, he is wrongly accused, leftists maintain, of a rape-murder in a case that symbolizes racial discrimination.

Though some airport service may start tomorrow, the opposition of conservative farmers and their left-wing allies, many of them hardened fighters from the 1960's, no longer students but professional agitators, will continue.

The leaders of the battle, mostly conservative peasants, are concerned solely with the effect on their farmland. Around the airport, largely with the help of their left-wing allies, they have built over 30 forts, towers and encampments, where the students live, permanently on guard. Revolutionary slogans hang from the towers and are emblazoned in red on oil drums.

Inconvenience to Travelers Stressed

The current phase of the struggle got under way in March. On the 26th, demonstrators broke into the control tower despite the presence of 13,000 policemen around the airport and smashed instruments, delaying yet another scheduled opening. "If the control tower is attacked again shortly after a plane departed," said Masaji Ishibashi, a farmer spokesman, "I am sure that will cause real trouble."

The farmers, hundreds of whom still work land near the airport that must be expropriated to build two more runways—there is only one of over 13,000 feet now—point out the inconvenience to travelers. "Imagine a foreign visitor who spends many hours in a plane to get here," Mr. Ishibashi said, "and then finds he must spend another few hours getting into Tokyo."

The trip downtown, which costs at least $50 by taxi, takes an hour and a quarter or more. Traffic jams have built up on the one narrow access road, even before the arrival of a passenger load estimated at 80,000 a day, so that two hours must be allowed, even by railway, which does not run right to the airport.

According to American officials, the airport may not have been needed since the present facility, Haneda, is operating at a third of the capacity of big airports in the West. The Transport Ministry took half-page advertisements in the press to rebut such suspicions, offering maps to show that extending Haneda by reclaiming Tokyo Bay would have been dangerous because traffic would have been too concentrated.

May 21, 1978

New Attacks Feared as Japan Starts Airport Service

By HENRY SCOTT-STOKES

TOKYO, Sunday, May 21—Japanese officials were fearful of new guerrilla attacks at the new international airport at Narita near here but nonetheless pressed ahead with plans to receive the first cargo and passenger flights today.

A Japan Air Lines cargo DC-8 from Los Angeles was the first flight to land this morning. The first passenger flight, a DC-8 from Frankfrt via Moscow, was scheduled to arive a few hours later. In all, 22 flights are scheduled for today.

Yesterday domestic air traffic at Tokyo's Haneda Airport was paralyzed for three hours, delaying 16,000 passengers, when leftists cut an underground air-traffic-control cable at three points in the western suburbs of Tokyo.

"We are really concerned about safety, everyone is worried," said a Japanese airline executive. "We can only just pray."

Leftists Take Responsibility

Responsibility for the cutting of the cable was taken by the Chukaku-ha, or Core Faction, an extreme left-wing group that was a center of violent student opposition to the Vietnam war in the 1960's.

In a separate attack last night, 300 helmeted left-wingers crashed two burning trucks against a gate at the Narita airport. The police fired tear gas and later reported that 21 policemen had been injured and that they had made 49 arrests, including 17 women.

Some 15,000 opponents of the new airport, including leftists and farmers from the area, attended a demonstration yesterday at which rocks and firebombs were thrown.

The airport is being protected by 13,000 riot policemen, one of the biggest antiterrorist forces of the postwar era.

Cost Put at $2.9 Billion

The police, according to the newspaper Asami, have stationed sharpshooters around the 12,000-foot runway at the $2.9 billion airport in case leftists put up balloons or kites or jam radio communications to hamper incoming flights.

"It's a little like landing a civil aircraft on the Ho Chi Minh Trail at the height of the Vietnam war," a foreign diplomat said.

The first scheduled arrival by an American carrier is a flight tonight by Continental Air Lines from Saipan.

Narita airport was formally declared open yesterday after a Shinto purification ceremony. All international carriers are to switch their flights from the old Haneda Airport to Narita by Tuesday, including Pan American World Airways and Flying Tiger, the American cargo line.

A Korean Air Lines flight to Los Angeles is scheduled to be the first departure from Narita on Monday morning. Chukaku-ha leaders have sworn they will stop that departure.

Issaku Tomura, the 69-year-old leader of the alliance of leftists and farmers opposed to the airport, said at the Narita rally yesterday: "Today's opening ceremony will turn out to be an occasion marking the death of the airport."

Mr. Tomura described the sabotage of Tokyo's air traffic control system yesterday as "an act of God," and he called for attacks on water, electricity and power supplies.

Officials of Nippon Telegraph and Telephone said that those who had cut the cables were "professionals." They knew exactly which cables to sever with hydraulic cutters after entering a manhole at Tokorozawa at 5 A.M. yesterday.

Leftists say they have 3,000 sympathizers among employees of public corporations. They obtain blueprints of public facilities, including Narita airport. They smashed the control tower there on March 26 after eluding thousands of riot policemen by gaining access through manholes and tunnels.

Becomes Political Issue

Opposition parties are making a political issue of Narita. The Socialist Party accused the Government yesterday of dealing with the issue only by force.

Transport Minister Kenji Fukunaga, in an attempt to isolate conservative farmers from radical leftists, has softened his stand and offered to consult with the farmers on planned expansions of the airport.

The Buddhist Komeito Party urged the Government to negotiate with the Narita farmers.

The Democratic Socialist Party charged that the Government's failure to negotiate with local residents had led to the troubles. But like Komeito and the Socialist and Communist parties, it denounced the violence of the radicals.

May 21, 1978

Tokyo Airport Showdown Is Quite Japanese

By HENRY SCOTT-STOKES

"Up until this affair started I was just a mere farmer and very obedient to the Government. I was just a plain farmer."
— MASAJI ISHIBASHI, leader of the farmers' revolt at Japan's Narita airport.

NARITA, Japan — One does not have to look far to find the origins of the conflict between local farmers and the Government over the $2.9 billion new international airport 40 miles northeast of Tokyo. The airport opened yesterday, seven years behind schedule, under the protection of 13,000 riot police who beat off an evening assault by hundeds of radical protestors armed with gasoline bombs and iron bars. Friday night, all flights over Japan were halted briefly after Narita's opponents cut a central air-traffic-control cable.

The bitterness behind the struggle of local farmers to defend their homes, their families and their livelihood goes back 13 years. Japan, in the midst of one of the remarkable economic advances of modern times, needed a second airport to serve Tokyo. Two stalwart politicians of the right, Ichiro Kono and Shoji Kawashima, both now dead, emerged to dispute the real-estate spoils. Prime Minister Eisaku Sato arbitrated, and Narita was chosen — without the consultation or consent of the farmers whose land was to be expropriated.

Mr. Sato, a former Transport Ministry official, had neglected a cardinal Japanese rule: Consult with everyone concerned before you take a decision and make sure that there is a consensus before you act. The conservative farmers tried legal means of protest. They appealed to the courts, made a petition to the Emperor and sent letters of protest to the Minister of Transport, all to no avail. Then the opposition parties got into the act. The first on the scene, the Japan Communist Party, was put off by growing radical student involvement. By the late 1960's, members of the radical Sekigun, or

Antiairport demonstrators set afire an electrical switchboard during yesterday's protests at the Narita airport.

Associated Press

The Political World

Red Army (long since driven out of Japan), took interest in Narita, and was joined by helmeted squads from other sects.

The farmers accepted the students' support because, as Mr. Ishibashi put it, "we can't keep fighting this kind of struggle simply by relying on political parties. That's the lesson we learned, we should defend ourselves by ourselves." Neither the Communist party, which shuns violence, nor the Socialist Party, joined the farmers in building concrete and steel towers to block flight-paths or fighting off riot police who came to take the towers. But there is also support from the general public. One morning recently the mailman handed Mr. Ishibashi, a registered envelope, containing a 10,000-yen note ($43) from a previously unheard-from well-wisher.

Many Japanese sympathize with the farmers because they are considered the victims of oppression by middle-class, white-collar residents of Tokyo who have little liking for the politics of left-wing radicals fighting at the farmers' side. That sentiment, too, goes back to the Government's decision to press ahead with Narita without consulting the people involved. "The Government made its mistake at the outset," said an elegantly suited banker and former Finance Ministry official at his office in Tokyo. "There is a Japanese way of doing things and you neglect it at your peril. And there's another factor. Once the two sides were dug in neither could give way because to do so would have been to lose face."

This "Japanese" explanation of events at Narita is one part of the story. There are folkloric elements to support it — the use by the radicals of bow and arrow in a medieval-style struggle to defend their feudal fortresses; the do-or-die, Guadalcanal-like resistance to the last, and the shrinking of the Government from loss of face. Takeo Fukuda is the fourth Japanese Prime Minister to have wrestled with that.

But fundamentally, the farmers and sympathizers have demanded a sense of justice, even Western democratic procedures. This elementary point is easily obscured. When Issaku Tomura, a local dealer in farm implements who is a sculptor of sorts, not long ago took a trip to Beirut and consulted with members of the Palestine Liberation Organization about tactics, Government officials suggested that the resistance to Narita is a Red extremist plot. Mr. Tomura, chairman of the

Sanrizuka Shibayama anti-airport alliance, the overall resistance group, is a leftwing ideologue. Mr. Ishibashi, vice-chairman of the alliance, is a former supporter of Mr. Fukuda's Liberal Democratic Party who doesn't approve of the Palestinian connection: "As far as the P.L.O. is concerned," he says, "I don't fully agree with the chairman because Palestinians are Palestinians and we Japanese are Japanese."

The fundamental issue, however, is where the will to fight on will come from now. The unique relationship between the conservative farmers and their radical allies is the key. Says Mr. Ishibashi: "The reason why farmers and students could come together is that we farmers do not study and we have little knowledge of politics and the law. . . . We can learn a lot from them and also they can learn something from us." Such as a sense of roots.

The way the struggle goes at Narita — a bloody affair in which five lives have been lost and thousands have been injured — the farmers cannot be in the vanguard. Unlike the mercurial, shifting radical students, they can be identified and prosecuted too easily. But morally, the farmers lead the fight. The relationship between the farmers and the students is evident on Mr. Ishibashi's farm. From the porch where he seated himself one hot afternoon beside a basket of scarlet cyclamen, he looked out across a garden of dwarf pines loaded with weights to make them grow in esthetic shapes toward the end of his yard. On one side were pigs, cattle and chickens in open stalls. On the other, in another outbuilding, were the students' quarters.

The struggle has not ended. Thirty student fortresses are still to be levelled. Flights out of Narita will be harassed. And how guerrillas are to be prevented from entering the airport with passengers remains to be seen. The Government also must extend the airport. A second and a third runway are scheduled to be built — over Mr. Ishibashi's garden of dwarf trees, and across the properties of hundreds of his fellow farmers. "When Japan Inc. fouls up," said a foreign diplomat, "it goes all the way."

Henry Scott-Stokes is a New York Times correspondent based in Tokyo.

May 21, 1978

Japan, Defying Leftists, To Repair Nuclear Ship

TOKYO, July 18 (Reuters) — The Japanese Government will go ahead with plans to move its controversial nuclear-powered ship Mutsu to Kyushu Island in the south for repairs, despite leftist threats of violence.

Tasaburo Kumagi, head of the government's Science and Technology Agency, said the 8,214-ton ship, laid up since a radiation leak marred its initial voyage in 1974, would move to Sasebo near Nagasaki in October.

There the ship, with its faulty reactor intact, will undergo repairs for three years in a shipyard that is in financial difficulty and needs the contract, he said.

July 19, 1978

Dissident Apparently Tries To Attack Japanese Leader

FUKUI, Japan, July 31 (Reuters) — A right-wing journalist opposed to the forced resignation of Japan's senior military officer apparently tried to ram the limousine carrying Prime Minister Takeo Fukuda today.

The unarmed man driving a small

sedan was blocked by a police vehicle a yard short of the bulletproof limousine in which Mr. Fukuda was riding through this port city.

The rightist, identified by police as Yoshihiko Uchiyama, fled from his car after shouting: "What are you going to do about the Kurisu issue?" The police said

that he was arrested later and charged with traffic offenses.

Last week, Gen. Eomi Kurisu was forced to resign as chairman of the Joint Staff Council of Japan's self-defense forces after saying that front-line commanders might take unilateral action in the event of a surprise attack on Japan.

August 1, 1978

Prime Minister Takeo Fukuda of Japan visits Secretary-General Kurt Waldheim at United Nations Headquarters.

Chapter 7

Japan's World Role

From defeat and devastation in World War II, Japan has come a long way in defining its world position. Although the nation is economically powerful, in reality the only advanced industrial power in Asia, it has failed to obtain the level of respect and recognition it seeks from Western countries for both its status and its achievements. Many critics, some of them Japanese, argue that Japan has, until recently, virtually ignored its international responsibility to contribute to as well as to take from the world community. During 1977-78 the number of loans made available by the Japanese government to foreign nations increased substantially. The recipients included Great Britain, Brazil, France and Mexico. Few developing nations, however, have been able to muster the strength to obtain such loans. In June 1978 Robert McNamara, president of the World Bank, approached the Japanese and urged them to contribute more aid to poor and developing nations. In subsequent talks between Fukuda and McNamara, a doubling of past development assistance from Japan was discussed as a priority for the period 1979 to 1982. This increase, it was believed, would also help to reduce Japan's enormous trade surplus.

Japan received some sharp criticism from around the world early in 1978 when fishermen in southern Japan were reported to have clubbed to death approximately 1,000 dolphins with the approval of the local Nagasaki government. The Japanese claimed that the dolphins were feeding upon their fish catches. Conscious of their recently strengthened position of influence in world affairs, the Japanese are acutely sensitive to international opinion. As often is the case in such matters, the Japanese responded to Western criticism with the contention that they had been thoroughly misunderstood.

Although Japan is aligned politically with the United States and the Western democracies, it has kept a low profile in dealing with Communist nations. Japan has relations on several levels with both the People's Republic of China and the Soviet Union in spite of the mutual enmity of both of these Communist powers. It also interacts with Taiwan and both Koreas.

Many U.S. military installations have been established in Japan since World War II. During the Cold War, these bases were vital to American military strategy in Asia and the Pacific. The U.S. military presence continues, particularly on the island of Okinawa where political control was returned to Japan in May 1972. In November 1977, however, the 1,450-acre Tachikawa Air Base complex, once the focus of most

American military activity in Asia, was closed down and its facilities reverted to Japan. The shutdown, part of an ongoing base consolidation effort, leaves 76 U.S. military facilities on the four main Japanese islands.

Projections of Japanese foreign policy guidelines for the years to come are still difficult to make. In 1977-78, Japan augmented her air force by one hundred F-15 jet fighters and forty-five anti-submarine planes, all purchased from the United States. Her defense budget has increased continuously since the end of the American occupation. Elements within the Japanese military, not content with civilian control of their functions, would like to see this budget rise even more substantially. As Japan becomes economically and militarily stronger and more confident, it seems likely that she will take a more independent stance in world affairs.

Japan Ponders Its Own Defenses
As U.S. Prepares Korea Pullout

By BERNARD WEINRAUB

TOKYO, July 31—The Japanese Government uneasy about the planned withdrawal of American ground troops from South Korea and the buildup of Soviet military strength in the Pacific, is in the grip of a major debate over the nation's security and fragile defense capability.

Although Defense Secretary Harold Brown, in a visit here last week, sought to assure Japanese officials that the United States would maintain "an active Asian role" and abide by its security commitments to Japan and South Korea, defense officials in Tokyo are plainly wary and puzzled about the phased withdrawal of more than 30,000 ground troops from South Korea over the next four or five years.

What concerns senior Japanese defense officials is that the United States has apparently received no assurance, or quid pro quo, from the Soviet Union or North Korea that the withdrawal would be accompanied by an easing of tension by the Pyongyang Government.

Moreover, Japanese officials express uncertainty about the reasons for the pullout, saying that Japanese and other Asian leaders have failed so far to receive "adequate explanations" for the withdrawal. They also say that the reduction of American troops in Northeast Asia is part of an overall retreat from the Pacific that will result in greater Soviet influence in the area.

U.S. 'Reliability' in Question

Compounding the uncertainty among the Japanese—a nation with a gross national product second only to the United States among industrial democracies—is "a profound uneasiness about American reliability," as a diplomat put it.

The so-called Nixon shocks of 1971, which included the major devaluation of the dollar and the abrupt announcement of the American move to improve relations with Peking, are factors that led Japan to reconsider her own foreign policy.

With the United States military withdrawal from Indochina, the fall of Saigon and now the withdrawal from South Korea, Japan appears to be almost reluctantly edging toward a more independent course. This includes efforts to improve relations with North Korea and to open links with Vietnam.

Perhaps the most subtle shifts, however, have occurred in defense. According to Western diplomats and some Japanese officials, the premise of American military superiority in the Pacific, which enabled Japan to enjoy a strong sense of security, has become cloudy.

Rise in Soviet Strength Seen

The Japanese point out that American naval tonnage and tactical air forces in the Pacific have declined while Soviet air and naval strength have grown steadily.

Japanese officials say that the Soviet Union has 120 submarines in the Far East, 45 of them nuclear.

Ironically, according to some diplomats, Japanese defense officials are reluctant to dramatize the increased Soviet presence because they believe that to do so would also dramatize the American weakness and raise questions about Japan's overwhelming dependence on military assurances supplied by the United States in a 1951 security treaty with Japan.

Nonetheless, officials are engaged in a debate that pits some politicians and senior bureaucrats, who want a slow increase in the proportion of defense expenditures, against those who insist that higher expenditures are unnecessary.

Japan's postwar Constitution bans a strong offensive armed force. Japan spends less than 1 percent of its gross national product to maintain a defensive force of about 200,000 air, naval and ground troops. Western intelligence experts estimate that Japan's Air Force might last 10 minutes in a war with the Soviet Union.

A further constraint on military spending is the potential anxiety and opposition in other Asian nations to an important military buildup in Japan.

August 1, 1977

VANCE AND JAPANESE DISCUSS PEKING TRIP

Areas of Conflict Between Tokyo and Washington Brought Up— Fukuda Asks Carter Visit

TOKYO, Aug. 26 (AP)—Secretary of State Cyrus R. Vance briefed Prime Minister Takeo Fukuda on his China trip today, and Japanese sources said Mr. Fukuda extended an invitation to President Carter to pay an official visit to Japan.

Mr. Vance told the Japanese that after his four days in China he felt as though he had "come back home" because of the "special relationship" between the United States and Japan.

But sources said the meeting also dealt with two areas of dispute between Japan and the United States—international economics and President Carter's concern over Japanese plans to operate a nuclear reprocessing plant.

Japanese officials said Mr. Vance told Prime Minister Fukuda today that the China mission had been "exploratory" and had not been aimed at finding a "final solution" to the question of establishing full ties with China.

A spokesman for Mr. Vance, Hodding Carter 3d, described the talks here as "warm, friendly and informative." Mr. Vance was scheduled to depart for Washington tomorrow.

In an apparent bid to reassure the Nationalists, Mr. Vance sent Richard C. Holbrooke, the Assistant Secretary of State for the Far East, to Taiwan to brief leaders on the Peking trip. Mr. Holbrooke later left for South Korea, where he was to confer with President Park Chung Hee.

Peking's demand that the United States sever its diplomatic and defense ties with Taiwan was a major theme of Mr. Vance's discussions in China. However, Mr. Vance gave no hint that the United States was prepared to abandon Taiwan in order to normalize relations with Peking.

August 27, 1977

JAPANESE FEAR HARDSHIP IN NEW FISHING LIMITS

WASHINGTON, Sept. 10 (Reuters)— Representatives of Japanese fishing interests said here yesterday that their country's fishing industry could be imperiled if the United States imposed proposed new restrictions on foreign fleets inside its 200-mile fishing limit.

Tomouoshi Kamenaga, the leader of a delegation that came to Washington for talks with Government officials, said at a news conference that if fresh restrictions were imposed on foreign fishermen, "perhaps we would not find the fishing industry viable." He said Japan had already paid about $550 million in relief to its fishing industry, on which the country relies heavily for food.

The Japanese visit was prompted by reports that United States fishing interests are advocating tough new regulations to the National Marine Fisheries Service, which is in the process of establishing catch limits for the 1978 season.

Under the current 200-mile fishing regulations, which the United States began to enforce earlier this year, the Fisheries Service allocated 1.2 million tons to Japan, with restrictions on certain species.

September 11, 1977

This Japanese fish market could be adversely affected by new restrictions on foreign fleets inside its 200-mile fishing limit.

Japan Air Lines

Japan Disappointed
Over Its Minor Role in U.N.

By PRANAY GUPTE

UNITED NATIONS, N.Y., Oct. 1—The Japanese here are observing the 21st anniversary of their country's admission to the United Nations, but they are not celebrating the occasion. In fact, they seem to be pretty glum.

"Our impact in the United Nations has perhaps been less than what we had hoped for," said Yoshin Okawa, the director general of Japan's mission here, the other day. "Our entry in the United Nations had meant to the Japanese people a readmission to the international community as a peace-loving nation."

"We used to feel like an international orphan in the years before our admission," Mr. Okawa continued. "We thought that the United Nations would be the solution to all the world's ills. But perhaps we were a bit starry-eyed."

A general sense of restlessness among members can be found at almost any time here at the United Nations, but the disappointment of Mr. Okawa and his colleagues is more than just pique. It is frustration that they feel.

"Our frustration stems from our belief that we can play a larger role in the United Nations and yet we feel that we are not being given the chance," said Yasushi Akashi, a minister in Japan's mission.

Specifically, the Japanese feel that although they are the third biggest contributor to the United Nations' financial pot —more than $120 million a year to the organization's budget and to various United Nations development agencies— they do not get much in return.

Take jobs, for instance, Mr. Okawa said. Of the 50 top positions at the United Nations, meaning those of assistant secretary general upward, Japan has been allocated only one—the one held by Genichi Akatani, the assistant secretary general who heads the Office of Public Information.

"There is one nation that contributes far less than us and yet it has four of these high positions," Mr. Okawa said.

Which nation, he was asked. Mr. Okawa appeared hesitant. When pressed, he replied almost inaudibly, "Finland."

He pointed out that until last year the Japanese share of the United Nations operating budget was 7.15 percent of the total, but that largely because of Japan's continuing economic prosperity, its budgetary contribution had been reassessed and it now paid 8.66 percent.

That increase represented the single largest jump in percentage points for any of the United Nations' 149 members. Thus, Japanese diplomats emphasize, their country pays more to the United Nations than either France or China, and almost double the amount now contributed by Britain.

In addition, Mr. Akashi noted, when Secretary General Kurt Waldheim recently appealed to member nations to contribute more money voluntarily so that the $100 million deficit of the United Nations could be eliminated, only three countries came forth.

They were Saudi Arabia and the United Arab Emirates, each of which paid about $1 million, and Japan, which donated $10 million.

"We see some injustice in that," Mr. Okawa said. "We feel that the responsibilities and privileges of member states should correspond to their contributions."

"Japan's contributions are a reflection of her economic standing in the present-day world, and she accepts this with good grace," he continued. "However, Japan feels she can and should be allowed to play a more prominent role in the political field as well."

The "political field" that Mr. Okawa was referring to is the United Nations Security Council. Japan's wish to become the first nonnuclear nation to be a permanent member of the Council is hardly a secret here.

But when asked to assess Japan's prospects for obtaining such membership, Mr. Okawa said: "I'm not optimistic. We have no illusions about the tremendous obstacles involved. But is it right that the present five permanent members are all nuclear powers? Won't it correspond to the reality of the world if nonnuclear members also have an important role to play in the Council?"

"We could be very useful in the Council," Mr. Okawa added, an assessment that was supported by diplomats from other Asian countries as well as from several African nations. These diplomats cited the leverage enjoyed by Japan in the developing world these days, largely because of the $1.1 billion it gives in aid annually, along with various kinds of technical assistance.

October 2, 1977

Japanese Criticism Stirs Dismay in Canada

By ROBERT TRUMBULL

OTTAWA, Oct. 7—Is the Canadian labor force overpaid, short on productivity and inclined to strike? Are corporate taxes too high? Environmental laws too strict? Is the United States a better place for foreign investors?

A business organization of leading industrialists in Japan says that the answer to all those questions is yes, and its blunt criticism of Canada as a place to build factories and otherwise invest in has caused a furor here, drawing rejoinders of outrage and denial.

The views were presented, apparently without much gentleness, to Premier William Davis of Ontario and his aides as they visited Tokyo last week on a trip to solicit Japanese investment. Mr. Davis was "stunned" by the comments, according to Canadian news dispatches from Tokyo.

Others shared in his dismay. Canadian economic analysts said that the

Associated Press
Premier William Davis

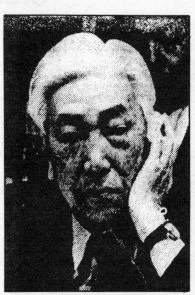

The New York Times
Eichi Hashimoto

adverse comments had been a contributing factor in a further slide of the Canadian dollar to less than 92 cents in terms of United States money, the lowest in seven years.

Minister Assails Organization

Canadian labor unions reacted with fury and Labor Minister John Munro said that the Japanese views presented a "greatly exaggerated" picture of Canada. He attacked the organization, which is called Keidanren, as a kind of industrial cartel that he characterized as at variance with free enterprise.

Several others, however, said they thought that the Japanese comments were on the mark. "We have been trying to tell Canadians the same thing for several years but very few would listen," said J. Laurents Thibault, the economics director of the Canadian Manufacturers Association.

What the spokesman for Keidanren said was that on every count conditions for Japanese investment in the United States were more attractive.

The spokesman, Eichi Hashimoto, is chairman of Mitsui & Company, a huge conglomerate. He said that Canadians approached by Mitsui for joint ventures in Canada had urged that proposed partnerships with Canadian participation be shifted to the United States because of lower taxes there.

'We Are Not a Charity'

"I suggested last year some proposals to your businessmen," he said. "But their reply was that it was not the time for investment in Canada. They would like to do something in your neighboring country."

"If we invest money," he said, "if we establish some enterprise, we have to make a profit. We are not a charity."

The Keidanren spokesman responded negatively when the Canadians on the Tokyo visit asked that Japan diversify investments in Canada, which are now concentrated in the development of mineral and forest resources. Although Canada bought more than $1.5 billion worth of goods from Japan last year, mostly fabricated materials. Canadian exports to Japan were nearly $2.4 billion, mostly raw materials, according to Government statistics.

Mr. Hashimoto cited an earlier report by Keidanren that had little good to say about the Canadian labor force and said that he believed the appraisal was still valid, although Mr. Davis assured him that conditions had improved.

Ronald Lang, research director of the Canadian Labor Congress, disputed the low Japanese opinion of Canadian labor. Mr. Hashimoto, he said, "just doesn't understand the Canadian economy at all or know what's happening to it."

The Canadian reception to the Japanese remarks filled many news columns and some editorials agreed with Mr. Hashimoto.

"These foreign criticisms are only echoing what Canadians have been saying for some time." The Globe and Mail of Toronto said. The Citizen, of Ottawa, commented that foreigners would have more confidence in the Canadian economy "when we do more for ourselves and stop hoping for others to bail us out with more capital investment."

The Minister for Industry, Trade and Commerce, Jack Horner, said he thought that the Japanese criticism was at least partly justified. "There's a lot of truth in what they say," he said in a radio interview, but added that conditions were "not near as bad as they say."

"The way it was put was perhaps a bit too forceful," Finance Minister Jean Chrétian said. Environment Minister Leonard Marchand denied that strictures enforced by his department were a factor in economic conditions.

And so it went. Proceeding to Hong Kong, the Ontario Premier received another shock when he presented his province as an investment lure to a meeting of Hong Kong businessmen.

The response was a denunciation of Canadian quotas on Hong Kong textiles, which were called a violation of previous trade agreements and discriminatory against poorer economies.

October 8, 1977

Japanese Official Says
U.S. Is Key to Asian Peace

By EMERSON CHAPIN

PRINCETON, N.J., Oct. 30—Continued political stability in the Far East depends on "the capacity and will of the United States to maintain the balance of power in that part of the world," Japan's top spokesman in the United States declared here last night.

Ambassador Fumihiko Togo declared that both in Korea and in Southeast Asia a continued American presence and commitment were vital to the maintenance of peace. He particularly expressed concern that the American withdrawal of ground forces from South Korea and the accompanying strengthening of South Korean forces should be carried out in such a way as not to weaken South Korean defenses and not to upset the "precarious balance" on the peninsula.

To this end, he expressed hope that the differences between Washington and Seoul that have arisen out of the efforts by South Koreans to influence American legislators, which have increasingly cast doubt on the American-aided buildup of the South Korean forces, be resolved "as soon as possible."

Ambassador Togo was the chief dinner speaker at the annual meeting of the mid-Atlantic regional organization of the Association of Asian Studies, attended by several hundred scholars and other specialists on Asian affairs over the weekend at Princeton University. His address was part of a recently intensified effort by Japanese officials to make Japan's positions and policies better known in this country and deflect criticism at a time when economic strains between Tokyo and Washington seem to be growing.

Shift Toward Positive Policy

This public relations effort comes at a time when some analysts discern a shift by Japan, under Prime Minister Takeo Fukuda, to a more positive international policy. Prof. Nathaniel B. Thayer, director of Asian studies at the Johns Hopkins School of Advanced International Studies, said today in one of the meeting's panel discussions:

"Japanese foreign policy is changing. Japanese diplomats now appear willing to take the initiative instead of waiting to respond to events. The initiatives are political, though often framed in economic terms."

Mr. Togo, who served as Deputy Foreign Minister before taking his present post early last year, touched only briefly in his talk on the developing strains with the United States, saying that it was Prime Minister Fukuda's aim that they be dealt with reasonably, as "economic issues," and not in emotional terms.

He spoke optimistically about Japan's increasing relations with China while suggesting that all was not well in relations with the Soviet Union. Moscow's refusal even to discuss the return to Japanese administration of four islands seized by the Soviet Union at the end of World War II "serves, in a way, as a constant reminder to many Japanese of Russia's behavior in the final days of the Pacific war," he said.

Citing the Soviet Union and China, he declared: "Japan and other free nations of Asia, having these two great powers with different social systems as neighbors, realize that the participation of the United States in Asian affairs is very important for maintenance of an equilibrium of power in that part of the world."

October 31, 1977

Pearl Harbor Plus 36

By James Reston

TOKYO—In a few days it will be 36 years since the Japanese attack on Pearl Harbor. This was the day, Franklin Roosevelt said, "that will live in infamy," but the world is so different now that Dec. 7 scarcely lives in memory.

Japan has become the third or perhaps even the second industrial nation in the world, with a trade surplus this year of around $17 billion, almost half of it at the expense of the United States. Accordingly, there are serious problems between Washington and Tokyo, including the threat of economic war.

But in the perspective of these 36 years, it is surprising that so few of the disasters so solemnly predicted after Pearl Harbor and the Vietnam War have come to pass.

There is no spirit of domination or revenge today in the relations between the United States and Japan. No revival of the Sino-Soviet alliance after the deaths of Mao Tse-tung and Chou En-lai. No collapse of American authority in the Pacific after the retreat from Saigon. No new naval alliance between Moscow and New Delhi in the Indian Ocean. No political swing to the left in Japan. Pearl Harbor itself is not worried about war in the Pacific these days but about a shortage of water in the Hawaiian Islands.

Prime Minister Fukuda looks cannily at this postwar world. He talks privately, not about the balance of power in the Pacific, but about the balance of trade in the world. For the first time in history, he says, we have a worldwide economic system in which every major nation's decisions influence the life of many other nations. This will take some working out and it will take time, he says, but he has no complaints he wants to make public.

Other Japanese officials, editors, bankers and business leaders are more forthcoming. They speak of the fragility of Japan—its vulnerability to decisions elsewhere in the world; the pricing of oil and other raw materials essential to Japan's economic stability; the rise of protectionism in the industrial countries, and of competition from the "new Japans" in Korea, Taiwan, and elsewhere in the Pacific Basin. They are particularly concerned about what they call the "uncertainty" of United States military, economic and financial policy.

They are also fascinated but puzzled by President Carter. They see him on their excellent national television system almost every night, but they clearly don't understand. Why, they ask, if he is a President of the Democratic Party, with a Democratic Party majority in the Congress, can't he get his policies on energy, Panama, welfare and taxes accepted?

They simply don't get the American Federal political system. Mike Mansfield, the former Democratic leader of the Senate, and now U.S. Ambassador in Tokyo, has tried to explain. He has put the photographs of Speaker Tip O'Neill and majority leader Robert Byrd of West Virginia along with other Congressional leaders up on his embassy wall, but the Japanese still feel uneasy about Washington's "unpredictability."

There is another problem between Washington and Tokyo. In the days of General MacArthur, Washington imposed its military and political control over Japan, but now MacArthur's spirit of domination has been replaced by Carter's spirit of accommodation, and the Japanese don't get that either.

If the Japanese could stop the world where it is at present, they would probably be satisfied. They are fairly free to compete in a reasonably secure military world and a fairly open trade world without contributing anything to its military security. But they seem anxious about the future.

The future of the Pacific in the last quarter of the 20th century depends on the relations among the four major Pacific powers—the United States, the Soviet Union, China and Japan, all of them powerful, self-contained continental nations except these fragile Japanese islands.

The Soviet Union holds the Japanese northern islands. Its Pacific fleet totals some 1,250,000 tons, including 75 submarines, while Japan's naval power is 190,000 tons and 15 submarines. China, with its 800 or 900 million people—nobody knows quite how many—is beginning to reach out for the modern technology of the West, and if it begins to compete for the export markets of the world, as Korea and Taiwan are already doing, what will happen to the "Japanese economic miracle"? This is what thoughtful Japanese are asking about the future competition of their Asian neighbors while they wonder about the rising opposition to their commerce in the United States and industrial Europe.

Prime Minister Fukuda shows little interest in these apocalyptic visions of the future. If Japan survived the defeat of the last World War after Pearl Harbor, he seems to say, it will surmount the economic and financial problems of the future. Nobody could have imagined at the end of World War II, or at the end of the Vietnam War, that things could be as hopeful in the Pacific as they are now. So Mr. Fukuda sticks to his optimistic view of the future, particularly to his faith in the United States, and on the 36th anniversary of Pearl Harbor, this is a happier prospect than seemed possible in 1941.

November 20, 1977

U.S. Handing Back to Japan Vast Air Base That Was Key to Military Operations in Asia

By ANDREW H. MALCOLM

TACHIKAWA, Japan, Nov. 27.—The paint is peeling now. The houses are empty and so are the barracks. The basketball hoops are gone. The unused ropes on the flagpoles bang forlornly in the winds. And grass grows on the runways.

Tachikawa Air Base is dead.

Once the focus of most United States military activity in the Far East, with a population of 40,000, this 1,450-acre facility is silent now. All the American planes and bombs and bullets are gone. All the wounded and families and troops have left. There are no more ammo flights to Korea or trooplifts to Southeast Asia or evacuation flights from either area.

Fight Over Real Estate Beginning

And on Wednesday, Nov. 30, more than three decades after the United States took over the facility from defeated imperial Japanese forces, Tachikawa Air Base will be formally returned to Japan, the latest step in a continuing United States base consolidation drive that leaves only 76 facilities covering 57,600 acres under American control on the four main Japanese islands.

However, Tachikawa will see further combat of a sort Local political infighting has already begun over disposition of this prime real estate situated on the outskirts of Tokyo, now surrounded by a city and valued at several hundred million dollars.

But these days the only thing left alive on "Tachi," as it is known to Americans, is a squadron full of memories.

"When I got here in 1945," said Norman Sapiro, a civilian employee of the Air Force, "these streets were filled with bomb craters and broken Zeros all over. We bombed the, uh, heck out of this place. The Japanese used to store supplies and make bombers here."

The base first opened 54 years ago this month. Korean and Chinese laborers slowly turned the rice paddies into

Tachikawa Air Base.

an airfield. In addition to aircraft production, Tachikawa housed a flight school, technical and research institutes and even a balloon squadron. A major item built here was the 97-Shiki transport, the conical-nosed plane that dropped Japanese paratroopers into Sumatra, among other battle zones.

Planes Sent to Berlin for Airlift

Emperor Hirohito, his two sons and other relatives visited the famous facility over the years. "We wanted to

tear out that traffic island over there," Mr. Sapiro recalled on his final visit here the other day, "but the Japanese told us we couldn't because the Emperor dedicated that big stone on it. So we didn't."

After the war Tachikawa became the area's chief United States logistical and equipment center with scores of C-46's, C-47's and C-54's. In 1948, after evacuating Americans from the Chinese mainland, the base's Globemasters disappeared to help run the Berlin airlift half a world away.

The Korean War saw American operations here grow even further, at first carrying out the evacuation of American civilians and then transporting the torrent of Allied military men and materiel flowing into the war zone. Around the clock the planes came and went. A typical flight might carry 35,000 pounds of hand grenades in and 80 war wounded out.

In fact, for the thousands of servicemen whose tours took them into, through or out of Tachikawa, the base hospital here became the best barometer of American military activities in the Far East. Sometimes several hundred soldiers lined the hallways there awaiting treatment. Everyone is gone now.

Across the base, mechanics worked through the night assembling jet fighters for aircraft carrier duty. And damaged planes came to this safe rear area for repair. "They came in here all shot up and full of holes," Mr. Sapiro said, "and we'd patch them up and send them back, the same with the wounded."

After Korea came the United States' quiet but sizable logistical aid to the French fighting in Indochina. "Even some of the Dien Bien Phu survivors came through here," Mr. Sapiro said.

A Busy Place in Vietnam War

"You should have seen this place during the Vietnam war," said Chief Warrant Officer Albert J. Rapplean, who has had four duty tours at Tachikawa. "Things were really hopping. If the transports refueled here instead of Okinawa, they could carry a lot more cargo. But we didn't talk much about all this then to avoid ruffling the Japanese."

"This was my first assignment in the Air Force," said Maj. Paul Sjordal. "It was 1963. I was a green second lieutenant fresh out of R.O.T.C. This was the big time. I remember everybody used to go down to the Shoppers Mart. They had everything there, I mean anything you could ever want, it was right there under one roof. And they had a sign that said: 'Through these portals passed almost everyone in the military.' It was true."

But the jet era had come by then and the planes needed more space than the 6,500-foot runway gave them. The only way to expand was through a Japanese neighborhood called Sunagawa whose residents resisted sometimes violently. Tachikawa had been scheduled to become the primary American air base in the Far East.

But the demonstrations blocked that, and by the late 1960's operations were slowly being transferred to Yokota Air Base, five miles away.

The last flight left here in 1969. The last family left the large housing complex in September. And Master Sgt. David Thaden will haul the last washing machine out this week.

The 'Old Days' Recalled

Now, roads with names like 10th Avenue and V Street stand empty. The vast Military Air Cargo Terminal, where millions of in-transit servicemen and women waited interminable hours for their flights to somewhere else, is void and lonely.

"You see those flagpoles over there?" Mr. Rapplean asked. "Well, I put 'em in a long time ago. I remember because we had a problem with the cement."

"Oh, and right over by that bridge," said Mr. Sapiro, "we were digging an irrigation ditch and someone struck metal. It was a 500-pounder. We kept finding them all over till just 10 years or so ago. I suppose we got them all."

"Those were some days, eh, Chief," Mr. Sapiro continued.

"We could do anything in those days. I remember old General Doyle would holler out his window, 'Hey Norm, can we do this and that.' And I'd say, 'Sure.' And we would."

Just outside the base, the notorious bar and nightclub quarter where Japanese children once fought over coffee grounds, has given way to clothing shops and television stores. The only remainder of another era is an English-language sign that proclaims: "Fatigues Tailor Made." A few blocks away is the railroad station where so many thousands of G.I.'s caught trains to the exotic downtown of Tokyo.

"I remember coming home," Mr. Sapiro said. "I'd get off the train and take a jinriksha back to the base. It cost me two cigarettes. You can't do that any more."

November 30, 1977

U.S. and Japan: Basic Conflict

Frictions Are Rooted In Cultural Differences

By ANDREW H. MALCOLM

TOKYO, Dec. 7—Economic bureaucrats and politicians are staying at their cluttered desks well after normal quitting time here these chilly days, struggling with the mounting trade controversy that has seriously strained relations between Japan and the United States, the non-Communist world's two largest economic powers.

News Analysis

But the government workers in Tokyo are not redesigning their economy, industrial structure or trading practices, as the United States would like. They do not admit the need for radical reforms. They will not drop the quantitive restrictions on imports of the 27 manufactured and agricultural items still protected here. Nor will they suddenly curb Japan's vast exports and open its protected domestic markets any more widely to foreign companies after the coming American-Japanese trade talks.

Instead, these professionals are drafting what they think of as "concessions" and "presents" to "satisfy" American critics, to "restore harmonious relations" and to prove Japan's "sincerity."

This, to the Japanese mind, is far more important in "clearing the atmosphere" and "refreshing" relations than the specific steps the Americans would like them to take. And it underlines what one diplomat calls the deep "cultural chasm" that still separates the mysterious East from what the Japanese regard as the equally mysterious West.

"Clear-cut, rational Western thinking just doesn't work in Japan," said one Western-educated Japanese official.

Decisions Seep Up

These cultural differences pervade daily life here. Governmental or corporate decisions, for instance, generally are not imposed from the top. They seep up from below in a gradual consensus-making process. So the simple change of a cabinet minister does not affect policy, as it might in a Western government.

Or when a company wants to apply to the Government for something, the last thing it does is file an application. The first thing it does is informally sound out every official involved. Only when everyone assents informally is the formal application made. This avoids the surprises and rejections that Japanese find so jarring.

This island nation of 113 million can sometimes seem superficially familiar to a Westerner. Japan's modern cities teem with cars, high-speed trains, subways, department stores, neon signs and English-language newspapers.

But in the same cities, a youngster with

blond hair can still attract a crowd with each person wanting to touch it. Businessmen heading overseas are often sent to special schools to learn not to slurp their food. Moviegoers in a crowded city laugh uproariously when an American cowboy says the nearest neighbor lives 25 miles away. And sales clerks may scream in surprise at the sudden sight of a foreign customer.

Still an Insular Society

The exposure to other influences by more than a million Japanese traveling abroad annually may bring accumulated changes. But the fact is that despite all the travel, all the overseas commerce and all the imported television shows and movies, Japan remains an intensely insular society. And this is now having serious repercussions in its diplomatic and trade relations.

The Japanese, said Prime Minister Robert D. Muldoon of New Zealand the other day, "have finally got to stop being so Japanese and become international citizens." But a Japanese politician observed, "To the Japanese, there are but two types of people in the world—Japanese and foreigners."

For centuries, until 1868, Japan shut itself off from the world. A comfortable homogeneity ensued with few of the frequently fractious and sometimes dynamic influences that mingle in polyglot cultures like that of the United States. The Japanese are the first to admit that a strong ethnocentrism has ruled here.

Trade Surplus Results

Such a "Japan first" policy has ruled trade. Eighty percent of the imports to Japan—a nation poor in resources—arrive as raw materials to produce jobs. The finished export goods have given Japan a $13.4 billion trade surplus so far this year.

Foreign critics, currently led by the United States, charge that Japan is not doing its share to shoulder the developed world's financial burden of deficits and help pull other nations out of the lingering recession. For the first time in postwar years Japan, in effect, is being asked to take an active economic and political leadership role commensurate with its economic stature.

For months Japanese officials have acknowledged that they must buy more abroad. But the concept of taking an assertive leadership role is foreign to the Japanese, whose idea of leadership is totally different. For instance, charisma here has little value; in fact, it is suspect. Charismatic men are seen as too assertive or ambitious.

Thus, Japanese leaders do not step from the crowd. Slowly, like decisions, they emerge—often simply through seniority —as men who can be trusted by the widest spectrum. The ideal leader, one Cabinet minister noted, is the best common denominator.

And for fear of upsetting the delicate domestic consensus, these men are unlikely to initiate what Westerners consider "bold" or "imaginative" steps. Being skillful politicians, however, they will react to external and internal political pressures, seeking an appropriate "present" or sign of "sincerity" to rebuild the common denominator. For they are well aware of the Japanese proverb: "The nail that sticks up is the one that gets hit."

December 8, 1977

Japan's Trade Policy
Is Self-Protective

By ANDREW H. MALCOLM

TOKYO—Richard Cooper, the United States Undersecretary of State for Economic Affairs, came to Japan to try to convince Japanese leaders to open their country more to foreign traders. At a Cooper news conference on the two nations' growing trade troubles, a reporter expounded on one Japanese position, and then asked critically what the United States was doing to match that particular effort.

The question didn't startle Mr. Cooper, but the phrasing did. It was a verbatim repetition of a Japanese official's statement and question just moments before in closed-door negotiations. "You seem very well informed," Mr. Cooper remarked.

The reporter was Japanese, a member of a "nation club" whose strong social unity explains much of the nation's success—and now, the growing trade troubles with other countries that led to the preparation last week of what the Japanese consider a trade liberalization package. In a world in which wars, emigration and immigration, education, and modern communication and transportation have mixed nationalities, traditions and customs, conservative Japan is still a country apart. It maintains its group-conscious individuality. The language has a revealing verb: "chigau." It is used to mean "to be wrong." Literally, it means "to be different."

Japan's social and cultural homogenity is derived from the centuries of enforced feudal isolation that ended little more than a century ago. Immigration into the country is still not permitted. No matter what their nationality, foreigners here are called "gaijin," or "outside people." In the 32 years since the destruction of Japanese cities and industry in World War II, that same cohesiveness has enabled a nation of 113 million, with no conventional natural resources and less space than United States Ambassador Mike Mansfield's home state of Montana, to forge the third most powerful economy in the world. By the 1960's, annual growth rates of 10 percent or more were taken for granted.

Japan's success in global competition was due in part to Government direction and investment-loan assistance to help turn its factories from guns to exports, in part to its easy access to cheap maritime transportation and, in large part, to its energetic and conscientious labor force. In the country's paternalistic corporations workmen such as Takashi Kinuta, a Honda automobile assembly line worker, "naturally" checks the windshields on Hondas he sees on the street to make sure the installation was right.

Workers' wages are low. (In the steel industry, for instance, $6.31 an hour last year, including benefits, compared with $12.22 in the United States.)

But Mr. Kinuta and workers like him are guaranteed lifetime employment. That means security. For the employer, it also means no layoffs, and difficulties in costcutting. And that helps explain why at times any export price, even one below cost (so-called dumping) is acceptable.

Japanese productivity is high. Labor-saving technology, plus diligence, enable Japanese steelworkers to produce 9.35 metric tons of finished steel per 100 manhours, compared to 8.13 in the United States. There are, however, no comparable figures for the output of Japan's politicians, an aging band of shifting factions dominated since 1955 by the Liberal Democratic Party (which is actually quite conservative).

The party now holds only a thin parliamentary majority. But the narrow margin matters less than it would in other countries with similar political systems. Japan's establishment of politicians and businessmen and bankers is closely linked through the conservatism, the elite university background (the most prestigious is Tokyo University) and, most important, by the fact that they are Japanese.. It produces a kind of national team spirit that causes Japanese reporters covering, for instance, the current United States-Japan trade negotiations to refer instinctively to the United States on the one hand and to "wanakuni," an evocative Japanese word that means "our country" on the other.

In Japan, decisions, whether governmental or corporate, are reached from the bottom up, a process of consensus-building that is lengthy but insures an unusual unanimity and efficient execution of a program. Thus, the impact of the Nov. 28 cabinet reshuffle by Prime Minister Takeo Fukuda was soley psychological; it never touched the vast bureaucracy that makes the real decisions. It was also designed to readjust power alignments in the liberal party. The ruling party's traditional base is in the declining rural areas and agricultural interests that lead the domestic struggle against liberalization of foreign trade, and the farmers' continued influence is reflected in the token agricultural concessions that Nobuhiko Ushiba, the new trade envoy, carries to Washington this weekend.

International criticism of Japan's instinctive insularity and trade policies has grown sharply. Recently, Robert Muldoon, New Zealand's Prime Minister, said it was time the Japanese were "dragged kicking and screaming" into the international community. As he put it: "They have finally got to stop being so Japanese and become international citizens."

Kurita & Habib/Gamma-Liaison; Green/Photo Researchers

Signs of Japanese prosperity: house in a wealthy Tokyo neighborhood.

Many Japanese regard such remarks as those of poor losers—or possibly racists—in less competitive, less organized countries. But strong criticism from abroad, especially from the United States, provides Japanese reformers with a reason and impetus for change. A handful of internationally-minded, self-confident and younger businessmen and politicians is slowly becoming more prominent in the island nation's hierarchical society. Privately, they believe Japan must better accommodate itself to an increasingly interdependent economic world. These men seem less concerned with the taint of "bata-kusai," the sour butter smell which Japanese generally associate with foreigners and Japanese too heavily influenced by foreign ways, and they are optimistic. But people with long experience here believe the Japanese will continue to deal with each crisis only under pressure, and only on an ad hoc basis, by offering, in what is a common expression here, "cosmetic concessions."

Andrew H. Malcolm is a correspondent for The New York Times based in Tokyo.

December 11, 1977

JAPAN SETS 12% RISE IN DEFENSE BUDGET

$2 Billion Will Go for New Planes, Ships and Arms — Concern Over U.S. Pullout From Korea Seen

By DREW MIDDLETON

Japan's defense budget for the fiscal year beginning April 1 will amount to $8.76 billion, with more than $2 billion going for new aircraft, ships and weapons systems.

The budgeted amount is 12.4 percent higher, in terms of Japan's yen currency, than that for the current fiscal year. The increase in dollar terms is higher because of an appreciation of about 15 percent in the value of the yen in the last year.

American officials feel the increase reflects to some degree Japanese uneasiness over the phased withdrawal of United States ground forces from South Korea.

Gen. John W. Vessey Jr., the American commander in South Korea, recently told a reporter for The Korea Herald of Seoul that the United States would retain "the capability to reintroduce ground combat forces" in the event of war.

The Japanese see American withdrawal as disturbing the delicate military balance in the area. Tokyo's view, which is shared by Peking, has been that American ground forces would be involved immediately in the event of any North Korean attack because of their proximity to the frontier. This involvement was seen as a strong deterrent to any North Korean aggression supported by the Soviet Union.

Assurances such as those of General Vessey that the United States Air Force in South Korea "will be strengthened" and that the Navy "will remain" apparently have not quieted the fears of the South Koreans, Chinese and Japanese.

The Japanese are concerned, a qualified source said, over Soviet expansion into South Korea in the event of war. This would increase the threat to Japan's maritime lifelines, including the oil traffic from the Middle East and Indonesia that fuels Japanese industry.

A large slice of the new Japanese defense budget—which still represents less than 1 percent of the gross national product, compared with 6 percent for the United States in 1976—will be spent on weapons systems that will improve Japan's defenses against sea and air attacks.

Procurement plans for this year include the purchase of 23 McDonnell Douglas F-15 fighters and 8 Lockheed P-3C anti-submarine patrol planes. Orders also are to be placed for new destroyers in the 3,900-ton and 2,900-ton classes.

The Japanese Defense Agency's long-term plans call for the purchase of 100 F-15's over the next 8 years and 45 P-30's over 11 years. Eight of the first 23 F-15's will be imported, eight will be assembled in Japan from parts suppled by McDonnell Douglas and seven will be manufactured by Japanese industry under license.

Of the eight P-3C's three will be imported, four will be assembled in Japan

and one will be produced by Japanese industry under license.

The three Japanese services will purchase 92 fixed-wing planes and helicopters.

Since ammunition stocks have fallen to 60,000 tons, from an original stock of 160,000, funds are provided to raise stock levels.

American military planners hope that the withdrawal of the Second Infantry Division from South Korea will be balanced by two developments. The first is improvement of the quality of Japanese forces. The second is improvement of South Korean forces through the introduction of more sophisticated American weapons. In addition, there will be an American program to train the South Koreans in use of these weapons.

General Vessey believes that these measures, which compensate for the American withdrawal, will result in improvements "which will make it clear to North Korea that an attack cannot succeed."

February 12, 1978

Advice to Japan

By Yukio Matsuyama

TOKYO—"If a country depends on military might, it does not have to worry about what other countries think about it. But isn't it the principle of the Japanese Constitution to maintain its safety by trusting in the justice and good faith of the peoples of other countries? Why are the Japanese unconcerned about the fact that Japan has come to be disliked by other countries?"

At a dinner party for the Trilateral Commission in Bonn, in October, a French businessman sitting to my right asked me the above questions.

It is reported that a Japanese Diet team which visited Washington about that time keenly felt the cold feelings of the American Congress toward Japan.

"Even if the Japanese islands sink, no one will go to save them." The man who uttered these words was Senator Daniel Inouye, who is considered to have very sound judgment in American political circles; so the situation is very grave.

Inouye added: "When I was a child, my grandparents taught me the traditional Japanese virtues of courtesy and consideration for others, and I was proud of the fact that I was Japanese. Now, however, when Japan only

takes and does not give, there are times when I am ashamed that I am Japanese."

To say that the worldwide criticism of Japan, which started as a result of the abnormal surplus in Japan's current accounts, makes for a situation similar to that on the eve of the Pearl Harbor attack seems somewhat wide of the mark. There is not a single person who believes that the situation can be resolved through war.

But the fact that Japan is rapidly becoming an international orphan is felt by everybody who has contacts with foreigners. Actually, the reason for the present crisis is the fact that, as pointed out by The Los Angeles Times, "the general Japanese public is astonishingly unconcerned about the kind of sufferings the policies of Japan are imposing on other countries."

When it was wrestling in the lower ranks of sumo, people overlooked the fact that Japan's wrestling style was somewhat lacking in dignity. But from about 10 years ago when Japan surpassed West Germany in gross national product and became No. 2 in the free world, strong criticism began to be voiced that Japan was not fit to be ranking wrestler.

Frankly speaking, it is not a difficult thing to point out that at the bottom of this distrust of Japan there lurks the racial problem.

Why is it that Britain only harps on the imbalance in British-Japanese trade despite the fact that its deficit in trade with Japan is smaller than its deficit in trade with West Germany? Why is it that no newspapers make a fuss when Canadians buy an American golf course but opposition is voiced when Japanese do the same thing?

But if we attach excessive importance to the racial problems and fail to see the effects of our actions, it will be a grave mistake.

The head of a Japanese diplomatic office in Europe said with a wry smile: "If Japan continues to repeat her vacillating, selfish activities, such as the 'concentrated downpour-type' exports [inundation of overseas markets by Japanese-made goods], her negative attitude toward liberalization and her reluctance to provide aid, it will only lose its friends and increase its enemies, not only among the advanced industrial countries, but also in the third world and in the Communist bloc."

He added, "My daily work is to defend the Japanese position, but if Japan were a person, he would certainly be the type of person I would least like to have as a friend."

The point that must be particularly considered in connection with Japan's not being liked by other countries is

Japan's World Role

Sharaku

the fact that other countries have the impression that Japan gives priority to profits and tries to evade its duties and responsibilities.

Because of the reaction to excessive emphasis on the "duties of subjects" before and during the war, there was good reason for people to pursue their rights rather than fulfill duties after the war. For more than 30 years we have exerted great efforts to keep our eyes open to rights.

But in comparison with other countries, the impression is that the Japanese pendulum has swung to one side and has not come back again. There is a big difference in attitudes toward rights and duties between Japan and those countries which have built themselves up through their own revolutions and countries where freedom and

religion have grown up together.

This selfishness is apparent in Japan's attitude toward other countries. Japan has shown practically no interest in seeing what it could do for the world and has been enthusiastic only about what it could take from the world.

The problem lies in the fact that the nations of the world are becoming mutually dependent at much faster tempo than surmised by Japan. Making demands in connection with the economic growth rate of another country in the next fiscal year would have been considered "interference in domestic matters" and "violation of sovereignty" only a decade ago. Unemployment, inflation, currency anxieties and hijackings—all these are grasped by the European countries and

the United States from the grave standpoint of "joint threats to democracy as a whole."

On the other hand, Japan, which has lived through the postwar years with the optimistic mood that "everything will come out all right somehow," has not taken things overly seriously and has tried to settle problems on a case-by-case basis. This has resulted in its being criticized for "specious deception" and having "free rides." These criticisms also result from a lack of ability and efforts to offer explanations to other countries.

Obtaining the trust of other countries does not mean being subservient to other countries. Rebuttals such as the following by chairman Toshiwo Doko of the Federation of Economic Organizations are desirable between friendly nations: "The United States attacks Japan as being unfair, but are the inequalities in the U.S.-Japan civil aviation agreement fair? Did the United States exert as much effort in exporting to Japan as it did in sending Apollo to the moon? Westerners should study the Japanese language more."

Japan follows the principle that "harmony is valuable" and is a poor talker, so it tries to avoid conflict at all costs. But in European and American societies it is actually normal for confrontations and struggles to exist, and the Japanese should become used to fighting without becoming panic-stricken or hysterical.

More than anything else, Japan must become used to considering things in fundamental terms and from a long-term viewpoint. It must throw off the reputation of being a country which "can only take makeshift steps as a result of outside pressure."

But overcoming the present crisis will have no meaning unless it is based on the "philosophical conviction" that it is the correct way, rather than on a feeling that Japan has been forced to act in a certain way.

If Japan continues *zensho* (making the best of a bad bargain) and "study in a forward-looking manner" and avoids hitting rocks by using a pole, the crisis will continue endlessly. Japan needs its own power. Let us attach an engine to the raft. For this purpose, Japan should restudy the question of strengthening the character of Japan itself and not fear the possibility that restrictions may have to be imposed on some established rights which have been considered only natural in the past.

Yukio Matsuyama, one of Japan's most prominent journalists, is a member of the editorial board of Asahi Shimbun, from whose English-language newspaper, The Asahi Evening News, this is adapted.

February 15, 1978

Japanese Slaughter 1,000 Dolphins

TOKYO, Feb. 24 (UPI)—Japanese fishermen clubbed and stabbed to death about 1,000 dolphins yesterday and today with the approval of a provincial government.

The bottle-nosed dolphins, sometimes called common porpoises in North America, are seagoing mammals of high intelligence who communicate with each other in an advanced pattern that is not fully understood by man. They are the same kind on those featured on the television series "Flipper" a few years ago. Those killed ranged from 12 to 15 feet long and some weighed more than 1,000 pounds.

"It's a pity to do this, but our livelihood depends on it," one fisherman told Japanese reporters at the scene on Iki-shima, an island fishing center in southern Japan. The fishermen call dolphins "gangsters of the sea" because they eat so many of the fish that might otherwise be caught.

The fishermen who planned the dolphin slaughter said that the value of their fish catch dropped last month to two-thirds of the $536,000 they earned in January last year.

They earn their living catching and selling cuttlefish and hamachi, a local fish.

Officials said a school of dolphins appeared off Iki-shima near the end of last year. When the catch declined, the islanders appealed to the Nagasaki government for permission to hunt the mammals.

Their appeal was granted, and the fishermen either captured the dolphins in nets or frightened them to shore where they were killed.

A fishing company in another part of Japan announced today that it had caught 40 dolphins of the same kind some 300 miles from Iki-shima and was shipping them to the Netherlands for $667 each. They are to be trained to perform in Europe.

February 25, 1978

Japan Upset by Foreign Reaction to Dolphin Killings

By ANDREW H. MALCOLM

TOKYO, April 29—Though it may surprise President Carter and his aides, the subject of Japanese fishermen's killing dolphins two months ago is high on the agenda for Mr. Carter's meeting in Washington next week with Prime Minister Takeo Fukuda, according to some people here.

It isn't, of course. A United States Embassy official said this week that "the two leaders have a couple of other little items to discuss, like the global economy, Asian security and multibillion-dollar trade surpluses." But nine weeks after the fishermen of a tiny southern island, Iki-shima, killed 1,000 dolphins that were "trespassing" on fishing grounds, the issue—or rather the Japanese reaction to foreign reaction—stirs strong feelings here.

"It's a classic microcosm of the situations Japan gets itself into internationally all the time," an experienced diplomat remarked. He outlined a typical pattern: Japan takes some action, such as hunting whales, exporting a flood of color television sets or killing dolphins. Criticism is aroused overseas, some of it emotional.

Magnified through Japan's news outlets, the criticism is taken much more personally here than in other nations, igniting indignation and a strong sense that once again Japan is misunderstood and wronged by the world, which the Japanese believe is always watching them closely.

Confrontations Are Avoided

Confrontations, verbal or physical, are usually avoided in Japanese society. As one result, for instance, oratorical debates using logical arguments are rare in Japanese, a vague language that usually favors ambiguity over specifics.

As another result, Japanese officials find themselves ill-equipped to dispute "logical" foreign criticism over a mushrooming trade surplus or the dolphin slaughter, except to declare that Japanese culture is misunderstood and that other nations have also killed wildlife brutally.

The stream of denunciatory letters, telegrams and phone calls to the Iki-shima fishermen and to Japan's embassies abroad continue to feed this concern, as do House hearings and Senate resolutions on the matter in Washington, and the threat of street demonstrations when Prime Minister Fukuda visits Portland, Ore., Washington, New York and Honolulu.

The Ikishima fishermen continue to kill the dolphins; they have slain 320 or so more since the publicized incident in February. In a telephone interview, Yoshio Tsukamoto, a director of the local fishermen's association, said his men did not like killing the dolphins, which are called "gangsters of the sea," but that it had been necessary to protect the livelihood of the association's 1,200 members. He cited statistics to show that the fish catch drops drastically when dolphins are present, although he said that water temperature and overfishing could also affect the harvest.

"These criticisms from abroad make us very angry," Mr. Tsukamoto said, "because they are so self-centered. Americans kill millions of cattle to eat, too." About 80 of the 1,000 slain dolphins have been sold for food and 120 frozen for future sale. The remainder were dumped offshore or buried on a nearby island.

Mr. Tsukamoto and others have criticized "sensational foreign news coverage" that depicted fishermen clubbing the dolphins to death in waters reddened with blood. According to photographs in Japanese magazines, the shallow bay's water turned red during the killing, but he said this was because the fishermen cut the carotid arteries of the dolphins, which channel blood from the heart to the brain, as the quickest, most humane means of slaughter. Cutting the carotids also helps preserve the meat for sale. The dolphins, he asserted, were not clubbed to death.

He said that the dolphin control program would continue, but that the fishermen had decided not to answer foreign criticism because their replies might be misunderstood. In addition, he said, the central Government has asked the fishermen to avoid "a big fuss for fear that President Carter will raise the issue" next week. Also, Mr. Tsukamoto said, it is impossible for those who are not Japanese to understand the issue.

However, he criticized the Fukuda Government for its inability to make Japan fully understood on the international scene. He said it was the Government's responsibility to take "the necessary public relations steps," but that this had not been done before the slaughter was reported overseas.

April 30, 1978

DEFENSE INCREASES URGED BY JAPANESE

Call for More Spending Follows Soviet Military Buildup and Reduction of U.S. Forces

By HENRY SCOTT-STOKES

TOKYO, May 13—A major defense debate has begun in Japan, inspired in part by President Carter's plans for withdrawing American combat units from South Korea, but more fundamentally by a drastic reduction in United States forces in the Far East and a rapid Soviet military buildup in the region.

The emergence in official circles of the debate, which is receiving a great deal of attention in the press, coincides with the first Far Eastern visit by Zbigniew Brzezinski, President Carter's national security adviser. He will travel to Peking, Tokyo and Seoul on a week-long trip beginning next Saturday.

The debate began in January, when Prime Minister Takeo Fukuda brought up defense issues in his speech opening Parliament. the first time since 1945 that the occasion had been used to raise defense questions.

It was further stimulated by an announcement from an opposition Buddhist political party, Komeito, that it was switching sides and would support the nation's 260,000-member armed forces, known as the Self-Defense Forces.

Animosity Toward Soviet Is Stirred

Since then the press, urged on by business interests eager for more defense spending, has stirred animosity against the Soviet Union by publishing articles that previously would never have seen the light of day. Tokyo Shimbun recently speculated that the only foreign power that could mount a naval invasion of Japan was the Soviet Union, and that

if it did so, its forces would land at Wakkanai or in Ishikari Bay, on the northern island of Hokkaido.

And Yomiuri Shimbun reported this week on its front page that officials no longer believed that the United States had the power to defend Japan. The bulk of the Pacific Seventh Fleet, it said, would be shifted to the Atlantic in the event of an emergency in Western Europe.

These articles have not aroused strong public reaction here, but a recent Yomiuri poll found that only 21 percent of Japanese people believed that America would defend Japan under the joint security treaty. Thirty-eight percent were skeptical that the United States would honor the treaty.

Similar polls have been published over the years with practically the same results, but now the press and an unprecedented series of official statements are focusing public attention on defense issues.

'The Sea of Russia'

The intensity of the issue was indicated in a speech given recently by Shin Kanemaru. Director General of Japan's Defense Agency. a position equivalent to Secretary of Defense, who remarked that "Russian warships and other vessels make such frequent appearances in the Sea of Japan these days that we might as well refer to those waters as the Sea of Russia."

Mr. Kanemaru, who was speaking at a seminar here at the Keidanren, the Japanese Employers Association, noted the huge disparity in Soviet and Japanese military air strength "The Soviet Union deploys 2,000 aircraft in the Far East." he said, "while Japan possesses only 400." Japan recently appropriated funds to buy 100 F-15 jet fighters and 45 P3C Orion antisubmarine aircraft from the United States at a cost of $4.5 billion. potentially the biggest Japanese aircraft orders ever.

Commenting on the imbalance between Japanese and Soviet forces, which the new aircraft would not greatly affect, Mr. Kanemaru said that Japan had nothing more than "bamboo spears against machine guns."

Some American officials have speculated that this debate is serving to prepare the ground for closer cooperation between the United States and Japan on military matters. Six years ago, Mr. Brzezinski in fact proposed such cooperation in a book on Japan titled "The Fragile Blossom." In the book, he called for "joint high-level civilian-military planning staffs" to be set up.

No Defense Coordination

At present there is virtually no coordination between the Self-Defense Forces and the 46,000-strong United States forces in Japan, spread over 130 bases and including 20,000 marines in Okinawa.

Japan spent $8.6 billion on defense this year, equivalent to nine-tenths of 1 percent of its gross national product, making it the biggest defense spender in Asia except for China. The United States spends 6 percent of its gross national product on defense.

Although the tactical mission of United States forces in Japan is offense, unlike that of the Self-Defense Forces, which are confined to such activities as earthquake and flood relief, some Japanese experts are asking whether the two should work together in an emergency.

Officials here envisage, in public at any rate, only that Japan pay more of the defense cost. Mr Kanemaru said recently that Japan could increase its contribution by $130 million from the current level of $500 million because the dollar has fallen against the yen.

But in June he will visit Washington and Brussels to inspect the workings of the North Atlantic Treaty Organization. These procedures have little relation to the level of coordination between the United States and Japan. but some American officials say that the gap should be closed.

Mr. Brzezinski. in his book on Japan. wrote that there must be "far greater meshing of minds on political-strategic trends in the region as a whole." and added that "under certain circumstances it could also involve NATO." That message is now receiving attention here.

May 14, 1978

Rally Asks an 'End to Hiroshimas'

Hundreds of Japanese women, many of whom were directly affected by the atomic explosions at Hiroshima and Nagasaki, represented a coalition of pacifist and feminist groups yesterday with an exhibit of wartime photographs at an International Women's Gathering in Stuyvesant Park.

The Japanese delegation included more than a third of the 1,000 women from a dozen countries who have come to New York during the United Nations Special Session on Disarmament to dramatize their increasing role in the internatioal peace movemet.

The largest of the groups represented, the Japanese National Delegation, announced that it would present Secretary General Kurt Waldheim with a petition, signed by 20,000 Japanese, calling for immediate world disarmament.

"We are a mother's movement," said Michiko Yonehara, a member of the Federation of Japanese Women's Organizations. "We are more interested in peace than in women's rights. We want a peaceful world for our children."

Conspicuous among the colorful banners was the canary-yellow hat of Bella S. Abzug, the presiding officer of the National Commission for the Observance of International Women's Year.

The former Congesswoman said she was pessimistic that the United Nations Special Session would have a real effect on the arms race.

"Meetings like this are just the start of a movement that is going to force the men in government to listen to us," she said. "We demand an end to Hiroshimas."

May 29, 1978

Japanese presenting the United Nations with a special appeal for complete nuclear disarmament.

United Nations/Photo by M. Grant

McNamara, Japanese Discuss Aid

Poor Countries Would Benefit

By JUNNOSUKE OFUSA

TOKYO, June 7 — Discussions are under way here between Japan and the World Bank on ways to implement their joint program to expand aid to developing nations in the next three years.

Since his arrival here yesterday, Robert S. McNamara, president of the bank, formally known as the International Bank for Reconstruction and Development, has had talks with Prime Minister Takeo Fukuda and other key Cabinet ministers on the aid plan.

The Japanese Government has already decided on a policy to double its official development assistance in the three years beginning in the 1979 fiscal year. However, no decision has yet been made on the amount of Japanese aid.

In talks with Tatsuo Murayama, Finance Minister, Mr. McNamara said that the World Bank would float a 75 billion yen World Bank bond issue, equivalent to $33 million, in the Tokyo money market next month to raise funds needed by the World Bank for aid to developing countries.

The World Bank's proposal for an increase in Japan's official development assistance provides for $2.25 billion during the three-year period from the fiscal years 1979 through 1981. Of the

Robert S. McNamara

Photo by Fabian Bachrach

total, Japan has been asked to extend $500 million in the first year, followed by $750 million and $1 billion in the second and third years.

Japan's official development assistance has been comparatively low in the past. According to official figures, aid to developing countries ranged from $3.9 billion to $4 billion a year from 1972-76. Of the yearly total, the Government development assistance ranged from to one-third to one-fifth of the nongovernmental aid.

The Japanese Government believes that the proposed increase in its official development assistance will serve a dual purpose. In sharply stepping up its

aid, Japan would satisfy the growing demand for assistance arising from developing nations, and, at the same time, reduce its mounting trade surplus.

A new aid program now under consideration by the Government provides that the country sharply increase its agricultural and food aid to developing nations over the next three years. Under the existing program, food aid is limited to rice only. The Government has purchased rice in markets in Thailand and Burma and supplied it to developing nations.

Under the new program, Japan proposes to buy - other agricultural products for aid, such as wheat from the United States or other agricultural products from such advanced agricultural countries as Australia and New Zealand for supply to developing nations.

June 8, 1978

Japan Will Buy 145 U.S. Planes To Expand Its Share of Defense

TOKYO, June 20 (AP)—Japan signed a $5 billion agreement today covering the purchase of 100 F-15 jet fighter planes and 45 antisubmarine patrol planes from the United States over the next 10 years, according to a spokesman for the Japanese Foreign Ministry.

The United States has been urging Japan to assume more responsibility for its own defense. Japan receives military assistance under the Japanese-American Security Treaty.

Some of the planes in today's agreement will be built in the United States by McDonnell Douglas Corporation and Lockheed Aircraft Corporation. Others are to be manufactured or assembled in Japan under license from the two American companies, the spokesman said.

June 21, 1978

Japan May Halt Loan Collection

TOKYO, July 11 (UPI) — Japan will stop trying to collect $448 million in loans to severely underdeveloped countries in a bid to end heavy criticism of its huge international trade surplus, the newspaper Mainichi Shimbun said today.

The newspaper said that Prime Minister Takeo Fukuda would announce his Government's decision not to demand repayment of the loans at the summit talks in Bonn next Sunday and Monday.

Similar action was taken by Sweden late last year when it announced it would not try to redeem $200 million in loans to underdeveloped nations, including India and Kenya.

The new measure, Mainichi reported, is part of Japan's package of economic measures to reduce its mushrooming trade surplus with the United States and West European countries. In the fiscal year that ended March 31, Japan had a trade surplus of $20 billion.

July 12, 1978

Japanese View of U.S.: Dwindling Respect

By HENRY SCOTT-STOKES

TOKYO, July 20 — Two weeks ago a Japanese Cabinet minister spoke out in criticism of the United States in a way that one has come not to expect from the Japanese since World War II. Kiichi Miyazawa, head of the Economic Planning Agency and the man who more than anyone else runs the Japanese economy, accused President Carter of inadequate leadership in advance of the economic summit meeting in Bonn, tore into Congress for "dragging its feet on the energy bill" and said Washington was mismanaging the American economy.

News Analysis

Since the end of the Allied military occupation in 1952, Japanese Government spokesmen — among whom Mr. Miyazawa now ranks only one rung below Prime Minister Takeo Fukuda — have usually been extremely cautious in offering even the most veiled criticisms of the United States.

"It is a great disappointment that President Carter seems to be coming to Bonn empty-handed," Mr. Miyazawa said in an interview with The New York Times. "It's not his doing. Congress is dragging its feet on the energy bill, particularly Part 5, but the bill is long overdue, and I certainly hope that the President will tell the Bonn meeting that by a certain date the U.S. will have its own comprehensive energy program."

Deficit and Inflation Noted

He continued: "Our Government has been doing its best under given circumstances to behave well while none of the fundamentals are being tackled in the U.S. Not only does your Government have the energy bill to complete, but you have a budget deficit of $60 billion, which is going to climb further, and you now have inflation of 7 percent, which is also going up."

The toughness of Mr. Miyazawa's remarks points to a change in Japanese opinion. In recent years, and especially since the end of the Vietnam War in 1975, many Japanese in government and in business have lost much of their old respect for all things American.

In private conversation senior officials ask brutal questions such as, "Is America really to be relied on in the future as a kind of big brother, guarantor of our security? Is the United States not withdrawing from the Far East as a whole in military terms, all protests notwithstanding?"

Business leaders are even sharper in their attacks, though always declining to be quoted by name. They have come to regard most of American industry as chronically noncompetitive and American workers as habitually lazy. Some go so far as to ask whether America, in view of its economic weakness, is "finished" as the leader of democratic forces in the world.

'High Time' for Such Criticism

"In a sense, it was high time that someone gave voice to this undercurrent of vicious criticism," said a close associate of Mr. Miyazawa. "It's just unhealthy that the Americans should remain in a state of ignorance about the way many Japanese actually feel."

The vehemence of Mr. Miyazawa's statements is explained in part by the timing. He was eager to influence the outcome of the Bonn meeting by putting the Japanese case in advance, encouraging the President to commit himself to getting an energy bill through Congress "by a certain date" and joining ranks with the West Germans. Chancellor Helmut Schmidt has been just as outspoken in bringing pressure on the United States.

This was purely tactical and may have contributed somewhat to the promise made by President Carter at Bonn to strengthen the dollar by saving oil and fighting inflation. But the more important feature of Mr. Miyazawa's remarks was that they were designed to lay bare long-term and keenly felt Japanese concerns.

Rise in Oil Price Feared

The lack of Congressional approval of energy legislation has a dual effect in Japanese eyes. First, it detracts from efforts to get the American balance of payments under control and hence helps to undermine the dollar. Second, it tends to reinforce those within the Organization of Petroleum Exporting Countries who want higher oil prices. Both these tendencies are of great concern to Japan, which would "lose more than anyone else from a rise in the oil price," according to Mr. Miyazawa.

This country is 99 percent dependent on imported oil, mainly from the Middle East. Japan paid $23.6 billion for its oil last year, and this accounted for one-third of all its imports. A 10 percent rise in the price of crude oil would cost Japan well over $2 billion a year.

The plunge in the dollar is crucial to Japan in other ways. It tends to snuff out economic growth in Japan, because it discourages companies from investing. Japan has committed itself to a 7 percent real growth rate this year, the highest target of any major industrial country. Prime Minister Fukuda repeated that commitment at the Bonn meeting.

But it is already certain that Mr. Fukuda will have to propose a big supplementary budget this fall to keep the Japanese economy fueled up. Without that extra budget the economy could go languid in the middle of this fiscal year, as it did last fall.

Record Trade Surplus

Japan's biggest concern, however, is that the United States could slip back into economic protectionism after the November elections. This could hit Japan much harder than an oil-price increase or even a further rise in the yen, which still looks enormously strong given that Japan is running a record trade surplus estimated at $23 billion this year and a surplus on current account estimated at $18 billion. The current account surplus last year was a record $14 billion.

For Japan it is just as vital that Robert S. Strauss, the President's trade negotiator, should be successful in his efforts first in getting a package of tariff cuts and other measures under the current "Tokyo round" of talks on the General Agreement on Tariffs and Trade and then in persuading the new Congress in early 1979 to vote for the package. "If Congress goes against the package, then the whole thing will collapse there," said Mr. Miyazawa in his interview.

From a Japanese viewpoint, the problem is that this country is running a record trade surplus with the United States, a surplus of $8.9 billion in the last fiscal year and probably considerably more in fiscal 1978, which ends next March 31. Japan has to make its contribution to international economic stability

by reducing its overall surplus. The flood of Hondas and Toyotas into the United States has to be checked. Only then will Congress be impressed.

Regulating Major Exports

"We are regulating exports of eight major items that account for over 50 percent of our exports to the U.S.," Mr. Miyazawa said. "This regulation is without any strict legal basis and is admittedly hard for the Ministry of International Trade and Industry, but still we've been doing it since April this year, and the record for April-May-June shows that

---

Criticism by Economic Aide Reflects New Worry Over Americans' Reliability

---

we've been able to restrict quantity exports of six out of the items and only two, cars and motorcycles, have gone up slightly over April-June last year.

"The rub is that pricing in the U.S. of export items tends to rise because of inflation in America, and our exporters have every motive to try to jack up prices, which Toyota has done six times in the past 18 months and is preparing to do for a seventh time, making a total price rise of about 26 percent," he continued.

"There's got to be a limit beyond which Americans cease to buy and switch to American cars. And this must eventually

diminish our dollar intake at long last."

A glance at the overall trade figures shows why the Japanese are primarily concerned about this aspect of American-Japanese relations. In fiscal 1977 Japan had a trade surplus on customs clearance figures of $12.9 billion, of which $8.9 billion, equivalent to two-thirds of the whole, was with the United States.

Meanwhile, Japan exported in the last fiscal year 1.89 million vehicles to the United States and imported from the United States only about 15,000 cars — a disparity of over 100 to one in favour of the Japanese car makers.

Japanese Surplus Will Rise

What disturbs men like Mr. Miyazawa and accounts primarily for his outburst may be the prospect that these figures will be still more unbalanced this year. The Japanese trade surplus with the United States is certain to leap once again to new records. Sales of Japanese autos are no longer rising, but in dollar terms they will be worth much more than last year's $5 billion plus.

The ultimate source of Mr. Miyazawa's concern is that Americans may observe that there is a relationship between trade and jobs. On a rough rule of thumb, $1 billion in trade is worth 100,000 jobs, though the figure varies greatly according to the industry involved. On this basis the loss of jobs in the Unites States because of Japanese products runs close to a million.

July 24, 1978

Prime Minister Fukuda visits President Carter at the White House.

Chapter 8

Trade Relations with the United States

Throughout most of the Tokugawa period, Japanese trade with the West was limited to exchange with the Dutch at only one port near Nagasaki. Fearful of the disruptive influence of foreign powers and wishing to insure tranquility in their homeland, shogun after shogun forbade any interaction with foreigners. This situation endured until Commodore Perry opened up Japanese ports to international commerce in the 1850s. Now Japan is the world's leading exporter.

During 1977-78, Japanese-American relations pivoted around the issue of Japan's enormous trade surplus. While this surplus vis-à-vis the United States grows, America is beset by the continuing increase of an already aggravated trade deficit. This trend is underscored by a rocketing yen and a sinking dollar in relative exchange values. The Japanese are publicly embarrassed, and American manufacturers are complaining. Imports are allowed into the United States much more easily than into Japan where the government, using the protection of native industries as its rationale, erects formidable trade barriers.

In December 1977, Prime Minister Fukuda announced a trade liberalization plan that Nobuhiko Ushiba, the special minister for external economic affairs, would bring to Washington for discussion with his American counterpart, Robert Strauss, the U.S. special representative for trade negotiations. The package specified that Japan would drop certain import restrictions, reduce a variety of tariffs, and limit its huge trade surplus. The day that Ushiba met Strauss in Washington, Foreign Minister Sunao Sonoda announced in Japan that his government's publicized trade liberalization plan was the maximum concession his nation could offer. Strauss found the program thoroughly inadequate. The U.S. wanted a 33%-40% reduction in Japan's $8.5 billion trade surplus with the U.S. over the following year. The Japanese, however, were contemplating a reduction of only one-third that amount.

Ushiba contended that the American demands for changes in Japanese trade policy were too radical. He insisted that Japan would never turn its trade surplus into a deficit as apparently the American delegates hoped it would. Arguing against increased U.S. exports of goods to Japan, Ushiba maintained that his country's sagging domestic economic situation would be harmed even further by the entry of American products for which there was no real demand. American officials argue that such a demand really exists and that it is thwarted because restrictive measures by the Japanese government militate against competition and give the Japanese consumer no choices.

The Japanese maintain that they work harder than others and save a greater proportion of their earnings than do citizens of other lands. They also consider themselves victims of American industrial inefficiency and the lack of an effective American energy-saving program. The United States insists that Japan must respond to the needs of the world economic system by stimulating its domestic economy and facilitating the consumption of imported goods by the Japanese. The December trade talks concluded with a joint resolution on general goals: Japan's domestic economic growth and surplus reductions in the international market. The bilateral gap, however, remained unresolved.

Despite the discussions, Japan's subsequent balance of payments and trade reflected an absence of governmental curtailment. Two weeks after the Strauss-Ushiba talks, the Japanese Finance Ministry announced the second highest monthly trade surplus in Japanese history. In early January 1978 Robert Strauss arrived in Tokyo and attempted to negotiate bilateral trade agreements with Ushiba. Once again Strauss considered Ushiba's concessions insufficient. The United States wanted further liberalization on import quotas by Japan, particularly in the areas of citrus fruits and beef. It also desired an end to other non-tariff barriers, an augmentation of import financing, and the elimination of specific Japanese export promotion measures. The mid-January trade talks marginally reduced the dissatisfaction on both sides. In March, however, Japan's trade surplus reached a new record high. The following month the Japanese government asked Japanese industry to curb its exports.

Several weeks later Fukuda arrived in Washington with a pledge to cut Japan's trade surplus by encouraging imports from the United States and reducing Japanese exports into the American market. In addition, a joint resolution emerged to strengthen procedures for consultation in monetary matters. Nonetheless, the consensus following the negotiations was that not much had changed. The Japanese trade surplus continued to grow while Japanese discontent over American concessions increased. In early July, just before the multilateral summit conference opened in Bonn, the Japanese were overtly critical of the trade positions of American officials and the U.S. Congress. In an unusually candid display of criticism, President Carter was attacked for coming to Bonn empty-handed, that is, without a workable energy policy. The stage was set for minimal results. At the conference, Japan once again promised to reduce its trade surplus. The Japanese government's protection of domestic agriculture emerged as a pressing point of disagreement. Both Japanese and U.S. negotiators were able to agree, however, about the gravity of the problem and concluded that full-scale talks on trade matters would continue to be a priority.

Secretary Kreps Warns Japanese Trade Imbalance Is Unacceptable

By ANDREW H. MALCOLM

TOKYO, Sept. 27—One day after her department reported the second largest monthly United States trade deficit in history, Secretary of Commerce Juanita M. Kreps warned businessmen here today that a continuation of such trade imbalances is "simply unacceptable."

Mrs. Kreps's message, one of the sternest yet delivered amid mounting United States-Japan trade frictions, came in a speech and news conference during the second day of her three-day visit to the chief American trading partner.

The Commerce Secretary is the latest in a series of Carter Administration officialss sent here to urge Japan to do more to rectify its lopsided trading surplus with the world in general and the United States in particular. This is Mrs. Kreps's first trip abroad as Commerce Secretary.

More Imports by Japan Urged

A primary solution offered by Mrs. Kreps and others from Washington is an increase of Japanese imports from the world in general and the United States in particular.

Mrs. Kreps noted that the United States, which reported a $2.7 billion overall August trade deficit, had had a trade deficit with Japan every year for the last decade. Finance Ministry officials here reported today that Japan's surplus in trade with the United States so far this year was $4.99 billion, including a $976 million Japanese surplus in August alone. For all of 1976, that surplus was $5.4 billion.

"Trade deficits of this magnitude and duration are simply unacceptable to the United States, both economically and politically," Mrs. Kreps said in a speech opening an exhibition here of data handling and communications equipment made in the United States.

She said the "principal purpose" of her trip was to meet with Prime Minister Takeo Fukuda whom she saw today, and other senior Government leaders here to discuss solutions to "this chronic trade imbalance problem."

At a news conference at the United States Embassy Mrs. Kreps said that the major threat of such imbalances was not to the economic strength of the United States as such, but rather that they feed "a strong sentiment for protectionism."

She said the Carter Administration wanted to encourage the flow of free trade. Mrs. Kreps added, however, "whether we could continue that is a moot point. We must try to find solutions in specially troubled areas like steel before they trigger heavier layoffs and lend credence to arguments for protectionism." And she noted the important role that a politically sensitive Congress plays in trade controversies.

Japan's 21-month-old economic recovery has been based largely on exports while consumer spending and domestic demand remain sluggish. Japan, the world's largest exporter of manufactured goods, shipped $50.4 billion worth of goods overseas in the first eight months of this year, a 22 percent increase over the same 1976 period

Japan's imports so far this year have totaled 40.6 billion, a 13 percent increase over the first eight months of 1976.

At the London economic summit meeting in May, leaders of the major powers agreed that the United States, West Germany and Japan should act as economic "locomotives" to help other nations out of the recession by buying more abroad. In the last year Japan's conservative Government has announced three economic spending packages designed to stimulate domestic demand, but no significant economic effect has resulted.

Mrs. Kreps noted the heavy preponderance of agricultural, forestry and other unprocessed goods in Japan's purchases from the United States, and she suggested an increase in the importation of American consumer goods as well as the reduction of high tariffs on items such as film and computers and a liberalization of import quotas on certain commodities.

Mrs. Kreps also urged greater efforts by American companies to sell in Japan. And in a meeting with Tatsuo Tanaka, Minister of International Trade and Industry, it was agreed today that the two nations would establish a Trade Facilitation Committee to examine the problems American exports encounter in Japan and to improve their sales.

September 28, 1977

Japanese Goods Swamp U.S. And Create Trade Tensions

By PAMELA G. HOLLIE

Five hundred million Japanese zippers, 30 million feet of Japanese chain and 3 million gallons of Japanese soy sauce are contributing to a record Japanese trade surplus with the United States this year.

The Japanese surplus or, to put it another way, the United States deficit is expected to reach $8 billion this year. As a result, the dollar is falling, the yen is soaring, American manufacturers are complaining and Government officials of both nations are wrestling with a disruptive international problem.

Yesterday, concerned about the embarrassingly large trade surplus on the one hand and the long-term threat to its exports implicit in the yen's climb on the other, the Japanese Government imposed controls designed to curb foreign speculation in its currency. [Page D3.] But despite such limited curative actions, on the trade as well as currency fronts, no solution to the basic imbalance has emerged. [Page D1.]

In a severe test of the United States' commitment to free trade, Japanese products have flooded American markets in recent years. Before this year is out. Japan will have shipped $18 billion in exports to the United States.

The result of this outpouring of goods, plus many millions of dollars in products manufactured by Japanese factories located here, is a veritable cornucopia of Japanese goods. Americans can use Japanese pens, drink Japanese whisky, drive Japanese cars, and fly in Japanese executive jets.

The United States trade deficit with Japan can be attributed in part to Japan's reluctance to import Western goods. But since the early 1960's, Japanese manufactures, whether imported or produced here, have clearly won a larger and larger place in American markets.

The Japanese trade surplus is thus apparent on every hand.

"We've gotten our business by taking it from other makers," said Shunji Takatori, assistant treasurer at YKK (USA) Inc. in Lyndhurst, N.J. In 10 years, the company's market share has grown to 20 percent of a rather stable $1 billion zipper market.

The American market generally absorbs 23 percent of Japan's total exports, but for consumer goods like television, the percentage runs as high as 50 percent. There are more than four hundred different Japanese companies competing for a share and thousands of products from ball bearings to soy sauce.

The reason for the Japanese presence in the American market is reasonably straightforward. The United States offers an open policy toward foreign investment and an enormous market, continental in scope, relatively free from economic controls and Government intervention.

By contrast to Japan, where domestic investment has been hampered by labor shortages, rising wage rates and a scarcity of land, the United States offers large supplies of energy, abundant natural resources, a talented labor force and advanced technological, research and development capabilities. Also, the Japanese, faced with an embarrassingly large foreign currency nest egg, have encouraged investment abroad.

Japan's spectacularly successful Sony Corporation set the pattern for Japanese business growth in the United States. Beginning in 1960 with about $1 million in radio, television and tape-recoding sales and 12 employees, the New York City based marketing subsidiary, Sony Corporation of America, now represents up to 30 percent of the parent company's $1.8 billion in sales and employs more than 3,000 persons in the United States.

"The United States is a large consumer market," said Harvey L. Schein, chairman of Sony of America. Like many Japanese companies, Sony says it "made headway by introducing something new to the market."

When America was thinking big, Sony introduced small products. In 1959, Sony marketed the world's smallest all-transistor radio, followed by the world's smallest all-transistor five-inch television in 1962. Then, in 1964, Sony made an even

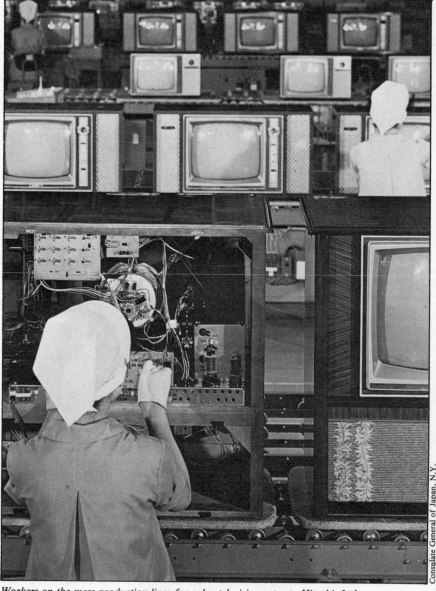

Workers on the mass production lines for color television sets at Hitachi, Ltd.

Consulate General of Japan, N.Y.

smaller television, a battery-operated model with a four-inch screen.

In the same vein, while American motorcycles were getting larger and bulkier, the Japanese introduced small, light, inexpensive motorbikes, then mopeds. And when the energy-conscious Japanese built cars, they built them to go farther on less.

Using technology to overcome the onus of "Made in Japan," which was associated with the shoddy goods made during the six-year American occupation, Japanese goods now represent the best the country can produce.

"We sell quality," said Fujio Mitarai, executive vice president of Canon U.S.A. Inc., a maker of business copiers, calculators and cameras. Like most Japanese companies, the research and development is a major part of the company's investment in gaining a strong market share. Canon, with headquarters in Tokyo, com-

mits to research and development 10 percent of its annual sales, which this year is an anticipated $600 million.

The practice of relying on technology to make the best product for less is behind a 300 percent sales growth in Canon's American business in the last three years, Mr. Mitarai said. "It is easy to make an excellent expensive camera," he said, but "nobody will pay $1,000 for a camera."

Certainly, price is a consideration. When Japanese companies first came to the United States market, their products sold well primarily because they were cheaper than American made goods. But, as Japan's economy recovered and wages escalated, Japanese products became more competitive.

"We once sold our product for about 20 percent below other bearing makers," said E.R. Wallenberger, president of the N.T.N. Bearing Corporation of America,

Des Plaines, Ill. "We were a disruptive force in the market," he said.

But now that N.T.N. Bearings' prices are competitive, the company has had to rely on its reputation as a reliable supplier and its high technology to hold a 3 percent share of a very competitive market.

Gaining and holding a share in the American market is not easy. In a typically cautious Japanese manner, the Kirin Brewery Company, Ltd. approached the market a little at a time beginning with Japanese restaurants on the West Coast. But, depending solely upon its reputation as a reliable supplier of a quality beer Kirin had trouble winning acceptance. Finally after nearly 13 years, the company has taken steps to adopt the marketing and advertising practices expected in the American market.

"If America can accept the Datsun, Sony and Toyota, why not a quality beer," said Clifford Thatcher, the American general manager of marketing. Hired to help Kirin attract a 10 percent share of a competitive imported beer market, Mr. Thatcher maintains that there is a shakedown coming in the imported beer business. "There are dozens of beers competing for a market share. We must be aggressive."

"America set the pattern for product advertising and marketing, which the Japanese have had to learn," said Fred Nakamura, executive vice president of Fuji Photo Film U.S.A. Inc.

After three unsuccessful marketing partnerships with American companies, Mitsubushi Aircraft International now handles its own United States marketing. With 18 salesmen in four territories to handle direct sales of its executive aircraft, sales have climbed 33 percent in 12 months.

Mitsubushi Aircraft now commands 15 percent of a $200 million executive aircraft market and expects a 20 percent share eventually. "We sell the fastest, quietest plane on the market anywhere," said a company spokesman.

While the share of the market varies greatly from product to product, Japanese companies have had greater success in recent years as they have spent larger amounts on advertising and marketing expertise.

Suntory Ltd. is spending $1.5 million to advertise its whiskies this year. Sponsoring a $124-a-head introductory party for its Signature brand whisky, which sells for $60 a bottle, the company is going all out to gain a market share for its spirits that include wines, a liqueur and a whisky especially blended for the lighter whisky taste Americans prefer. The company's goal is one million cases of whisky exported to the United States annually.

While the Japanese are gaining increasingly large market shares, the competition is no pushover. Facing a formidable competitor like Kodak, Fuji Photo Film, at one-fifth the size, is not overestimating its ability to tackle the giant. It is enough to "establish ourselves as a good reliable second source of supplies," a spokesman said.

Fuji, at $1 billion in sales worldwide, estimates it has a 5 to 7 percent share of the American film market now. "It would be unrealistic to aim at one-third of the market," he said. "Perhaps a 10 percent share is a possible and reasonable target."

The handicap for many Japanese companies has been the time and cost of importing materials from Japan. Kirin's beer takes 21 days to travel the 7,000 miles. "It is hard to maintain high quality with such a lag," a spokesman said.

Only by negotiating duty agreements and operating an open shop can Mitsubushi Aircraft keep its costs down. About 29 percent of its materials and labor are Japanese. The skin and airframe of its executive aircraft are sent by freighter to San Francisco then by railcar to San Angelo, Tex., where the planes are assembled.

Until recently, Japanese companies depended heavily on imports from Japan, but as conditions change, more and more products are produced in the United States. "The United States Government is closing the door to foreign merchandise," said Yoshiya Abe, representative for Pentel of America Ltd., Fairfield, N.J Facing a 25 percent duty on its pen parts, Pentel imports only the point from Japan The other 95 percent of the company's parts and labor are American.

"It didn't take long for us to realize that with duties of up to 35 percent it made sense to begin operations in the United States," said Masahiro Yoshida, executive vice president of the YKK Zipper company. Five years ago, the company built a $15 million manufacturing facility in Macon, Ga. "Nearly all of the company's United States sales are produced here," he said.

So far, as the market has grown, Japanese companies have tended to reinvest their earnings in expansion rather than repatriating them.

Sony of America, for example, has grown at rates of up to 35 percent annually, but the company has never paid a dividend to its parent, despite an investment of over $100 million. This does not mean, however, that the parent does not receive a substantial return on parts and products sold or on royalties paid for technical know-how.

On occasion, the sale of technical know-how becomes a market disadvantage. Canon Inc., Tokyo, licensed its technology to Saxon Industries Inc., which makes copiers in the United States. Saxon is competing with Canon U.S.A. in the same market.

"It is very hard to claim you are the best, when your competitors know the same technology you do," said a Canon U.S.A. spokesman. "That is very bad for business."

November 18, 1977

The Big Japanese Trade Surplus

No solution has emerged in the campaign to deflate Japan's ballooning trade surplus. There has been much dialogue in the last few years about the incendiary nature of the problem. Strong exhortations have been made on both sides of the Pacific to allow the yen to appreciate sharply to try to eliminate the competitive advantage of some Japanese goods. And through the

The Economic Scene

influence of so-called trade-facilitation committees in Tokyo and Washington, some curbs have been arranged on shipments of electronic products here, especially color television sets.

Instead of shrinking, however, Japan's trade surplus has about doubled this year to a $20 billion annual rate and the favorable balance with the United States has swelled. Moreover, it has occurred despite a big rise in (the value of the yen. The currency rose this week

to a postwar high of around 244 to the dollar, compared with the range of 285 to 295 little more than a year ago.

What's the answer?

"The trouble is that we and the Japanese are passing each other on different levels," a high official of the Carter Administration said this week in discussing the cleavage between the United States and Japan on mutual trade problems.

"Our views are quite far apart. We want the yen to appreciate further to make their exports more expensive so that the flow can be reduced, and we want them to open their import doors much wider. They say that too many problems are wrapped into that solution and that the way to go is for them to invest more in this country."

●

Japanese viewpoints also came from several sources in recent days. For example, Yoshizo Ikeda, president of Mitsui & Company of Tokyo, said at the National Foreign Trade Council's convention in New York that he believed the best way to narrow Japan's favorable trade balance with the United States was to have Japan step up its direct investment here. And the Yamaichi Research Institute of Securities and Economics said the surplus of trade would widen unless the Japanese Government adopted sweeping measures to stimulate the economy.

Makota Hara, chief economist for the Bank of Tokyo, who is stationed in New York, said resentment was rising in Japan over United States pressures but added that he favored a multifaceted program to improve trade relationships encompassing a lower value for the yen, increased domestic stimulus of the Japanese economy and more imports by Japan, particularly from the United States.

Despite a series of meetings between top officials of both countries all year, with more being scheduled for coming weeks, the trade rift has been widening. It could become much worse, according to knowledgeable sources on both sides.

● ● ● ●

Mr. Hara, who is one of Japan's leading economists and a former official of a Japanese Government overseas economic organization, said that current economic relations between his country and the United States were more strained than at any time since the end of World War II. An American official indicated that Mr. Hara's assessment was not exaggerated.

Tensions have been running high among Japan's leading businessmen, bankers and Government officials about the trade pressures from the United States for some time. A little more than a year ago, Japan was showing a worldwide trade surplus of almost $10 billion, more than half of it from dealings with the United States. The yen was then fluctuating at from 285 to 295 to the dollar and the Government wanted it to stay in that range.

Nevertheless, Japan agreed to undertake some stimulative measures to try to bolster the domestic economy in the hope that greater imports would be encouraged. Tax cuts wee instituted, and an increase of $4.8 billion was authorized in Government spending for public works and residential construction. It helped create a deficit of about 8,500

The New York Times/Paul Hosefros

Japanese products are prospering in the American market place. Cameras and film are among them. These six different brands of cameras were photographed at Willoughby-Peerless here yesterday.

The Trade Gap Widens
(in billions of dollars)

U.S. Imports from Japan

U.S. Exports to Japan

20
15
10
5
0

70 '71 '72 '73 '74 '75 '76 1977*

*Based on Commerce Dept. and N.Y. Times estimates

Source: U.S. Dept. of Commerce

The New York Times/Nov. 18, 1977

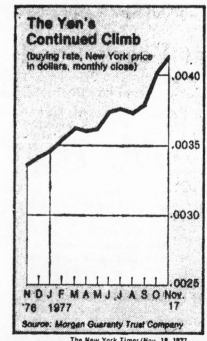

The Yen's Continued Climb
(buying rate, New York price in dollars, monthly close)

.0040
.0035
.0030
.0025

N D J F M A M J J A S O Nov.
'76 1977 17

Source: Morgan Guaranty Trust Company

The New York Times/Nov. 18, 1977

billion yen, representing about 30 percent of the budget.

Mr. Hara feels that the appreciation of the yen by some 17 percent—half in the last month or so—to the 245-to-the-dollar area—has gone too far. If it continues to hold in that range, he said, "there will not only be a serious impact on smaller Japanese exporting companies, but also on the major exporters, such as producers of steel, autos and electronics." He said that a value of 270 yen to the dollar "might be a reasonable level at this time."

The United States' view, however, is that Japan's exports will not be reduced to any major extent unless the rate gets to 200 or 210 to the dollar.

• • •

While Mr. Hara maintained that Japanese exports must continue to expand to assure growth for the economy, he conceded that steps should be taken to increase imports.

He said it was likely that the Japanese Government would agree to increase imports by $3 billion through special measures, probably by December. The increases, he predicted, would come in imports of aircraft, petroleum and food.

The economist also said he believed there would be tax cuts for individuals as well as increased expenditures for public works in the next Japanese budget—a $10-billion program overall. "The proper measures to adjust the imbalance of American trade," Mr. Hara said, "are not only to put pressure on the yen exchange rate but also to solve the fundamental oil problem and, more importantly, the structural problems in American industries."

That is a view shared among economists in this country as well, and it's a message that American industry, labor the Administration and the Congress should constantly keep in mind. But there is also a message for Japan, namely that it is time to do something drastic to lower its import barriers, which have been almost impenetrable in many fields for too long. There will have to be give on both sides to heal the deteriorating trade relations of two nations that need to be linked closely, economically and politically.

November 18, 1977

Japan Ready to Cut
Its Tariffs 40%
Over 8 Years for Trade Accord

By VICTOR LUSINCHI

GENEVA, Nov. 29—Japan announced today that it was ready to cut its tariffs by an average of 40 percent over eight years as part of the projected international pact on the lowering of world trade barriers now under negotiation here.

The announcement by Ambassador Masao Sawaki at the start of the annual meeting of the 83-nation General Agreement on Tariffs and Trade aligned Japan with the United States and the European Economic Community in the initial approach to the bargaining for tariff cuts at the world trade talks.

But at the same time Mr. Sawaki informed the GATT members that Japan was "actively considering" making some tariff cuts without waiting for the conclusion of the so-called Tokyo round of bargaining for trade concessions in the hope that this would speed the negotiations.

While officials in Tokyo have indicated that such action was contemplated, Mr. Sawaki's statement was the first confirmation of it by the Japanese Government in an international trade forum.

The Japanese statement was welcomed by an American spokesman, who said Washington was pleased by both Japan's approach to the tariff-cutting negotiations and the consideration it was giving to the early lowering of some duties on imports.

The United States has been encouraging Japan to take appropriate action to ease the entry of foreign goods in view of its large trade surplus, the spokesman noted. This surplus, coupled with the record-level United States trade deficit, is the major reason for the recent strength of the Japanese yen and weakness of the dollar, financial experts say.

No tariff-cutting formula has been formally agreed upon at the trade negotiations, which were officially started in Tokyo four years ago.

Last September, however, the United States and the European Economic Community tentatively agreed to use as a working hypothesis a Swiss-suggested formula. This would reduce tariffs of most industrialized countries by about 44 percent, or midway between the higher average arrived at under an initial American proposal and the lower figure that the community had submitted.

The tentative accord reached by the United States and the community on a yardstick for preparing the initial offers on tariff cuts on industrial goods that the trading partners propose to exchange on Jan. 15 allowed a margin of five percentage points on either side of the basic average figure within which the partners would seek to stay.

With its announcement today, Japan has subscribed to the working hypothesis developed by the other two major trading powers. Earlier, Japan had proposed a formula under which, it said, its tariff cuts would average 38 percent.

The negotiations on trade in industrial and farm products are scheduled to enter the active give-and-take bargaining stage in January, when the initial positions of the trading partners on tariff cuts, the administrative and other non-tariff measures that hinder trade flows, and on rules to govern the conduct of trade are to be on the agenda.

Stressing the danger of a retreat into protectionism, the chairman of the GATT assembly, George A. Maciel of Brazil, urged that every effort be made to achieve "substantial results" at the negotiations as soon as possible.

"The future of international trade and of trade relations between our countries depends on the success of the Tokyo round," he said.

___

Strauss Expects Substantial Development

WASHINGTON, Nov. 29 (AP)—Robert S. Strauss, Special Representative for Trade Negotiations, said today he expected that there would be "something substantial to announce" in the near future as the result of negotiations to rectify Japan's huge trade surplus with the United States.

Mr. Strauss would not provide any hint at a news conference on what Japan might do to slash the surplus, which is projected at about $7 billion this year. But he made it clear that the United States would not be easily satisfied.

"We expect substantial results in our bilateral negotiations with the Japanese," he said.

Mr. Strauss said recently that he thought United States trade with Japan might be nearly in balance beginning in about a year, and confirmed that Japanese officials were expected in Washington early next month to disclose a package of measures Japan said it would use to cut its trade surplus.

November 30, 1977

Japanese Adopt a Major Portion
Of Trade Liberalization Package

By ANDREW H. MALCOLM

TOKYO, Dec. 6—Prime Minister Takeo Fukuda and his economic cabinet ministers today adopted a major portion of a package of proposed trade-liberalization measures that an envoy will carry to Washington soon in an effort to ease the mounting trade tensions between the two allies.

The contents of the economic package were not announced publicly. And the proposals are still subject to amendment and augmentation before Nobuhiko Ushiba, special Minister for External Economic Affairs, leaves for Washington, probably this weekend.

But initial indications were that the Japanese proposals—involving for instance increased imports of such minor items as smoked herring—fall far short of the "basic," "drastic" and "extraordinary" measures demanded by United States officials during a recent series of bilateral consultations.

Thus, if the final package presented in Washington is similar in scope to what is known so far of its contents, the outlook is for a further deterioration in trade relations between the United States and Japan, the noncommunist world's two largest economic powers.

In Europe, meanwhile, Western European heads of government undertook to make a concerted attempt of their own to persuade Japan to bring its trade with Europe into balance, a move that could further exacerbate the American-Japanese dispute. [Page D1.]

In the Tokyo foreign-exchange market, the dollar fell again against the yen today as exporters and Southeast Asian sources sold the American currency heavily. The dollar closed at 241.525 yen, down from 242.625 Monday, after hitting a low of 241.48 yen earlier in the day.

American officials have warned Mr. Fukuda that a continuation of Japan's massive trade surplus with the United States and other nations seriously threatens relations between Washington and Tokyo. In the first 10 months of 1977 Japan had a trade surplus of $13.36 billion with other countries including a $5.4 billion surplus with the United States.

American officials in a series of trade talks throughout the fall have warned of a rapidly growing protectionist movement in the United States, Japan's chief foreign market. Last month, in blunt statements that shocked some Japanese officials, United States representatives demanded that Japan take a variety of major economic restructuring steps aimed at decreasing exports, expanding imports and moving its trade accounts to at least a balanced position, if not a deficit. This, the Americans said, was Japan's responsibility as a major economic power to help pull other nations out of their economic doldrums.

For the Japanese, who have based their own two-year-old economic recovery almost solely on vigorous expansion of exports, such measures represent a direct challenge to traditional procedures. Last week Mr. Fukuda reshuffled his cabinet to confront the chore. But many Japanese speak indignantly against what they regard as the American ultimatum.

An American rejection of what is being portrayed here as a maximum Japanese effort to open its protected domestic markets to major foreign infiltration would almost certainly increase antagonisms here.

Tonight one Western diplomat intimately familiar with the stands of both sides noted, "there's a very wide gap between them."

Key American Demand

Perhaps the most important American demand was that Japan publicly commit itself to turn its current account surplus into a deficit by an early and specific date.

Japanese sources said this evening such a commitment was not a part of the economic program approved today and have emphasized the difficulty in promising specific results from a diverse, free economy.

Another United States demand was that Japan drop the quantitative restrictions it maintains on 27 import categories, mostly agricultural products.

But according to informed sources, the present economic package only liberalizes the quotas on some minor items like potato flour and smoked herring. Some more citrus product imports may be permitted in certain seasons and a few thousand tons more foreign beef may be allowed in, although only for purchase by hotels. Anthracite coal imports would be liberalized.

Tariff reductions are also expected on about 90 items. Some unconfirmed reports say the tariff on autos will be cut from 6.4 percent to zero, on computer terminal equipment from 22.5 percent to 18 percent and on color film from 16 percent possibly to 11 percent.

In background briefings Japanese officials said these other areas were discussed in the economic package:

¶A "positive approach" by Japan in the multilateral trade negotiations in Geneva where, critics charge, Japan has been a passive participant.

¶"Improvement of import-financing facilities".

¶Progress in removing non-tariff barriers.

¶Maintenance of an "orderly" export program.

¶"Promoting of foreign aid".

¶"One-shot purchases" of raw materials such as oil and uranium to increase stockpiles and help right the trade surplus. Officials declined to elaborate before the plan is presented in Washington.

Japanese officials said they could not estimate the impact such changes would have in increasing the amount of imported manufactured goods, which the Americans say total only 20 percent of Japan's overseas purchases.

But the Japanese portrayed the last two weeks of hasty economic planning as including "very harsh discussions" between political and bureaucratic factions.

On the economic side, this pits those advocating vigorous Government financial efforts to stimulate the economy and increase imports against fiscal conservatives concerned with the heavy deficit financing this would require.

On the philosophic side, the debate pits a relative handful of internationally-minded bureaucrats against Japan's own powerful protectionist lobbies, which are strongest in agricultural areas that have traditionally been the political mainstay of the governing Liberal Democratic party.

"These days," said one politician, "the pressures are very great."

Yet to be included in the package are economic-growth estimates for next year and detailed domestic stimulation measures, focusing heavily on public works construction. Mr. Fukuda has ordered the drafting of a 15-month budget, a combination of a second 1977 expansionary supplemental budget and the regular 1978 budget. Japan's fiscal year ends March 31.

"Unless we have greater domestic demand," one Japanese official said, "some minor changes in the (import and export) system will not have much effect."

December 7, 1977

JAPANESE INDICATE THEY CANNOT MEET U.S. TRADE DEMANDS

USHIBA BARS DEFICIT PLEDGE

Official Going to Washington Talks Says Tokyo Won't Commit Itself on Shifting From Surplus

By ANDREW H. MALCOLM

TOKYO, Dec. 8—Japan has no intention of making a public pledge to turn its massive trade surplus into a deficit, Nobuhiko Ushiba, Japan's new Minister for External Economic Affairs, declared in an interview here.

Mr. Ushiba, a former Ambassador to the United States, will travel to Washington this weekend to deliver Japan's answers to a series of economic demands made by the United States in recent weeks. In good part, Mr. Ushiba indicated he will stress that the American demands are beyond his Government's power to deliver.

Meanwhile, American officials here reiterated that a deficit commitment, including a target date for its accomplishment, remained the single most important item of any economic package to halt rising protectionism in the United States and reduce the growing trade difficulties between the two nations.

The United States is urging that Japan commit itself to a deficit in its "current account," which includes payments for services as well as goods. By that broader measure, Japan's surpluses are smaller than its trade surpluses—which simply cover goods—but they are nevertheless huge, perhaps more than $10 billion this year.

Most Serious Situation

With both sides expressing displeasure and disappointment with the stands of the other, even before the sessions open, Americans here were pessimistic that next week's meetings would produce appreciable progress toward resolving the economic troubles, which Prime Minister akeo Fukuda has said form the most serious situation in Japan's postwar history.

The United States, which expects a deficit of around $30 billion this year, has said it is the responsibility of the major industrialized nations to incur trade deficits now to help pull many other lands out of their lingering recession. Japan amassed a trade surplus of $13.36 billion for the first 10 months this year.

During a series of increasingly blunt bilateral consultations this fall, United States officials demanded "drastic" and "basic" economic restructuring in Japan to stimulate the domestic economy and ease the purchase of imports here, especially of manufactured goods, to right the trade balance. Not to do so would seriously threaten relations between Japan and its trading partners, American officials told Mr. Fukuda.

A Cabinet reshuffle, including the appointment of Mr. Ushiba to the new post, and some hasty economic planning devised a package of measures including tariff reductions on some 90 items, some small increases of minor items, mostly agricultural under quotas, and other steps to increase some purchases abroad.

There were signs that Mr. Ushiba himself was disappointed with the package. "The Prime Minister told me," Mr. Ushiba said during the interview last night in the Foreign Ministery, "to do my best even if the package is not as large as I hoped for."

No Commitment on Deficit

He declined to discuss details, but did disclose that there would be no public commitment to seek a current account deficit by a specified date. "Who can do that?" he added, "No country in the world. You know exporting and importing are done by private companies."

He said there were some improvements in Japan's economic offerings, but added, "You cannot expect something dramatic. Maybe the United States can take dramatic measures but other countries, no, I don't think so."

Much of his presentation, he said, would consist of his outlining for American officials the economic and political problems and constraints of Japan, such as strong domestic opposition to trade liberalization. "I must tell [the Americans] again and again and again," he said. "Maybe they don't understand."

He said the package emphasized three main areas: stimulation of the domestic economy, improving the trade environment through a variety of tariff, Government procurement and import financing measures for foreign concerns to do business in Japan and an "extra emergency purchase plan" of overseas commodities such as United States wheat.

Specific Japanese plans for stimulating the domestic economy will be forwarded to Washington during the meetings, Mr. Ushiba said. Mr. Fukuda, who promised during the London economic summit meeting to stimulate the Japanese economy to grow at a 6.7 percent rate this year, now acknowledges the final figure will be more like 5.8 or 5.9 percent. The Americans have suggested 8 percent for next year.

Together, the minister said, such steps would certainly reduce Japan's surplus some but by how much he could not say. A Government report issued here today predicted that, without major measures, the trade surplus would balloon to $20 billion next year. Government officials, however, talk of cutting this year's surplus in half, a step American authorities termed "worth discussing."

But Mr. Ushiba was not optimistic over increasing the amount of imported manufactured goods, which total only 20 percent of Japan's total imports. "How can we force our people to buy foreign manufactured goods if there's no demand?" he asked.

He described himself as surprised that the trade controversy had progressed so far and said one goal of his visit was to cool the atmosphere for less emotional future talks free of current "tensions."

"I'm not going there to solve everything," he said. "That's quite clear. I hope people are not too much excited about the current outcome."

In background briefings, meanwhile, American officials said the slim Japanese package showed that "a wide gap remains to be bridged." Other Western diplomats called the package "cosmetic."

'Now That's a Gap!'

"The Japanese are still talking about reducing a surplus," said one American, "and we're talking about achieving a deficit. Now that's a gap!"

They said they realized the Japanese Government was going through a delicate process of balancing conflicting domestic and foreign forces but that the final Japanese plans had to be substantial. "We want to be able to go to the Congress," said one official, "and tell them, 'The Japanese are no longer part of the problem; they are working with us.'"

"Unfortunately," one American added, "I think [the Japanese] perception of the seriousness of the situation is on the short side." Diplomats of other countries agreed. They said that in their conversations with local officials, the Japanese indicated a strong belief that the Americans were bluffing about the threat of protectionism and Congressional reaction against Japanese exports.

December 9, 1977

Japan's Doughty Trade Aide at U.S. Talks

By ANDREW H. MALCOLM

TOKYO, Dec. 12—When Nobuhiko Ushiba was a boy, he watched his father's raw silk business slowly decline and die as imports, foreign competition and other economic forces pressed in from the world outside Japan. Now those factors are again closing in on Japan as her trade partners around the world, especially the United States, demand basic economic restructuring and costly domestic stimulation within this island nation to balance Japan's lopsided trade surplus and give foreign business a better chance here.

Man in the News

Thus, the 66-year-old Mr. Ushiba (pronounced oo-she-bah with no accented syllable) began his first assignment as Japan's new Minister for External Economic Affairs. It is expected to be a full week of less than tranquil trade talks in Washington between the two Pacific allies.

"It will be rather difficult, I am afraid," the veteran diplomat said in an interview before his departure, "but then government officials must do difficult things sometimes."

His immediate plan is to offer some minor tariff and quota concessions, an explanation of the strong domestic forces militating against liberalization within Japan and a broad outline of the planned 1978 expansionist government budget.

Knowing the new minister plus some of the thinner aspects of Japan's package, an American diplomat commented, "Ushiba will be as good as he is allowed to be. But he can't be any better."

Across the table will be Robert S. Strauss, President Carter's Special Trade Representative, who has a reputation here for his downhome bluntness.

"I've never met Mr. Strauss," Mr. Ushiba said. "I don't know how to satisfy him."

It is not the first difficult diplomatic encounter in Mr. Ushiba's 45-year foreign service career. There were the complex textile talks with the Americans during the early 1970's, which Mr. Ushiba led as Japan's Ambassador to the United States.

And then there was the little-known Ushiba incident in 1971, when President Richard M. Nixon suddenly produced his diplomatic rapprochement with China without much warning to Japan, the chief Asian ally of the United States.

When Secretary of State William Rogers tried to reach Mr. Ushiba just before the announcement, he found that the Ambassador was again out

Nobuhiko Ushiba

Consulate General of Japan, N.Y.

in the American countryside, meeting Americans and speaking on Japan, a task Mr. Ushiba felt was a primary mission. As a result, the telephone connection with Washington was delayed. And Mr. Ushiba's subsequent urgent message arrived in Tokyo only three minutes before the American announcement. The short notice is still bitterly recalled here.

Mr. Ushiba, who was born Nov. 16, 1909 the third of four sons of Tetsuro Ushiba, was picked for his new post in large part for his knowledge of and rapport with Americans, although he says he will be dealing with many other nations in the coming months. Though accented, his English is fluent. But at times his mind runs faster than his tongue, causing him to swallow the last half of a sentence on the way to he next.

Among his diplomatic counterparts, he is considered a skilled negotiator and creative thinker.one of a small group of internationally minded Japanese more open to a less insular and traditional approach to foreign affairs. "He's quick, very quick," said a diplomat. "He understands fast. Unlike many Japanese, he gets to the point right away, and he has a knowledge of the details as well as the broad outlines."

A 1932 graduate of the Law School of prestigious Tokyo University, Mr. Ushiba promptly joined the diplomatic service, where he was assigned to Britain and Germany. As a minor official in Berlin, he learned fluent German and worked on the prewar Axis alliance

between Japan and the Nazi regime.

During postwar bureaucratic struggles, he was once exiled from the Foreign Ministry to the Ministry of International Trade and Industry, where he assiduously acquired much of his respected economic background. He returned to the Foreign Service in 1954 as a counselor in Burma, became Ambassador to Canada in 1961, Vice Minister in 1967 and Ambassador to the United States in 1970.

Three years later, Mr. Ushiba retired to become an adviser to the ministry and a director of the Sony Corporation and the Taisei Tourist Company, which owns the famous Hotel Okura here. "I had to do something to earn a living," he said.

Tall and heavyset for a Japanese, Mr. Ushiba was an athlete in university, especially as lead oarsman in eight-man rowing crews. He is a voracious reader, especially of history books. Also, he is, what a close friend called, "a hasty golfer," briskly attacking the course in early daylight even after a midnight return from yet another government economic survey mission to Europe.

He has maintained his diplomatic contacts. His wife, Fujiko, like most Japanese wives, keeps in the background. A fervent mah-jongg player, Mrs. Ushiba as a girl lived several years on Long Island while her father was assigned to New York with a Japanese concern.

The Ushibas have three daughters and a son, who is a reporter for Sankei Shimbun, a Tokyo newspaper. They live in Setagaya, a generally affluent area of Tokyo.

Next weekend on his return to Tokyo, Mr. Ushiba will face yet another difficult negotiation—carving a bureaucratic sphere for his newly created "ministry." So far, it consists of only two assistants, a secretary and a borrowed office down the hall from the Foreign Minister.

The other day when Mr. Ushiba entered the Prime Minister's office as an avid golfer and emerged as Japan's chief economic spokesman to the world, flustered officials suddenly realized that the new minister had no car to go home in.

Despite his new responsibilities, Mr. Ushiba retains a sense of humor. After parrying a reporter's questions about Japan's economic package, its tariff barriers and its protectionism, especially in agricultural areas subsidized by artificially high prices, Mr. Ushiba noted that he was leaving for the United States, where meat prices were about one-sixth of Japan's. With a straight face he looked at the American and asked, "Can I bring you back some beef?"

December 13, 1977

JAPAN'S TRADE PLAN CALLED INADEQUATE BY U.S. NEGOTIATOR

STRAUSS CITES 'MINIMUM GOALS'

Says Ushiba Proposals Fall Far Short—Tokyo Holds Package is 'Maximum Possible' at Moment

By CLYDE H. FARNSWORTH

WASHINGTON, Dec. 12 — Japan presented to American officials today its proposals for dealing with the severe trade imbalance between the two nations, but the Americans promptly said that the proposals "fell considerably short" of what was needed.

The presentation, marking the beginning of a critical round of talks here on how to reduce Japan's huge trade surplus, was made by Nobuhiko Ushiba, Japan's new Minister of External Economic Affairs.

Robert S. Strauss, chief American trade representative, said Mr. Ushiba's offers of trade liberalization fell short "of what I sought as minimum goals."

This was an implicit reference to rising Congressional pressure to put up trade barriers and protect American jobs if the Japanese don't make substantial concessions to reduce this year's expected $8.5 billion trade surplus with the United States.

Ushiba Under Strong Pressure

Mr. Ushiba, on the other hand, a former Ambassador to Washington who was given the external economic post just two weeks ago, is under strong pressure from a number of groups in Japan to go slow on concessions.

As an indication of that, Sunao Sonoda, Japan's new Foreign Minister, said in Tokyo today that the proposals Mr. Ushiba was presenting represented the "maximum possible package" Tokyo could offer at the moment.

Mr. Ushiba arrived here with the specifics of a package put together by the new Tokyo Cabinet last week, proposals for cutting tariffs on about 300 items and reducing nontariff barriers on other industrial and agricultural imports.

Congressional Interest Noted

After meeting Vice President Mondale, who noted the intense Congressional interest in his visit, the Japanese envoy conferred with Mr. Strauss for four and a half hours.

Mr. Strauss later told newsmen that, while the discussions were positive in tone, the Japanese offers were insufficient to meet the minimum goals.

The United States wants a Japanese commitment, American sources reported, to reduce the surplus by one-third to 40 percent over the next 12 months. The value of the Japanese concessions, the sources said, was only one-third what the United States is asking.

The United States is also demanding faster Japanese economic growth so that consumption of imports will increase.

The official forecast for this year had been a Japanese growth of 6.7 percent, but Prime Minister Takeo Fukuda noted recently that the figure might fall below 6 percent. Japan's growth had been at double digit rates before the oil price increases four years ago.

Slower than expected growth of both the Japanese and the West German economies poses a danger to the world economic recovery, many economic officials here and abroad believe. But conservative electorates in both countries have been resisting economic stimulation, fearing it would aggravate inflation.

In addition to reducing its surplus with the United States, the Carter Administration has been demanding that Japan commit itself to move into a current account deficit with the rest of the world. The current account is a broader measure of the foreign economic position of a nation including both trade and services.

Japan is expected to run a trade surplus with the rest of the world this year of $15 billion and a current account surplus of $10 billion. The current account is lower because Japan ships its exports on foreign vessels and must buy abroad such other essential services as insurance.

A mission to Tokyo last month led by Richard Rivers, general counsel in the Office of the Special Trade Representative, discussed specific target dates for reaching a current account deficit.

But the Japanese have not yet accepted this demand, and the Tokyo press has lashed out against "dictatorial American policies." Japan has said only that it should "broadly" aim at restoring equilibrium in its overall balance of payments, which includes trade, services and the flows of long-term capital.

Initially, the Carter Administration's efforts were concentrated on getting a higher valued yen. The theory was that this would reduce exports by overpricing them and make imports more competitive with domestically produced goods.

Although Japanese automobiles and other goods have been marked up in price, the effect of what has already been a sharply upvalued yen have been to make the Japanese even more competitive by reducing inflation and increasing productivity, many Administration economists believe. Meanwhile, trade barriers combined with a penchant of the Japanese consumer to save more than he consumes has restrained imports.

Last month, therefore, the Carter Administration drastically altered its strategy and began making specific demands for import liberalization rather than stressing currency alternatives. In effect, Treasury Secretary W. Michael Blumenthal, pitcher of the yen game, was benched and replaced by Mr. Strauss for the trade game.

Mr. Ushiba remains in Washington for four days. Some time before Congress reconvenes the new year Mr. Strauss is expected to lead a mission to Tokyo to wrap up a trade package with the Japanese. Should he fail, there is little doubt Congress will act.

"We are hoping to make considerable progress" Mr. Strauss told newsmen today, despite his initial disappointment with the Japanese offers. "This is not the last of the ninth, but only the seventh inning stretch."

'Maximum Possible Package'

Special to The New York Times

TOKYO, Dec. 12—Japan's new Foreign Minister, Sunao Sonoda, said today that his nation's trade liberalization proposals being presented in Washington this week represent the "maximum possible package" at the moment. But he expressed some doubt that the package would be acceptable to the United States and said a failure of the talks would be "quite serious" in bilateral relations between the two Pacific allies.

Meeting with foreign correspondents in one of his first public appearances since becoming Foreign Minister Nov. 28, Mr. Sonoda a former paratrooper in World War II, also outlined in broad terms his desire to solve economic frictions with Japan's European trading partners next year as well as to promote relations with its Asian neighbors, especially China and the Soviet Union.

But, he said, the current trade tensions with the United States were the "most urgent of Japan's diplomatic challenges." It is important to keep economic issues from becoming political ones, the 64-year-old minister said, because "friendly and cooperative relations" with the United States are the "pivot of Japanese diplomacy."

"All the nations of the world today are experiencing economic stagnation and confusion," the Minister said, "at and confusion," the minister said, "at and pursues its own selfish interests and blames its own woes upon others, then economic chaos might very well lead into political chaos."

December 13, 1977

Did Japan Mislead Carter?

By James Reston

WASHINGTON, Dec. 13 — Last spring, when Prime Minister Takeo Fukuda of Japan came to Washington, he told officials here that Japan would have an overall trade "deficit" this year of about $700 million. Instead his country will have a trade surplus of over $13 billion, about $8.5 billion with the United States alone.

This is why the Carter Administration is taking such a hard line with Mr. Fukuda's new External Economic Affairs Minister, Nobuhiko Ushiba, who is now in Washington. Officials here are not saying so in public, but privately they are saying that Mr. Fukuda either made a wild misjudgment of Japan's trading position or, what's worse, deceived the United States Government—not only in the spring in Washington but at the summer summit in London where officials say he repeated the $700 million figure.

"I can't believe this was a deliberate act of deception," one official here said. "I prefer not to believe it, but there is a pattern here of protracted unfairness, which has to be corrected if we are to avoid extremely awkward political consequences."

It is recalled here that President Carter, Vice President Mondale, and Zbigniew Brzezinski, head of the National Security Council, were all enthusiastic about the development of the Trilateral Commission, which helped bring Japan into close consultation with the industrial nations of North America and Europe.

In fact, there is reason for supposing that the meeting of these three at a Tokyo conference of the Trilateral Commission, long before Carter was nominated for the Presidency, contributed to Mr. Carter's decision to choose Mr. Mondale and Mr. Brzezinski for these key positions.

Accordingly, the Carter Administration is now putting the following argument before Messrs. Fukuda and Ushiba in quite specific terms:

¶You know that we are very strong friends of Japan. You know that some of us have worked for five or six years to make Japan an equal partner with the United States and Europe in dealing with global economic and political problems of mutual concern.

¶You also know that we back you for a permanent seat on the United Nations Security Council (Tokyo has a special envoy working on this objective). You can therefore also be sure that we're not going to pull a Nixon or a Connally shock on you.

¶This having been said, the Administration's message continues, we are telling you very frankly that we will have to take steps unless you yourselves take really major measures to reverse what has become a pattern of sustained unfairness. So it should not be a shock to Japan if this happens because we're telling you right now we're going to do it. This is being told to you by friends who want you to play a major role, and we still wonder what happened last spring.

In speculating on "what happened last spring" when Mr. Fukuda predicted the $700 million "deficit," officials here have two theories:

First, either Mr. Fukuda's prediction —some officials here regarded it as a "promise"—was made in good faith, in which case the Japanese internal political and economic structure is so complicated that they cannot handle it without severe outside pressures, which Washington is now applying.

Or second, there was an element of misleading the Carter Administration, which officials don't want to think is true but can't help considering.

There is perhaps a third possible explanation: Japan's economy, despite her vast trade surplus, is confronted by many serious problems. Her steel industry is operating at only 70 percent of capacity. She no longer has the competitive advantage she had of much lower wages and prices; in fact, Korea, Taiwan and Singapore are now underselling her in the simpler electronic product markets. And she was able to absorb the shock of the oil revolution by exporting enough more goods to pay for the higher priced oil: in effect exporting the oil cost to the United States and other countries.

At the last Trilateral Commission meeting in Bonn, Germany, Yukio Matsuyama, a former Washington correspondent of the Asahi Shimbun newspapers, made these observations about the Japanese situation:

"Since the defeat in the Pacific war, the Japanese attitude . . . has been timid and passive, partly because of the legacy of the occupation and partly because, compared with other nations, the Japanese have been so fortunate as to be content with the status quo. . . . She was interested only in what the world could do for her and not what she can do for the world.

"However, Japan has had a rude awakening through changes in the international climate. . . . When we think of our meager endowment of natural resources, we cannot help but think: 'Frailty, thy name is Japan. . . .'"

The Ushiba mission here is only the latest part of that Japanese "rude awakening"—calculated by the Carter Administration here in the belief that Prime Minister Fukuda cannot make major trade accommodations without it. So both sides are now acting in response to severe political pressures at home, and playing high-risk politics with one another, but there is a limit to this game as both nations should have learned in 1941.

December 14, 1977

Japan-U.S. Trade Backlash

Dangers Exist of Nationalistic Reaction by Tokyo And an Ultraprotective Response in Congress

By CLYDE H. FARNSWORTH

WASHINGTON, Dec. 13 — There are dangers of a backlash in the present trade confrontation between the United States and Japan that could cause both sides to retreat for a little tranquil reflection

Economic Analysis

after Nobuhiko Ushiba, the new Japanese Minister of External Economic Affairs, leaves Washington Thursday. His offers to reduce the size of his nation's huge trading surplus were immediately deemed insufficient by his American interlocutors, and yet if the United States presses too hard it may trigger in Japan a vehement nationalistic reaction against being pushed around.

This could have myriad consequences for the global economic and political system. Some Japanese newspapers have already accused the United States of trying to dictate terms.

There are dangers even of a backlash in this country, generated out of the creation of expectations that cannot be realized. This could spark a nationalistic, ultra-protective response in Congress.

"The important point is that we are all in the same economic boat, says Japan's Ambassador here, Fumihiko Togo, "and the worst remedy to resort to is to start restricting our trade with each other; we went down that road in the 1930's."

The Japanese, many analysts believe, cannot be expected suddenly to dissolve their giant trading surpluses, which a nation almost totally lacking in fossil energy reserves regards as its cushion against an uncertain future.

The Japanese have traditionally taken pains to provide for the future, a concern that is evidenced by the highest savings rate in the world. The Japanese save a quarter of what they have available to spend, against the little more than 5 percent that Americans put aside.

The Tokyo Government is being urged to stimulate the economy to spur consumption, but unlike their American counterparts, Japanese consumers are not that eager to consume. To a degree, the trade surplus embodies the collective penchant for saving.

Ingenuity and Hard Work

It also grows out of ingenuity and hard work. One example of industrial inventiveness occurs in the export of automobiles. The cars are not finished when they leave a plant. Finishing takes place on slow factory boats to the export markets.

Yet, as Ambassador Togo remarked, the Japanese are in that same economic boat with other nations, and their surpluses—$15 billion this year in trade, $10 billion in the current account, which covers trade plus such services as insurance and shipping purchased abroad—are straining the world trading system.

A quarter century ago, when Japan was beginning its amazing reconstruction from the ashes of World War II, it was already running a trade surplus of roughly the same size as today's—in proportion to the overall size of its economy.

The effects then were hardly noticed or noticeable. The economy was a bamboo shoot, compared with the towering stalk of today, the world's second largest trading power.

Already Undermined System

A difficult maneuver is under way today to get the Japanese to accept a greater responsibility for the workings of a world system, already undermined not simply by Japanese surpluses but also by the petrodollar surpluses of the oil exporters who quadrupled their prices four years ago. Although American officials deny that they are using strongarm tactics on the Japanese, the Americans emphatically point out that Japan can no longer play by the narrowly drawn rules of 25 years ago, when its trading position hardly mattered.

Japan's $10 billion current account surplus this year is hardly the only strain on world finances. It comes on top of the $40 billion petrodollar surplus. And these enormous sums are reflected in debts of other nations, some of which are already so deeply in debt they must take severe austerity measures to have any hope of raising new money.

The belt-tightening that countries such as Britain, Italy, Peru, Zaire, Turkey and Portugal have had to undergo saps consumption and acts as a drag on world trade. Yet, healthy trade is what the Japanese must count on to keep their own economy sound.

Stimulation and Relaxation

The United States feels that the Japanese have an obligation to the world system to stimulate their economy so that Japanese consumers will buy more from abroad. Washington also believes the Japanese must make far greater efforts to relax tariffs, quotas, discriminatory regulations and other barriers to imports.

Perhaps most difficult, the United States is seeking a restructuring of the complicated Japanese marketing and distribution network, dominated by large trading companies. Americans say the network is itself an impediment to penetration.

In reply, the Japanese contend that the United States does not fully appreciate what Tokyo has already done. They argue that the United States is simply looking for a scapegoat to deflect attention from its own inability to control energy imports, which is the largest component of what is expected to be a $30 billion American trade deficit this year.

December 14, 1977

Tokyo and U.S. Still Split As Trade Discussions End

But Japan's Tariff Cuts and Growth Goal of 7% Improve Hopes of Reducing Its Surplus

By CLYDE H. FARNSWORTH

WASHINGTON, Dec. 15—Japanese and American negotiators, concluding four days of talks here, are still far apart over what actions are necessary to reduce an $8.5 billion trade surplus with the United States but said two recent Japanese Cabinet decisions had improved prospects for successful conclusion of the dialogue.

Nobuhiko Ushiba, Japan's Minister for External Economic Affairs, led a delegation that has been talking to the American chief trade negotiator, Robert S. Strauss, as well as to members of both Houses of Congress and leaders of American industry.

At a joint news conference, Mr. Strauss said that Mr. Ushiba, a former Ambassador to Washington, "hasn't hit a home run with us, but he hasn't struck out either."

The most important Tokyo action, apparently influenced by the pressure Mr. Ushiba has been feeling here, was to set a 7 percent growth target for the Japanese economy next year. If this goal were met, it would be by far the best economic activity of any industrialized nation.

The Japanese said they would enlarge their budget deficit substantially, borrowing 37 percent of what they will spend, which would break through what had been a traditional debt ceiling of 30 percent. Housing and public works are among the sectors that would be stimulated.

The expectation is that the greater activity will draw in more imports from the United States and other countries the Japanese trading surplus with the rest of the world, which is expected to reach $15 billion this year.

Japan had aimed for 6.7 percent growth for the current fiscal year, but,largely because of the depressing effects of the sharp appreciation of the yen in recent months, actual output is now expected to rise by only 5.3 percent.

Mr. Strauss said the new target for 1978 and the apparent Japanese willingness to commit new resources to meet it would have a "very positive effect, and I view it with great encouragement."

The second action involves advance tariff cuts the Japanese are making on 318 items as part of the multilateral trade negotiations in Geneva.

Though the value of the cuts in terms of increased export potential for the United States was termed "peanuts" by one American official, and "insignificant" by Mr. Strauss, the gesture was seen as important in the long-range efforts to continue trade liberalization.

The cuts were seen as both an indication of a willingness to move more broadly and as a step to advance the Geneva negotiations, which the major trading nations are counting on to halt the present slide toward protectionism in many countries.

Mr. Strauss said that, although there was still a wide gap between the United States and Japan over ways to narrow the trade imbalance between the two countries, Mr. Ushiba's visit had defined he differences more sharply.

He said the two Governments would now study the positions and determine whether the differences can be narrowed.

"If we are able to close the gap," the American negotiator commented, "I would plan a trip to Tokyo, but there is no point in going unless the trip is meaningful."

A Strauss mission to Tokyo some time before Congress reconvenes next Jan. 19 had been under consideration.

Mr. Ushiba also conferred with President Carter, inviting the President to visit Japan on behalf of Prime Minister Takoe Fukuda. Mr. Carter said that if he could not go to Japan he would send Vice President Mondale. Mr. Carter is planning a foreign tour beginning Dec. 29, but Japan is not on his itinerary.

The President termed the Ushiba mission a "good first step" toward resolving the bilateral trade problems, adding, "We hope to make progress in the future." Mr. Ushiba met with representatives of United States business who complained about restrictions in selling to Japan and with members of both Houses of Congress who said American jobs were being lost because of the influx of Japanese goods.

Representative Charles A. Vanik, chairman of a House trade subcommittee, said he and Mr. Ushiba had spoken about the growing pressures in Congress for protectionist legislation.

The pressures may be difficult to contain if the Japanese "failed to address themselves to this problem very, very quickly," said the Ohio Democrat, whose state has been hit by layoffs in the steel industry.

The Japanese have indicated that they are aware of the threat of mandated trade restraint. "Our relations with the United States must be kept in good form," Mr. Ushiba said today.

December 16, 1977

Getting Tough With Japan

Echoing some loud cries of distress from industry and labor, the Administration has lately been warning that Japan must rapidly eliminate its giant trade surplus with the United States lest the domestic pressures for protection against Japanese imports become unstoppable. The surplus is certainly large—some $8.5 billion this year, part of Japan's global trade surplus of $15 billion—and the pain to particular industries considerable. But Washington's reaction has perhaps been too blunt and too panicky. The brewing mini-crisis between the two governments could do serious damage to the international trading system and to the relationship between the United States and Japan that has been crucial to stability in Asia since World War II.

During the first quarter-century following the war, that relationship was marked by a tacit tradeoff. In exchange, first, for economic aid and, later, for American toleration of one-sided Japanese protection of its industries, Japan became an anchored aircraft carrier and supply ship at the center of our system of Asian alliances. But the American military presence in Asia has shrunk; American and Japanese interests have changed, and the economic relationship now seems undesirably one-sided, at least to the United States.

●

In the present atmosphere of mutual fault-finding several things should be kept in mind. First, large Japanese trade surpluses with the United States are not immutable. The surplus in 1972 was $4.4 billion. In each of the next three years it was roughly $1.5 billion. Then it climbed to $5.3 billion in 1976. The trade balance has more to do with the general health of the world economy, especially Japan's, than with specific practices on either side. Moreover, it is misleading to focus merely on the bilateral trade balance. Given the structure of industry in the two countries, a Japanese trade surplus with the United States is probably inevitable and—from the point of view of the American consumer—even desirable. The same is true of American trade surpluses with other parts of the world. The significant indicator is a country's overall accounts, rather than any bilateral trade balance.

There is a second consideration to keep in mind. It is probably true that thousands of Americans are out of work as a direct result of competition from Japan. But aggregate employment in this country is likely to suffer rather than benefit from higher obstacles to trade. The best way to put Americans back to work is to increase demand worldwide to a point where new jobs are generated in all industrial countries.

Over the past several weeks, Japanese officials have spoken of increasing their growth rate to 7 percent next year from virtual stagnation over the past 12 months. That would be most welcome, as would a similar effort by West Germany. When the three leading market economies—those two and the United States—are working together, the entire international economy will benefit. That is why recent hints that Tokyo is having second thoughts about the 7 percent growth target are dismaying.

In announcing plans to stimulate growth, Tokyo also announced some measures to liberalize imports. They are inadequate, and Washington is right to say so. Yet, even a rapidly growing Japan free of many present import restrictions is not likely to be a major market for industrial production from the West. It should, however, increasingly become one for the lower-cost products of the developing states. When Japan liberalizes its import policies, the chief beneficiaries are likely to be not the United States or the United Kingdom, but countries like South Korea, China and Brazil for manufactured products, and Australia and New Zealand for grains and meats.

•

Japan should do more to help the world's economy; by doing more it would also help its own. Doing more, however, requires not only Government decisions to spur growth but also changes in entrenched habits among Japanese industrialists and consumers. It means as well the goring of some sacred cows, such as the agricultural interests that play so important a role in the councils of the ruling Liberal Democratic Party. None of these steps are easy, and they are made even harder by obvious pressure from abroad. Ultimatums are seldom useful among close allies, and the Japanese are right to see something akin to an ultimatum in recent American statements. What is needed now from Tokyo is firm follow-through on good intentions. What is needed from Washington is less panic and a longer view.

December 27, 1977

Japan's Trade Surplus 2d Highest; New Commercial Mission in U.S.

The battle between the United States and Japan on the trade front moved another step forward yesterday with the arrival oof an important Japanese trade mission in Washington and the announcement of a new batch of balance of payments and other economic statistics here.

The most startling of the developments was the announcement by the Japanese Ministry of Finance that Japan's overall payments surplus in November was $1.83 billion, the second highest figure in Japanese history, after the $3.3 billion total recorded in the crisis month of August 1971.

The extraordinarily large surplus, which includes trade, a service and capital items, was largely accounted for by an inrush of short-term funds seeking to profit from a sudden rise in the value of the yen against the dollar.

Meanwhile Prime Minister Takeo Fukuda Monday summoned leading cabinet ministers for an urgent session on Japan-United States trade problems. After the meeting, officials said that Japan would offer new concessions to America on Japanese import of key agricultural items —high quality beef and citrus products.

Another element in the situation was the finding by the Organization for Economic Cooperation and Development in Paris that the world economy would continue to grow slowly in 1978 unless Japan and West Germany expanded their domestic economies more rapidly.

Pressure for concessions from Japan— both on import quotas and on the broad economic front—has mounted against the background of unofficial predictions that this year Japan may have a trade surplus of $10 billion with the United States alone.

The predictions contrast with previous estimates that the Japanese trade surplus with America this year would be $8 billion.

The latest Japanese trade mission to go to Washington, which is composed of four members of the ruling Liberal Democratic Party, was hastily assembled on Sunday night, and is another reflection of the urgency with which the Japanese regard the trade crisis.

The purpose of the mission, which is led by Takami Eto and Tsutomu Hata, former high officials of the Agriculture and Forestry Ministry, is to meet Congressional leaders and Administration officials to explain the damage that would be done to Japanese agriculture if Japan were to make major concessions to United States demands for liberalization of imports of beef and citrus products.

Last week, the United States called on Japan to raise the import quota for high quality beef served in hotels to 10,000 tons from 1,000, but so far the best offer by the Japanese is to raise that quota to only 3,000 tons. The United States side also demanded that Japan step up imports of orange and grapefruit juice to 50,000 tons from 1,000 tons.

The Japanese trade mission will be reinforced by yet another mission this week led by Saburo Fujita, chairman of the Japanese Farmers' Federation Union.

The urgency that Prime Minister Fukuda attaches to obtaining agreement on an only moderate increase in Japanese imports of farm products is explained by the fact that his Liberal Democratic Party is overwhelmingly dependent in parliamentary elections upon support from agricultural constituencies.

While the Japanese are still trying to get away with making only a token offer on agricultural imports—which would, all agree, make only a minute contribution anyway to cutting the huge Japanese trade surplus with America—the publication of the latest batch of economic statistics in Tokyo can only cause the United States side to stiffen its demands for concessions.

The statistics include:

An overall trade Japanese surplus of $1.7 billion in November, after seasonal adjustment, compared with $1.36 billion in October. In November, exports totaled $6.8 billion, up 24 percent from November '76, while imports rose by a mere 4 percent to $5.2 billion.

A record industrial production index figure of 133.4 in November, surpassing the previous November 1973 high of 132.9 on the index, which is based on 1970 at 100.

A record November motor vehicle export figure of 396,317 units, worth $1.3 billion, up 23 percent from the November 1976 level on a unit-volume basis and up 41 percent in value.

The ruling party in Japan is "caught in a crossfire," observed a senior Japanese diplomat, between United States demands for what amounts to a "symbolic' gesture" on imports of agricultural goods and grass-roots Liberal Democratic Party opposition to concessions of any size.

Mr. Fukuda's anxiety to find a solution to the problem is reflected in his decision to offer new concessions on farm goods before the year's end, but the chances are that the Japanese offer will once again be construed as minimal by the United States.

Japan is driving ahead with its bid to raise exports and remains unwilling or unable to get the domestic economy moving faster as the O.E.C.D., the 24-nation group in Paris to which leading industrial countries belong, would like. In Eastern Europe, Japan has just made a move intended to increase exports by offering a $140 million syndicated loan to East Germany as well as official finance for two petrochemical plants worth $800 million.

It remains to be seen whether Robert S. Strauss, the president's special trade representative, will go through with his plan to visit Japan early in 1978 for trade talks. Last week's visit to Washington by Nobuhiko Ushiba, the Minister for External Trade Affairs, Mr. Strauss's counterpart in Tokyo, would appear to have been largely disappointing.

December 28, 1977

U.S. Optimistic That Japan Will Halve Its Trade Surplus

By CLYDE H. FARNSWORTH

WASHINGTON, Jan. 5—A Commerce Department official's coffee mug is emblazoned with the patriotic legend, "Be American. . .Buy American," but below, in smaller type, are the words: "Made in Japan."

That mug, as well as pocket calculators, color television sets, microwave ovens, cameras, watches and myriad other products contributed to what is now estimated as a $9 billion Japanese trade surplus with the United States last year—a surplus that has aggravated problems of the dollar, of unemployment, and of protectionism.

Heavy pressure has been applied by Washington to get the surplus reduced, and with negotiations expected to culminate next week in Tokyo, American officials now believe there are fairly good chances the Japanese surplus will be halved over the next 12 months.

On the basis of trade concessions the Japanese have already made or are expected to make shortly, the American special trade representative, Robert S. Strauss, is hoping to put the final touches on an agreement in Tokyo next Thursday and Friday that would undercut threats of a protectionist backlash in Congress.

Follows Cabinet Reshuffle

His mission to Tokyo follows a Japanese Cabinet reshuffle, and the subsequent trip here last month of the new Minister of External Economic Affairs, Nobuhiko Ushiba, who was warned repeatedly of an American protectionist reaction if the Japanese did not both open up their markets to more American—and foreign—products and check their export enthusiasm.

Mr. Ushiba came here with some concessions but they were immediately labeled insufficient by Mr. Strauss.

Nevertheless, the former Democratic Party chief, who has close ties with many in Congress and is one of the few persons who can see President Carter on short notice, insisted that the Japanese had taken a step in the right direction.

Mr. Ushiba, the trade negotiator said, had neither hit a home run nor struck out in his Washington visit. Mr. Strauss will now be aiming for the stands in Tokyo.

Budget Most Encouraging

Of all the measures the Japanese have announced, the United States regards a reflationary budget for the 1978 fiscal year as the most encouraging. A heavy dose of deficit spending, much of which has been earmarked for public works, is intended to lift the 1978 growth rate to 7 percent. But the experience of 1977 casts some doubt on the possibility of reaching the 1978 target.

Japanese exports to the United States have resulted in a $9 billion Japanese trade surplus.

Consulate General of Japan, N.Y.

The Japanese had earlier said their 1977 growth rate would be 6.7 percent. The final figure, largely reflecting the depressive effects of the yen's appreciation on domestic consumption, will be closer to 5.3 percent.

The higher the growth rate the greater the demand for imports, according to conventional economic theory.

But as Frank A. Weil, Assistant Secretary of Commerce for Industry and Trade, has noted, Japan's small imports of manufactures have been the result of such additional factors as an historical anti-import bias, non-tariff barriers arising from administrative rules, a high propensity to save, the complexities of the distribution structure and the close linkage between Japanese manufacturers and trading companies.

Mr. Strauss sent a deputy, Stephen Lande, to Tokyo last week to try to determine whether the budget will be sufficiently expansionary to make the 7 percent target attainable.

Another deputy, Alan Wolff, is leaving for Tokyo on Monday to prepare further ground for the Strauss visit. This week Mr. Strauss was in Europe with President Carter. The presence of the special trade negotiator was intended to impress upon the Europeans the importance the United States attaches to the multilateral trade liberalization negotiations that are expected to reach a crucial stage late this month in Geneva, a key American official reported.

The United States is counting on an active leadership role by the Japanese in the Geneva round. During the Ushiba visit here last month the Japanese Cabinet agreed on making advance tariff cuts on more than 300 products, a positive sign of its interest in further trade liberalization.

While the value of the cuts will mean no more than $50 million to $75 million of additional American sales to Japan annually, according to American estimates, Washington welcomed the Japanese action as a move in the right direction.

Here, as far as is known, is the state of play on other American demands:

¶Liberalization of import quotas— The United States wants freer access for citrus products, concentrated juice and beef, and the Japanese have already indicated they will go along. While the dollar volume of trade is relatively small, the states involved in the trade—California, Texas, Florida and Arizona—are especially important politically.

¶Abolition of other non-tariff barriers—The United States has demanded liberalization of import licensing rules and safety and health standards, used either directly or indirectly to keep out American products. Examples are emission standards for trucks and other vehicles and the ban on a fungicidal spray wax on citrus fruits. American officials report a fair amount of progress in breaking down some of these barriers.

¶Expansion of import financing— The Ministry of Trade and Industry has the same authority to grant credits for imports as for exports. The United States has demanded the authority be used, and the Japanese are considering the demand.

¶Elimination of certain export promotion measures — The United States is asking that some of these programs be cut back or eliminated. Again the Japanese have shown themselves sympathetic, according to American officials.

The Japanese have also offered to enlarge stockpiles of agricultural products, which would help American farmers get rid of surpluses, and to expand foreign aid programs, which would pump more money into third world development, and indirectly spur exports from the United States.

American officials point out that some of the fault lies with American companies themselves and their inability to communicate effectively with Japanese associates and customers.

In New York City alone there are 20,000 Japanese businessmen, most of whom speak English, all of whom are actively promoting and selling their products in the United States market. Yet, in Tokyo there are only 1,000 American businessmen. Few speak Japanese or fully understand the culture.

January 6, 1978

U.S. and Japan Pressing
for Accord in Trade Dispute

By ANDREW H. MALCOLM

TOKYO, Jan. 9—Amid a stream of bilingual news conferences and bilateral lobbying sessions, Japanese and American officials opened a new round of working-level discussions here today in an effort to settle, at least for the moment, their continuing trade dispute.

Alan W. Wolff, United States deputy special trade representative, began three days of meetings with his Japanese counterparts in several ministries. They are expected to clarify details of Japanese trade liberalization proposals, Japan's new economic stimulation plans and a joint strategy for the renewed multilateral Tokyo round of tariff negotiations scheduled to open in Geneva next week.

On Wednesday Robert S. Strauss, President Carter's special trade representative, is scheduled to arrive for two more days of talks culminating in an expected settlement announcement on Friday.

"It won't be a surprise package," said an American official, "but I think the contents will be significant."

Rather than including any bold new details, sources said, the plan will be a collection of Japanese measures announced since the bilateral trade dispute began late last summer, when the size of Japan's 1977 global trade surplus (around $15 billion) and its surplus with the United States ($8 billion) became apparent.

Growth of 7 Percent Held Unlikely

These measures include tariff reductions on 318 items, modest quota liberalization on a few of the many agricultural products still under quantitative import restrictions and an expansionist government spending budget for fiscal 1978, beginning April 1. The last is designed

to pull in more imports and push Japan's economic growth from the 5.3 percent expected for 1977 to 7 percent for 1978. Diplomatic critics praised the tariff steps, but found Japan's other proposals falling far short of the basic economic restructuring that this country's trading partners feel is necessary for Japan to assume its full international responsibilities as the noncommunist world's second largest economic power.

As for the 7 percent growth rate, virtually no independent economic observers here believe it is possible this year.

American officials have stressed the need for significant Japanese trade concessions to quell "protectionist pressures" which, they say, are mounting in Congress and labor in the United States during this election year.

Japanese officials, on the other hand, say the Americans should do more to correct their own trade imbalance and that Japan has already made the maximum concessions possible, given its domestic protectionist pressures and the slim numerical hold in Parliament of Prime Minister Takeo Fukuda's Liberal Democratic Party.

Publicly and privately, in restaurants, meeting rooms and hallways, officials of both sides these days are courting officials, legislators, reporters and the public of the other to present their case. Numerous delegations from Japan's Parliament and the United States Congress have crisscrossed the Pacific in recent days to meet their counterparts, raising suspicions that the trips and accompanying pronouncements were more for domestic consumption back home than international edification.

Today, Representative James R. Jones, Oklahoma Democrat, calls for development of a "genuine two-way street" in trade between Japan and the United States. "The perception in America," the Tulsa Congressman warned, "is that Japan is a closed market because of bureacratic red tape and other nontariff barriers to American products."

On Friday Senators Carl Curtis of Nebraska and Clifford Hansen of Wyoming,

Republicans, held a joint news conference in the United States Embassy to label as "totally unacceptable" and "cosmetic" Japan's proferred increases in beef and citrus product imports. Although representing only a minute fraction of the value of total United States-Japan trade of $26 billion, beef and oranges have somehow become the symbols of concession to both sides. Tomorrow Senator S. I. Hayakawa, California Republican, has scheduled a news conference to talk about the citrus issue.

The American legislators criticized Japans's beef cartel that sets prices at six to 10 times world prices and Japan's "inefficient" cattle industry. "They call

it an 'industry' to have one or two cattle in a pen out back," said Senator Hansen, who owns 1,500 head of his own on a Wyoming ranch.

For the first time in the recent months of trade tensions here, a specific method of retaliation was mentioned.

"We don't need Japanese automobiles," said Senator Hansen. But, asked what kind of motor vehicles he owned on his ranch, he responded: "Japanese, five of them."

"That's what I mean," he said, "we're all in this together. The concept of gradual change over time is strong here. But that's no good anymore. The pressures are building. We have constituents, too, and we're going to clamp down."

January 10, 1978

U.S. AND JAPAN OPEN TWO-DAY DISCUSSION OF TRADE PROBLEMS

NEWS CONFERENCE SET TODAY

Indications Are That the Americans Have Been Unsuccessful in Bid to Liberalize Tariff Setup

By ANDREW H. MALCOLM

TOKYO, Jan. 12—Robert S. Strauss, President Carter's special trade representative, opened two days of critical talks with Japanese officials here today with the aim of settling a series of major trade issues between these two economic superpowers.

There were indications tonight that the Americans have so far been unsuccessful in their attempts to get Japan to take trade liberalization steps significantly greater than those announced during last month's bilateral sessions in Washington. At that time, Mr. Strauss called the Japanese quota increases and tariff cuts "insufficient."

Joint Announcement Expected

A joint news conference is scheduled for late tomorrow by Mr. Strauss and Nobuhiko Ushiba, Japan's Minister for External Economic Affairs. The announcement of the details of some form of agreement is expected then

But a conceptual problem appears to be arising between the two allies. The Americans view the measures, expected to be modest, as only the beginning of a major long-term economic restructuring aimed at opening Japan far more to for-

Robert S. Strauss, President Carter's special trade representative.

Photo by Fabian Bachrach

eign goods and making the country play a greater global leadership role economically.

Japanese officials, on the other hand, see the "settlement" as an end in itself and are resisting United States demands for future trade commitments.

"As long as we can get the Strauss visit over with and get the settlement," one Japanese official said today, "then we can get United States-Japan relations back on an even keel."

The strained trade relations became evident late last summer when the mushrooming size of Japan's 1977 trade surplus (about $17 billion) became apparent. About $9 billion of that stems from trade with the United States.

Drastic Measures Called For

With uncharacteristic bluntness, the American Administration demanded a variety of "drastic" economic steps by Japan, which 18 months ago had assured its trading partners that its imports would grow to help balance its massive exports. "Dramatic" steps were necessary, the Americans said, to quell mounting protectionist pressures in the United States against Japan.

In a series of meetings throughout the fall, visiting American officials and the United States Ambassador, Mike Mansfield, told the Japanese Government—in what was publicly described as "friendly advice"—that it must make a public commitment to achieving a balance in its international payments, take a much more active role in the Geneva multilateral trade talks, consider a broad range of tariff cuts on significant products, drop 27 quantitative restrictions on imports, reconsider its "aggressive" export promotion program, stimulate the domestic economy to draw in more imports and improve access to the Japanese market for foreign goods, especially manufactured goods, which total only 20 percent of Japan's imports.

Common Market Demands Expected

Failure to do these things, the Americans said, would seriously jeopardize relations between Tokyo and Washington. The countries of the European Economic Community are expected to make their own demands later.

Trade with the United States

'So far, the Japanese have agreed to cut tariffs on 318 items, liberalize imports of some minor sub-items still officially protected by quotas and stimulate the 1978 domestic economy with the aim of achieving a growth rate of 7 percent, compared with the 5.3 percent estimated for 1977.

Today, Mr. Strauss, his deputy Alan Wolff and Ambassador Mansfield visited several Government offices where the tables were decorated with tiny American and Japanese flags. One official called the exchanges "constructive and unreserved." Another called them "heated."

The Americans reportedly sought a public Japanese commitment to vigorous participation in the Geneva talks. They also were said to have sought larger tariff cuts on items such as computers and color films and to have expressed dissatisfaction with the size of planned increases in the import quotas on high-quality beef and orange juice.

Japanese officials were said to have agreed to increase beef imports from the present 1,000 tons to to 3,000 tons and to raise the limit on oranges from the present 22,500 tons to 45,000 tons. Although such agricultural items represent a small part of the total import picture, they have become symbols to many of Japan's basic protectionist policies in many areas.

American Congressmen visiting here in recent days have said such "token concessions" would not satisfy protectionist forces in the United States and might prompt retaliatory trade moves.

Warning by Senator Kennedy

In a speech today to the Foreign Correspondents Club of Japan here, Senator Edward M. Kennedy, Democrat of Massachusetts, warned that it was "extremely unlikely" that Congress would "continue to support an open trade policy on the part of America when a variety of restrictive policies continue to be practiced on the part of Japan."

The Senator recalled Japan's concern with American trade barriers during the early 1960's. In those days, it was the United States that had the bilateral surplus

"Now the tables are turned," he said, adding: "Japan has the surplus and it is the United States that is concerned. The role of Japan has also changed. As a leading economic power in the modern world, Japan is now being asked to share the responsibilities, as well as the benefits, of creating and maintaining a healthy global economy."

Mr. Kennedy, who is returning from a visit to China, said he was confident Mr. Strauss would leave for Washington tomorrow with "some kind of agreement." but added that the important factor was the reaction in Congress.

Mr. Strauss is to continue his round of meetings tomorrow, ending with a 30-minute afternoon talk with Prime Minister Takeo Fukuda.

January 13, 1978

U.S. AND JAPAN REACH AN ACCORD ON EASING OF TENSIONS IN TRADE

Strauss Is Enthusiastic, but More Restrained Tokyo Officials See New Economic Issues Arising

By ANDREW H. MALCOLM

TOKYO, Jan. 13—The United States and Japan announced agreement today on a package of economic measures that, American officials predicted, would open a new and more liberal era in the trading relationships of the nonCommunist world's two largest economic powers.

The steps, agreed to after six months of increasing tensions over Japan's mounting trading surplus, covered Japan's previously announced decisions to reduce tariffs on about 300 items, liberalize quotas on some agricultural imports and stimulate the domestic economy to achieve a 7 percent growth rate for 1978.

But the understandings also included numerous new commitments by Japan for "a marked diminution" in its current account surplus, "a sweeping review" of ways to relax its foreign exchange controls, "substantially increased opportunities" for foreign suppliers seeking Japanese Government contracts, increased foreign aid by Japan and concrete arrangements to monitor progress in fulfilling the pact.

American officials, who had said a dramatic agreement was needed to stem protectionist pressures in Congress, cited in particular Japan's commitment to achieving "basic equity" between itself and other major trading countries in opening domestic markets to foreign businesses. Japan has come under very strong international criticism for its policies of protecting its domestic producers from foreign competition.

Robert S. Strauss, the American Special Representative for Trade Negotiations, appeared enthusiastic about the agreement, which was still being drafted in a ministerial meeting at 1 A.M. today. "We have really redefined the economic relations between our two great nations," he said at a news conference before his return to Washington. "This agreement represents a change in direction and philosophy."

Japanese officials, who face strong domestic protectionist forces themselves, especially from agriculture producers, were considerably more restrained. "I do believe," Nobuhiko Ushiba, Minister of State for External Economic Affairs, said of the likely adverse reaction in Japan, "that, whatever present dissatisfaction or confusion there may be, Japan can overcome it."

Later, Mr. Ushiba warned Japanese reporters that the new agreement was not an end in itself. "The conclusion of the present negotiations," he said, "is merely a temporary pause, and Japan has to expect that new economic issues will arise one after another from now on."

"It will be necessary," he added, "for Japan to open more of its domestic market to foreign goods."

These widely quoted remarks are viewed as part of a Government effort to prepare the Japanese public for Japan's assuming greater economic leadership in the world. In the past, the Japanese, with their sheltered economy, often tended to feel "wronged" or "misunderstood" under a barrage of foreign criticism or demands.

Other sources expressed considerably more skepticism than the Americans, saying the pact was too heavy on generalities promised as future steps and too light on specific and immediate Japanese reforms.

"There is a big difference," one diplomat noted, "between being able to promise something and being able to fulfill that promise." Like others, he cited previous Japanese commitments that failed to materialize.

These earlier pledges included Prime Minister Takeo Fukuda's promise last spring at the London economic summit meeting that Japan's economy would grow at a 6.7 percent rate in 1977 and that i ts current accounts—which include the flow of goods and services between Japan and other countries—would register a deficit of several hundred million dollars. The actual figures are estimated to be 5.3 percent and a surplus of $10 billion.

The agreement pledges that Japan will take "all appropriate steps" to increase the volume and overall percentage of imports of manufactures." Such purchases help create jobs in other lands but at present they account for only 20 percent of Japan's total imports, compared with more than 50 percent in other industrialized nations. Japan's progress is to be reviewed in the "joint trade facilitation committee," a three-month-old body designed to ease American access to the Japanese market.

In the agricultural area, Japan set increases in orange imports to 45,000 tons from the previously offered 22,500 tons and a total increase of 10,000 tons in beef quotas for all countries. Japan also agreed to dispatch missions to the United States to consider expanding Japanese forestry im-

ports and the purchase of electric and nuclear power plant machinery. There is also to be a joint Government and industry buying mission to the United States soon and a citrus study group to consider; among other things, seasonal quotas for American citrus exports.

The agreement said Japan would soon announce some simplification of import inspection requirements and expansion of import credits. And it set several further consultations this year to review the agreement's progress. This includes another Strauss-Ushiba meeting in October.

Both countries promised to cooperate during the coming multilateral trade negotiations in Geneva.

Mr. Ushiba said that the provisions together with the yen's appreciation in recent months, enabled his Government to set a goal of a $6 billion current account surplus for Japan's 1978 fiscal year, which begins April 1. With such a "marked diminution," the carefully worded seven-page communiqué said, Japan would continue all reasonable efforts, "under present international economic conditions," to fur-

ther reduce its current account surplus, "aiming at equilibrium with [a] deficit accepted if it should occur."

Mr. Strauss said he arrived in Tokyo Wednesday night expecting "a C-plus or B-minus effort" to emerge today. Instead, he said, "I grade it as an A result, a major move on a new enlightened course, and I so informed President Carter on the phone this morning."

The agreement carries a transcending significance for other countries. If fully carried out, it commits two of the world's three largest economic powers to coordinate an expansion of their economies in an effort to stimulate business in many lands and counter the world's current sluggish economic growth. West Germany has notably resisted stimulative measures for fear of inflation.

It remains to be seen whether the agreement will stem what the American negotiators continually referred to as "a rising tide of protectionism" in the United States. I do not think we have eliminated these forces," Mr. strauss said, "but had we not reached agreement, they would have become much stronger."

January 14, 1978

Text of Communique Issued by U.S. and Japan on 2 Days of Trade Talks

TOYKO, Jan. (AP)—Following is the text of the joint communiqué issued today at the conslusion of two days of trade talks between the United States and Japan:

On Jan. 12 and 13, 1978, the Government of Japan and the United States of America, through their representatives, Minister of State for External Economic Affairs, Mr. Nobuhiko Ushiba, and the President's Special Representative for Trade Negotiations, Ambassador Robert S. Strauss, consulted upon a series of policies and measures designed to contribute to global economic expansion and to strengthen their economic relations. The objective of the consultations was to develop common policies which would facilitate constructive adjustment to changing world economic conditions and the economic relationships between Japan and the United States.

In particular, Minister Ushiba and Ambassador Strauss agreed that a new course of action, building on the steps outlined below, was necessary to avert increasing unemployment and a worldwide reversion to protectionism.

INCREASED ECONOMIC GROWTH

Both sides agreed to take major steps to achieve high levels of non-inflationary economic growth. The Government

of Japan reiterated its recently adopted real growth target of 7 percent for Japan fiscal year 1978, and stated its intention to take all reasonable and appropriate measures, including those previously announced with respect to public expenditures, in order to achieve this target.

The Government of the United States confirmed its intention to pursue policies aimed at the maintenance of substantial, non-inflationary economic growth, as will soon be detailed by President Carter.

Both sides agreed that in the present international economic situation, the accumulation of a large current account surplus was not appropriate.

Marked Diminution of Surplus

Accordingly, Japan has undertaken steps aimed at achieving a marked diminution of its current account surplus. The Minister added that in Japan fiscal year 1978 Japan's current account surplus would be considerably reduced through the expansion of domestic demand, the effect of yen appreciation in recent months, and a series of new measures for improving the access of foreign goods to the Japanese market.

In Japan fiscal year 1979 and thereafter, under present international eco-

nomic conditions, all reasonable efforts would be continued with a view to further reducing Japan's current account surplus, aiming at equilibrium with deficit accepted if it should occur.

The United States stated its intention to improve its balance of payments position by such measures as reducing its dependence on imported oil and increasing its exports, thereby improving the underlying conditions upon which the value of the dollar fundamentally depends. The Ambassador expressed confidence that in the next 90 days an effective energy program would be enacted by the Congress.

To preserve and strengthen the open

world trading system, both sides fully support the acceleration and early conclusion of the Tokyo round of the Multilateral Trade Negotiations, each making substantial contributions in full cooperation with other participants to reduce or eliminate tariff and non-tariff barriers to trade.

Both governments agreed that their joint objective in these negotiations is to achieve basic equity in their trading relations by affording to major trading countries substantially equivalent competitive opportunities on a reciprocal basis.

Trade with the United States

To achieve parity in their trading relations and equivalent openness of their markets, deeper than formula tariff reductions would be utilized.

Interests of Third Countries

In this connection, both sides expressed their intent in the course of the Multilateral Trade Negotiations to consider favorably taking deeper than formula tariff reductions on items of interest to each other with the aim of seeking to achieve comparable average level of tariffs taking into account non-tariff measure at the end of the Multilateral Trade Negotiations, taking fully into account the interests of third countries.

The Government of Japan intends to take all appropriate steps to increase imports of manufactures. The Government anticipated that the total volume of imports of manufactures, as well as the share of these imports in total Japanese imports, would continue to increase steadily. Both sides agreed to review progress in these matters in the joint trade facilitation committee or other appropriate forums and to take whatever corrective actions might be necessary.

The Minister stated that Japan is taking the following significant actions to increase imports:

¶Advance tariff reductions on $2 billion of imports effective April 1.

¶Removal of quota controls on 12 products.

¶As regards high-quality beef, we shall make mutual efforts to exploit demand so that within the hotel and general quotas there will be an increase in importation by 10,000 tons on a global basis beginning in the Japan fiscal year 1978.

¶A three-fold increase in orange imports to 45,000 tons.

¶A four-fold increase to 4,000 tons in the quota for citrus juice.

¶Conducting a sweeping review of its foreign exchange control system and planning a new system based on the principle that all transactions should be free unless specifically prohibited. As a forerunner of the new system, certain immediate measures of liberalization are to be announced soon.

¶Formation of an inter-industry citrus group to study the present state and future developments in the citrus situation including juice blending and seasonal quota, to report to their governments by Nov. 1, 1978.

¶Dispatch of a forest products study group to the United States Northwest with the objective of expanding and upgrading this trade.

¶Dispatch to the United States of a mission to explore the possibility of purchasing electric power plant machinery and equipment including nuclear plant components and equipment.

¶Dispatch to the United States of a Government-industry buying mission sponsored by the joint trade facilitation committee.

¶A Japanese Cabinet decision to secure for foreign suppliers substantially increased opportunities under Government procurement systems.

¶Simplification of inspection requirements on imports.

¶Expansion of credit for imports into Japan.

¶Relaxation of rules for the standard method of settlement.

¶Cooperation in international efforts to curb excessive competition in export credits.

ECONOMIC COOPERATION

Referring to Official Development Assistance, the Minister reaffirmed the intention of the Government of Japan to more than double its aid in five years and noted that, as part of such efforts, the proposed Official Development Assitance for the Japan fiscal year 1978 had substantially increased, and that the quality of Official Development Assistance had improved through an increase of grant aid. He added that the Government of Japan would pursue its basic policy of general untying of its financial assistance.

Ambassador Strauss welcomed these developments and noted that the President would seek legislation to increase substantially United States bilateral and multilateral aid to developing countries.

REVIEW PROCEDURE

In addition, both sides agreed:

¶To coordinate closely with each other and their trading partners including the European communities in multilateral and bilateral forums.

¶Improve access to Japanese markets, by making every effort to assure the success of the joint trade facilitation committee in its work, to increase imports of manufactures, and resolve concrete problems encountered in trade with Japan including the aim of overcoming non-tariff barriers by applying liberal approach.

¶To continue regular technical exchanges on growth problems and prospects through the joint economic projections study group.

¶To review global and bilateral economic policy this spring in Washington at the next meeting of the sub-Cabinet group.

¶To review progress made in all these areas at a meeting between Minister Ushiba and Ambassador Strauss next October.

January 14, 1978

Questionable Protection

By William Safire

CHICAGO — For every automobile America's free economy sells in Japan, that nation's government-monopoly economy — "Japan, Inc." — sells one hundred automobiles in the United States.

That slight imbalance is not merely the result of our plant inefficiency or high wage scales: It is caused partly by a level of Japanese protectionism that amounts to a form of economic warfare against the United States.

For example, Japan—and some other industrial nations—have been producing more steel than they can use. Rather than cut back production and suffer the local outcry at unemployment, the governments have been underwriting company losses and "dumping" steel on the American market.

That's against our law. A foreign government cannot subsidize a product and then unfairly compete in our markets, forcing us to close mills and effectively transferring their unemployment to our workers.

What has been our reaction to this international trade lawlessness?

First, Mr. Carter's special trade representative, Robert Strauss, has been smilingly shaking hands and accepting Japanese assurances of improved relations, like Cordell Hull on Dec. 6, 1941.

Second, our Deputy Treasury Secretary for Monetary Affairs, Arthur Solomon, at the request of the steel industry's 120-Congressmen caucus, has come up with a scheme called "trigger pricing." His idea is to fix a "fair" price for steel imported from abroad, based on normal production costs without subsidy, with penalties triggered by price-cutting.

The Strauss gladhanding is harmless, but the Solomon decision is truly Solomon-like: It cuts the baby in half. In the guise of keeping the Congress from fighting "dumping" with quotas

183

or tariffs, its "trigger" effectively places the basic United States industry under Presidential price control.

When the Government creates a bureaucracy to regularly control the price of imports, it gains absolute control of the price of the United States product.

Amazingly, many leaders of the steel industry — tired of being called nasty names by Presidents for acting like real entrepreneurs—much prefer the rosy glow of good public relations to the rough-and-tumble of competitive capitalism. Wearing their new image, brows furrowed at the closing of mills and the loss of jobs at inefficient plants, they long to relax into a world of Government-administered prices.

"Trigger pricing" is a solution far worse than the problem. The Carter men love it: The State Department types can tell our trading partners they were saved from Congressional retaliation for dumping, and the economic planners have a life-and-death control of American steel through the creation of what amounts to a foreign Carter cartel.

We cannot afford either foreign dumping or backdoor price control. One answer would be for Congress to put teeth in our antidumping statutes, penalizing proven dumping with automatic imposition of punitive quotas.

Another answer is to begin thinking the unthinkable about Japan. One of that nation's greatest assets is a free ride on defense spending. Unburdened by any substantial armed force, its economy is far more productive. The United States, with its nuclear umbrella, is Japan's defense.

Might it not be time, a third of a century after World War II, to have a good, public, agonizing reappraisal of that commitment? Our Ambassador to Japan, Mike Mansfield, would understand that approach: the "Mansfield amendment," threatening to withdraw United States troops from Europe, has been an invaluable spur to get our allies to bear their fair share of defense costs.

If tiny Panama can renegotiate its canal treaty with us, can we not renegotiate our peace treaty with Japan? The very consideration of requiring a conventional arms buildup in Japan, in order for them to keep our nuclear guarantee, would have salutary fallout:

The Soviets would not like it a bit. They want to dominate Japan, and the possibility of the birth of a defense budget there might cause them to shed SALT tears.

The Chinese would be deeply concerned. They want United States power in the Far East to counter the Soviet Union, and have historical cause to fear a Japanese military buildup. If we dramatize our willingness to continue to make that restraint possible, shouldn't that be a spur to Sino-American normalization? We ought to get some credit for what we're already doing.

The Japanese would get the message that we are not coming to them hat in hand, begging for them to stop the dumping and exporting their unemployment. The specter of folding the nuclear umbrella at some far-off date (a "Church amendment"?) might just capture their attention.

Let's drop the Carter-cartel price-control route, which steelmen and union officials are so shortsighted to embrace. Instead, let us remind "Japan, Inc." and others that by protecting themselves from United States products, they call into question their taken-for-granted protection by the United States.

January 19, 1978

Mansfield Defends Trade Moves by Japan as Genuine

By HENRY SCOTT-STOKES

Mike Mansfield, the United States Ambassador to Japan, said yesterday that Japan had made "genuine and not merely cosmetic" concessions in trade talks with the United States last month.

In a speech at the Japan Society in New York, the Ambassador appeared to be trying to allay American doubts that Japan gave much ground at talks conducted in Tokyo by Robert S. Strauss, President Carter's special trade representative.

"The steps Japan has decided to take entail genuine sacrifice, painful adjustment in wide sectors of its economy, and significant political risk. They were not easy or empty concessions," said Mr. Mansfield.

An Apparent Disagreement

The Ambassador did note the problems raised by "Japan's huge worldwide current account surplus," about $11 billion in 1977, and "massive surplus in our bilateral trade," which was $8 billion last year according to the Department of Commerce.

"Within the next two to three years, there should be a sizable reduction in their current account surplus," Mr. Mans-

American Ambassador Mike Mansfield.

Department of State Photo/Robert E. Kaiser

field said at a news conference preceding his speech.

Mr. Mansfield and Mr. Strauss appear to have different ideas about the speed with which Japanese measures will have an effect on the huge Japanese trade surplus.

"The ultimate effect of these efforts by Japan will not be evident for some months," said the Ambassador. But Mr. Strauss said that "we are not going to change [trade situation] overnight."

Mr. Strauss appearing before a Senate Finance subcommittee Wednesday, said that United States trade with Japan would only "reach parity in an eight-year period."

Backing up Mr. Strauss, David Rockefeller, chairman of the Chase Manhattan Bank, said in Hong Kong yesterday that he saw "no immediate prospect" of a reduction in the huge United States-Japan trade deficit.

"I have a feeling both governments recognize the seriousness of the problem and are going about solving it in an amicable and serious way," said Mr. Rockefeller, who visited Japan this week. "But as of now we're sort of on dead center and as far as I know there's no immediate prospect of change."

The burden of Mr. Mansfield's address

Trade with the United States

here was that given the political situation in Japan the Japanese had tried hard to find solutions.

"Many sectors of the Japanese economy are in trouble; the Japanese Diet represents and defends the position of constituents who feel themselves threatened by American 'demands'. . .These were bold measures by the Japanese Government.

We, and our European colleagues, must give Japan full credit," said Mr. Mansfield.

The Ambassador noted that Japan, America's largest overseas trade partner, had agreed to increase imports of agricultural products from the United States, had allowed the yen to appreciate sharply, thus making imports cheaper, and had

lowered tariffs on cars and computers.

The former Democratic Senator from Montana also said that "Japan has acknowledged that the eventual result of these measures should be a sharp reduction in its surplus or even equilibrium in its overall current account surplus."

February 3, 1978

Potential Export Advantage For U.S. Dollar-Yen Rate

When a buying mission of prominent Japanese industrialists was nearing the end of a whirlwind American tour last week, the group leader suddenly tossed a baseball to a high-level trade official of the Carter Administration, who had arranged the historic visit.

The Economic Scene With that gesture on a New York television program, Yoshizo Ikeda, president of Mitsui & Company, the giant trading organization in Tokyo, suggested that he and his 91 associates had done their part on behalf of better economic relations between the two countries. Now, he indicated to Frank A.Weil, an Assistant Secretary of Commerce, it was the turn of the United States.

Without any sybolism, a similar message has been candidly conveyed recently by Japan's Finance Minister, Tatsuo Murayama, and private Japanese businessmen, who think the time has come for a close cooperative effort among the United States, West Germany, Switzerland and Japan to deal with the unabated turmoil in the international currency markets stemming from the dollar's weakness. Their concern heightened as the value of the yen touched a postwar peak at 230 to the American dollar.

"It was very unusual for any country to send a big buying group like ours abroad," Mr. Ikeda said in a recent interview here. "Usually, countries are sending missions to sell their own products, not buy from others. I believe, however, that our buying mission was very successful. We came out stronger than we thought we would, expecially in our buying of consumer goods here, which now should double or triple in the near future."

The next inning of the ball game is clearly an aggressive American follow-up sales campaign in Japan. The 20 percent decline of the dollar in the last 12 months—and the consequent rise in the yen—has provided American exporters with a potential advantage they did not previously have.

Yoshizo Ikeda, President of Mitsui & Co., Ltd.

The unrelenting decline of the dollar in relation to those other major currencies in the last year has become a source of growing irritation and worry, not only in the affected nations but also throughout the non-Communist world. Some observers think the Western nations may be approaching another major financial crisis, unless order is soon restored in the monetary realm.

In addition to the export problems and inflationary pressures caused by the instability of the foreign exchange markets, some countries have had to engage in costly dollar-support activities to try to limit the precipitous slide of the dollar and the simultaneous rise of the yen, the mark and the Swiss franc.

Last Monday, for instance, the Bank

of Japan had to buy an estimated $400 million to moderate the speculative activity. Makoto Hara, chief economist for the Bank of Tokyo, one of the county's largest private banks, recently noted the $7 billion increase in the foreign-exchange and gold reserves of the Japanese central bank during the year ended last Feb. 28 and said that most of that gain "represented Japan's effort to support the dollar."

In the same period, of course, the United States, West Germany and some other nations have also intervened extensively in the currency markets for the same purpose, but the extent of those operations is not known.

While United States commitments have been large, banking officials believe they have not reached the level of some of the other countries, which are obviously motivated by the desire to retain competitiveness for their own products in world trade.

The persistence of the adverse foreign-trade figures for the United States has prompted the current vigorous American-Japanese effort to redress the imbalance favoring Japan (about $8 billion this year). It may also lead fairly soon to a new initiative by this country to develop a multifaceted policy to expand American exports sharply to other parts of the world as well as to Japan.

It was the latter objective that brought Mr. Ikeda and his group to the United States at the beginning of this month. In two weeks of visits to 17 cities, they met with representatives of some 3,000 American companies seeking products they might purchase on behalf of their companies at home.

When they returned to Japan last weekend, they reported that they had signed contracts here for more than $300 million of American goods and had made tentative commitments to be completed in the next six months for an additional $1.6 billion of industrial goods, raw materials, processed foods and fashion and leisure products.

What was most important, according to both Japanese and American sources, was the demonstration to United States companies that there are greater opportunities in the Japanese market than many previously believed.

Of course, a buying mission of that type can only make a small contribution to the solution of the massive trade problems of the two countries. There is much still to be done to widen entry of foreign goods into Japanese markets by eliminating or minimizing many tariff and non tariff barriers, and enlarging the potential market through greater overall growth for the Japanese economy.

But the buying mission may have helped reduce what has been termed the ultimate non tariff barrier to United States products—the ignorance of American exporters on how to do business in Japan. And it may be further reduced when a large American selling group goes across the Pacific this fall.

March 22, 1978

JAPAN ASKS CURBS BY KEY INDUSTRIES ON MAJOR EXPORTS

TRADE SURPLUS SETS RECORD

Hold on Shipments to 1977 Levels Is Urged—Goods Sent to U.S. Up 11 Percent in March

By JUNNOSUKE OFUSA

TOKYO, April 15—The Ministry of International Trade and Industry appealed to exporters today to reduce shipments of automobiles, steel, television sets, ships and other major products.

The appeal was issued as the ministry announced that Japan's trade surplus had reached a record high of $2.45 billion in March. Japan's shipments of goods to the United States rose by 11.1 percent, while imports from the United States dropped 24.5 percent.

Move to Ward Off Criticism

The huge trade surplus could provoke further criticism of Japan, especially by the United States and the European Economic Community. The surpluses have been a major factor behind the dollar's plunge in value against the yen.

In an apparent move to ward off such criticism, the ministry said it would take prompt action if exports of certain items become the cause of international trade issues. It also urged exporters to try voluntarily to cut shipments of such products as motorcycles, copying machines, watches and cameras. The ministry said that it would keep a close eye on the export of other products.

In Japan's system of close relations and cooperation between business and Government, the ministry's proposals, and what the Japanese call administrative guidance, often have the impact of administrative direction or law. The ministry has often taken the role of economic planner.

'Request' to Exporters

Under today's directive, industries will be required to file their export schedules with the ministry every quarter to prevent a sudden and sharp rise in shipments, officials said. A committee to monitor the plan, headed by Deputy Minister Toshinobu Wada, was set up.

A ministry official said that the Government was making a "request" to the exporters, adding: "We're hoping that they'll think about the situation we're in and make appropriate decisions." The industries named by the ministry accounted for about 40 percent of exports last year.

The nation's trade surplus for the entire 1977 fiscal year, which ended March 31, reached a record high of $13 billion, compared with a $3.3 billion surplus for the previous year. The ministry expressed hope that it could trim the nation's current-account surplus to $6 billion in this fiscal year.

Booming vehicle exports last year played a major role in building up the trade surplus. The ministry said that it would attempt to keep vehicle exports this year within the level of the 4.62 million estimated to have been exported last year.

Today's announcement by the ministry was the latest in a number of moves taken by Japan and its trading partners to redress the trade imbalance. In January, after six months of negotiations, the United States and Japan announced a new trade agreement in which Japan agreed to lower its tariffs and quotas to stimulate imports. On the American side, the manufacturers of color television sets won an orderly marketing agreement to limit the number of imports of Japanese sets and the Administration devised a trigger-price system for the American steel industry to curb steel imports deemed to be too low in price.

The appreciation in the value of the yen—30 percent against the dollar since the beginning of the year—has been making Japanese exports more expensive. Toyota, for instance, has increased the price of its cars in the United States six times in the last 12 months, the latest increase announced yesterday. Despite the increased cost of Japanese products, exports have continued to rise rapidly.

The March trade surplus, for example, compared with the previous monthly high of $2.2 billion last December. Exports came to $8.78 billion, up 22.9 percent from a year earlier, while imports remained depressed at $6.33 billion, down 0.9 percent. Exports for the year amounted to a record $84.63 billion, up 19.9 percent, while imports also reached a record $71.63 billion, up 6.3 percent.

In the 1977 fiscal year, Japan had a trade surplus of $8.9 billion with the United States and a $4.6 billion surplus with the nine-nation European Common Market, both the largest ever recorded, the Government said.

April 16, 1978

The Odd Man Out
Confronting Japan's Trade Surplus

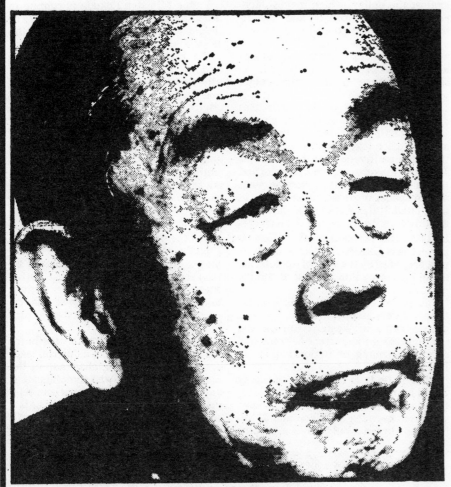

Prime Minister Fukuda: trying to cut back a dangerous trade surplus.

By CLYDE H. FARNSWORTH

WASHINGTON — In the jigsaw puzzle of world trade Japan is coming increasingly to be recognized as the piece that doesn't fit. The reasons stem from the essential structure of the Japanese economy, and there is little that Japan or the rest of the world can do in the short run to alter those conditions.

What Japan, the United States and their trading partners do hope to accomplish, however, is a reshaping of the central — and dangerous — symptom of the

Clyde H. Farnsworth is a reporter in the Washington bureau of The New York Times.

misfit, Japan's huge trading surpluses. The surpluses will be high on the agenda when Prime Minister Takeo Fukuda meets in Washington this week with President Carter and Administration officials. Mr. Fukuda will be offering assurances that his nation is doing just about everything it can to reduce the surpluses, which have over the last year led to harsh words between the two countries.

There is much at stake over the issue, for the world in general and for the United States in particular. A trade imbalance between two nations has the effect of taking jobs from the country in deficit and giving jobs to the country in surplus. In the last 12 months Japan ran a surplus with the world of $12.9 billion; its surplus with the United States was $8.9 billion.

The danger is that if Japan doesn't act to reduce the surpluses, restrictive actions will be taken by its trading partners to stop the Japanese goods from coming across their borders. This could unleash a protectionist fury, and some see an even more serious threat.

"There is an atmosphere of August 1914 about world trade today," says Sir Roy Denman, British negotiator in the Kennedy Round of trade talks and now a high trade official in the Common Market secretariat in Brussels.

The Carter Administration is basically sympathetic to Mr. Fukuda's efforts to trim the huge surplus, but the atmosphere in Congress is less friendly. Representative James Jones, an Oklahoma Democrat and the new chairman of a Congressional task force monitoring the American-Japanese trade agreement, put it this way: "Congress is looking for success in balancing trade between our country and Japan. Unless we can show progress, I am afraid that protectionist legislative action will surely result in this Congress."

Just last week the House Ways and Means Committee gave Mr. Fukuda a signal of the Congressional state of mind with a vote that just failed to override President Carter's decision on the nut and bolt industry. The President had come out against providing that industry with import relief.

The Japanese economy is very different from that of Japan's trading partners. More than any other people, they must export to survive. They have virtually no raw materials or fossil fuels. There is a local agriculture, but it does not produce enough to feed a population of 113 million. This vulnerability makes them both aggressive exporters and cautious consumers, and leads to the kind of trade surpluses that have so roiled other nations.

The Japanese have talked about a number of ways of dealing with the surpluses, up to and including strategies for vastly expanding their direct investment in the United States. One of their offerings, which has come to be known as the 7 percent solution, targets a 7 percent growth in their economy this year.

Theoretically, faster growth draws in more imports, increasing Japanese consumption and thereby narrowing the trade surplus.

"Only through a substantial increase in economic growth," says Charles L. Schultze, chairman of the Council of Economic Advisers, "can these surpluses be reduced." But growth was also projected at 7 percent for last year, and it turned out to be closer to 5 percent.

The Fukuda Government is talking about curbing Japanese exports. The Ministry of International Trade and Industry has already announced deceleration guidelines to curb overseas shipments of motor vehicles, steel, color television sets and ships so that they fall at or below the total for the fiscal year ended March 31.

But American and European officials are not too happy about such moves. They see export restraints as a variation on the protectionist theme, causing a reduction in the growth of world trade. They prefer that the Japanese act more vigorously to spur imports.

Tokyo replies that it is doing this as well, with a specially targeted program of import incentives. Foreign currency loans at low interest rates to importing companies now help finance purchases of everything from cigarettes to machine tools.

There are a host of other emergency import promotion measures, some worked out earlier this year in a bilateral agreement with Robert S. Strauss, Washington's Special Representative for Trade Negotiations. Altogether, says Trade Minister Toshio Kemote, they could produce an additional import flow of $10 billion. But American officials are wary of such figures, having been burned by optimistic trade projections from Tokyo early last year.

Though the yen has been falling a bit in recent days in response to the generally better tone of the dollar, the yen's dramatic appreciation since early last fall is also expected to have some moderating effect on the trade surplus.

The yen had risen some 20 percent against the dollar, which makes Japanese goods more expensive and, theoretically at least, less competitive in world markets. The price tags on Toyota cars and trucks went up by an average of $253 a unit, or 5.4 percent, in mid-April, the second increase in less than eight weeks.

But so far, at least, the price increases don't seem to be hurting Japan's car sales in the United States. It is uncertain at what price level Japanese cars lose their competitiveness, but the major Japanese makers — Toyota, Nissan and Honda — are seriously assessing what the prospects of direct investments in the United States would be if that point should come. Some idea of the intractability of the problem of the Japanese surpluses is gleaned from an internal report prepared by the staff of the International Monetary Fund for use at coming meetings.

The paper takes current foreign-exchange rates, assumes reasonably good growth rates in Western Europe and then forecasts the current or trade and service accounts of major nations in 1981.

What it finds is that West Germany would be running a deficit of $2 billion, Britain, France and Italy would have surpluses between $1 billion and $2 billion and Japan would have a surplus more than $4 billion.

As for the United States, its current account deficit would drop from $20 billion last year to a range of $6 billion to $7 billion. Management of the dollar poses no problem at such relatively modest levels.

The Japanese surpluses would be smaller than this year but still unwieldy.

Prime Minister Fukuda is coming to Washington with the express purpose of defusing protectionist reactions to the imbalances.

His message to the Administration and to Congress is that Japan is a loyal ally and that in the critical economic and trade sector it has taken American advice to heart by ordering rapid expansion to raise consumption of imports.

Administration officials are sympathetic. They had hectored both Japan and Germany to accept greater responsibility for the health of the world trading system. Here is the way one Administration official sizes up the situation now: "The Japanese are really making an all-out effort."

Yet the pressures the 72-year-old Mr. Fukuda is working against in the United States are enormous, as evidenced by the recent statement by Representative Jones, whose panel will analyze actions taken both by Japan to increase its imports and by the United States to promote its exports.

Keeping the protectionist fires burning in Congress are such industrial leaders as John J. Nevin, chairman of the Zenith Corporation, who complains that Japanese success in the American television market is accounted for by unfair competition, not greater Japanese efficiency. "The dumping [selling at a

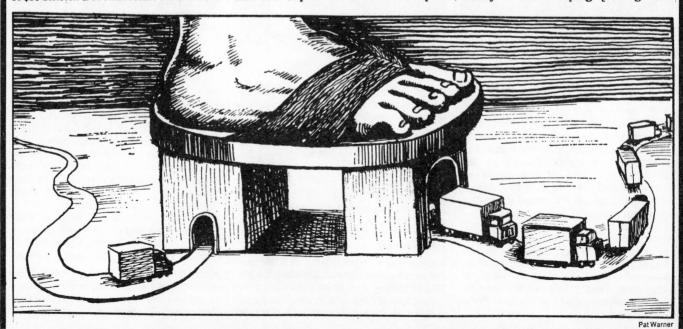

Pat Warner

lower price in the United States than the production cost in Japan] that has plagued this industry for 10 years has not been stopped," he said at his company's annual meeting last week.

Mr. Fukuda calls good relations with the United States the "pivot" of his foreign policy. And many American officials are telling the Japanese that, apart from whittling down the surpluses, one thing they can do to improve relations is to invest more in the United States.

Mr. Strauss, the special trade negotiator, recognized as much last January when he was wrapping up the trade agreement in Tokyo. Volkswagen had finally invested in the United States after years of wavering. So Mr. Strauss tried to get commitments from Japan's leading auto makers to build multimillion-dollar assembly plants in this country.

Mr. Strauss and other analysts agree that the economics of yen appreciation are pushing the Japanese in this direction. When Mr. Strauss was in Tokyo in January the dollar was at 240 yen. In March it was at 230 yen. Earlier this month the dollar fell as low as 218 yen, and it is now trading at between 225 and 230.

A move by Tokyo to cut exports has displeased the U.S.

Ryuzo Yamazaki, executive managing director of Nissan, which manufctures Datsun cars, said in an interview here that with a rate of 210 yen to the dollar there would be no turning back from a massive investment in the United States by his company, probably somewhere in the East.

Why the East? Mr. Yamazaki, who was a member of a Japanese buying mission here, explained that despite price increases the company could probably continue to supply the West Coast profitably from Japanese plants. But it would be impossible to absorb the freight cost of shipping cars to the Atlantic Coast.

As Nissan goes, so goes Toyota, according to a Japanese maxim. The two companies keep a close watch on each other.

Japanese auto makers today ship about one-fourth of their production to the United States. One out of every two cars on the West Coast is Japanese-built. If Toyota or Nissan were to manufacture in the United States on the scale necessary for full efficiency, the investment for one plant alone would be between $800 million and $1 billion. Thousands of new jobs for Americans would be created.

While trying to stimulate imports, many Japanese representatives maintain that one of the major difficulties in reducing their trade surplus is not so much Japanese protectionism as the failure of foreign companies to study the Japanese market and distribution system. The buying habits of Japanese consumers are different from those of Western consumers.

It takes time and money to sell goods in Japan, a requirement that conflicts with the pressures on Western companies to show immediate profits.

This points up one of the deeper problems: While Japan has exploded into Western industrial society, culturally it is still a light-year away.

April 30, 1978

Why American Exports Have Lagged

By ANTHONY M. SOLOMON

In 1977 Japan's surplus on current account — the difference between its sales of goods and services to foreigners and its purchases from them — reached a record $11 billion. In anticipation of the strain this imbalance would place on the international monetary and trading system, American and Japanese officials began urgent discussions on how best to reduce it.

As part of the multifaceted agreement reached in January between Robert S. Strauss, America's Special Representative for Trade Negotiations, and Nobuhiko Ushiba, Japan's Minister for External Economic Affairs, the Japanese promised to take steps, both immediately and in the future, to open their markets to imports from all nations.

For the short term, Japan agreed to enlarge its quotas on a number of products, make unilateral tariff cuts and work to increase imports of manufactured goods. For the long term, Japan agreed to make major reductions in trade barriers at the multilateral trade negotiations being held in Geneva under auspices of the General Agreement on Tariffs and Trade, in order to open Japan's markets to the degree prevalent in other industrialized nations.

To support the American effort to promote exports to Japan, the Japanese Government announced it would send a buyers' mission to the United States. Further, both nations agreed to push the work of the Trade Facilitation Committee, which they jointly established last October. Subsequently the United States announced it would develop a program to strengthen American export competitiveness. As part of this effort, the Treasury Department has made a study of the barriers that hinder sales of American-made goods in the Japanese market. We find continuing real barriers for which only the Japanese Government is responsible. At the same time, however, we find significant psychological barriers on the part of United States exporters. These psychological barriers must be assigned part of the blame for our lagging export performance.

Japanese Barriers

In spite of the recent pledge by Japan to ease import restraints on certain products of special interest to the United States, several restrictions continue to limit potential American exports to that country. The Japanese restraints are both formal and informal. They include:

● Residual import quotas in 27 product categories, 22 of which are agricultural commodities.
● Tariffs on manufactured goods that generally average several percentage points more than those of other industrial nations.
● High protective tariffs in such important sectors as computer equipment, film, photographic equipment and some semiconductors.
● Approval procedures (for imports of manufactured goods) that require product testing in Japan and then take as long as 18 months to complete.
● Strict Government procurement rules for a wide range of products from computers to radio equipment.

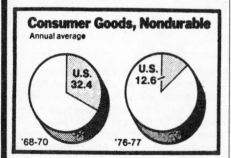

Consumer Goods, Nondurable
Annual average

U.S. 32.4   '68-70

U.S. 12.6   '76-77

● Several restrictions on imports by Japanese public corporations, such as those in the telecommunications, tobacco or railway business.

● Special import restraints for politically sensitive, labor-intensive and regionally concentrated industries.

The most tightly closed areas of the Japanese economy are the public-corporation sectors and the labor-intensive sectors, including agriculture, leather goods, textiles, banking and insurance. Competition in these industries is severely limited, and progress in opening them up to imports is extremely slow.

The United States Government will continue to press forcefully for a reduction in these Japanese tariff and nontariff barriers. We think that concessions must be made by the Japanese Government, not only at the multilateral trade negotiations in Geneva but also on a unilateral basis as Japan's contribution to the health of the international economic system.

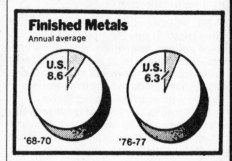

Finished Metals
Annual average

U.S. 8.6   '68-70

U.S. 6.3   '76-77

straints on imported goods remain in some areas, especially those of color

---

A Treasury study finds that U.S. companies have steadily lost market share in Japan. Not all the barriers are on Tokyo's side.

Changing Economics

Some existing barriers are slowly giving in to the laws of economics. The older basic industries, which enjoyed strong protection and generous Government support in the past, are now more open to imports. To be sure, these industries are still closely tied to the Japanese trading companies, which control distribution within the country and determine import levels for basic raw materials and energy. But the concept of "Japan Inc." is slowly losing relevance as markets for basic and semiprocessed materials are opened to import competition. Aluminum and pulp provide good examples of the new trend.

The modern manufacturing industries — sophisticated machinery, consumer durable goods, electronics and chemicals — were once totally protected in Japan, but import restraints are significantly weaker today. Domestic competition is much stronger in these industries, and the Japanese companies are highly efficient. Indeed, these companies have recently served as the engine of Japanese export growth, and they will continue to drive that growth in the foreseeable future. At the same time, domestic Japanese markets for modern

manufacturers are largely open to foreign competition. But stringent restraints on imported goods remain in some areas, especially those of color film and computers. Arbitrary Government standards and burdensome approval procedures can considerably dampen the enthusiasm of American exporters.

U.S. Businessmen

The causes of the United States trade imbalance with Japan cannot be found entirely in Japanese import restrictions. The fact is that the United States share of most of the export markets in Japan has been shrinking for a number of years. Businessmen from other countries face the same barriers to marketing in Japan as American businessmen do, but they have increased their market shares at our expense. The Americans' market loss has extended virtually across the board, affecting raw materials, fuel and food as well as manufactured products.

In raw materials, this trend is most clearly seen for a product that the United States has in abundant quantity — coal. Between 1968 and 1970 the United States supplied 58 percent of Japan's coal import needs. By 1976-77, however, this market share had fallen to 32 percent. Other exporters, especially

Australia, increased their market shares in coal at the expense of American exporters. Australia, Canada and other Pacific-basin countries achieved similar results in other commodities.

The relative decline of United States exports to Japan is even more pronounced in manufactured goods, involving every important category of such products. Compared with 1968-70, the United States share of total imports by Japan in 1976-77 fell from 32.4 to 12.6 percent for consumer nondurable goods, from 39.5 to 27.2 percent for consumer durable goods, from 61 to 51.3 percent for capital equipment and by lesser amounts in other categories.

United States exporters are losing out in the manufactured-goods market in Japan, primarily to exporters in the developing nations of Asia. Western Europe's market shares in Japan have also declined but to a smaller degree than those of the United States. And this has happened despite the fact that the United States has advantages over other suppliers: a history of close trade ties with Japan and a high-technology economy.

In part our shrinking market shares

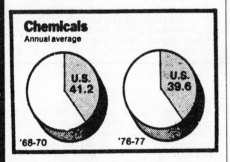

Chemicals
Annual average

U.S. 41.2 '68-70

U.S. 39.6 '76-77

may be a problem of psychological perception. Japan in the past did maintain severe restrictions on virtually all imports and foreign investment projects. But the situation has changed, and the Japanese economy is now more open in many significant sectors. Even so, many American businessmen, recalling the tremendous difficulties they once experienced, seem to ignore new export opportunities. Some businessmen are still intimidated by the image of "Japan Inc." — that of a huge, centrally directed economy that foreign businesses cannot possibly crack. Today this image is faulty. The Japanese economy is indeed huge and complex, but it is not a coordinated, xenophobic monolith where competition by foreigners is im-

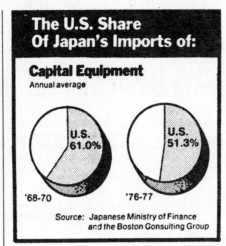

The U.S. Share Of Japan's Imports of:

Capital Equipment
Annual average

U.S. 61.0% '68-70

U.S. 51.3% '76-77

Source: Japanese Ministry of Finance and the Boston Consulting Group

possible. Case studies done for the Treasury Department by the Boston Consulting Group argue that loss of United States market shares in Japan for specific products has often resulted from lack of aggressiveness or innovation by American suppliers. Large refrigerators are an example. American suppliers dominated this market until 1973, but they actually sold fewer refrigerators each year after 1974, even though total annual domestic sales in Japan more than tripled from 1973 to 1977.

Faulty pricing and marketing strategies appear to have been a major cause of the decline in the Americans' market share.

United States businessmen also cite marketing difficulties as a reason for not selling in Japan. But a number of

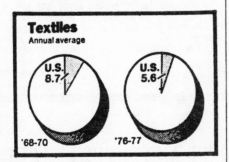

Textiles
Annual average

U.S. 8.7 '68-70

U.S. 5.6 '76-77

American companies have exported very successfully to Japan, proving that it can be done.

What is required is a strong commitment to develop the potential of the Japanese market, a willingness to incur the high cost of entry and the development of effective marketing channels.

From Here on Out

The recent surge in United States imports of Japanese goods, combined with sluggish United States exports to Japan, has drawn the attention of both governments.

The Strauss trade mission accomplished a first step in helping to open up the Japanese market for certain agricultural products and in obtaining tariff cuts on about $2 billion in imports. Still deeper cuts will be pursued in the multilateral trade negotiations in Geneva.

For United States exporters, the most meaningful feature of the Strauss-Ushiba agreement is the new willingness on the part of Japan to accept more imports.

The immediate challenge ahead is for United States businessmen to be aggressive in actively exploring, producing for and winning markets in Japan.

This means using available Export-Import Bank credits where needed. It means taking advantage of the Trade Facilitation Committee, led by Washington's Commerce Department and Tokyo's Ministry for International Trade and Industry, both to gather in-

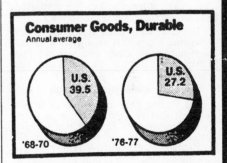

Consumer Goods, Durable
Annual average

U.S. 39.5 '68-70

U.S. 27.2 '76-77

formation and to cut red tape.

American exports to Japan will not improve simply because the Japanese remove trade barriers. Competitors from the Pacific basin and Western Europe will be ready to rush in as Japanese barriers come down.

Markets in Japan must be won. The challenge to the Japanese Government is to open the door. The challenge to American business is to walk in first, not last.

Anthony M. Solomon is Under Secretary of the Treasury for Monetary Affairs.

April 30, 1978

FUKUDA, IN U.S. TALKS, SAYS JAPAN WILL CUT HUGE TRADE SURPLUS

ECONOMIC ISSUES DOMINATE

Prime Minister Says Imports Will Be Increased and Shipments to U.S. Will Be Curbed

By CLYDE H. FARNSWORTH

WASHINGTON, May 2—Prime Minister Takeo Fukuda of Japan insisted today to members of the United States Cabinet and Congress that his country was determined to reduce huge trading surpluses by raising its growth rate to increase imports and by curbing shipments of certain major export items such as automobiles.

Mr. Fukuda arrived last night with Japan's Foreign Minister, Sunno Sonoda, and the Minister of External Economic Affairs, Nobuhiko Ushiba, for a Japanese-American conference. The Prime Minister will see President Carter tomorrow.

The talks have been dominated by the economic issues that arise from a $9 billion surplus in trade and services that Japan ran with the United States last year.

Mansfield Arranged Talks

The figures have been translated into job losses in areas hard hit by imports, raising the specter of protectionist legislation in Congress. In an effort to avoid this, Mike Mansfield, the former Senate Majority leader who is now the Ambassador to Japan, organized meetings between Prime Minister Fukuda and Congressional leaders, which took place this afternoon.

Replying to questions on trade from Senator Abraham A. Ribicoff, Democrat of Connecticut, and Representative Charles A. Vanik, Democrat of Ohio, Mr. Fukuda reported that Japan expected to reduce shipments of steel to the United States this year by 10 to 20 percent.

"Your people like our cars," he told Mr. Vanik, "but even so we will endeavor to hold sales this year to 1977 levels or less." The Japanese sold 1.9 million cars here last year.

In color television, he said, there would be a cutback in shipments this year amounting to 30 percent below 1976 levels.

In return, Mr. Fukuda urged the United States to do something about its inflation, which, he noted, had caused the dollar's international value to weaken against the Japanese currency. He had wanted a commitment from the United ship through intervention in the exchange market, but American officials told him even before the visit began he would not get this.

The Japanese had been pressing for an accord similar to one the United States reached with West Germany under which the United States actively intervenes by selling German marks to check the slide of the dollar.

Senator Jacob K. Javits, Republican of New York, came away from the closed meeting at the Capitol convinced, he told a reporter, that the Japanese really wanted to do something about their surpluses. "Fukuda realizes it's their big problem and they have to deal with it," he said

Senator Edward M. Kennedy, Democrat of Massachusetts, whose state has been especially hurt by imports, added "We're obviously hopeful of being able to export more."

The Finance Committee Chairman, Russell B. Long, a Louisiana Democrat, said that Mr. Fukuda seemed receptive to additional purchases from the United States.

He also said the point was raised that Japan should be spending more for defense, which would mean more purchases of military hardware from the United States.

Japan spends less than 1 percent of its output of goods and services on defense, compared with 5 percent for the United States.

Senator Long said the argument had been raised in the past that the Japanese constitution, written by the United States after World War II, prevented expansion of military activities. But he added: "We are no longer interested in that condition."

Japan today relies almost completely on an American defense shield. One of the suggestions to ease the burden on the United States is that Japan pick up payments for Japanese personnel on American military bases.

Mr. Fukuda had a breakfast meeting with Treasury Secretary W. Michael Blumenthal, Special Trade Representative Robert S. Strauss and other members of the economic cluster of Mr. Carter's Cabinet at Blair House, across the street from the White House. They then lunched with Secretary of State Cyrus Vance, who told reporters he too was confident of further progress in balancing the trade accounts.

"The relationship between our two countries is excellent," Mr. Vance said. "The strength of that relationship is the cornerstone or pillar on which our Asian policy is founded and it will remain so."

American officials described the meetings as "courteous but frank." The frankest points came during talks that Mr. Strauss had with Mr. Ushiba over trade specifics.

May 3, 1978

CARTER AND FUKUDA AGREE TO BOLSTER MONETARY PROCESS

Prime Minister Seeks a Sharing of Burden of Reducing Tokyo's Current Account Surplus

By CLYDE H. FARNSWORTH

WASHINGTON, May 3—President Carter talked about trade surpluses, the dollar and general world economic and political conditions with Prime Minister Takeo Fukuda of Japan today and heard about Japan's plans to accelerate purchases from the United States.

Though Mr. Carter told reporters that the three hours of meetings, including

Trade with the United States

a working lunch, "went well," neither the Japanese nor the Americans were completely satisfied with the outcome.

The two leaders announced a strengthening of monetary consultative procedures, but this was far less than a commitment for foreign exchange market intervention, which the Japanese had sought from the United States.

The new consultative procedures are little more than what already exists between the monetary officials of the two countries, Japanese and American officials agreed privately.

Japanese Withhold Specifics

The Japanese, for their part, refused to be specific in terms of the amount by which they would seek to reduce their current account (trade and services) surplus in the current fiscal year which began April 1.

In their 1977 fiscal year, the Japanese achieved a massive $14 billion surplus and last January, in a Japanese-American trade accord, a figure of $6 billion was cited as the target for the current fiscal year.

Significantly, Mr. Fukuda, declined to reaffirm the target in his talks with Mr. Carter and American economic officials, insisting that the outcome would depend not only on what Japan did, but on what the United States did as well.

Sharing of Burden Sought

Japanese officials emphasized that the value of the dollar in relation to the yen, the rate of American inflation and other forces governed by the United States were also at work in determining the size of the surpluses. In other words,

Mr. Fukuda was contending that even though Japan was willing to take specific actions of redress, the burden of the surpluses should be shared.

The Prime Minister is turning around an argument used often by the United States—that other countries share with it a responsibility to reduce American trade deficits.

To mollify the United States and try to reduce protectionist pressures in the Congress, Mr. Fukuda came here to announce that his country was stepping up its purchases of specific American goods, curbing shipments of major export items, such as automobiles, and was on track to meet the 7 percent growth target for the current fiscal year.

With a deficit spending program channeling funds into public works and other domestic consumption expenditures, the Japanese intend to spur economic growth even though they will be holding down the exports that contribute heavily toward that growth. The Japanese explain that their domestic consumption will more than compensate for the export curbs.

There are many skeptics—in the United States and Japan. In their 1977 fiscal year, the Japanese said that they would grow by 6.7 percent and actually achieved 5.3 percent.

In stepping up purchases, Japan is buying more DC-9's for its domestic airline, known by the initials TOA, paying in advance for uranium enrichment services from the United States and increasing

its stockpiling of nonferrous metals, Mr. Fukuda told American officials.

In addition, he said that Japan would be doubling its overseas development assistance in the next three years—instead of five years as originally scheduled.

In a speech tomorrow in New York before the Foreign Policy Association and the Japan Society, Mr. Fukuda will announce a $10 million grant to the United Nations to help resettle Vietnamese refugees.

Japanese sources said the Prime Minister would announce an easing of restrictions to permit some of the refugees to resettle in Japan. In the past Japan has been unwilling to admit them.

The Japanese position on the economic questions was described by Japanese Government sources as cooperative but not overly conciliatory.

"Mr. Fukuda did not come here to get scolded," said a Japanese source.

Japanese officials were disappointed by the American refusal to go as far as they wanted in a monetary accord. The Japanese had been pressing for something similar to what Washington agreed with Bonn earlier this year—active intervention to try to prevent further erosion of the dollar's value.

In other developments, the Prime Minister pledged that Japan would play a leading role in insuring the success of international trade negotiations in Geneva and a July economic summit meeting in Bonn.

May 4, 1978

Price Rises Stem Car Imports

By REGINALD STUART

Last month's sales decline for foreign cars, the first in nearly two years, may be the first tentative sign that the boom in imported models—particularly from Japan—is flagging because of higher prices.

In Greensboro, N.C., for example, Garson L. Rice, one of the South's most successful Toyota dealers, says the emphasis these days is on "the hard sell and discounting." A sign on his display window offers a $1,000 discount on higher-priced Toyota models.

Dealers in southern California, where sales of foreign cars traditionally have been strong, are maintaining an optimistic front, but admit that they are stressing product quality these days rather than price.

Pessimism in Japan

In Japan, major automobile manufacturers say they are pessimistic about export prospects, and point to a succession of price increases, which have followed sharp appreciation of the yen.

Another complicating factor: the prospect of the Japanese Government imposing quotas on the sale of Japanese cars — Toyotas, Datsuns and Hondas—in the United States.

Since the yen began to rise in the fall of 1977, Japanese car makers have raised retail prices by 20 to 22 percent. As a result, they say they are having difficulty competing effectively in the United States with American car

prices.

Honda, smallest of the so-called big three Japanese makers sold in this country, says it already has agreed to a 10 percent reduction in shipments to the United States, and its two larger competitors also are reported exercising restraint.

Exports Dropped 15 Percent

Over all, Japanese manufacturers do not expect their car shipments this year to exceed the 1977 level, which was up 28 percent from the previous year, and it could be significantly lower. The Japanese Ministry of International Trade and Industry reported recently that the nation's car exports in April dropped 15 percent to 400,000 units from March.

At the United States headquarters of the two leading foreign car distributors, Toyota and Datsun, the chief sales executives said in recent interviews that the latest price increases averaging about 5 percent—may have increased the possibility that their parent companies might locate manufacturing or assembly plants in America to reduce the cost of making and marketing their cars. Volkswagen began producing its Rabbit model in the United States this spring under similar circumstances.

As for the current market, Norman D. Lean, Toyota's vice president for general operations in the United States, said he hoped to attract new customers with a campaign to raise $1 million in contributions for the United States Olympic Committee. The money would be used to train American athletes for the 1980 summer Olympics in Moscow. Tied in to the promotion is a sweepstakes, requiring a "no obligation" visit to the showroom to register for a variety of prizes—condominiums in Aspen, his-and-hers Toyotas and trips abroad.

Dollar's Decline to Blame

One Toyota dealer, however, observed cynically that the promotion would help sell cars about as much as giving away hot dogs and Coke.

Foreign car sellers and buyers, accustomed to small cars that are low priced, sharply styled and high on gas mileage, agree that such cars simply are not cheap anymore. The declining value of the dollar in such countries as Japan and West Germany, home of Volkswagen, has caused the prices of top selling foreign cars to match those of some American vehicles.

A fully equipped Toyota Corona, for example, can sell for as much as $7,000, about the same as a modestly equipped Chevrolet Caprice or Oldsmobile Cutlass.

Further complicating life on foreign car lots, is mounting competition from domestic car makers. The push is on from company headquarters in Detroit to get small cars moving briskly this summer.

Competition Heats Up

Foreign car dealers also are pushing hard, following a 9.5 percent decline in foreign car sales in the United States last month. Citing a 12 percent year-to-year decline in unit sales last month,

to 40,255 units from 47,702, Mr. Lean of Toyota said: "Dealers are coming around to the point where they realize they're going to have to sell. It's getting competitive."

At Datsun, where sales last month fell 13 percent to 33,728 units on a year-to-year basis, Robert O. Link, the American distributor's vice president and general manager of sales, said: "I think we'll lose some traffic, but on a value analysis, I think we're still competitive."

Mr. Link, who recently disclosed in Memphis that the American Datsun distributor was placing a "near moratorium" on dealership expansion until the current uncertainty was resolved, said little could be done about car

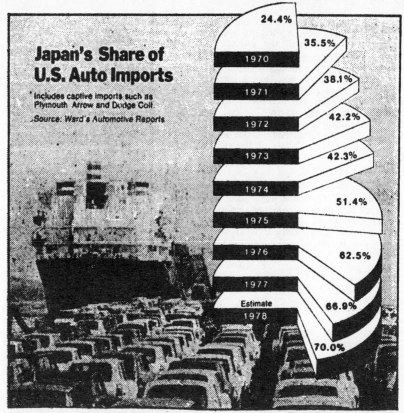

Japan's Share of U.S. Auto Imports

Includes captive imports such as Plymouth Arrow and Dodge Colt.

Source: Ward's Automotive Reports

Year	Share
1970	24.4%
1971	35.5%
1972	38.1%
1973	42.2%
1974	42.3%
1975	51.4%
1976	62.5%
1977	66.9%
Estimate 1978	70.0%

The New York Times/May 24, 1978

Toyotas roll off the assembly line for export.

Japan Air Lines

prices because importers could not dump cars (sell them below actual cost) or control the price increases.

Dealers Must Cut Corners

He said Datsun was staging sales training programs at an accelerated pace, offering new selling strategies and other types of services. But, he said, much will be left to the dealers who will have to cut corners to minimize price increases on the retail level.

"If there's a slump, there's nothing we can do about pricing," said Mr. Link. "But we have to do something."

Hiromichi Osuga, spokesman for Toyota, said in Japan that as a result of the rise in retail prices, the company's car shipments to the United States had declined 16.5 percent in April from a year earlier. Toyota, he said would consider itself successful if its 1978 exports to the United States equalled the 560,000 cars it exported there in 1977.

A spokesman for the Nissan Motor Company, which makes Datsun cars, said in Japan that shipments of Nissan's automobiles to the United States (which reached 483,216 units in 1977) registered a 10 percent decline in April.

Honda Raises Prices

The Honda Motor Company said in Japan that at the beginning of 1978 the company drafted a program for car exports to the American market calling for up to 275,000 units, up 10 percent from 1977. It has since raised retail prices by 20 percent, following the yen's sharp appreciation. A spokesman for the company said the impact of the price rise was expected to be felt in the coming months, so it would be very difficult to attain its goal this year.

The spokesman declined to make any comment on Prime Minister Takeo Fukuda's recent commitment to President Carter to hold down auto exports, or on plans by Japan's Ministry of International Trade and Industry to hold Japan's car shipments to the United States at or below 1977 levels.

May 24, 1978

Wider Japan Surplus Expected

By HENRY SCOTT-STOKES

TOKYO, June 9 — Kiichi Miyazawa, head of the economic planning agency, and Nobuhiko Ushiba, Minister for External Economic Affairs, leave for Western capitals this weekend for further talks on the simmering dispute over this nation's huge trade surpluses.

The soaring trade surpluses will break more records this year, according to a forecast made by Mr. Miyazawa's agency this week. In the calendar year 1978, the total will be about $23 billion, according to the estimate, compared with a 1977 level of $17.3 billion, also a record.

The latest forecast, based on a May 20 survey of 33 big trading companies, contrasts with an earlier official estimate — for the fiscal year ending March 1979 — that the trade surplus would drop to $13.5 billion. Results for calendar and fiscal years can naturally vary widely, but the latest prediction suggests that the figures for the fiscal year that began in April will be disappointing from a Japanese viewpoint.

Arguments to Be Advanced

With the new estimates in mind, the two Japanese officials will put up a spirited defense of national interests based on the following arguments, advanced in telephone interviews:

¶Real Japanese economic growth, after adjustment for inflation, will be about 7 percent this fiscal year, the highest of any big industrial country, raising the nation's total output of goods and services close to $1,000 billion, or about half the American total.

¶Japan will restrain exports of staple trade items as promised by Prime Minister Takeo Fukuda when he met with President Carter in early May. Sales of cars, steel, television sets and ships will all be held back.

¶Even if Japan's surplus in trade and payments on current account (including trade, service and transfer items) are high, they will be drastically reduced by greatly increased export of long-term capital.

These points will be made by Mr. Miyazawa and Mr. Ushiba first in Washington early next week and then at a ministerial-level meeting of the Organization for Economic Cooperation and Development to be held in Paris on June 14 and 15. The O.E.C.D. meeting is to have the two Japanese ministers as its co-chairmen.

There is nothing especially new in the Japanese arguments, but a subtle change of emphasis is apparent. It is now conceded that a higher Japanese growth rate and voluntary controls on exports will in fact make no impact on the huge trade surpluses.

Exports to the United States alone, for example, rose 35 percent in May to $2.2 billion, with sales of cars up 55 percent in dollar terms.

The Japanese fall-back position is that exports of long-term capital will be increased to cut back the surplus on overall balance of payments, which includes both current-account and long-term capital items.

Mr. Miyazawa said that the debate on Japan's position should "not concentrate on the current account we should discuss the basic balance."

The difference may be judged by 1977 figures. Last calendar year Japan's payments surplus on current account was $10.9 billion, but its basic balance, after $3.2 billion in long-term capital exports, was just $7.7 billion.

Controls Loosened

This year, the traditionally restrictive Ministry of Finance has dramatically loosened its taut controls to allow a greatly increased outflow of long-term capital, largely through the issuing by foreigners of yen-denominated bonds. Foreign yen issues here, which climbed to the equivalent of $1.47 billion last year, may this year soar to around $4.5 billion.

Japan, Mr. Miyazawa said, is "in a similar situation to West Germany." That is, Tokyo has become a major source of international capital by virtue of low interest rates and a very strong yen.

Mr. Ushiba, in a more cautious vein, said that Japan must still underline efforts to cut back its surplus on current acount, but he also stressed the greater contribution that Japan would make to world growth by increasing economic aid.

Robert S. McNamara, World Bank president, who is on a visit here, yesterday supported Japan's aid efforts, saying he believed Japan would achieve its goal of doubling official development aid from about $1.7 billion in 1977 to $3.4 billion by 1980.

June 10, 1978

Honda Refuses to Cut Its Auto Exports to U.S.

Motorcycle parts being manufactured at the Honda Motor Company.

Consulate General of Japan, N.Y.

A vice president of the Honda Motor Company said yesterday that the company planned to adhere to its original goal of selling 260,000 cars in this country even though the Japanese Government had asked it to limit car imports to last year's level of 223,000 to help reduce the United States trade deficit with Japan.

Michihiro Nishada, the executive vice president of Honda, in an impromptu news conference here, acknowledged that Japanese officials had made the request to keep exports to the United States to 1977 levels. He said the officials had "left it up to us" to decide what to do and that the company had decided to stay with its original target.

Mr. Nishada, who with other top company officials met with security analysts here, also said that Honda was seriously considering constructing an auto assembly plant in the United States but had not made a final decision.

Honda Auto Sales In the U.S.

In thousands

1975	102
1976	
1977	223
1978	260*

*Estimate

The New York Times/June 21, 1978

The executive drew a square on a tablecloth in one of the dining rooms of the New York Society of Security Analysts to illustrate that the company had an option to buy 270 acres next to the 217-acre site in Marysville, Ohio. The company is constructing a plant to assemble 60,000 motorcycles a year at the site. The plant is expected to employ about 500 persons.

Mr. Nishada also said the company planned to make an effort to import more from the United States to help offset the American trade deficit, which in May ran 36 percent above May 1977 despite attempts by the Japanese Government to cut exports to the United States.

Honda has moved up to third place among the car exporters to this country in the last five months, surpassing Volkswagen. The largest exporter is Toyota, followed by Datsun.

June 21, 1978

Court Calls Import Duty Optional, Probably Averting a Price Spiral

By WARREN WEAVER Jr.

WASHINGTON, June 21—The Supreme Court today averted an increase in the prices Americans pay for Japanese electronic products that would almost certainly have affected many other imports and touched off an inflationary spiral.

The Justices ruled unanimously that the Secretary of the Treasury was not required by a 1897 law to impose a "countervailing duty" on Japanese television and stereo sets even though Japan gives preferential tax treatment to such exports.

The Department of Justice had warned the Court that raising this new tariff barrier "would risk a significant breakdown in international trading agreements and retaliatory actions from our trading partners" and undermine flexibility in pending multilateral trade negotiations.

Others Would Have Acted

For the consumer, today's decision blocked an otherwise certain price increase in Sony, Panasonic and similar products that would have spread, as other industries sought protection under the alternative interpretation of the law, to steel, automobiles, Japanese cameras, French wine and most imports from West Germany, the Netherlands and Canada.

In particular, the steel industry was expected to act, as both the United States Steel Corporation, the industry giant, and the Bethlehem Steel Corporation, the No. 2 producer, had joined the suit, brought by the Zenith Radio Corporation, as friends of the court. Neither steel company had immediate comment on today's ruling.

At the Zenith headquarters in Glenview, Ill., a spokesman said that "we are naturally very disappointed" and predicted that the company would have no further comment in light of the unanimity of the ruling.

According to the Department of Commerce, about half of current American imports — or $50 billion worth — comes from countries such as Japan that exempt their exports from indirect taxes. A decision subjecting all this trade to countervailing duties could thus have raised prices here by an estimated $10 billion or more.

15 Percent Rise Sought

The case decided today (Zenith Radio Corp. v. U.S., No. 77-539) represented an attempt by Zenith to meet Japanese competition by forcing up import prices by approximately 15 percent, the size of the Japanese excise tax from which such Japanese exports are exempt.

For the previous decade or more, mounting Japanese imports had worried domestic television manufacturers, finally capturing about a third of the American market. Under heavy economic pressure, several United States manufacturers have been taken over by foreign companies or merged with other domestic producers, but a substantial active industry remains here that could have benefited considerably had the Court ruled for Zenith.

The unanimous opinion written by Associate Justice Thurgood Marshall turned largely on the intent of the turn-of-the-century Congress that approved the first broad requirement for imposition of countervailing duties.

The 1897 statute ordered the Treasury Department to levy an equal countervailing duty when any foreign country pays a "bounty or grant" to an exporting manufacturer. Zenith contended that the remission of the 15 percent excise tax on electronic products by Japan constituted such a bounty or grant.

For the last 80 years, the Treasury Department had interpreted this law as requiring imposition of a duty only when the exporting country gives the exporter a benefit that exceeds the value of the remitted tax. Justice Marshall wrote that "this long-standing and consistent administrative interpretation is entitled to considerable weight."

'Shared Assumptions' Cited

"In deciding in 1898 that a nonexcessive remission of indirect taxes did not result in the type of competitive advantage that Congress intended to counteract," Mr. Marshall said, "the department was clearly acting in accordance with the shared assumptions of the day as to the fairness and economic effect of that practice."

"The theory underlying the department's position was that a foreign country's remission of indirect taxes did not constitute a subsidization of that country's exports," he added. "Rather, such remission was viewed as a reasonable measure for avoiding double taxation of exports — once by the foreign country and once upon sale in this country."

Noting that Congress has since reenacted the statute five times without modification and that the Treasury position was incorporated in the General Agreement on Tariffs and Trade in 1947, Mr. Marshall concluded that "the Secretary's interpretation of the countervailing duty statute is as permissible today as it was in 1898."

A 1970 request by Zenith that the countervailing duty be imposed was rejected by the Commissioner of Customs in 1976. Zenith then filed suit in the Customs Court, which ruled for the corporation, largely on the basis of a 1903 Supreme Court decision dealing with sugar imports from Czarist Russia. The Court of Customs and Patent Appeals reversed that decision by a 3-to-2 vote, finding that the 1903 case dealt with a different and more complicated trade issue.

The Supreme Court also handed down today two unanimous decisions involving class actions that postponed a plaintiff's right to appeal a denial of class-action status until after his trial is over.

In one case (Coopers & Lybrand v. Livesay, No. 76-1836), purchasers of securities suing an accounting firm contended they should be allowed to appeal a denial of class certification directly because they would not be able to pursue their claims individually.

The United States Court of Appeals for the Eighth Circuit agreed, but the Supreme Court reversed that decision, saying that requiring the courts to decide such a question separately "would have a seriously debilitating effect on the administration of justice."

In the other (Gardner v. Westinghouse Broadcasting Co., No. 77-560), the Justices ruled that an order denying class status to a woman who charged an employer with discrimination based on sex was also not appealable separately. Associate Justice John Paul Stevens wrote both opinions.

June 22, 1978

Japan Asks
For Accord On Trade

Seeks Concessions Before Bonn Parley

By HENRY SCOTT-STOKES

TOKYO, June 27 — Nobuhiko Ushiba, Japan's top negotiator at the current world trade talks, warned today that action was needed soon on Japanese concessions to insure the success of the talks.

Mr. Ushiba, who is also Japan's Minister of External Economic Affairs, warned that "we don't have much time left" and asked for "the cooperation of the ministers concerned."

The urgency of Mr. Ushiba's appeal, which followed a Cabinet meeting to discuss the trade issue, stems from the fact that broad agreement on a "package" of tariff cuts and other items by the United States, Japan and the European Economic Community is due be-

fore next month's economic summit meeting in Bonn. The current negotiations, being held here under the auspices of the General Agreement on Tariffs and Trade, have become known as the "Tokyo Round."

Mr. Ushiba faces bitter resistance, however, from Japan's nationalistic Ministry of Agriculture, as well as the Ministry of International Trade and Industry, at which his appeal was mainly aimed.

The key remaining points to be settled, officials said, are Japanese import quotas on oranges, which the United States wants raised, and Japanese tariffs on 15 industrial items such as computers and color film, which the United States wants cut. Japan's powerful agricultural lobby, which includes a large minority of conservative members of the Diet, or Parliament, from rural areas, is violently opposed to the lifting of quotas on oranges, taking it as a forerunner to the relaxation of other import restrictions.

The package is being put together by Mr. Ushiba, Robert S. Strauss, Presi-

dent Carter's trade representative and domestic coordinator of anti-inflation efforts, and Wilhelm Haferkamp, representing the European Economic Community.

The final agreement is to be presented to heads of government at the July 16-17 summit meeting in Bonn. But some Japanese officials are already warning that the trade issues will not be resolved by the time of the summit.

Prime Minister Takeo Fukuda is known to believe that a failure in the current trade talks could be fatal to Japan, leading to a bout of world protectionism in which his nation, more dependent on trade than the others involved, would suffer most.

A refusal to concede to the largely symbolic actions on oranges and industrial items demanded by Mr. Strauss, he is said to feel, would be especially untenable given the huge trade surplus that Japan continues to run up. This year's surplus is expected to reach $2 bilion.

June 28, 1978

Japanese Leader Attacks
the U.S. On Trade Issues

By HENRY SCOTT-STOKES

Economic Planning Chief Sees a Lack of Direction

TOKYO, July 8 — The head of Japan's Economic Planning Agency says that this country has been disappointed with American leadership preceding a major seven-nation economic conference to be held next weekend in Bonn.

The planning chief, Kiichi Miyazawa, who is generally regarded here as the man who runs the economy for Prime Minister Takeo Fukuda, also said during an interview that he regrets the failure of

Congress to enact energy legislation and is fearful of a protectionist trend in the United States after elections this fall.

In unusually severe remarks in advance of the July 16-17 session in West Germany, Mr. Miyazawa expressed "great disappointment that President Carter seems to be going to Bonn empty-handed." The Japanese official said Mr. Carter and his trade negotiator, Robert S. Strauss, "are really unfortunate, they don't have anything to give, it's all take."

Energy Bill Called Long Overdue

The normally cautious Mr. Miyazawa accused Congress of "dragging its feet on

the energy bill," which he described as long overdue under the terms of a communique agreed to in January by Japan's Minister of External Economic Affairs, Nobuhiko Ushiba, and Mr. Strauss.

In the interview, which took place at his office, Mr. Miyazawa called on President Carter to get the energy bill back on the road by a bold statement at the economic conference, which Mr. Carter will attend together with heads of government from Japan and five West European nations.

"We would certainly hope that the President will tell the Bonn meeting that by a certain date the U.S. will have its own comprehensive energy program," Mr. Miyazawa said, stressing the words "by a certain date".

Reflecting the disappointment of Japanese business and government leaders over the delay in enactment of the energy bill, which the Ushiba-Strauss communique said should be passed in 90 days, Mr. Miyazawa also said the American economy was being mismanaged.

"Not only does your Government have the energy bill to complete," he said, speaking in English, "but you have a big budget deficit of the order of $60 billion, which is going to climb further and you now have inflation of 7 percent, which is also going up."

Mr. Miyazawa had few kind words for the United States, but he did try to avoid direct criticism of President Carter. "It's not his doing that Congress is holding up the energy bill," he said.

He described the attitude of American negotiators, mainly Mr. Strauss, in advance of the Bonn meeting as "very tough," adding that "they are very much worried that they may lose in the Congress" early next year when they present a package of tariff cuts and other measures negotiated in the Tokyo round of the trade talks under the General Agreement on Tariffs and Trade. The package is due to be approved in outline in Bonn, with the exception of some agricultural items.

"If Congress goes against the package, then the whole thing will collapse there," Mr. Miyazawa said. "The Administration

is really worried."

Asked whether it was not unusual for a Japanese minister to criticize the United States in such unvarnished terms, Mr. Miyazawa, who is a former Foreign Minister, said, "If I were at the Foreign Ministry, it might be a different affair, but in my present position I can speak frankly."

He added that he was sure his American friends appreciated frankness, and he said, "My belief in American democracy presses me to speak without reservation."

His criticism of the United States extended to the trade unions. "The labor unions used to be free traders, like the United Auto Workers," he said. "Those were the days when America had a great edge over any other country. Now that industry is losing ground, it's a different matter and the same is true of your steel workers."

"Youngstown was the beginning of the whole thing," he said, alluding to the closing of a steel plant at Youngstown, Ohio last autumn in the face of Japanese competition.

Fear of Protectionism Expressed

Repeatedly, Mr. Miyazawa came back to the topic of the Bonn meeting and the danger of protectionism.

"At the Bonn summit, if we stopped rowing the boat, then the boat would not stay still in the river," he said. "It would stand a real chance of going backward,

back to a waterfall of protectionism."

His remarks reflect anxiety in Japan over a number of matters that he did not mention, notably Japan's unwillingness to increase farm-product imports from the United States, the surge of the yen close to a rate of 200 to the dollar, a corresponding tendency for the Japanese economy to dip, and the expanding Japanese trade and payments surplus.

Japanese leaders are steeling themselves for a clash with the United States after the fall elections when Congress ends its recess. The two governments are hoping that the trade figures will have turned around by then, but so far, despite Japanese restrictions on major categories accounting for over 50 percent of exports, they show little sign of doing so.

This year to the end of next March, when the Japanese fiscal year ends, Japan will have a record trade surplus of $23 billion with the world, the Economic Planning Agency predicted recently, with nearly half the surplus in trade with the United States.

In addition a government forecast that Japan will have a current account surplus, including exports, imports and service items, of $6 billion is likely to be a wild underestimate, according to the unofficial Japan Economic Research Center which put the expectable surplus at $18 billion, up from $14 billion in 1977.

July 9, 1978

Japan Plans Imports to Trim Surplus

TOKYO, July 12 (Reuters) — Japan said today that it planned to trim at least $4 billion from its huge trade surplus by initiating emergency imports, including $1 billion worth of enriched uranium ore from the United States. Of the amount, $1.2 billion is definitely set, and the rest is almost certain.

The announcement came on the eve of Prime Minister Takeo Fukuda's departure for the economic summit meeting of leading non-Communist industrialized nations in Bonn, where Japan's record trade surplus is expected to come under attack again.

A spokesman for the Government's Economic Planning Agency said that the $4 billion estimate included all the emergency imports the Government could think of to cut the surplus.

One official, Shintaro Abe, the chief Cabinet secretary, said at a news conference that the Government had already decided on $1.2 billion of emergency imports, including $680 million

for civilian aircraft, $120 million for uranium ore and $220 million for iron ore pellets.

An additional $2.2 billion is considered "virtually certain" and would include advance payment of $1 billion to the United States for uranium ore enrichment, $430 million for crude-oil stockpiling and $597 million for ships built by Japanese subsidiaries abroad.

Japan also hopes to spend $500 million for aircraft leasing.

Japan exported $20.42 billion worth of goods more than it imported in the 1977 fiscal year, which ended last March. The surplus included about $9 billion to the United States alone.

Private economists said that the new measures announced today appeared far too small to make substantial cuts in the balance of trade, even though Japan believes its surplus will drop to $13.5 billion in 1978.

Because Japan's exports are still in-

creasing despite a sharp rise in the value of the yen, a leading private economic research organization here forecast the 1978 surplus could exceed $24 billion.

The $4 billion is also $6 million below the amount Toshio Komoto, the Minister of International Trade and Industry, last month said was needed to made a real dent in the surplus.

Imports Up 8.1% in Half-Year

TOKYO, July 12 (AP) — Japan's dollar-based licensed imports for the first half of this year rose 8.1 percent from the first six months of 1977 to some $38.06 billion, the Ministry of International Trade and Industry said today.

Dollar-based licensed imports in June this year were $6.89 billion, up 3.4 percent from $6.67 billion in May and up 15.1 percent from May 1977, the ministry said.

July 13, 1978

7 INDUSTRIAL NATIONS PLEDGE TO SPUR JOBS, CURB INFLATION; U.S. READY TO CUT OIL IMPORTS

CARTER IS 'PLEASED'

Aid for Dollar Is Goal— Tokyo to Sell Less as Bonn Sets Growth

By FLORA LEWIS

BONN, July 17 — Leaders of the largest industrial democracies agreed today on a modest package of moves to help combat worldwide unemployment "without rekindling inflation."

President Carter, like the six other heads of government at the fourth annual economic summit conference, said that he was "very pleased with the results." Later, an American spokesman said the President thought it was more productive than last year's London summit meeting, where far more ambitious promises were made but never delivered on, because careful consideration of the individual pledges of action from the seven made it more likely the pledges could be fulfilled.

The key commitments were the American promise to strengthen the dollar by saving oil and fighting inflation, Japan's affirmation that it would buy more foreign products and sell fewer exports and West Germany's agreement to prime its economic pumps and spur growth.

Better 'Than Expected'

Chancellor Helmut Schmidt of West Germany, Prime Minister James Callaghan of Britain and others said the results were much better "than expected," and Mr. Schmidt said several govern-

ments, including his own, had gone further to contribute to the package than they had planned. In addition to the United States, West Germany, Britain, Japan, Italy, France and Canada took part in the meeting. In addition, Roy Jenkins, president of the Common Market's executive commission, was present.

But, except perhaps for Japan, the specific commitments made by each country were no larger than had been discussed in preparatory meetings in recent months. A high American official pointed out that the two-day meeting was "not a negotiation, but a discussion," and that the leaders had not actually "made concessions".

The seven leaders appeared, two hours late, to report on their views in turn to reporters who had been assembled long before in Bonn's angular, new, brown-glass municipal theater.

Most of the reporters had had no chance to get anywhere near them during the summit sessions and activities, so stern were the security precautions, with green-uniformed troops manning light tanks and machine guns in sandbagged emplacements to protect all Government ministries. The journalists were conveyed from a temporary press center in nearby Parliament offices, where they had watched the proceedings on closed-circuit television, to the theater in army buses, many painted with a large red cross.

The final communiqué was not ready. Mr. Schmidt, his sometimes scolding face relaxed in evident relief and pleasure that all had gone well, without serious incident, apologized, saying participants had been working very hard until the last moment on wording the one summit document not drafted beforehand, a declaration establishing sharp new sanctions against countries that give refuge to aircraft hijackers.

Only Fukuda Stern-Faced

The European and North American leaders, brought up in a culture where

people smile to convince others of their confidence, were all beaming. Only Prime Minister Takeo Fukuda of Japan was stern-faced and tight-lipped.

The crux of the "comprehensive strategy" laid down by the seven was the endorsement of the once-contested principle that both the strongest and the weakest of the industrialized trading nations must "contribute" to restoring balance to the world economy by changing its own economic course. Each of the seven countries made a separate declaration of what it planned to do, in addition to the joint commitment to cooperate in solving what the communiqué called "a long-term problem, which will only yield to sustained efforts."

None of them added up its promises into an overall growth target, however, as they had all done in vain in London last year.

Japan offered the most precise new measures. Mr. Fukuda said with a sigh that his country's balance of payments was "too good, and that is the cause of our headache." Nevertheless, he promised to reduce Japan's huge trade surplus within a year.

He said Japan would:

¶Seek to increase domestic demand for the 1978 fiscal year by 1.5 percent above last year's performance — in other words, actually achieving the 1977 goal. In the next month or two, he forecast "appropriate measures" if trends did not show the target was being met.

¶Take a temporary and "extraordinary step" of voluntarily restraining exports to keep the volume for the 1978 fiscal year "at or below" 1977. American sources said there were specific promises to hold back sales of cars, ships, steel, and television sets, although the dollar value of exports probably will not decline for some time because of the increased value of the yen.

¶Make "emergency purchases" of enriched uranium, civilian aircraft and crude oil to keep down its trading sur-

Trade with the United States

plus. The promise provoked reports of an understanding with President Carter to buy Alaskan crude, but American officials said nothing had been specifically settled on that issue. The United States is presently legally barred from exporting Alaskan oil.

¶Double its official aid to developing countries within three years.

Previous Pledges Repeated

The United States, on the other hand, promised to reduce its dependence on imported oil. President Carter repeated previous pledges that oil-import savings of 2.5 million barrels a day would be achieved by 1985, and that measures "will be in effect" to achieve this "by the end of the year." By 1980, he promised, American oil prices will be raised to the world level.

However, there were no public pledges, and American officials insisted that there had been no private ones either, on what steps the President would take if Congress failed to pass his full energy bill, including the controversial import equalization tax.

The American aides said passage of the first four points of the bill would bring import savings up to 1.8 million barrels daily, and the noncontroversial parts of the fifth point would make the total 2 to 2.3 million, implying that executive action could then cover the difference.

But the government heads did not exact details from each other on how they would meet their undertakings, the officials said, leaving it up to each to decide later just which steps would be taken. This applies to Mr. Carter's oil promise as well as to Mr. Schmidt's promise of economic expansion and most of Mr. Fukuda's pledges.

United States energy commitments also specified a one-billion-barrel strategic oil reserve, a two-thirds increase in coal production, and a ceiling of 0.8 in the ratio between the growth of gross national product and the growth in energy demand. The other countries made a similar pledge to hold down the rate at which economic expansion increases their appetite for energy, a reversal of previous trends.

West Germany said it would have measures prepared for its Parliament by the end of August amounting to "up to 1 percent of gross national product" (about $6 billion) in increased growth and demand stimulation. One report said Mr. Schmidt had offered to pledge additional overall growth of five-tenths of 1 percent, but the other countries preferred the communiqué's final wording, which mentioned only "quantitatively substantial" measures in hopes that Bonn could do better than that.

French Offer Slight Easing

France, which has been on a deflationary austerity program that is beginning to pinch severely, offered a slight easing with an increase of five-tenths of 1 percent of gross national product in its 1978 budget deficit.

Canada, still obliged to counter inflation, said it would try to expand employment and increase output up to 5 percent.

Britain and Italy, both emerging from grievous inflationary and currency troubles, modestly pledged to keep on present courses.

While none of these plans represented dramatic new steps, the acceptance that no single country or group of countries could be expected to bear the brunt of an overall effort was the source of the intense satisfaction among the leaders.

Once again, although with appropriate hedging and escape clauses for their various domestic constituencies, they resolved to ward off protectionism, promote a balanced expansion of trade, stabilize currency relations, create more jobs and fight inflation.

As Chancellor Schmidt, the host, pointed out at a brief appearance of the group before reporters, all the leaders govern "democratic states and all have to get parliamentary majorities."

The meeting's emphasis on relations with developing countries was put on improving the investment climate, a discreet way of noting that they will have to be enabled to provide the markets for further growth among the industrialized group, and, therefore room will have to be found for their exports.

Among themselves, the national leaders managed to generate an impression of euphoria at their demonstrated ability to open sensitive domestic issues to discussion with foreigners, and accept close mutual responsibilities. They will meet again, probably in Tokyo, at "an appropriate time" next year, they announced.

July 18, 1978

Wakayama Plate Mill of the Sumitomo Metal Industries, Ltd.

Chapter 9

The Steel Controversy

Steel was one of the few trade issues about which the United States and Japan reached agreement during 1977-78. Steel became an issue of contention in October 1977 when U.S. Treasury Department ruled that five Japanese exporters of carbon steel were "dumping" their products on the American market, that is, selling at prices below cost. The five companies were Kawasaki Steel Corporation, Kobe Steel, Ltd., Nippon Kokan, the Nippon Steel Corporation and Sumitomo Metal Industries. To avoid strong protectionist reactions from the American steel industry, the Carter Administration sought self-imposed temporary steel export quotas from the Japanese.

The Japanese government immediately promised a substantial reduction of steel exports to the United States. All importers of Japanese steel were, at the same time, required to post bonds of 32% of the declared value of any new shipments to the U.S. The Japanese steel companies accused of dumping refused to reveal production costs, but it was proved that they were selling at approximately $75 per ton below a cost-justified price. Fumihiko Togo, Japan's ambassador to the United States, relayed the extreme displeasure of the Japanese steel industry with American laws. These laws, the industry felt, would impair competition when the situation really called for improvements in American steel production techniques.

The major U.S. steel companies suffer from outmoded plants and production methods. With sizable decreases in their recent earnings, they are not now in a position to pump capital into rebuilding their factories. By 1976-77 steel imported from Japan had amounted to 20% of the total American steel market and accounted for 60% of all steel imported to the U.S. Japanese steel plants, rebuilt after World War II, are probably the most efficient in the world. In addition, labor costs in the Japanese industry are thought to be half of those in the United States. According to U.S. government figures, American labor costs were $136.53 per metric ton of steel while Japan pays only $62.99.

In December 1977 the United States, Japan and several Western European nations met in Paris to resolve some of the worldwide problems facing the steel industry. A plan was adopted to monitor trends in international trade in steel. It was also agreed that older, inefficient steel plants needed to be phased out.

Ninety days after their initial ruling on dumped steel, the American Treasury Department issued guidelines on market prices for steel. Under a system of "trigger prices," imported steel selling below an average of $330 per metric ton would trigger a

203

Treasury investigation into whether the steel products were priced below the legal levels. Six months after the U.S. Treasury Department's first ruling on dumping, the U.S. International Trade Commission confirmed that importation of carbon steel plate from Japan was detrimental to the American producers of the same product. Thus the Commission set increased duties on foreign steel imports to afford American producers a more competitive standing in the domestic market. In May 1979 the Treasury Department determined that the five Japanese companies accused of dumping steel had, in fact, dumped $175 million worth on the American market annually since the early 1970s.

The Steel Controversy

U.S. Rules 5 Japanese Exporters Dump Steel on American Market

By CLYDE H. FARNSWORTH

WASHINGTON, Oct. 3—The Treasury Department, in its first ruling in memory against "dumping" by the Japanese steel industry, issued a finding today that five exporters of carbon steel plate were selling in the American market at prices substantially below their costs.

The decision, a preliminary one, came amid rising protests from the domestic steel industry and a newly formed steel caucus in Congress demanding import restraints in the wake of increasing layoffs in the industry.

Reacting to this pressure, the Carter Administration indicated last Friday that it was considering negotiating temporary steel import quotas with the Common Market and Japan in efforts to head off more radical protective action by Congress.

The antidumping finding, though limited in this case to a specific product, could have the effect of reducing imports by sharply increasing the American tariff on the structural steel that comes from the five Japanese suppliers.

In today's administrative action, which is still subject to further hearings over a period of 90 days before it becomes final, the Treasury assessed a "dumping" duty of 32 percent, which compares with the present 7½ percent tariff on carbon steel plate. Last year the United States imported $174 million worth of carbon steel from Japan.

One further administrative action, a finding by another Government agency,

the International Trade Commission, that there has been injury to the domestic industry, is required over a subsequent 90-day period before the antidumping duty would actually go on the tariff books.

But as of today, importers of the Japanese plate are required to post a bond equivalent to 32 percent of the declared value of new shipments, to show the money is there to pay the higher duties, if they finally obtain. This itself could be a deterrent to new shipments.

Today's action came as the result of a complaint filed by the Oregon Steel Mills division of the Gilmore Steel Corporation. The United States Steel Corporation, the industry giant that has filed a much broader antidumping complaint against the entire Japanese industry, issued a statement today in Pittsburgh noting that the Treasury's finding supported its case. The statement went on to say: "Unfair trade practices have given foreign steel producers an advantage which has resulted in the loss of almost 20 percent of the domestic steel market this year."

Within the last two weeks an antidumping complaint covering merchant rods from France was filed by the Georgetown Steel Corporation. Meanwhile, it was learned that broader antidumping charges against the European industry are being prepared by at least two large domestic producers.

A Japanese economic spokesman in Washington said his government was "certainly concerned" about the development but would have to study it very carefully before issuing any formal comment. The spokesman insisted that exports were not the sole cause of the American industry's problems.

This view is shared by President Carter and others in the Administration who are preparing a package of measures that may include some import relief as well as investment tax credits and Government guaranteed loans to help the domestic industry improve its efficiency.

President Carter's Special Trade Representative, Robert S. Strauss, notes that in the last two decades the world steel industry has been completely restructured, except in the United States.

President Carter is expected to invite soon a group of steel industry specialists, from labor, management, financial and other organizations, to a series of White House meetings to discuss the industry's problems.

While issuing its antidumping ruling against the five Japanese steelmakers—the Nippon Steel Corporation, Nippon Kokan K.K., Sumitomo Metal Industries., the Kawasaki Steel Corporation and Kobe Steel Ltd.—the Treasury today ruled against a complaint by the Armco Steel Corporation against an Italian company allegedly getting what Armco said was "extraordinary subsidization" of exports.

The Terni Steel Company of Italy supplies an electrical steel, known as silicon steel, to the American market. Armco said it intended to appeal the Treasury's decision to the United States Customs Court.

In ruling against the Japanese, Treasury officials said they got little cooperation from the Japanese steel companies in seeking to determine what their true costs were.

The Treasury figured that a reasonable price for Japanese steel in the American market should be $285 a ton. The Japanese are charging only $210 a ton for the carbon steel plate, according to the Treasury figures.

October 4, 1977

Japanese See a Sharp Reduction In Shipments of Steel to U.S.

Importer Says Treasury's Finding of Dumping in U.S. Will Virtually End His Taking of Orders

By AGIS SALPUKAS

Officials of several large Japanese trading companies said yesterday that the Treasury Department's finding of "dumping" would severely cut imports of steel from Japanese producers.

As of Monday's preliminary decision, importers of Japanese plate steel must post bonds equivalent to 32 percent of the declared value of new shipments. One official of a major Japanese trading company, which is a large importer of Japanese steel, said in an interview that this level was "very inhibiting" and that his company would virtually stop taking orders for Japanese steel.

The official did not want his company or himself to be identified.

If the preliminary finding of the Treasury Department is upheld, the money from the bonds would be used to pay the higher duties on the steel. A decision is expected in six months.

Japanese Unhappy

Japanese officials, unhappy with the finding, pointed out that the decision was based on estimates by American officials and analysts of what it costs the Japanese mills to produce steel. The Japanese

companies named in the finding—the Nippon Steel Corporation, Nippon Kokan K.K., Sumimoto Metal Industries, the Kawasaki Steel Corporation and Kobe Steel Ltd.—refused to disclose production costs to the investigators.

Fumihiki Togo, Japan's Ambassador to the United States, said last night in Cleveland that the Japanese steel industry was "very unhappy with your laws."

"The right remedy for an industry faced with import competition," he said, "is to become more competitive."

American steel officials, who generally reacted with enthusiasm to the decision, said in interviews that the Treasury finding would enable them to do just that —become more competitive with the Japanese.

The finding of dumping (selling abroad cheaper than at home) affects only carbon steel plate, which is produced in rolling mills. The plates, which can run as large as 12 feet by 40 feet by 6 inches thick, are used in heavy construction, shipbuilding, offshore oil rigs and other heavy products such as construction machinery.

For the first seven months of 1977 about 4,461,000 tons of carbon steel plate were sold in the United States market with 21.4 percent coming from the imports and 8 percent, or 359,000 tons, shipped from Japan.

G. H. McClure, senior vice president of commercial steel at the Armco Steel Corporation, said in an interview yesterday that the action by the Treasury Department would take pressure off two

of his company's plate-rolling mills—one in Houston and the other in Ashland, Ky.

He said that both mills shipped to the Southwest and West, where the Japanese were selling their steel at $60 to $70 lower than the average of $325 a ton that Armco was charging its customers. The 32 percent bond, he said, "evens things out."

Other Foreign Mills

He added that the decision would "undoubtedly" lead to the recall of some of the laid-off workers at the mills. About 150 workers were laid off at the Ashland plant and 1,400 at the Houston plant, he said, primarily because Japanese competition had cut into their markets.

Mr. McClure and other steel officials conceded that producers from countries such as Britain, Italy, West Germany, South Korea and India, whose industries are beset by low demand, might try to move in and take over the steel customers of the Japanese.

But John Cutler, a lawyer who handled the dumping complaint for the Gilmore Steel Corporation, on which the Treasury finding was based, said in an interview that, in past cases Gilmore has won, "a finding on one country has a very inhibiting effect on other foreign manufacturers as well."

Before the antidumping duty actually goes on the tariff books, a second Government agency—the International Tariff Commission—must find within 90 days that there has been injury to the domestic steel industry.

October 5, 1977

Slapping a Penalty on Japanese Steel

After years of appeals by American steel makers for protection against low-priced imports, the Treasury Department last week issued its first ruling in memory against "dumping" by five Japanese steel makers and ordered that they immediately begin posting a bond equivalent to a "dumping" duty of 32 percent.

But while allaying some of the anxieties of America's troubled steel industry, the move exacerbated fears among advocates of trade liberalization that a rising tide of protectionism both in the United States and Europe could doom the ongoing world trade talks in Geneva.

Using independent cost estimates, the

Treasury said that the five Japanese steel makers—Nippon Steel, the world's leading producer; Nippon Kokan; Sumitomo Metal Industries; Kawasaki Steel and Kobe Steel — were selling carbon steel plate in the American market for $210 a ton, some $75 below a cost-justified price. Carbon steel plate is used in heavy construction, shipbuilding, oil rigs and machinery.

Last year the United States imported $174 million of carbon steel from Japan, and altogether imports now account for almost 20 percent of the American steel market.

The Treasury decision is subject to 90 days of hearings. Before a perma-

nent 32 percent duty could go into effect, the International Trade Commission would have to find that there had been substantial harm to domestic industry and an additional 90 days of hearings would ensue.

But spokesmen for Japanese trading companies indicated that because of the immediate bond the decision would result in an immediate cutback in steel shipments to the United States, a move that American exporters fear could result in retaliation against their own products.

Robert S. Strauss, the United States's special trade negotiator, said that one in six American jobs depended on ex-

The Steel Controversy

ports, and one third of American farm produce is exported.

Fumihiki Togo, Japan's Ambassador to the United States, said in Cleveland, "The right remedy for an industry faced with import competition is to become more competitive."

Most experts agree that the United States industry suffers from outmoded plants and practices, but at present the industry finds itself in no position to make improvements. United States Steel, the industry leader, suffered a 52 percent earnings drop in the first half, while No. 2, Bethlehem declined 86 percent. Furthermore, thousands of steel workers across the country have been laid off and U. S. Steel forecasts further layoffs of workers and administrative personnel.

American steel makers contend that the Treasury decision will enable them to become more competitive by capturing a greater market share, thereby earning enough money to plough more into improved plant and equipment.

In one gain for protectionist forces, Representative Charles A. Vanik, Democrat of steel-producing Ohio, called on President Carter to hold steel imports to 18 percent. Calling himself an advocate of free trade, Mr. Vanik, chairman of the House Subcommittee on Trade, said the steel industry, nevertheless, needed special help. Some observers have expected protectionists to find similar allies in states affected by imports of shoes, TV sets and textiles.

October 9, 1977

The United States International Trade Commission has found that carbon steel plate from Japanese steel mills injures domestic producers.

Japan Trade Center

Japan Steel Efficiency Stirs Problems

Low Production Cost Behind Rift With U.S. on 'Dumping'

By ANDREW H. MALCOLM

TOKYO, Nov. 22—Earlier this fall NHK Japan's semi-Governmental television network, dispatched a film crew to Youngstown, Ohio, to get local reactions to the steel-import controversy rising between the United States and Japan.

The Japanese team so interested a Youngstown television station that it dispatched its own film crew to cover the Japanese film crew. This local interest so impressed the Japanese that they as-

signed another cameraman to film the American cameraman filming the Japanese cameraman filming Youngstown steel subjects.

The incident underlines the compelling international interest that the steel issue carries for both nations and the threat it now poses to their close relations.

For the United States, which has the non-Communist world's largest economy, foreign steel has become an emotional "dumping" issue allegedly costing the jobs of thousands of Americans.

Seen as Corporate Survival

For Japan, the No. 2 economy, steel exports are widely considered as a matter of corporate survival. Last year this nation's mammoth steel industry, with about 340,000 workers in six dozen companies, shipped overseas 52.1 million tons, or 44 percent, of its 118.4 million

tons of crude steel production. The export total is more than twice the volume of West Germany, Japan's closest export competitor. There is little doubt that Japan's steel companies are generally the world's most efficient—production costs run 15 to 20 percent less than in the United States. And although they are severely troubled today, they also enjoy some unique historical and geographical bonuses as well as a continuing substantial cost advantage in lower wages.

Historically, the Japanese Government has worked closely with developing industries.

Following the devastation of World War II, steel, along with shipbuilding, power, coal, and chemicals, got special Government startup assistance, since diminished. Generally, this involved Government loan guarantees that allowed the steel companies to pay below-market interest rates. Production for exports also received special emphasis.

In the last two decades worldwide production of crude steel globally has grown 153 percent to 753 million tons a year. In the same period, United States production increased just 9 percent while Japanese output soared 1,038 percent.

In 1955, the United States had 39.3 percent of the world's crude steel production while Japan controlled only 3.5 percent. Twenty years later the United States had 16.4 percent while Japan had 15.8 percent.

The United States had become, meanwhile, the world's largest importer of steel products (15 percent of domestic consumption in the first half of this year) and Japan's largest single steel customer, taking one-fifth of this nation's output. Even the United States's new Alaskan oil pipeline was built with Japanese steel.

The steel industry here basically consists of two tiers. The top tier comprises the so-called "Big Six"—Nippon Steel, Nippon Kokan, Kawasaki, Sumitomo, Nisshia and Kobe—whose vast integrated coastal complexes are run largely by computer. Men only monitor.

Ore arrives in giant bulk carriers at one end of the company and is loaded as finished product into other giant carriers at the far end. According to the Japan Iron and Steel Federation, in such plants 83 percent of production is by the more efficient oxygen converter versus 61 percent in the United States. Ten of the world's 15 largest blast furnaces are in Japan.

The great majority of Japanese steel companies, however, are much smaller and precariously financed, largely by the hustling trading companies that do their marketing and buying.

While the larger companies deal generally in long-term set contracts with both customers and suppliers, the movements of the smaller companies are more volatile since, in part, they concentrate so heavily on the widely fluctuating structural steel market that mirrors the world's economic ups and downs.

Wherever a market opens up—for instance, when one nation's domestic prices move up—these smaller Japanese makers move in quickly as a group. One foreign businessman here called it "a pack."

Because so much of their capital is borrowed—80 percent is not uncommon in Japanese businesses—regular heavy payments are required. In Japanese, the companies are called "Jitensha Sogyo," literally, "bicycle operators," meaning, "if you stop pedaling, you fall."

"Given the stagnant domestic economy," one diplomat said, "they have simply got to export to survive."

Their export success is due to a variety of factors including the use of newer equipment built when costs were lower, previous declines in the costs of raw materials and increased efficiency and reduced costs in the maritime movements of these raw materials and finished products.

These are efficiencies that Japan as an island nation is in a good position to exploit to the maximum. The opening of the St. Lawrence Seaway in 1959, for instance, increased Japanese steel competitiveness by allowing ocean-going vessels a straight run from Yokohama to the American heartland.

However, the major factor, in the steel success story according to experts here, has been Japan's lower wages and increasing productivity.

Japanese manufacturers are reluctant to release production data, but according to American calculations, labor costs were 65 cents an hour in 1957 and 85 cents in 1964 at a time when comparable American costs were $3.22 and $4.61 respectively. Last year, including benefits, one manhour of labor averaged $12.22 in the United States. And $6.31 in Japan.

Costs have been held down here in part because of the increasing use of "contract workers," who number about 42 percent of the payroll and are paid less than those hired under Japan's traditional system of lifetime employment.

Simultaneously, new facilities and labor-saving technology saw Japanese steel output per manhour rise 166.4 percent between 1964 and 1975 while the comparable United States rate increased only 17.5 percent. Thus, for instance, in 1975 Japanese steel workers produced an estimated 9.35 metric tons of finished steel per 100 manhours versus 8.13 metric tons in the United States.

Put another way, this means that the United States 1975 labor costs $136.53 per metric ton compared with 62.99 in Japan.

November 23, 1977

STEEL REFORM PLAN REACHED WITH JAPAN

U.S. and West Europe to Join Tokyo in Monitoring Industry Trends

By PAUL LEWIS

PARIS, Nov. 30—The United States, Western Europe and Japan agreed today to work together in attempts to reform their troubled steel industries, burdened by inefficient plant and excess capacity, in order to preserve free-world trade in steel.

They also undertook to start monitoring trends in the world steel industry more closely next year, hoping the exercise would serve both as an "early warning system" to spot incipient problems and as an aid to steel producers in planning new investments.

But these countries acknowledged that any restructuring of their steel industries would be "difficult and often painful" to carry out and may only prove politically feasible if there is a sustained economic upturn in the industrial world.

Today's agreement came at the second meeting of the special committee set up last summer by the 24 industrial member countries of the Organization for Economic Cooperation and Development to review the world steel industry, after a rash of plant closures and layoffs in the United States brought the long simmering steel crisis to the boil.

The chief United States delegate at the talks, Deputy Assistant Secretary of State William G. Barraclough, said he was "highly satisfied" with today's agreement, which had "contributed to the mutual understanding of the difficult problems facing all participant steel industries."

The communiqué issued at the end of the meeting committed the United States and the other participant countries to observe the following three "general principles" in their efforts to help their steel producers.

¶Top priority must go to reforming and restructuring national steel industries in order to promote "a rational allocation of resources," though without "shifting the burden of adjustment from one producing country to another."

¶All measures, both immediate and longer term to help steel producers must preserve the "free and fair flow of trade" and avoid "quantitative restrictions" on steel imports.

¶But no country can be expected to accept "large quantities of imports and unjustifiably low prices to the detriment of domestic production and employment." However, measures taken to deal with such "dumping" should take account of "customary trade patterns."

The most important aspect of today's agreement may be its recognition that any permanent solution to the steel industry's problems must involve phasing out inefficient plants and the equally frank acknowledgement that this could prove politically impossible at a time of generalized recession.

December 1, 1977

Japan Backing U.S. Plan on Steel; Big Trade Concessions Pledged

WASHINGTON, Dec. 2 (AP)—Japan, a major supplier of steel to the United States, announced support today for a Carter Administration plan to assist American steel producers.

The Japanese position was outlined at a news conference by Naohiro Amaya, a senior official of the Ministry of International Trade and Industry.

Meanwhile, in Tokyo, Nobuhiko Ushiba, Japan's new minister in charge of external economic affairs, said that his country was prepared to make major concessions to the United States to help resolve the trade imbalance between the two nations.

The statements by the two Japanese officials were among the most conciliatory so far in the trade discussions that have been under way informally for several weeks. A focal point of the talks has been the impact of low-cost imported steel on the American steel industry, where plant closings and personnel lay-offs have aroused demands for Government intervention.

An interagency Administration task force has developed a plan that would include the setting of minimum prices for imports of steel. The prices would be based on the costs of the most efficient foreign steel producer—most likely Japan itself.

"The reference price system is acceptable to us," Mr. Amaya said. "We want full cooperation with the United States to get the reference price system workable and successful."

Japan's decision to accept the American plan was seen as evidence of a desire on the part of that country to remove an issue that has hindered economic relations between the two countries.

The United States Treasury Department has tentatively accepted for investigation an allegation by the Gilmore Steel Corporation that Japanese makers have engaged in the dumping of steel on the American market. A much larger dumping claim has been filed by the United States Steel Corporation.

Mr. Amaya said he had no idea how the American steel plan would affect Japanese exports, but most officials believe the impact will be minimal.

In the early months of 1977, Japanese makers had a 60 percent share of American steel imports but in recent months that figure has declined to about 35 percent.

Mr. Amaya denied that Japanese companies have engaged in dumping. "We have been very careful about price as well as quantity," he said. "We have wanted to be careful not to aggravate the situation here."

100% Solution 'Impossible'

TOKYO, Dec. 2—Nobuhiko Ushiba, the

Japan and the U.S. have agreed to a system of "reference prices," minimum prices for steel imports, designed to assist American producers. Japanese steel manufacturers, using newer technology, operate 15%-20% more efficiently than their American counterparts.

new minister for external economic affairs,' said today that Japan would make

"large concessions" to the United States as a step toward solution of the current bilateral economic problems.

"However, a 100 percent solution of these problems at this time is impossible," Mr. Ushiba said. "This is not the aim of the negotiation. We will have to defer several things for the future. Some of them will be taken over by the GATT [General Agreement on Tariffs and

Trade] negotiation at Geneva and some others at a summit conference next year,' the minister noted.

Mr. Ushiba spoke at a news conference. He is expected to visit the United States with a package proposal to be worked out by the Government by next Tuesday to find a breakthrough in the economic conflict.

When asked to comment on a statement by Robert S. Strauss, United States Spe-

cial Trade Negotiator, Thursday that Japan must make large concessions to solve the bilateral economic issues, Mr. Ushiba said that the concessions Japan would make would be large, "even from the U.S. point of view."

He said, however, that the package Japan was drawing up would be an "almost finished one" to be subject to further negotiations with American officials.

December 3, 1977

Steel-Price 'Dumping' Guide Issued

By EDWARD COWAN

WASHINGTON, Jan. 3 — The Treasury Department announced today most of the minimum prices it has devised to provide an early warning of the illegal "dumping" of foreign steel in this country at unfairly low prices.

The system of reference or trigger prices is meant to speed up Federal action against foreign producers illegally selling steel in this country below their production costs. Imports priced below the new minimums would trigger a Treasury investigation into whether the steel products were in fact priced illegally low. If so, a punitive tariff could be imposed.

The average of the separate "reference" prices established for nearly a score of different steel products was $330 a ton, the Treasury said. That was $20 a ton, or 5.7 percent, below the average price of comparable American steel products in the eastern United States.

Steel company executives today generally declined to comment on the Treasury's trigger prices, saying they needed time to study them. The average of $330 a ton was decidedly below the $360 a ton recommended last Dec. 8 by David M. Roderick, president of the United States Steel Corporation. It was not immediately clear, however, whether the two composite figures were precisely comparable.

The trigger prices "should allow domestic manufacturers to recapture a substantial share of the market lost to imports," the Treasury predicted, but it also stressed that their effect "will depend in part on the pricing practices of American firms."

In that regard, most major American steel companies recently announced plans to raise prices about 5.5 percent effective Feb. 1 and March 1.

The trigger prices are the principal response of the Carter Administration to complaints from American steel compa-

nies and the United Steelworkers of America that the domestic industry is being badly hurt by cut-price imports from foreign mills that sometimes get subsidies from their own governments.

It is already illegal for imports to sell below their production costs if domestic companies are injured. As Treasury officials reiterated at a briefing today, the new system gives American industry no higher price protection that it already enjoys under the Antidumping Act.

Instead, the new system is meant to prompt the Treasury to begin investigations on its own initiative. In the past, the Government has investigated only after receiving a complaint from a domestic steel producer claiming injury from imports.

Before the Government will impose a countervailing or extra duty on the import complained of, two findings must be made. The first is a Treasury finding that the item has been "dumped," that is, sold here below cost or below the exporter's home-market price. If dumping is found, then the International Trade Commission is asked to inquire whether the dumping has injured the domestic industry.

Obtained From Japanese

The trigger prices for 17 types of steel-mill products were calculated from Japanese cost data obtained through the Japanese Government. Robert Crandall, deputy director of the Council on Wage and Price Stability, said that Japan was chosen because it was the low-cost producer among major steel-exporting nations.

The trigger prices include the cost of production in Japan, including overhead and profit margin, as well as shipping, insurance, handling, and routine customs duties.

Peter D. Ehrenhaft, deputy assistant secretary of the Treasury for tariffs, said in response to questions that the Treasury could impose the countervailing duty retroactively, and without having notified the importer of that possibility when the merchandise cleared through customs.

Could Prove to Be Illusory

This has always been possible under

the law. The effect of the Treasury's new emphasis on dumping is to notify importers and domestic steel consumers that any bargain they think they may be getting on foreign steel could prove to be illusory if extra duties are imposed months after a shipment arrives.

Mr. Ehrenhaft said that the Treasury would compile data on costs and prices so that it can make dumping findings in 60 to 90 days, several months faster than has been the case.

The Treasury compared the trigger prices of five major steel categories, plus duties, with present East Coast list prices of domestic manufacturers. For two lines, tin plate and hot-rolled bars, the American price was lower. These are also the two most costly types of steel of the five.

The three lines for which the American list price exceeded the trigger price plus duty were cold-rolled sheet, hot-rolled sheet and plate.

Mr. Ehrenhaft said that the trigger prices went into effect tody but that a companion importer's invoice that would facilitate price comparisons would not be in use before mid-February, at the earliest. In any event, the publication of the trigger prices merely invites comparisons. It does not mean that any extra duties will be imposed on any shipment.

The Treasury offered the following details of how it calculated the trigger prices: cost data came from six major integrated Japanese steel companies and some smaller, electric furnace steelmakers. The Treasury and the Council on Wage and Price Stability compared the data with figures from American and European trade sources and concluded "that the figures provide a reliable basis for computing costs of production."

The calculations were based on an assumed operating ratio of 85 percent of capacity in Japan. Although the present rate is only 70 percent, the rate has averaged more than 85 percent "over normal business cycles since 1956." The higher rate meant lower average costs and hence a lower level of protection for the American industry.

The Treasury listed the following factor

The Steel Controversy

costs: raw materials, $165.19 a ton of finished steel; labor, $68.56; and other costs, chiefly overhead, $64.05. To the total production cost of $297.80 the Treasury added $17 for depreciation, and $34 for interest and profit. The Treasury said the $50.62 return to capital was equivalent to 13 percent of total assets, a ratio that "compares favorably with the better years for the United States industry in the past decade."

To the basic cost figures the Treasury added average costs for freight to the East Coast, insurance and handling. Similar calculations will be made for the West Coast, where Japan has a better advantage because of lower shipping costs.

The Treasury said that, when imports include "extras," such as charges for special sizing or finishing, the trigger prices would be increased by amounts for extras that the Treasury will publish shortly.

In addition to the 17 prices listed today, the Treasury said still to come are prices for wire, tubular products, cold-finished bars and alloy products.

January 4, 1978

Imported Japanese steel has had harmful effects on the American steel industry, forcing plant closings and layoffs.

Japan Trade Center

Workers in the machine control room at a mill of the Yawata Iron and Steel Works.

Consulate General of Japan, N.Y.

JAPAN'S STEEL FOUND HURTING U.S. MAKERS

I.T.C. Ruling Means Duties Can Be Imposed on Carbon-Plate Imports

By CLYDE H. FARNSWORTH

WASHINGTON, April 13—In a finding of major significance in restraining American imports of steel, the United States International Trade Commission agreed unanimously today that carbon steel plate from Japan injures domestic producers.

The 4-to-0 vote by the independent trade monitoring body is part of a complex bureaucratic process that will ultimately subject Japanese steelmakers to sharply higher duties on the steel they sell here.

The commission was ruling in a case brought by the Oregon Steel Mills Division of a small West Coast manufacturer, the Gilmore Steel Corporation, whose complaint that the Japanese were selling in the United States below fair value focused public attention on the matter of the "dumping" of steel in the Ameri-

The Steel Controversy

can market.

Gilmore and other American steel companies said the unfair foreign competition was causing unprofitable operations and rising unemployment.

As public pressure mounted, President Carter established a special short-cut method of assessing duties on imports of cheap steel to lift prices closer to the domestic level. This so-called trigger price method of assessing dumping duties has checked imports but at the same time led to price increases by the domestic industry.

The trade commission's finding of injury means that the Treasury will now assess higher duties on the carbon steel plate of between 4 and 18 percent, depending on grades and quality. The figures are arrived at on the basis of constructions by the Treasury of what it costs to produce the steel in Japan and ship it to the United States market.

Under antidumping laws, relief can be obtained only after two conditions have been met. The Treasury must find that the goods have been dumped or come in at "less than fair value," and the International Trade Commission must determine that the shipments harmed domestic industry.

These two conditions have now been met for imports of carbon steel plate. Japan sold $173 million worth of this product in the United States in 1976, but it is expected that, when the figures are in for last year and this year, the volume will turn out sharply lower.

One reason is that, as soon as the Treasury issues a preliminary dumping finding, the importers have to post a bond to cover the potential punitive duty that would be assessed.

The Treasury's preliminary finding in the Gilmore case came last October. According to trade reports, it led to an almost complete freeze of the import traffic. The preliminary decision called for additional duties of 32 percent. Bonds had to be posted to cover that additional liability, which acted as a powerful deterrent to new shipments.

In January, however, as the Treasury was working out the trigger price mechanism to shorten the formal dumping proccedure, the agency said it got additional information on Japanese costs that permitted it to reduce the duties to the range of 4 to 18 percent.

It was the preliminary decision by the Treasury last October that brought the Gilmore case to public notice. The Treasury had never before made a dumping finding in basic steel.

Today's determination by the trade commission found injury to the domestic industry from carbon steel produced by these Japanese companies: the Kawasaki Steel Corporation, Kobe Steel Ltd., Nippon Kokan, the Nippon Steel Corporation and Sumitomo Metal Industries.

April 14, 1978

Japanese Steel Ruled Dumped

WASHINGTON, May 25 (AP)—The Government made a final decision today that the Japanese steel industry had been illegally dumping, or selling at below cost, the $175 million worth of carbon steel plate it exports to this country each year.

The ruling, though a foregone conclusion, represented a victory for the domestic steel industry in its fight against Japanese imports. The Treasury ruled in favor of a complaint brought by the Oregon Steel Mills division of the Gilmore Steel Corporation.

Five Japanese steel companies will have to pay tariffs of 5.4 to 18.5 percent on imports of the product since October 1977. But, since the Treasury reached a tentative decision last October, importers have been posting bonds covering the tariffs. Carbon steel plate is used in buildings, bridges and ships.

The Treasury Department now has a trigger-price system under which it begin investigations automatically if steel-import prices fall below a certain level In refining the system today, the Treasury took steps to make it easier for importers to ship steel to West Coast ports but more difficult to get it to Great Lakes ports.

The department said the handling charges used to calculate trigger prices of steel mill products entering through West Coast ports would be increased to $7 per metric ton from the present $3, effective for shipments brought in on or after May 31.

May 26, 1978

A Malaysian learns to operate a combine from a Japanese instructor.

Chapter 10

Trade and Diplomacy with Asia and the U.S.S.R.

Trade, not politics, has been the major issue underlying Japanese-Asian relations in the postwar period. Traditionally, Japan has relied upon Southeast Asia for most of its raw materials. In August 1977 Prime Minister Fukuda outlined the preliminaries of a new economic development program which his government would sponsor for Japan's trading partners in Southeast Asia. It included the financing of industrial projects and the removal of certain Japanese trade barriers.

While Japan may trade with other Asians, however, it maintains a restrictive policy in regard to immigration from surrounding nations. In March 1978, after months of serious debate and notwithstanding pressure from the United States and the United Nations, Japan finally decided not to admit a boatload of 104 Vietnamese refugees who were attempting to disembark at Kobe harbor. In a similar case, four Laotians were held in a Japanese jail for 18 months as illegal aliens.

Relations between Japan and the People's Republic of China improved significantly during 1977-78. In February 1978, Japan and China signed an eight-year, $20 billion trade pact involving industrial goods and fuel. For the Japanese, the agreement promises an early entry into the alluring Chinese market, as well as an abundant supply of badly needed oil and coal.

In June and July 1978 China and Japan began to lay the groundwork for a treaty of peace and friendship—ultimately signed in August and ratified in October—that would facilitate economic and industrial cooperation for years to come. Some analysts see this move as a reflection of Japan's increased diplomatic self-confidence, inasmuch as the Soviets were displeased, as expected, by the Sino-Japanese rapprochement. In years past, a major obstacle to the treaty has been China's demand for a clause condemning attempts at regional "hegemony" by any nation, referring directly to the Soviet Union. Fearful of angering the USSR, the Japanese negotiators were able to insert an article providing that the treaty will not affect relations of either party with third countries, thus mitigating the effect of the anti-hegemony clause. In view of China's abundant labor force and Japan's advanced technology, both sides seem eager to exploit the benefits of cooperation. Sino-Japanese relations appear to be entering a new phase in which fuel, heavy industry and arms will play a major role.

Russo-Japanese relations in 1977-78 were marked by hostility over a number of issues: Japan's refusal to return a MIG defector to Russia in 1976; fishing disputes which, according to one Japanese official, would certainly have meant war in years past; disagreements over four islands north of Hokkaido; and the Sino-Japanese peace talks. The Russian press reported progress on the Sino-Japanese peace accord with a heated denunciation of the "anti-hegemony clause" and pointed references to unspecified retaliatory measures. In February 1978 the Soviets published the draft of a peace pact offered to Japan—and subsequently rejected—a month earlier to woo her away from China. A Soviet press barrage against Japan's "anti-Soviet foreign policy" and "Japanese imperialism" ensued.

In spite of the enmity between the Soviet and Japanese governments, trade between the two countries is significant and continues to grow. Since 1970, trade has risen three-fold to a level of $3.36 billion annually, centered around a massive enterprise directed by Japan to exploit the natural resources of Siberia.

8 NATIONS' LEADERS DISCUSS TRADE TIES

5 Southeast Asian Countries Seek Loans, Lowering of Barriers by Japan, Australia, New Zealand

By DAVID A. ANDELMAN

KUALA LUMPUR, Malaysia, Aug. 6—The prime ministers of three major economic powers in the Asian-Pacific region, Japan, Australia and New Zealand, met today for the first time with the leaders of the five non-Communist countries of Southeast Asia, exchanging a series of pledges to remove the economic barriers that have traditionally divided them.

"The developed countries have a great responsibility," Prime Minister Takeo Fukuda of Japan told President Suharto of Indonesia, President Ferdinand E. Marcos of the Philippines, Prime Minister Lee Kuan Yew of Singapore, Prime Minister Hussein bin Dato Onn of Malaysia and Prime Minister Thanin Kraivichien of Thailand.

"If the advanced countries succeed in reviving their economies," Mr. Fukuda added, "it would give great impetus to the developing countries. I stressed this when I met with President Carter. And we agreed that we should endeavor to restore economic activity and health based on the principle of free trade."

Today's first, closed-door session, which also included Prime Minister Malcolm Fraser of Australia and Prime Minister Robert D. Muldoon of New Zealand, was largely devoted to a general exploration of world and regional economic conditions. Yet it seemed to some analysts here that Mr. Fukuda might be laying the groundwork for what could turn out to be some disappointments for the five leaders of the Association of Southeast Asian Nations, known as ASEAN.

During the association's meeting over the previous two days, the five Southeast Asian leaders indicated that they planned to present a broad range of requests to Mr. Fukuda and, with some variations, to Mr. Fraser and Mr. Muldoon.

Specifically, the association's leaders want about $1 billion from Japan to finance a series of five regional industrial projects, some broad tariff concessions and pledges from Japan to contribute to commodity stabilization arrangements.

Among themselves, however, the five leaders were unable to agree on any firm timetable for the industrial projects, and Mr. Fukuda is understood to be somewhat reluctant to move quickly on either tariff concessions or commodity arrangements. These two issues are part of a far broader range of questions that are being discussed in the discussions between industrially developed and developing countries known as the "north-south dialogues," and which could have a serious impact on Japan's faltering economy.

Imports of Raw Materials

Japan is faced with a difficult situation in Southeast Asia. It continues to rely on the raw materials and commodities that the region supplies—oil, tin, rubber, palm oil, teak and a variety of agricultural commodities.

At the same time, Japan's repeated demands for a lowering of tariff barriers by the United States ring hollow among the nations of Southeast Asia, which for years have suffered from the high tariffs Japan has imposed on the manufactured products of the region.

The eight leaders have agreed to confine their discussions, which are all being held in private, to economic matters. But it is clear that the intentions of the new Communist governments in Indochina are lending whatever urgency there might be to the sesssions.

The countries in the association, Mr. Muldoon is understood to have told today's session, are serving as the "buffer" to prevent "Communism from spreading from the north."

Vietnam has repeatedly criticized the association as a hostile military pact, a charge that the leaders of the five Southeast Asian countries continue to deny.

This morning, Thailand's Prime Minister Thanin called a news conference to denounce what he said were the "aggressions" of the Indochinese countries against Thailand. He also said fighting was continuing among the Indochinese countries themselves, along the Vietnam-Cambodian border and the Cambodian-Laotian border. On the Thai-Cambodian border he charged that the Cambodian Communist troops had "intruded into Thai territory 400 times since Jan. 1."

But he said that Thailand could deal with the situation by itself, without any military assistance from either the ASEAN countries or the three industrial countries.

August 7, 1977

JAPAN CONSIDERS AID FOR SOUTHEAST ASIA

Fukuda Gives Region's Leaders List of Economic Programs but Avoids Commitments

By DAVID A. ANDELMAN

KUALA LUMPUR, Malaysia, Aug. 7—Prime Minister Takeo Fukuda of Japan told the leaders of five non-Communist nations in Southeast Asia today that Japan would consider a broad range of economic concessions and aid programs to help stabilize the economy of the region, but refused any of the solid commitments the five nations had hoped to obtain.

Mr. Fukuda met for more than three hours this afternoon with President Suharto of Indonesia, President Ferdinand E. Marcos of the Philippines, Prime Minister Lee Kuan Yew of Singapore, Prime Minister Hussein bin Dato Onn of Malaysia and Prime Minister Thanin Kraivichien of Thailand. The five nations make up the 10-year-old Association of Southeast Asian nations, known as ASEAN.

"Until now, the relationship between Japan and ASEAN has been based on the exchange of money and goods," a Japanese Government spokesman quoted the Prime Minister as having said during the private talks. "But from now on, we want to establish a new heart-to-heart relationship with the ASEAN countries."

Japanese Commitments Given

An 11-page communiqué was published tonight spelling out what Japan was prepared to offer, and it was clear that Mr. Fukuda, who faces severe economic problems at home, could not be moved to

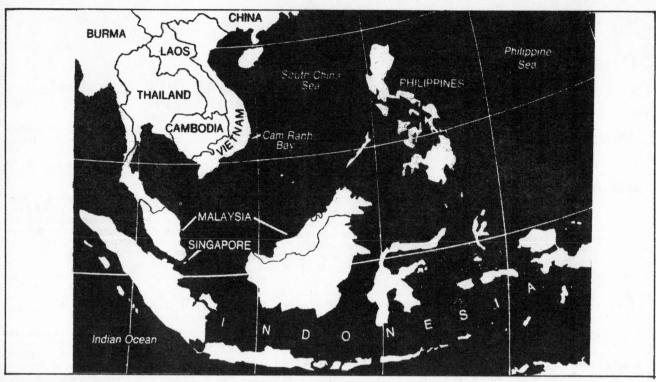

Japan's Southeast Asian trading partners.

make any more concrete commitments than the following:

¶An agreement by Japan to "consider favorably the request for the total amount of one billion U.S. dollars" to finance a series of five regional industrial projects—one in each of the five countries—provided that the "feasibility was confirmed" for each such project. No such feasibility studies have yet been completed and the economic viability of several of the projects, which include fertilizer and diesel engine plants, have been called into question during the talks among the five Southeast Asian leaders.

¶An agreement to further examine the bloc's requests for "removal and-or relaxation of tariff and nontariff barriers" and to study the improvement of Japan's generalized system of preferences. But all changes would come within the context of the much broader "Tokyo round" of tariff discussions. The Southeast Asian countries had hoped for specific tariff concessions by Japan for the entry of their products.

¶Agreement to "conduct a joint examination on the various problems in connection with the stabilization of export earnings from primary commodities." The Southeast Asian countries had hoped for the establishment of a system similar to the European Economic Community's that would compensate member countries for foreign exchange losses due to fluctuation in prices of export commodities.

¶Japanese agreement to "cooperate closely" in the establishment of a common fund for commodity price stabilization that had been proposed in the discussions between the developed and underdeveloped countries, known as the "north-south dialogues."

Japanese Aid to Double

Mr. Fukuda restated his position that foreign aid to the five countries as well as to other developing nations would more than double within the next five years. From 1971 to 1975, Japanese grants and loans to developing countries totaled $3.4 billion of which 43 percent, $1.5 billion, went to the Southeast Asian countries.

This year, Japanese aid is expected to reach a billion dollars, of which 46 percent will go to Southeast Asia.

Mr. Fukuda presented no concrete timetable for the future aid increases. He is expected to disclose some of the figures in talks over the next 10 days with each of the Southeast Asian leaders in their own capitals.

In general, Mr. Fukuda seemed to have achieved many of his goals in the two days of meetings here: to continue what Japan considers its special relationship with the countries that supply much of its raw materials and commodities, and

at the same time to improve its somewhat miserly image.

Mr. Fukuda and the five Southeast Asian leaders also discussed the need to strengthen the economy of the region against any further political or military dislocations.

No Suggestion of Military Aid

But a Japanese Foreign Ministry official emphasized tonight that at no time was there any suggestion that Japan would provide any military assistance or grants.

The spokesman also quoted Mr. Fukuda as saying that Japan was "prepared to

give economic assistance to the Indochinese countries in order that these countries be freed from poverty and difficulties."

The five Southeast Asian countries have been particularly sensitive about the question of aid to Indochina, particularly to Vietnam, which has repeatedly criticized their association as a hostile military pact.

Some officials have indicated that the United States may be asked next month at a meeting in Manila to provide the Southeast Asian nations with the same aid and trade package that it may give to Vietnam.

The meeting with Mr. Fukuda followed a similar session this morning with Prime Minister Malcolm Fraser of Australia during which he agreed to increase by $100 million the level of aid to the Southeast Asian countries, to $208 million a year, and to allow more of the aid to be used to buy locally produced products rather than Australian goods.

But Mr. Fraser refused to discuss liberalizing tariff restrictions noting that over the last five years, Southeast Asian exports to Australia had increased "at the healthy rate of 30 percent per year."

Tomorrow, New Zealand's Prime Minister, Robert Muldoon, will meet with the five leaders. And Mr. Fukuda and Mr. Fraser have scheduled a morning discussion on several outstanding trade disputes between their two countries.

August 8, 1977

North Korea Safeguarding
200-Mile Fishing Limit

TOKYO Aug. 13 (AP)—North Korea has apparently banned all Japanese fishing boats from within its 200-mile economic zone, the Maritime Safety Agency said today.

A spokesman said the 50-ton squid fish-ing boat Shinyo Maru No. 1 was ordered out of the zone on Thursday by a North Korean warship.

Crew members said today on returning home that they had been told by loud-speakers: "Get out of our fishery zone quickly. If you enter it again, we shall not forgive you."

The sailors said the ban applied to all Japanese fishing craft.

August 14, 1977

North Korea Says It Has Freed
Japanese Boat Seized Off Coast

TOKYO, Nov. 12 (AP)—North Korea today released a Japanese fishing boat and 10 crew members seized earlier in the week for allegedly violating North Korea's military sea zone, the Pyongyang radio reported.

The broadcast from the North Korean capital, monitored in Tokyo, said that North Korea had released the 197-ton Chidori Maru No. 87 "in consideration of friendly relations with Japan."

A North Korean patrol boat seized the fishing craft on Thursday five nautical miles inside the zone, the broadcast said. It said that more than 76 Japanese fishing boats had violated the zone in October.

The Pyongyang Government established what it called a "military sea boundary" on Aug. 2 and said most foreign ships and planes would be banned from entering the zone without permission. Sunao Sonoda, Japan's Chief Cabinet Secretary, said then that he believed the zone "runs counter to international law and practice."

November 13, 1977

Fukuda Begins Visit to Thailand;
Pledges Peaceful Role for Japan

BANGKOK, Thailand, Aug. 15 (UPI)—Prime Minister Takeo Fukuda of Japan, pledging that his country will never "become a military power again," arrived in Thailand today for a two-day visit.

Mr. Fukuda was welcomed at the air-port with a 19-gun salute by Prime Minister Thanin Kraivichien and Foreign Minister Uppadit Pajariyangkul. Japanese children waved flags of the Rising Sun and the tricolor of Thailand. The 72-year-old Japanese leader is scheduled to meet with King Phumiphol Aduldet tomorrow.

He arrived aboard a special Japan Air Lines flight after a 24-hour stay in Singapore, where he spoke on the 32d anniversary of the Japanese surrender in World War II.

August 16, 1977

Japan Asks 'Mutual Trust' in Asia

MANILA, Aug. 18, 1977—Prime Minister Takeo Fukuda of Japan ended his 10-day tour of Southeast Asia here today with a speech outlining Japan's new doctrine of peaceful cooperation with its neighbors based on mutual trust.

"As a true friend of the countries of Southeast Asia," Mr. Fukuda told a large farewell gathering at the newly renovated Manila Hotel, "Japan will do its best to consolidate mutual confidence and trust, covering not only political and economic areas but also social and cultural."

The Japanese leader reaffirmed his country's rejection of a military role and its desire to be "an equal partner" of the Association of Southeast Asian Nations in the task of development. Earlier he pledged a billion dollars in aid to the Southeast Asian group's members, Indonesia, Malaysia, Singapore, Thailand and the Philippines.

Mr. Fukuda also expressed the hope that the United States would maintain its military and economic presence in the region. He added he had discussed this with President Carter during his recent visit to Washington.

The Prime Minister and Mrs. Fukuda left Manila International Airport for Tokyo this afternoon aboard a special Japan Air Lines plane.

As with his arrival yesterday afternoon, the Japanese leader's departure was festive, with Filipino well-wishers lining the way to the airport and waving Japanese flags. The sun-emblazoned white banners reminded many Filipinos of an era now long past, the occupation of their country by Japan during World War II.

Referring to these memories, President Ferdinand E. Marcos told his guest at today's farewell, "there had been fears of Japan rearming but these have been laid to rest by the Prime Minister's doctrine of peace."

Mr. Marcos said he and other ASEAN leaders looked to Japan, as well as the United States, as a catalyst for development and free trade in the region.

The Philippine President will next meet with an official delegation from the United States to discuss ASEAN problems. Mr. Marcos has been designated ASEAN's spokesman in the dialogue, which is to start in Manila Sept. 7.

August 19, 1977

Japan ● '79

MORE SHIPS IGNORING VIETNAM'S REFUGEES

Captains Said to Spurn Appeals for Fear of Red Tape and Losses

By HENRY KAMM

KOBE, Japan, Aug. 21—The three groups of Vietnamese refugees sheltered in a Roman Catholic home in this port city have been recovering from their arduous escapes by small boat since May.

The 104 persons—about one-third of them children—spend their time learning English from a priest, watching television in a language they don't understand, reliving awful memories and waiting for an embassy to give them a visa to a place of permanent refuge.

Since Japan refuses to consider asylum for anyone, their hopes center on the United States, France and Australia. They have vaguely heard of the American decision last month to admit 7,000 "boat people," but no official has talked to them about it, and they can only hope.

Their memories are of fears of being caught, of drownings, of death of hunger, thirst or exposure and of constantly bailing out their rickety craft while retching with seasickness.

Those were the dangers they expected when they set out. And they can speak of them matter-of-factly. But they cover with smiles and little laughs their embarrassment over the anger they feel about the many ships that passed them by while they were adrift at sea.

Asian Countries Reluctant

Before they were rescued—each group by a Japanese merchant vessel—they had all tasted the bitterness of having ship after ship ignore their pleas and SOS signals and abandon them to the sea, with food, water and fuel running low, passengers ill and the coast far off.

Since the heavy refugee flow from Vietnam began last year, there have been increasingly frequent reports of violations of the traditional requirement that all ships encountering others in distress come to their rescue.

In shipping circles here and in Southeast Asia, it is recognized that the violations have become everyday occurrences and suspicions are voiced that some companies may have ordered their captains not to pick up "boat people."

The reason is that almost all Asian countries are reluctant to grant refugees even temporary shelter and have made serious difficulties for captains wishing to let these passengers off at their next port of call.

Great losses of time, danger to cargoes and governmental bureaucratic complications have ensued for shipping lines. How many lives have been lost because of the reluctance of ports and ships to rescue these refugees will never be known.

Merchant vessels are not the only suspected offenders. The leader of a group of 28 refugees that set out from Saigon May 8 said that on May 10 their boat flashed an SOS to the Australian naval vessel Vendetta. The vessel pulled up by the fishing boat. The Vietnamese group leader—he did not want his name printed for fear of reprisals against his relatives in Vietnam—asked for help and said that some people aboard were ill.

Passed by 21 Ships

While Australian sailors leaned over the rail to photograph the scene, the captain replied that he regretted he could not take the refugees aboard because his ship was on patrol. The refugee leader said the Australians then lowered medicines, water and fruit juice to them and a map indicating that Malaysia was 20 hours away. The Vendetta, a large destroyer that is listed as carrying a crew of 320, returned to its patrol.

"We had hoped to be invited aboard," the refugee leader said.

The next day, said the leader, a former Education Ministry specialist, 21 ships passed within their sight in 12 hours. The Vietnamese signaled with flares and homemade flags, but no ship acknowledged the signals.

"I thought that they were busy, or because they had to feed us, or because they had difficulties with governments for political reasons," the refugee leader said in apology for those who failed to try to save the lives of his group, which included three young children and a pregnant woman.

Members of one group that left Vietnam from Cam Ranh on July 12 reported having passed within 50 yards of a ship bearing an Esso band around its smokestack on July 14 and being ignored by its crew. The 56 refugees on the boat later narrowly escaped capture by Chinese in the Paracel Islands, where they stopped to ask for drinking water before being rescued by a Japanese freighter.

August 25, 1977

JAPAN WEIGHS EASING CURBS ON REFUGEES

U.S. and U.N. Applying Pressure but Only Slow Improvement Is Foreseen for Vietnamese

By HENRY KAMM

TOKYO, Aug. 25—Prodded by the United States and the office of the United Nations high commissioner for refugees, Japan is considering liberalizing its restrictive polices toward accepting refugees from Vietnam who arrive in Japanese ports after having been rescued at sea by ships heading for Japan.

But highly placed officials of the Foreign Ministry and the Immigration Bureau foresee only slow change, if any, in existing attitudes. Long delays and insistence on firm guarantees that the refugees will not remain indefinitely in Japan have made captains of ships hesitant to rescue the "boat people" who flee from Vietnam in small fishing craft. Many of those upon whom the ships turn their backs are likely to perish at sea.

Katsuyoshi Yamano, chief of the entry division of the Immigration Bureau, disclosed in an interview that last month the Japanese Embassy in Washington had been informed by the State Department that the United States would like Japan to act more liberally in granting temporary entry permits, reconsider its absolute refusal even to consider granting permanent asylum and increase its contribution to the United Nations refugee body.

Mr. Yamano said these points were still under study in various departments of the Government. He indicated that any decision would be slow in coming.

Assurance From U.N.

The official also disclosed that the United Nations high commissioner had urged Japan to liberalize its temporary entry procedure based on a United Nations assurance that the refugees would be permanently resettled elsewhere eventually.

Japan now requires that before a ship

220

can land refugees, either the country in which it is registered or the one in which it is owned must guarantee that it will take responsibility for resettling the refugees elsewhere if no other country can be found that will accept them.

This requirement causes delays of about two weeks, during which the rescuing ship is immobilized at great cost to its owners and to the shippers of its cargo.

Japan also requires that facilities be available to care for and shelter the refugees. But despite its position as Asia's wealthiest nation, Japan provides no governmental aid for feeding and sheltering refugees, leaving this task to private charities, principally the Roman Catholic organization Caritas.

"There are no suitable facilities at the moment," said Mr. Yamano, explaining his country's failure to provide housing for the refugees.

The total number of Vietnamese refugees in Japan amounts to 606 in a nation of 113 million.

The immigration official said Japan could not agree with the high commissioner's suggestion that the United Nations' assurances alone should suffice to grant a landing permit. "The rescuing country should have a responsibility," he said.

However, it has been difficult to get countries such as Liberia that provide "flags of convenience" for shipowners to take the necessary diplomatic step to issue a guarantee.

Contributions to Refugee Agency

A well-placed Foreign Ministry official said that the ministry hoped to increase Japan's contribution to the United Nations refugee agency, but that this would still have to be approved by the Finance Ministry and in any event could not go into effect before the next budget year beginning next April 1.

"Our impression is, frankly speaking, that we are very much surprised," said Mr. Yamano in reaction to criticism of the Japanese attitude. He was commenting on a recent case that has caused despair among persons close to refugee matters and anguish to a group of 20 refugees.

They were picked up last month by the Greek ship Krios, which was carrying a cargo of coke from Poland to North Korea. Because the master of the vessel was unwilling to deliver refugees from one Communist-ruled country to another, he asked to be allowed to make a special call in the Japanese port of Nagasaki to discharge the 20.

But from July 10 to 13, the Krios was denied entry into Japanese territorial waters, while its Vietnamese passengers worried about whether they would soon be handed over to the Government in Pyongyang.

Guarantee From Greece

Finally, on July 13, the Greek Government gave its guarantee and on the following day the ship was allowed into port. Only on July 15 were the refugees allowed ashore. They are still in Japan.

"I would like even a symbol of helpfulness," said the Rev. Robert Kimura, a Jesuit from California who has taken Japanese nationality. He runs the largest refugee shelter in Japan, in the port city of Kobe. "But they live by the book, and this is not in the book," he continued, describing the attitude of Japanese authorities.

Official Japanese sources ascribe the official reluctance to help refugees to a fear that such an attitude would encourage the 650,000 Koreans and 50,000 Chinese in this ethnically nearly monolithic country to insist on a greater degree of assimilation into a society that strongly discriminates against them.

"This is not a quantitative but a qualitative question," a Foreign Ministry official remarked when reminded of the small number of Vietnamese in Japan.

August 26, 1977

Japan Decides to Keep
Its Curbs on Vietnamese Refugees

By ANDREW H. MALCOLM

KAMAKURA, Japan, March 10—Prodded by the United States and the United Nations High Commission for Refugees, Japan decided late last summer to reconsider its highly restrictive policy on acceptance of Vietnamese refugees who are picked up at sea by ships bound for Japan.

Now, six months later, interviews with Government officials and refugee workers here reveal that Japan has decided not to change its policy toward these so-called "boat people." They will still be forbidden to settle permanently. And before freighter captains can bring in refugees they have picked up at sea, they will still be required to obtain a written guarantee from their home government assuming responsibility for resettling the refugees elsewhere. Japanese ships arriving with refugees are required to get the guarantee from the United Nations Commission.

This time-consuming and costly process has made many captains reluctant to pick up the refugees. Thus many are left to an uncertain future at sea.

In a Sept. 13 speech in Tokyo, Foreign Minister Iichiro Hatoyama promised "an appreciable measure" concerning the acceptance of refugees by Japan. But in an interview this week, Katsuyoshi Yamano, chief of the Immigration Bureau's Entry Division, said, "There is no change. And we don't have any prospect for change."

The Japanese Point of View

Japanese officials have expressed surprise at criticism of these policies. They maintain that immigration is not part of the Japanese tradition or social structure and is not possible in the crowded conditions of this island nation of 113 million. There are now 369 Vietnamese refugees in Japan, and 864 have left, primarily for the United States.

The Japanese Government has declined to support refugee operations in Japan directly. But money for food, $3.85 per person per day, comes from the United Nations commission, to which Japan donated $80,000 this fiscal year.

Housing is provided privately at 15 locations, mainly by churches such as this city's Yukinoshita Catholic Church, which turned over its retreat center to 30 Vietnamese whose rickety boat washed ashore in southern Japan last fall. Clothing has come from the Salvation Army, religious groups and schools for foreigners.

This nation's policies have drawn increasingly bitter comments from relief workers here who see the stand of Japan, Asia's most affluent nation, as setting a standard of what is acceptable for other Asian lands.

New Flow Is Expected

Despite a reported crackdown by the Vietnamese Government, a new flow of boat people is expected next month as the Pacific's seasonal storms subside. No exact figures are possible, but experts here estimate that because of the weather and the refusal of some captains to pick up refugees, only half the refugees who flee by boat survive.

"We figure 10,000 are at the bottom of the ocean," said the Rev. Martin Clarke, a refugee relief leader. "People round the world get all excited about the Japanese killing dolphins but not about these poor people dying at sea because the ships are afraid to pick them up."

Hirotaka Yoshizaki/The New York Times

The Reverend Martin Clarke, a refugee relief leader, with Sister Kathleen Stack, left, and Vietnamese families among those being housed at the Yukinoshita Catholic Church relief center in Japan.

A 64-year-old Catholic priest, Father Clarke has spent the last third of his life in Japan. As a young man, he was a fireman then a priest in New York City, where relatives ran the P.J. Clarke's bar.

Now he and Sister Kathleen Stack of Kansas City and eight other workers for Caritas, the Roman Catholic relief organization, monitor refugee living conditions and help the people with the paperwork required to enter Japan, stay temporarily, gain asylum abroad and leave.

"These Government people," said an impatient Father Clarke, "all they see are the books. You know, the law is for people, not the other way around."

He said it was ironic for Asian refugees to be refused asylum in Asia.

The Most Recent Group

No new refugees appear to have made it to Japan since October, when a Taiwanese freighter carried a boatload of 86 into Japan's southern territorial waters after the Taiwan Government took nine days to decide to refuse them entry.

The refugees had left Vietnam on Aug. 18. They said they had been terrified of

being shot and the children had gotten seasick. "But after the Communists came, there was no freedom," said one farmer. "You needed permission just to go to the next village."

Five days after leaving, their fuel ran out and they drifted. Two ships appeared, one registered in Liberia and the other in Panama. "We knew they could pass us by," said one refugee, "but we hoped they wouldn't." They did. Days later, the Taiwan ship stopped.

Another boatload of refugees here spent 20 days at sea and saw 23 ships pass. Two of those refugees died.

How They Pass the Time

"We are very sorry to be such a burden on everyone," said Nguyen Phuoc Dong, who like most of the refugees in Japan is waiting for approval to go to the United States. "Maybe," he said, "it is a little too much to expect that I could be a farmer again."

The refugees spend their days studying English with volunteer foreign teachers. The children play in the chill air of their first winter outside the tropics. The wives

wash clothes and buy food from neighborhood merchants like Takeo Kikuchi.

"They are good customers," he said. "They certainly do like peppers a lot."

According to Mr. Yamano, the immigration official, the Japanese Government has not given the refugees permission to work but has decided "not to mind" if they find temporary jobs. However, due to the language barrier and the refugees' generally remote locations, only five have been successful.

Hitoshi Mise, associate officer of the United Nations Refugee Commission in Japan, confirmed that Japan has not changed its entrance regulations, although it has promised to increase its contribution in the next fiscal year to $1.5 million. "The Japanese Government is studying the refugee problem," he said. "They are very much afraid of a lot of new arrivals."

Father Clarke, meanwhile, said his workers expected more than 1,000 new boat people this year, beginning next month.

March 15, 1978

Japan and China Sign 8-Year Pact For $20 Billion Industrial Deals

By ANDREW H. MALCOLM

TOKYO, Feb. 16—Japan and China signed a $20 billion trade pact in Peking today that sets the scene for marked improvements in their diplomatic and political relations and is a welcome economic plum for Japan.

For Japan, the major eight-year pact, technically an agreement between the Chinese Government and a group of private Japanese industrialists, provides a handsome headstart into the vast Chinese market for Japanese manufacturers, many of whom are still riding out a lingering recession at home and sharp criticism abroad of their exports. Officials spoke today of a "new era" and "spectacular growth."

For China, the pact promises a source of foreign exchange and assures supplies of steel, modern equipment, plants and advanced industrial technology as that nation pushes its own economic development.

For both China and Japan the agreement, in negotiation for almost a year, represents the most dramatic single link since the two countries normalized their diplomatic relations in September 1972. Diplomats, politicians and journalists here are also agreed that it smooths the way for final completion, possibly by late spring, of the long-stalled treaty of peace and friendship between China and Japan, with populations of about 850 million and 112 million, respectively.

For the Soviet Union, another Asian power that has long opposed such links between its ideological rival and Japan, the rapprochement may come as a direct affront and eventually prompt some form of retaliation, perhaps through restricting Japan's prized access to the Soviet Union's fertile fishing grounds in the Pacific. Another multibillion-dollar economic agreement, between Japan and the Russians to develop Siberia's vast natural resources, has never gotten off the ground.

There is still no World War II peace treaty between Tokyo and Moscow, which drove an embarrassingly tough bargain with Japan during recent fishery negotiations. Until Japan's defeat in World War II, relations between Japan and China in this century were marked by economic exploitation and military aggression on the part of Japan.

Today's Japan-China agreement was signed in the Shanghai Chamber of the People's Great Hall with Yoshihiro Inaya-ma, president of the Japan-China Economic Association and chairman of Nippon Steel, signing for the Japanese side and Liu Hsi-wen, a Deputy Foreign Trade Minister, for China.

Steel Mill for Shanghai

During the first five of the pact's eight years, starting immediately, the agreement sets Japanese sales of plants and technology to China at $7 billion to $8 billion. Included is a large integrated steel mill in Shanghai. Two other steel mills, one in Hopei Province and the other in Shansi, are being considered for later. But the Chinese have not specified what other purchases they plan.

Construction materials and equipment form the rest of Japan's sales share at between $2 billion and $3 billion.

In return, China would sell to Japan a five-year total of 47.1 million tons of oil, up to 5.3 million tons of coking coal and up to 3.9 million tons of other coals. Exact costs were to be determined later based on "rational international prices and practices." Sales volumes for the pact's final three years will be negotiated after 1981.

Such definite long-term oil purchase commitments, the first of their kind between Japan and China, represent a further effort by a resource-poor Japan to diversify its sources of petroleum imports. With virtually no oil resources of its own, Japan last year imported 236 million tons of oil.

The oil agreement also marks a decision by the Japanese industry to adapt its refineries to handle China's oil, which has a low sulfur but a high paraffin content.

Trade Slow in Recent Years

Trade between Japan and China had suffered in recent years because of domestic political uncertainties in both countries, natural disasters and adverse economic conditions. However, preliminary figures for last year showed that trade recovered to $3.5 billion, a 14.9 percent increase over 1976. This was attributed largely to the gradual recovery of economic order in China after the turmoil over the so-called Gang of Four. The agreement today is seen as a strong reflection of the new development policies of the new post-Mao leadership.

The new agreement does not, however, limit other economic activities. A steady stream of officials, businessmen, technicians and others make the 1,300-mile flight between Peking and Tokyo. A new 480-circuit coaxial cable has also improved communications. There are sales of computers and other items. An exchange of transportation technicans is likely in coming months as China seeks to modernize its railroads. And informational seminars proliferate with Chinese participants expressing growing interest in learning how Japan managed its rapid postwar economic recovery.

Thanks to the new trade agreement, the future also holds new hope for Japan's steelmakers, who have had to bank up to a third of their less-efficient capacity. This year, experts say, Japan's steel exports to China may exceed steel sales to the United States, which bought 7.1 million tons last year compared with China's 4.5 million tons.

This development is not likely to hurt the political fortunes of Prime Minister Takeo Fukuda, whose popularity has sagged in recent months over Japan's economic and export problems. Conclusion of this economically beneficial agreement is also likely to reduce the opposition to better relations with China among pro-Taiwan members of Mr. Fukuda's conservative Liberal Democratic Party. Mr. Fukuda has been meeting quietly with influential party members seeking to build a consensus on concluding the treaty of peace and friendship with mainland China.

Treaty talks broke down three years ago over China's insistence on including a clause opposing efforts by other countries to seek regional "hegemony." The Japanese feared offending Moscow, but officials here now appear ready to accept some form of that statement. And Japan's Ambassador to Peking, Shoji Sato, met Tuesday with Han Nien-lung, Deputy Foreign Minister, to discuss preparatory details for the resumption of treaty negotiations.

Opposition to the treaty within Japan appears to be fading fast. This is seen as a consequence of Japan's traditional cultural affinity with China, economic pressures for expanded overseas sales and as a reflection of continuing frictions with the Soviet Union, which unlike China has no influential lobby in Japan.

The Russians were angered by Japan's temporary detention of an advanced MIG-25 flown here by a defecting pilot. The Japanese have also demanded the return of four Kurile islands seized by the Soviet Union in August 1945, but the Russians have maintained that the matter is closed.

February 17, 1978

Japanese-Chinese Dispute on Isles Threatens to Delay Peace Treaty

By ANDREW H. MALCOLM

TOKYO, April 14—An unusual, long-simmering territorial dispute over five uninhabited islands erupted today between Japan and China, threatening to further delay a peace and friendship treaty that both sides regard as vital to their future relations.

The focus of the dispute is the Senkaku Islands, five islets and three reefs with a total area of 2.5 square miles, about the equivalent of two Central Parks. No one lives on these islands in the East China Sea, 215 miles southwest of Okinawa in the Ryukyu chain.

On Wednesday, for unexplained reasons, 38 Chinese fishing boats, some armed with machine guns, entered the waters around the islands and anchored. They are not fishing, according to witnesses, but crewmen shout and carry signs supporting China's territorial claims.

A growing number of Japanese patrol boats accompanied by aircraft are now circling the Chinese boats and using loudspeakers to order them to leave immediately. Today in Peking, Mitsuro Donowaki, minister of the Japanese Embassy, formally demanded at the Chinese Foreign Ministry that the boats be withdrawn. There was no immediate reply.

In Tokyo late tonight, a spokesman for the Chinese Embassy said: "The islands are part of the territory of the People's Republic of China as outlined in a Chinese Foreign Ministry statement on Oct. 31, 1971. This is all we can say for the moment." That earlier statement simply cited China's claim to the islands. But the latent dispute was shelved by both nations when they established diplomatic relations in 1972.

So far, neither side has mentioned what is probably the real reason for the dispute: the unexplored potential for oil and minerals in the surrounding seabed.

But one almost definite diplomatic result of this somewhat bizarre maritime shouting match is the scuttling, for the moment at least, of what had appeared to be an imminent resumption of treaty negotiations between China, Asia's most populous nation, and Japan, Asia's most economically powerful nation.

The treaty talks stalled three years ago over a Chinese demand for a clause denouncing hegemony, namely by the Soviet Union. Japan has maintained that such a clause must have universal application and not be aimed at a single nation.

Economic and political momentum for again trying to reach an accord had appeared to be increasing here in recent months. China signed an eight-year, $20 billion trade agreement with Japanese industrialists in February, and preliminary diplomatic talks had been held on resuming treaty negotiations. In addition, leaders of the ruling Liberal Democratic Party had started a series of "consensus-making meetings" to convince this conservative party's more conservative members to support or at least accept resumption of the treaty talks.

Pro-Taiwan Lobby Gains

In recent days, however, the party's pro-Taiwan lobby, including many members of Prime Minister Takeo Fukuda's own faction, have seemed to gain strength. And a trip to Peking by Foreign Minister Sunao Sonoda, originally scheduled for this week, has been postponed indefinitely.

Political and diplomatic observers here and in Peking speculated today that perhaps the Chinese had decided that no treaty with Japan was possible while Mr. Fukuda remains at Japan's helm. And they perhaps decided to drop the issue for now by reasserting previous claims to the islands, which the Chinese call Tiao Yu-tai. There were also reports that the boat incident was in retaliation for trips to Taiwan by some prominent Japanese politicians to attend a recent memorial service for the late Chiang Kai-shek. Chinese officials here refused to discuss their Government's motives.

The confrontation is certain to please the Soviet Union, which has long opposed the treaty. So far, Taiwan, which also claims the islands and occasionally sends working fishing boats into the area briefly, has remained silent.

A source in Japan's Foreign Ministry said today that the islands are part of the nation's "inherent territory." He said 132 foreign fishing vessels, mostly from Taiwan and South Korea, had entered the waters around the islands last year, but all had left after warnings from Japanese patrol craft.

At the end of World War II, the islands came under American occupation. When a peace treaty was signed in 1951 in San Francisco, the Foreign Ministry official said, China made no claims to the islands. Nor did it make any claim in 1972, after Okinawa, the largest of the Ryukyus, was formally returned to Japan alone with the rest of the chain.

However, Chinese students abroad have demonstrated, notably in various United States cities, against Japan's claim to the islands.

Japanese officials call the movements of the fishing boats "unlawful" and "very strange." Prime Minister Fukuda told a Cabinet meeting he was seriously concerned over the incident and planned further political consultations. Foreign Minister Sonoda told Parliament, "Without disposing of the issue of the violation of territorial waters, Japan cannot reopen the treaty negotiations."

April 15, 1978

The New York Times/April 15, 1978

Senkaku Islands, focus of a dispute between Japan and China

China, Russia and Japan

Only Delicate Diplomacy Can Square the Asian Triangle

By FOX BUTTERFIELD

HONG KONG — The sudden appearance of a cluster of 140 Chinese fishing boats around a small group of uninhabited islands claimed by both Japan and China has threatened to set back one of Peking's cherished foreign policy objectives. Until the arrival of the boats around the Senkaku Islands 12 days ago, China seemed about to win a complex triangular game among Tokyo, Moscow and Peking.

Both China and the Soviet Union have come to see Japan as an invaluable partner in their drive for economic development and for security against each other. Both Peking and Moscow have lavished a series of inducements on Tokyo — a $20 billion term trade agreement from the Chinese, a chance to share in the exploitation of mineral-rich Siberia from the Russians. Neither Asian Communist power has been above trying to manipulate Japanese politics to its advantage.

Although Japan's leaders have sought to maintain a policy of rough equidistance from their two neighbors, in many ways it has been an uneven contest. Most Japanese have a favorable, almost romantic predisposition toward China. There is the two nations' cultural affinity, born of Japan's millenial history of borrowing from Chinese religion and writing, and a guilt complex deriving from Japan's invasion of China before and during World War II. On the other hand, Japanese share an almost pathological hatred and fear of the Russians dating to Czarist times and the Russo-Japanese war. They recall also Stalin's last-minute attack on Japan in Manchuria at the end of World War II, the prolonged detention of hundreds of thousands of Japanese prisoners and the seizure of four Japanese islands north of Hokkaido.

Earlier this month Japan's Prime Minister, Takeo Fukuda, had signaled that the triangular competition might be nearing a climax and that Japan was ready to resume long-stalled talks on a treaty of peace and friendship with China. Peking has insisted that the treaty include a controversial clause pledging Japan to resist hegemonism, China's code-word for Soviet influence. Tokyo had earlier balked at the clause for fear of antagonizing the Russians. But the appearance of the Chinese fishing boats, which touched off stormy debate in the Japanese Diet, forced Foreign Minister Sunao Sonoda to postpone a scheduled trip to Peking last week to resume the talks. For the Senkakus, which lie between Okinawa and Taiwan and which may overlie rich deposits of oil, are an emotional issue on which most Japanese agree.

Why did the Chinese fishing boats, some armed with machine guns and signboards proclaiming China's right to the barren islets, show up in the Senkakus? Did China think the move might force Mr. Fukuda to act more promptly? Or was it a stratagem by dissidents in China seeking to embarrass the new moderate leadership in Peking, as some Japanese speculated? Will the incident have any permanent effect on the emerging close relations between Peking and Tokyo?

Analysts in Hong Kong had no immediate answers to these questions. Peking itself insisted that the boats strayed into Japan's new 12-mile territorial limit around the Senkakus by accident. Deputy Prime Minister Keng Piao told a visiting Japanese delegation that the boats had merely been pursuing a school of fish. He did not explain why many of the boats were not fishing, Japanese officials said, nor why some of them stayed close to the Senkakus after his statement.

The episode was in striking contrast to China's previous successful record of diplomacy with Japan and its other non-Communist neighbors in the year and a half since the death of Mao Tse-tung. The trade agreement with Japan, for example, guaranteed Japan a market for its goods at a time of growing world protectionism and assured China the technology it needs for an ambitious development program. Under the accord, Japan will deliver $10 billion worth of steel, factories and advanced technology to China over the next eight years while China will ship an equal amount of oil and coal to Japan. Several Japanese firms are reportedly close to signing other contracts to help China modernize its railways and its iron and steel and chemical industries.

The only recent precedent for such large-scale economic involvement by another country in China is the Soviet aid of the 1950's, during the halcyon days of relations between Moscow and Peking. Since Mao's death, his successors have repeatedly reaffirmed their own belief in his policy of suspicion toward Russia and indicated that while there may eventually be some small improvement in state-to-state ties, the fundamental dispute will continue. Last month Peking rebuffed a half-hearted overture from Moscow to issue a joint statement on relations, calling on the Russians to first withdraw many of their estimated one million soldiers from the Sino-Soviet frontier and agree to negotiate the status of border territory disputed by China. In evident response, Soviet leader Leonid I. Brezhnev made a tour of the Soviet Far East, significantly watching military maneuvers near the Chinese frontier.

Russia's Asia policy over the last decade, which has concentrated largely on trying to contain China, has been singularly unsuccessful, most analysts agree. It is Russia rather than China that has been isolated, though Moscow has established close ties with India and Vietnam. While Russian diplomats have cultivated right-wing Japanese who oppose the peace treaty with China and Japanese fishermen who must operate in Russian waters, most Japanese believe that the Soviet Union is a greater threat to their security than China.

China has helped foster this belief by inviting a number of senior officers of Japan's military establishment to Peking in recent months and urging them to strengthen their defense ties with the United States. In China's eyes, the Washington-Tokyo alliance remains the best guarantor of their own safety in Asia, though Peking has begun to openly doubt the steadfastness of the Carter Administration in the face of continued Soviet military expansion.

China has also expressed disappointment with the slowness of President Carter's moves toward normalizing relations with Peking. United States officials say, however, that Mr. Carter is considering ways to reach a step-by-step understanding with China that he hopes will amount to normalization. "There are glimmerings, some faint suggestions, that the President has rediscovered China," one official remarked.

April 23, 1978

Four Laotians Held by Japan for a Year Underline Vast Legal Morass Over Refugees

By ANDREW H. MALCOLM

TOKYO, May 2—Japanese authorities have held four Laotian refugees behind bars for a year to a year and a half without filing charges against them or giving them any legal recourse.

The men, who fear returning to their homeland, now under Communist control, are not accused of any crime but have been imprisoned behind a barbed-wire fence and are under constant television surveillance by armed immigration officials at the Yokohama Detention Center.

When a reporter attempted yesterday to visit the men, who are officially considered "illegal aliens," permission was denied to "protect the men's privacy."

In a Legal Vacuum

But immigration authorities began hurried attempts to place the men in private refugee centers, which handle a growing number of "boat people" the Indochinese refugees found adrift at sea.

Although at odds over the treatment of these men, refugee workers and officials here agree that the four cases underline the little-known legalistic and bureaucratic morass that has enveloped hundreds, and possibly, thousands, of Indochinese refugees overseas who do not qualify for the special attention now being given to the boat people by many countries, primarily the United States.

There are about 150 boat people in Japan now, but five times that many other Indochinese refugees are estimated to be marooned here in a legal vacuum so far ignored by any government. Primarily, these are college students, many now graduated. As the non-Communist governments of Cambodia, Vietnam and Laos fell, the students and other nationals became stateless.

They cannot return to their homelands free of fear or suspicion. They generally cannot go to other nations unless they have relatives there. And legal barriers here prevent them from establishing a normal life. For instance, they cannot marry in Japan without a passport from their new Communist Government.

The four Laotians are Thao Sangsith Savath, 29 years old; Thao Aroune, 19;

Nai Pane, 20, and Vanna Bouathoug Outhai, exact age unknown. Japanese officials forbade interviews and refused to discuss details or dates.

However, some facts about the men were gathered from friends and from pleas for help written to relatives and to American officials.

France Refused Two

Some details are sketchy, but Thao Sangsith Savath and his cousin, Thao Aroune, say they originally fled from Laos to Taiwan, where they applied for American visas. They were told this would take six months. They heard unofficially that France would admit them and, under pressure to leave Taiwan, purchased one-way plane tickets to Paris.

French authorities, however, refused to admit them without round-trip tickets and forced Korean Air Lines to fly them out of the country. Upon landing in Tokyo in April 1976, Thao Sangsith Savath says, airline officials told them to "get lost."

They entered Japan on 72-hour visitor's visas and picked up odd jobs for about seven months until they were apprehended as illegal aliens. Thao Sangsith Savath said they were placed in the Yokohama Detention Center on Nov. 10, 1976. Nai Pane says he was placed there on Feb. 28, 1977. Vanna Bouathoug Outhai, a former soldier, has grown increasingly moody in custody and does not answer many questions, but he once mentioned that he arrived in 1976.

"The appearance of the center may be similar to a prison," says Tsutomu Yamabe, director of the Immigration Bureau's enforcement division, "but the actual living there is no different from normal life."

"No one here can go anywhere," said a guard, "the prisoners can do nothing. No school. No work. It is like a prison. They are just waiting."

There are four men to a room. Every few seconds, television cameras flash pictures to a ground-floor monitoring office where an array of holstered pistols and night sticks hang on one partition.

Twice a day the men are allowed outside in a large yard screened by trees from nearby apartments. The yard is surrounded by a 10-foot-high fence topped by four strands of barbed wire. The windows have metal bars and slats.

Medical care is available. They may bathe twice a week.

An Unexplained Delay

"These people once had legal status in Japan," Mr. Yamabe explained in an interview, "but that has expired now and their future stay is regarded as illegal. According to the law, we should force them out. But in the meantime we are protecting them. I don't think 'detain' is the right word."

He said the Government had asked the United Nations High Commissioner for Refugees here to declare the men refugees so they could be released. He said this bureaucratic designation had been delayed but could not explain why. He said efforts to find sponsors among Japanese families and organizations had failed because "they all want to help refugees and technically these men are not refugees." People classified as refugees so they could be released. He said tions subsidy.

Officials of the United States, which has accepted more than 170,000 Indochinese refugees, have said that only Thao Sangsith Savath might qualify for admission after his brother, who lives in Poughkeepsie, N. Y., becomes a United States citizen. Another possibility might be to obtain a special work visa, but this requires having a specific job. The men say they have no particular skills.

The embassies of other nations have not responded to written appeals to consider the men's cases.

Today, after learning of a reporter's inquiries, Mr. Yamabe asked the Roman Catholic charity organization Caritas to move the men to a refugee center, and that move was being planned.

But still unanswered is the question of where the men may go eventually.

May 3, 1978

Brzezinski Tells Japan's Premier Peking Is Pressing for Peace Pact

By HENRY SCOTT-STOKES

TOKYO, May 23—Zbigniew Brzezinski,

the White House national security adviser, arrived here today from Peking to brief Prime Minister Takeo Fukuda on his talks and tell him that the Chinese

leaders wanted a peace treaty with Japan.

Peking's prodding, which was disclosed by Japanese sources, came as the Cabinet decided in principle to resume talks on a treaty. The talks had been suspended in 1975, and Mr. Fukuda has been feeling his way toward a resumption since the New Year.

His attitude on relations with China is cautious. A statement released by the American Embassy after the meeting said only that "Prime Minister Fukuda described the present state of Japan-China relations, including preparations for the conclusion of the peace and friendship treaty between the two nations."

American Sees Sonoda Today

Tomorrow Mr. Brzezinski meets with Foreign Minister Sunao Sonoda, who favors a treaty with China. However, the Japanese, despite encouragement from President Carter in his talks with Mr. Fukuda in Washington on May 3, are expected to make haste slowly. "The Chinese just want to lay down terms," a

Zbigniew Brzezinski.

The White House Photo Office

senior minister said recently. "They don't want to negotiate."

That statement reflected a caution that is shared by Secretary of State Cyrus R. Vance, as distinct from Mr. Brzezinski's enthusiasm for closer relations with China.

"There are basically three factions in Peking," said one minister last week.

"They are lead by Hua Kuo-feng, by Teng Hsiao-peng, the senior Deputy Prime Minister, and by the chief of state, Yeh Chien-ying, representing the older generation.

"These three factions are constantly on the alert against one another, and none of them can afford to be out ahead of the others, approving a peace treaty with Japan, so you are left with a very low common denominator."

May 24, 1978

JAPAN AND CHINA SET NEW TALKS ON TREATY

Agree to Resume Negotiations for Peace Pact in Peking Next Month, but Early Accord Is Unlikely

By HENRY SCOTT-STOKES

TOKYO, June 14—Japan and China agreed today to resume negotiations on a peace treaty that were first proposed six years ago but were suspended in late 1975 after Japan refused to accept an anti-Soviet "hegemony" clause in the treaty that was sought by China.

The negotiations will start again in Peking early next month against a background of conflicting interests among the great powers. The Carter Administration strongly supports the treaty and the Soviet Union vehemently opposes it.

The proposed treaty, agreed on in principle by Prime Ministers Chou En-lai of China and Kakuei Tanaka of Japan, in 1972, is of considerable potential importance but it is not likely to be concluded soon, diplomatic sources said.

Economic ties between China and Japan, which established full diplomatic relations in 1972, are becoming steadily closer as shown by a trade understanding reached here today under which China may this year import more steel from Japan than will the United States. For many years the United States has been Japan's best customer for steel.

Initial Talks May Be Brief

A spokesman for a top leader of the governing Liberal Democratic Party said

that the "working-level talks" between the Japanese Ambassador in Peking, Shoji Sato, and Han Nien-lung, a Deputy Foreign Minister of China, should be concluded within a week. Foreign Minister Sunao Sonoda may then go to Peking to conduct full-scale "political" negotiations with the Chinese and try to settle the matter of the "hegemony" clause, the spokesman said.

Japan is expected to insist that a rider be inserted in the treaty to make it clear that any clause on "hegemony"—a code word used by the Chinese to refer to what they perceive as a Soviet threat—is not directed against a specific third country.

The Japanese strategy for the negotiations, as outlined by a spokesman for elements within the governing conservative party who support the treaty, seems to indicate that Government of Prime Minister Takeo Fukudo is not yet ready to conclude a peace treaty. It was believed here that the chances of Peking's agreeing to dilute the "hegemony" clause—which President Carter urged Mr. Fukuda to accept when they met on May 3 in Washington—are no better than they were in 1975.

Kiichi Miyazawa, who was then Foreign Minister, tried at that time to negotiate with his Chinese counterpart, Chiao Kuan-hua, a four-point "antihegemonism" formula devised by the Japanese, but the Chinese would have none of it.

Though conclusion of the long-sought treaty would be a significant accomplishment, diplomatic sources said, it is still unclear just how it would serve the long-term interests of Japan.

Foreign Minister Sonoda is believed to be at odds with a large part of his own ministry on the matter and Mr. Fukuda himself

heads a faction in the Liberal Democratic Party that has always preferred friendship with the Chinese Nationalist Government on Taiwan to closer relations with the Communist regime in Peking.

The Japanese Foreign Ministry is characteristically extemely cautious. Since the end of the United States military occupation more than 25 years ago, the ministry has consistently avoided creative policy proposals in favor of nimble adjustments to outside pressures.

Japanese diplomats, mirroring public opinion, are known for their dislike of the Soviet Union. But this nation never needlessly seeks to antagonize powerful foreign nations, diplomats here point out, particularly the Soviet Union and the United States.

The key matter is the attitude of Mr. Fukuda, who stands well to the right of center in the governing party and whose personal following includes many of the conservative politicians who have close relations with the Chinese Nationalists.

Fukuda Walking a Tightrope

Mr. Fukuda thus is performing something of a tightrope act in agreeing to resume talks with China. He faces strong competition from Masayoshi Ohira, a senior leader of the party and former foreign minister, who favors a treaty with China, for leadership of the party—and consequently the prime ministership—in a party election to be held late this years. The party itself enjoys only a narrow margin of support in Parliament over its rivals.

Mr. Fukuda must not alienate his own close supporters by leaning too far toward China. But he must also be ready to steal Mr. Ohira's pro-China policy should the domestic political winds suddenly blow in that direction.

While the diplomatic impasse has continued, economic ties between China and Japan have grown steadily closer, as is shown by the trade understanding reached here today. After weeks of negotiation, a visiting Chinese mission is

near formal agreement on importing from Japan at least 2.4 million metric tons of steel in the second half of 1978, bringing total purchases this year up to 5.5 million metric tons. United States imports from Japan are expected to be at about the same level.

Earlier this year Japanese interests

concluded a $20 billion long-term trade agreement with the Chinese under which Japan will buy mainly oil and coal while China will get industrial plants and technology.

Japanese Parliament ratifies oil treaty with South Korea. Page Dvv.

June 15, 1978

Japan Showing New Self-Confidence in Talks With China

By HENRY SCOTT-STOKES

TOKYO, June 23—The Japanese decision to press on with talks on concluding a peace treaty with China in the teeth of Soviet opposition indicates a growing self-confidence in this country, long regarded as too timid to have a foreign policy of its own.

News Analysis Japan formally informed China yesterday that it was ready to resume negotiations on a treaty of peace and friendship on July 3 in Peking. Only three days earlier the Soviet Union had made a protest in Tokyo against Japanese plans to move ahead toward conclusion of the long-delayed treaty.

Skeptics may say that Japan is going ahead with the talks simply because the United States favors the pact. But officials here say the Tokyo Government is acting on its own volition, and is not merely reacting to American encouragement—given to Prime Minister Takeo Fukuda by President Carter at their meeting in Washington last month—or just responding to American plans to accelerate the pace of talks aimed at establishing normal relations between the United States and China.

Whether the peace treaty will actually be concluded in the months ahead remains to be seen. But the pace that Japan proposes to set in the talks with China is impressive. Newspapers here are already reporting that Foreign Minister Sunao Sonoda may go to Peking early next month to pursue the negotiations.

Japanese Diplomats Less Reticent

There has also been a marked change in the attitude of Japanese diplomats, who until recently were reticent in their comments on the treaty talks and gave an impression that there was a difference in views between Foreign Minister Sonoda, a politician who is deeply and personally committed to the treaty, and career diplomats serving under him.

The diplomats now say there is a "consensus"—a key Japanese concept—in favor of concluding a treaty. They say

there is no reason why it should not be signed in the coming months following a delay of nearly six years since Kakuei Tanaka, who was then the Japanese Prime Minister, issued with the late Prime Minister Chou En-lai a joint communiqué that called for a treaty.

The key provision of that declaration was the establishment of full diplomatic relations between Japan and China. There had been no formal diplomatic ties since the Communist regime came to power on the mainland in 1949. The communiqué also incorporated a Japanese apology to the Chinese, referring to "Japan's responsibility for causing enormous damages in the past, to the Chinese people through war."

And Section 7 of the communiqué stated that "normalization of relations between China and Japan is not directed against third countries. Neither of the two countries should seek hegemony in the Asia-Pacific region and each country is opposed to efforts by any other country or group of countries to establish such hegemony," it said.

This clause was significant in that the word "hegemony" is always construed in current Chinese diplomatic parlance to refer to a presumed Soviet threat to China. The clause became a contentious issue between Japan and China when Moscow exerted pressure on Japan to refuse to endorse such a notion.

When talks on the peace treaty finally began in late 1974—much later than the Chinese and Japanese had expected—the Russians multiplied diplomatic pressures on Tokyo to agree on a treaty with China only on condition that the "hegemony" clause be eliminated or drastically toned down.

At talks in New York in the fall of 1975, Foreign Minister Kiichi Miyazawa tried, unsuccessfully, to get Chinese agreement to a wording that would be much less offensive to Moscow. Thus for years the Soviet Union has had its way, effectively suspending the Chinese-Japanese talks.

Further snags in the treaty negotiations are still possible. The Japanese say that the central issue will still be "hegemony." But on the other hand Japan appears to have modified its position since the un-

succesful talks in New York nearly thrǝ years ago, when Mr. Miyazawa w trying to wriggle away from Clause of the 1972 communiqué.

Tokyo now appears to have fallen back on a softer stand. Precisely what draft Japanese diplomats will take with them to Peking is not known, but they may well have "fallback" positions that the Chinese can accept.

The key is the attitude of Prime Minister Fukuda, for whom the basic consideration is that he be re-elected to the presidency of the governing Liberal Democratic Party, which carries with it the prime ministership, at a party election to be held in the fall. Mr. Fukuda belongs to the conservative wing of the party and has many pro-Taiwan associates, but to ward off a challenge from former Foreign Minister Masayoshi Ohira, he may need the China card, since the treaty with Peking seems to be favored by the country as a whole.

Mr. Fukuda will not say now what his view of the Japanese-Chinese treaty is. But the more positive comments of Japanese diplomats suggest that word has come down from on high to pursue the treaty as fast as possible—unless the Chinese suddenly dig in their heels.

What seems clear is that the Japanese Government has taken a positive stand on the treaty without specific reference to the United States, without giving much attention to the sharper tone in United States-Soviet relations, and almost regardless of American plans for speeding the pace of talks to conclude diplomatic relations between China and the United States.

For the first time since World War II Japan thus appears to be moving toward a quite independent foreign policy. This is most obvious in Southeast Asia, an area where Japan and China logically contend for influence.

Last year Mr. Fukuda made a trip through the five countries that belong to the Association of Southeast Asian Nations, known as ASEAN, which Japanese diplomats say was an indication that their country was seeking to play a political, not merely an economic, role in Asia. Western diplomats accept this interpretation of the "Fukuda doctrine," under which Japan offers long-term aid to the region.

The bases of Japan's greater self-confidence and its move toward the ASEAN countries are primarily economic: the huge growth in the Japanese economy, almost twice the size it was in dollar terms only two years ago, at close to a trillion dollars this year; large ASEAN trade deficits with Japan, and the proximity of Japan, as compared with the United States, to Southeast Asia.

The most striking development here, however, is Japan's diminished fear of Soviet retaliation in the event a treaty is concluded with China. Diplomats say that the Soviet Union has almost no support for its foreign policy in East Asia outside Mongolia, and they question whether the rapid growth in the Soviet military presence in the Far East—notably an increase in the Russian naval commitment—adds up to a major threat to Japan.

Although the prospects for a Japanese-Chinese treaty are still unclear, it is evident that after three decades of seeming subservience to great-power demands, from America and the Soviet Union in their different ways, Japan is unmistakably beginning to choose its own way forward.

June 24, 1978

CHINA STRENGTHENS ITS TIES WITH JAPAN

Initiates Joint Economic Projects by Inviting Weapons Makers and Oil and Rail Experts

By HENRY SCOTT-STOKES

TOKYO, July 20 — A new era appears to be opening up in China's economic relations with Japan. The two major Oriental powers, which remained at arm's length for nearly 29 years after the 1949 revolution in China, are planning a mass of joint industrial projects.

Whatever comes of these plans — the initiative for which has come largely from the Chinese — the tone of Chinese-Japanese relations is changing for the better as one Japanese industrial mission after another visits the mainland.

China and Japan are about to resume their long-suspended talks on a peace treaty in Peking, and the Japanese seem optimistic that this time there will be agreement. The treaty was first proposed in 1972 when the two nations established diplomatic relations. [The talks resumed on Friday.]

"What has changed is that the Chinese side is much more positive," said Toshio Kimura, a former Japanese foreign minister, who is now a senior figure in the governing Liberal Democratic Party, in an interview. "That is why I am much more optimistic than even a month ago."

Major Moves by China

China has recently made three major moves:

¶It has proposed for the first time that Japan join China in development of the potentially huge offshore oil fields under the East China Sea. China had previously suggested only that Japan should give technical and financial aid in offshore oil development.

¶It has invited representatives of Japanese arms manufacturers to visit Peking this fall with a view to buying arms from Japan — a nation that has so far banned arms exports as incompatible with the "peace" Constitution imposed on Japan by the United States in 1947.

¶The Chinese have informed a mission led by Yoshizo Ikeda, president of Mitsui & Company, one of the world's largest trading companies, that in the future they would accept bank loans from abroad to finance industrial development. This is an abandonment of the longstanding policy that China should not accept foreign loans.

Each of these developments is an important change in policy. Taken together, they suggest that prospects for Chinese-Japanese economic cooperation — which were already much brighter following conclusion of a $20 billion trade agreement early this year under which Chinese oil and raw materials would be traded for Japanese plant and technology — had progressed far beyond all expectations.

Heavy Two-Way Traffic

Evidence of the rapprochement between Japan and China does not rest merely on recent pronouncements by China and on the record trade agreement. There has also been heavy two-way traffic in economic missions. Bank of China experts have visited Japan to study the its automated banking system, for example, while engineers from Japan National Railways have gone to China as advisers on the construction of a new national railway system.

During the first six months of this year, 50 Chinese missions visited Japan, compared to 73 in all of 1977 and 39 in all of 1976. The number of Japanese visitors to China meanwhile leaped from 8,000 in 1972, the year that diplomatic relations were established, to about 30,000 last year.

The overall pattern, now that Chinese objections to close cooperation with a capitalist neighbor appear to have been removed, is determined by the complementary character of the two economies. China has the labor and Japan has the technology, and the old atmosphere of "never the twain shall meet" is evaporating.

But it is too early to say what will happen. Japan and China did only $3.5 billion in two-way trade last year compared with $3.9 billion between Japan and Taiwan. The Chinese-Japanese peace treaty has yet to be signed and it contains a troublesome "hegemony" clause that Japan has so far hesitated to accept because it implies hostility toward the Soviet Union. And the Chinese have not yet approached the Japanese Government itself on joint development of offshore oil; this week's talks in Peking have been with Japanese oil company executives.

Arms List Reportedly Offered

In addition, Japanese companies cannot export arms. They can only supply China with items like trucks and vessels that the Chinese may use for naval purposes. Officially, it is none of Japan's business what China does with such purchases. In any event, there have been no detailed talks on arms-related deals between China and Japan, so far as is known, although a Tokyo newspaper, Sankei Shimbun, reported recently that China had approached Japan about arms purchases three years ago and had even submitted a list of the arms it wanted to buy. That report could not be confirmed.

But what is clear from a wealth of evidence is that China and Japan are in contact on many levels to get their economies moving faster and in tandem. Hitachi, a shipbuilding, engineering and electrical equipment company, received a $55 million order for oil rigs for use in the East China Sea last month. Nippon Kokan, a steel company, has been asked to help China expand a Peking steel mill to a capacity of 6 million tons, while Nippon Steel, the world's largest steel company, is helping to build another mill of the same size in Shanghai.

There are other big Japanese deals in the air. Hitachi and Toshiba, a leading electrical company, are negotiating the sale to China of a color television plant worth about $125 million, the companies confirmed last week. If a contract is concluded, this could become China's first color television facility. The same two companies are competing to supply a power station to Shanghai.

July 23, 1978

Japan ● '79

Japan Cites Soviet Air Intrusion

TOKYO, Sept. 7 (AP)—Two Soviet bombers violated Japan's airspace today over the Goto islands west of Kyushu, defense officials said. A protest was lodged with the Soviet Union, they added.

The Soviet aircraft, both described as Tupolev TU-95 bombers, flew over the islands about two minutes until Japanese jet fighters scrambled, the officials said.

September 8, 1977

Soviet Warns Japan On Treaty With Peking

MOSCOW, Nov. 26 (AP)—The Soviet Union warned Japan today that Tokyo could face "retaliatory measures" if it signed a pending peace and friendship treaty with China containing a clause vehemently opposed by Moscow.

The warning came in a commentary appearing in the Soviet Communist Party newspaper, Pravda. The article was signed "Observer," indicating that it reflected high-level Kremlin thinking.

The clause in question would pledge Japan and China to resist efforts by any third country to achieve "hegemony" in the northwestern Pacific region.

"Japan, whether it wants it or not, is being pushed onto the road that leads to aggravating relations with third states, and the latter are entitled to take retaliatory measures in case China and Japan should undertake actions on the level Peking is now trying to impose," the article said. It did not specify what form the "retaliatory measures" would take.

November 27, 1977

Soviet-Japanese Fishing Accord

MOSCOW, Dec. 21 (Reuters)—The Soviet Union and Japan have decided to extend for one year a temporary agreement on fishing catches in each other's 200-mile coastal zones, leaving quotas unchanged from 1977, the press agency Tass said today. It added that the accord allowed Soviet ships to take 650,000 tons from Japan's zone and Japanese fishermen to catch 850,000 tons in Soviet waters. The two sides are discussing a longer-term treaty.

December 22, 1977

Soviet Issues Pact It Offered Japan

MOSCOW, Feb. 23 (Reuters) — The Soviet Union published today the draft of a treaty of good-neighbor relations and cooperation that it offered to Japan last month.

The release of the draft, by the Government press agency Tass, followed the delivery yesterday in Tokyo of a message from Leonid I. Brezhnev, the Soviet leader, to Prime Minister Takeo Fukuda.

According to reports from Tokyo, Mr. Brezhnev said in his letter that Moscow wanted an accord because of what he called a third force that sought to damage Soviet-Japanese relations. This appeared to be an allusion to China, which is also pressing for a treaty with Japan

Japan has refused to conclude a World War II peace treaty or a good-neighbor pact with the Soviet Union until the Russians return a small group of islands at the southern end of the Kuril chain, which was part of Japan until 1945.

The published draft treaty consists of 14 articles and is similar to a Soviet-West German pact signed in 1970. It commits both countries to settle disputes by peaceful means and to refrain from the threat of force.

Under one clause, the Soviet Union and Japan would not allow use of their territories "for any actions that could prejudice the security of the other party." The provision may apply to the presence of American military bases in Japan.

The draft affirmed the intention of both countries to continue talks on an eventual peace treaty. This clause probably was included to counter Japanese critics of the Soviet proposal. They have portrayed it as an attempt to shelve the question of a peace treaty and, with it, the issue of the disputed islands.

The islands, situated off the northeast coast of Hokkaido, the northern Japanese island, are the Habomai Islands, Shikotan, and the two larger islands of Kunashiro and Etorofu.

The Soviet Union contends that they are part of the Kuril chain. Japan says they have closer historical ties to Japan than the more northerly Kuril islands.

February 24, 1978

MOSCOW'S RELATIONS WITH TOKYO COOLING

Soviet Heightens Its Denunciations as Japan Moves Toward Closer Political Ties With China

By CRAIG R. WHITNEY

MOSCOW, April 9—Japanese-Soviet relations, which have never been warm, are growing rapidly cooler as Japan moves toward closer economic and political ties with China.

Japanese diplomats here expect the deterioration to accelerate if, as expected, Tokyo and Peking decide this month to resume negotiations later on a treaty of peace and friendship. The talks were suspended in 1975 after the Chinese insisted on a clause rejecting attempts by third powers to achieve "hegemony" in Asia—by which they meant their main ideological and territorial adversary, the Soviet Union. At present the Soviet reading—which reports from Tokyo indicate is correct—is that the Japanese are willing to accept some form of the clause even if it displeases the Russians.

Last January Moscow tried wooing the Japanese with a friendship treaty of its own. In February, after Tokyo rejected it, the Soviet press published the text and began a barrage of denunciations. In the last two weeks the Japanese have been accused of militarism, have been warned against an "anti-Soviet foreign policy" and have been accused of secretly preparing to arm themselves with atomic weapons. The Soviet Army newspaper, Krasnaya Zvezda, said, "Japanese imperialism is rearing its head."

Only the United States among other capitalist countries has come in for as much abuse here this year.

Concern With China the Focus

Politics has not interfered with Soviet-Japanese trade the way it has with Soviet-American trade. Japanese officials say Soviet trade amounted to $3.36 billion last year, double Soviet-American trade in 1977.

The preoccupation of the Russians with the Chinese has increased considerably since then, as the new leadership under Hua Kuo-feng and Teng Hsiao-ping has disappointed whatever hopes Moscow had for an ideological and political reconciliation after Mao Tse-tung died.

The stepped-up Russian campaign against Japan is largely a reflection of this concern, though relations have long been troubled by the legacy of the belated Soviet entry into the Pacific theater in World War II, nine days before the Japanese surrender in August 1945. The Russians still hold four small islands just north of Japan in the Kurile chain that were seized then, and they insist after 33 years that Japan has no claim to them. Successive Japanese governments have refused to conclude a peace treaty until the islands—Kunashiri, Etorofu, Shikotan and Hamobai—are returned. Moscow last rejected the demand in January, during a visit by Foreign Minister Sunao Sonoda.

A month later the Soviet press published the draft of the treaty on "good neighborliness and cooperation," which Mr. Sonoda has reportedly refused to discuss until a peace treaty is agreed on. The publication—highly unusual for the Russians—seems to have offended the Japanese. "Reaction at home was very critical," a Japanese diplomat said, "and I think it backfired."

MIG-25 Issue Still Rankles

For their part Soviet officials have still not forgiven the Japanese for welcoming a Soviet pilot who defected in September 1976 with an advanced MIG-25 plane, which the Japanese gave to American intelligence experts for analysis despite strong Soviet objections.

Since then Japan and China have moved closer to a treaty of reconciliation, in abeyance since 1975 because of Chinese insistence on the hegemony clause. In February they concluded a $20 billion trade agreement for the next eight years. Now Prime Minister Takeo Fukuda is apparently preparing the way for the treaty talks to reopen: Mr. Sonoda will be going to Peking shortly.

Unlike the United States, both Japan

and the Soviet Union have strictly separated their political quarrels from their trade relations, the $3.36 billion figure for last year being only slightly below 1976 while American-Soviet trade declined from $2.5 billion to $1.86 billion.

"Your big problem," said Masaaki Ninomiya, Moscow representative of Mitsui Trading, "is that your Export-Import Bank can't give credits for your exports here. Ours does." Japanese officials say there are $3 billion worth of Government-underwritten credits for exports to the Soviet Union, which rose from less than $500 million in 1973 to $2.5 billion in 1976. In 1974 Congress forbade the Export-Import Bank to grant such credits until the Soviet Union relaxed its restrictions on emigration.

Most Obstacles Are Nonpolitical

Most of the obstacles in the way of greater Soviet-Japanese trade are not political but practical and economic, except for a long-simmering dispute about fishing in the northwestern Pacific, where both countries claim 200-mile coastal zones. Since 1973 Soviet officials have tried to interest Japanese concerns in multi-billion-dollar deals to exploit natural gas, coal and oil reserves in remote Siberia in return for part of the production.

Like West European companies, Japanese traders have done a big business in recent years in industrial plants, chemical manufacturing equipment and pipe for the gas lines the Russians are building to Eastern Europe, but orders have fallen off in the last year. This year, the Japanese believe, price rather than politics will decide whether trade picks up again. They are worried about the decline in the dollar, the Russians' preferred medium of foreign exchange, because it forces them to raise prices.

"I think trade can help solve our political problems," a Japanese businessman said. Kamenobu Orita, manager of the Mitsubishi office, said, "So far our business hasn't been affected by politics, and I hope it stays that way."

April 10, 1978

Soviet Warns Japan Against China Pact Aimed at Moscow

TOKYO, June 19—The Soviet Union issued a stern warning to Japan today that this nation would be drawn into the current Soviet-Chinese conflict if it should conclude a peace treaty with China "aimed against the Soviet Government."

The Soviet Government, in a 400-word statement delivered to the Foreign Ministry by Ambassador Dmitri S. Polyansky, said that such a treaty might result in a reversal of the present relationship between Japan and the Soviet Union.

Last week, Japan and China agreed to resume their long-interrupted negotiations for conclusion of a treaty of peace and friendship. The proposed treaty contains a controversial clause, sought by the Chinese, opposing "hegemony" by a third country in the area, which Moscow regards as directed against the Soviet Union.

The Soviet statement said that it was up to Japan how it conducted its relations with China but that the Soviet Union "cannot be an onlooker regarding a matter that may directly affect its own interest."

"Peking leaders are attempting to bring Japan into an anti-Soviet line," it continued, "by concluding a treaty aimed against the Soviet Government. Should a treaty containing a clause directed against the Soviet Union be signed, the Soviet Union would have to make a necessary amendment to its own policy regarding its relations with Japan."

The statement asserted that China's leaders had elevated their hostility toward Moscow to the level of a national policy. They have stepped up "a policy of undermining progress in détente, fanning the menace of war and plotting conflicts between nations," it said.

The Soviet statement concluded by urging Japan to refrain from taking steps that might result in damaging relations between Tokyo and Moscow.

Prime Minister Takeo Fukuda, speaking at a meeting of the Foreign Correspondents Club here today, said that Japanese-Chinese relations were one thing and Japanese-Soviet relations another. He said he expected that the treaty negotiations with China would be concluded successfully.

June 20, 1978

Japan and Soviet, Despite Tension, See Booming Trade

By HENRY SCOTT-STOKES

TOKYO, July 6 — At the Foreign Ministry here, a special room on the sixth floor is reserved for receiving Soviet diplomats.

The conference room is similar to many others in the building. It has a brown sofa, armchairs and a single window on an inner courtyard. On one wall, however, hanging above the sofa, is a huge map of several eccentric-shaped islands studded with volcanoes and lakes. One of the islands, much larger than the rest, stretches diagonally across the map.

This is Etorofu Island, called Iturup by the Soviet Union. One of Japan's "Northern Islands," which the Russians assert are part of the Kurile Island chain, it is 126 miles long and 28 miles wide. It was taken from Japan by the Soviet Union in 1945 along with the three other principal islands in this group: Kunashir, Shikotan and Habomai.

A Japanese diplomat, referring to Soviet visitors, remarked: "At first they objected to the map, but we told them it was an essential part of the décor, and eventually they gave way."

Concern Over Soviet Relations

The Foreign Ministry's taste in "art" reflects the concern here over the Soviet Union, with which its relations are severely strained. Yet the two are bound together by trade, which has grown rapidly, and by a common interest in vast economic projects in Siberia that began in the 1960's. Since 1970, trade between the two has risen from $822 million to $3.36 billion last year, with a balance of $512 million in Japan's favor in 1977.

The strongest economic tie between the two nations, which have the second and third largest economies in the world, is their seven major joint ventures in Siberia, aimed at exploiting that region's seemingly unlimited natural resources. The largest project, to develop natural-gas deposits in Yakutia, in the interior west of the Lena River, progressed in May when Japanese, Soviet and American planners agreed to a contract involving a Japanese and United States investment of nearly $4 billion.

So far, only $25 million has been committed by the United States. This is a small sum compared with the $1.47 billion already lent to the Soviet Union by Japan for projects in Siberia to cut and ship lumber, build ports, mine coal and prospect for oil off Sakhalin Island.

But the companies involved in the Yakutian natural-gas plan are sufficiently large to guarantee that it will continue. Under the agreement, liquefied gas is to be shipped to Japan and the United States by 1985.

Large Steel Companies Included

The companies include the largest steel concern in the world, Nippon Steel, three other large steel companies here, six major trading companies, also the biggest in the world, and nine major Japanese banks. The American partners are El Paso Natural Gas and Occidental Petroleum.

"The only question," according to a Japanese diplomat, "is whether the United States will allow that much gas to be imported. That is the key on which the whole project hinges." He was referring to plans for shipping abroad a good proportion of the nearly 700 billion cubic meters of gas found in Yakutia.

Whatever the United States decision — and the 1974 Trade Act prohibits the use of Export-Import Bank loans for the project — economic ties between Japan and the Soviet Union remain strong enough to counterbalance to a great degree the tension between the two countries. This strain centers on the Northern Islands, which are situated between Hokkaido and the Kurile chain.

There is little prospect that the Soviet Union will hand these back. The Russians assert that Japanese public opinion does not care about them very much, and is simply being agitated by a "third power" — the United States.

Japanese Resentment Increased

The resentment felt by the Japanese, which was articulated by the conservative Government of Prime Minister Takeo Fukuda, has been aggravated by Soviet attempts to stop Japan from going ahead with its long-term aim of concluding a peace treaty with China. Talks on the treaty were due to start today, but have been deferred until July 21, when they are scheduled to resume in Peking after a gap of nearly three years. Chinese-Japanese negotiations ground to a halt in 1975, principally because the Soviet Union skillfully countered a rapprochement between the two nations, largely by diplomatic methods.

The new development here is that this time, the Japanese appear resolved to brush aside Soviet objections to the treaty, which were restated in a diplomatic note delivered to the Foreign Ministry on June 19. The Soviet objection is that the Chinese-Japanese peace treaty will contain a clause that rejects "hegemony" by any power in the region, which is generally believed to refer to Soviet ambitions.

Trade with Asia and the U.S.S.R.

During the last three weeks, a series of rumors have surfaced in Tokyo suggesting that the Russians will retaliate sharply against Japan if it concludes the treaty, a document intended only to reinforce ties with China, with which Japan has had diplomatic relations since 1972.

The first of the rumors was a foreign news report that the Soviet Union was conducting a major military exercise on Etorofu, or Iturup. That report, which came from the chief of the Japanese Joint Staff Council, Gen. Hirumi Kurisu, was later denied in Parliament here.

Report of Fishing Talks Cut Off

The Japanese press meanwhile reported that the Soviet Union had broken off fishing negotiations with Japan in retaliation for the announcement that the Government here wanted to resume peace talks with China. This also turned out not to be the case. "They just postponed the talks for interministerial talks in Moscow," said an official.

Another rumor had it that the Russians were building a missile base on Etorofu. A senior Self-Defense Forces official replied that although the report had not been confirmed, "Russian transport planes and naval vessels have visited Etorofu several times since the end of May." Fifteen years ago, the Soviet Union kept a full division on the island; now it has only two tactical air squadrons. The main Soviet missile bases are in eastern Siberia and in the Kuriles further north from Etorofu.

Japan has on the whole reacted calmly to such rumors, and to the overall Soviet military buildup in the Far East, although this has come at a time when the American military presence has been reduced. But as one diplomat remarked, "What can they do, land troops on Hokkaido? I don't think so."

The Far Eastern Economic Review, a Hong Kong weekly, also reported last month that the Soviet Union has 125 submarines in its Pacific fleet, including 50 under nuclear power, operating out of Vladivostok and other ports.

Soviet Deployments Reported

The review, which cited intelligence sources, probably in the United States, said that the Soviet Sixth Airborne Division at Khabarovsk had been reinforced. Just under a third of the Soviet Naval Air Force, with 355 aircraft, it said, had been assigned to the Far East, while intermediate-range ballistic-missile sites were being established at Irkutsk, Ulan-Ude, Chita, Magdagachi and Komsomolsk.

The Japanese, however, are not intimidated. "They are not directed specifically at Japan," said one official. "It's part of the worldwide competition with the United States — they divide their forces in three and send one-third to the Far East."

The assurance of officials here appears genuine. It is based partly on a view of the Soviet economy that one explained this way: "In 1961 Khrushchev boasted that by 1980 Russia would surpass America in per-capita gross national product. Then the growth rate was 10 percent a year. Now it is 4 to 5 percent, dropping to 3 or 3.5 percent."

Thus, as the yen goes higher and the dollar falls, and Japan emerges as a source of international capital comparable to West Germany — the two nations are respectively the second largest and the largest capitalist nations trading with the Soviet Union — Japanese self-confidence and inclination to act independently of the great powers has become more evident.

July 7, 1978

Japanese Report Says Soviet Fleet Poses Growing Danger

TOKYO, July 28 — Recent reinforcement of Soviet naval forces in the Far East has "intensified the confrontation between the U.S. and the U.S.S.R." in the area according to a Japanese Government report approved by the Cabinet here today.

The annual defense "white paper" said that the Soviet Union has 125 submarines in the Far East, of which 50 are nuclear-powered, and concludes that this concentration of force has "intensified" pressure on Japan.

The report, which was prepared by a team under Atsuyuki Sassa, a defense adviser at Japan's Defense Agency, said that enhanced Soviet activity" appears to be aimed at increasing political and psychological influence over this area.

The white paper said that given this increase in Soviet forces in the area, the United States Seventh Fleet did not have the strength to fully protect Japan's vital sea lanes.

Growing Anti-Soviet Tone

The report marks an increasingly anti-Soviet tone in Government statements here at a time of mounting debate over military policy and in effect identifies the Soviet Union as Japan's principal potential enemy, unlike previous papers.

It takes by far the hardest line in an official document published here and is much tougher than Japanese Foreign Ministry reports. Previous defense white papers have been relatively innocuous.

Commenting on the defense report in a telephone interview, Mr. Sassa said that in the Far East the Soviet Union was "menacing the absolute safety of island countries such as Japan." This country is dependent on imported oil, raw materials and food.

"Even if they did not use nuclear weapons," Mr. Sassa said, "their forces are strong enough to destroy us, especially by hitting our sea lanes."

July 29, 1978

233

Index

Index

Index